A CITY'S ARCHITECTURE

Ashgate Studies in Architecture Series

SERIES EDITOR: EAMONN CANNIFFE, MANCHESTER SCHOOL OF ARCHITECTURE, MANCHESTER METROPOLITAN UNIVERSITY, UK

The discipline of Architecture is undergoing subtle transformation as design awareness permeates our visually dominated culture. Technological change, the search for sustainability and debates around the value of place and meaning of the architectural gesture are aspects which will affect the cities we inhabit. This series seeks to address such topics, both theoretically and in practice, through the publication of high quality original research, written and visual.

Other titles in this series

Losing Site
Architecture, Memory and Place
Shelley Hornstein
ISBN 978 1 4094 0871 0

The Political Unconscious of Architecture
Re-opening Jameson's Narrative
Nadir Lahiji
ISBN 978 1 4094 2639 4

Architecture and Science-Fiction Film
Philip K. Dick and the Spectacle of Home
David T. Fortin
ISBN 978 1 4094 0748 5

Symbolic Houses in Judaism
How Objects and Metaphors Construct Hybrid Places of Belonging
Mimi Levy Lipis
ISBN 978 1 4094 2104 7

African Identity in Post-Apartheid Public Architecture
White Skin, Black Masks
Jonathan Alfred Noble
978 0 7546 7765 9

Neo-historical East Berlin
Architecture and Urban Design in the German Democratic Republic 1970–1990
Florian Urban
ISBN 978 0 7546 7616 4

A City's Architecture

Aberdeen as 'Designed City'

William Alvis Brogden

ASHGATE

© William Alvis Brogden 2012

All rights reserved. No part of this publication may be reproduced, stored in a retrieval system or transmitted in any form or by any means, electronic, mechanical, photocopying, recording or otherwise without the prior permission of the publisher.

William Alvis Brogden has asserted his right under the Copyright, Designs and Patents Act, 1988, to be identified as the author of this work.

Published by
Ashgate Publishing Limited
Wey Court East
Union Road
Farnham
Surrey GU9 7PT
England

Ashgate Publishing Company
Suite 420
101 Cherry Street
Burlington, VT 05401–4405
USA

www.ashgate.com

British Library Cataloguing in Publication Data
Brogden, W. A.
    A city's architecture : Aberdeen as 'designed city'. – (Ashgate studies in architecture)
    1. Architecture – Scotland – Aberdeen – History. 2. Aberdeen (Scotland) – Buildings, structures, etc. 3. City planning – Scotland – Aberdeen – History.
    I. Title II. Series
    720.9'4123–dc22

Library of Congress Cataloging-in-Publication Data
Brogden, W. A.
    A city's architecture : Aberdeen as 'designed city' / by William Alvis Brogden.
      p. cm. – (Ashgate studies in architecture)
    Includes bibliographical references and index.
    ISBN 978–1–4094–1147–5 (hardback : alk. paper)
    1. Architecture – Scotland – Aberdeen. 2. City planning – Scotland – Aberdeen.
    3. Aberdeen (Scotland) – Buildings, structures, etc.
    I. Title. II. Title: Aberdeen as 'designed city'.
    NA981.A23B77 2011
    720.9412'3–dc22
                                                                                    2011012516

ISBN 9781409411475 (hbk)

Reprinted 2012

Printed and bound in Great Britain by the MPG Books Group, UK

In Memoriam

Edna Earle Jones Brogden
(17 October 1920–5 April 2010)

Jessica Emily Alice Smart
(2 May 1982–9 November 2008)

Contents

List of Figures		*ix*
Preface		*xv*
A Note on Sources		*xix*
Prologue		*xxi*
1	The Landscape	1
2	The Legacy of the Mediaeval Town	17
3	Early Improvements	57
4	The Designed City	83
5	From Classic to Caledonian	115
6	Architecture for Everyman	161
7	Granite City	205
8	Learning from the City	221
Bibliography		*253*
Ilustration Credits		*275*
Index		*281*

List of Figures

Prologue

0.1   Camillo Sitte, Piazetta and Piazza of St Mark, Venice (woodcut, *Town Planning on Artistic Principles* (French edition 1911)

0.2   Bridge Of Dee, Aberdeen (19th-century photograph City Library)

1   The Landscape

1.1   Pictish Stone, Monymusk (John Logan, drawing 1819, Royal Commission on the Ancient and Historical Monuments of Scotland)

1.2   Peterculter with Culter House and Grounds in the centre, and the site of the Roman Marching Camp to the left at Oldtown (part of Gen William Roy's MS *Great Map* 1747–55, National Library of Scotland and the King's Maps, British Museum)

1.3   Stephen Switzer, part of a *Forest or Rural Garden* (print from *Ichnographia Rustica* 1718)

1.4   Monymusk, showing Grant's improvements (part of Gen William Roy's MS *Great Map* 1747–55, National Library of Scotland and the King's Maps, British Museum)

1.5   Alexander Milne, *A Plan of the City of Aberdeen with all the Inclosures surrounding the Town to the adjacent Country* (printed map 1789 Aberdeen Art Gallery/Maritime Museum)

2   The Legacy of the Mediaeval Town

2.1   St Nicholas Kirk (print 1822, City Library)

2.2   James Gordon, *The Newtown of Aberdeen* (part of printed map *Abredoniae utriusque Descriptio* 1661, National Library of Scotland)

2.3   Benholm's Lodging, Netherkirkgate (19th-century print City Library)

2.4   Shiprow with Provost Ross' House, looking south-west (19th-century print City Library)

2.5   Wharf (drawing by George Taylor, *Design of a Road…1793* Aberdeen Art Gallery and Museum Collections)

2.6   The Odds Quarter and the Green Quarter (part of Gordon's *Abredoniae* 1661, National Library of Scotland)

2.7   Bow Brig and The Green, looking east (19th-century print City Library)

2.8   Schoolhill and Upperkirkgate, looking east (drawing 1865 City Library)

2.9   Ross' Court looking south to Upperkirkgate (19th-century print City Library)

2.10   Gallowgate and Broadgate, the Spine of the Mediaeval Town; Odds Quarter to west, Evens Quarter to east (part of Gibbs' *Plan* a printed map of 1864, Aberdeen Art Gallery and Museum Collections)

2.11   John Slezer Old Aberdeen (detail of print 1692, Royal Commission on the Ancient and Historical Monuments of Scotland)

2.12   Old Aberdeen (part of Gordon's *Abredoniae* 1661, National Library of Scotland)

2.13   Prospect of Aberdeen looking south from the Spital (part of Hutton's drawing, circa 1750, Royal Commission on the Ancient and Historical Monuments of Scotland)

2.14   Broadgate with gateway to Marischal College left and Cistern in centre (19th-century photograph City Library)

2.15   Byron's House Broad Street (drawing by R. Strachan 1899 City Library)

2.16   Broadgate, west side, also known as Guestrow (19th-century photograph City Library)

2.17   85 Broad Street, Grant's Emporium for Tea (Building Warrant 1887, Aberdeen City Archive)

2.18   34 Broad Street at Queen Street, Hutcheson's Bakery (Building Warrant 1890 Aberdeen City Archive)

2.19   73–5 Broad Street Proposal for Henry Gray's 2nd premises (Building Warrant 1902 Aberdeen City Archive)

2.20 & 2.21   Guestrow, Ragg's Lane and Broad Street (Building Warrant 1898 Aberdeen City Archive)

2.22   Guestrow showing parts to be demolished 1926 (print Aberdeen Art Gallery and Museum Collections)

2.23   Provost Skene's House (print City Library)

2.24   Ragg's Lane (19th-century print City Library)

2.25   New Loan Company 29 Broad Street, detail of plan (Building Warrant 1903 Aberdeen City Archive)

2.26   Design for Esslemont and Macintosh's store, Broadgate and Netherkirkgate (Building Warrant 1902 Aberdeen City Archive)

2.27   Café Royal, section (Building Warrant 1897 Aberdeen City Archive)

2.28   Entry to Broadgate from Union Street (19th-century photograph City Library)

2.29   Longacre being demolished for further extensions to Marischal College (19th century photograph City Library)

2.30   Marischal College (1822 print City Library)

2.31   The Castlegate in 1661 (part of Gordon's *Abredoniae* National Library of Scotland)

2.32   South Prospect of Aberdeen (part of John Home's map of *Aberdeen Harbour* 1769 Aberdeen Art Gallery and Museum Collections)

3   Early Improvements

3.1   Castlegate, detail from painting by Hugh Irvine of Drum, 1800 (print Aberdeen Art Gallery and Museum Collections)

3.2   William Adam, Robert Gordon's Hospital (print 1822 City Library)

3.3   Tolbooth, Townhouse, New Inn and Mercat Cross, West end of the Castlegate, early 19th century (print City Library)

3.4   Wharf and Marischal Street with Tolbooth (Home *Map* 1769 Aberdeen Art Gallery and Museum Collections)

LIST OF FIGURES

3.5 W.S. Percy, Marischal Street Bridge with Virginia Street in 1932 (drawing City Library)

3.6 Old Aberdeen Town House and High Street (drawing Aberdeen Art Gallery and Museum Collections)

3.7 Castlegate from Rotten Row (late 18th-century drawing City Library)

3.8 Robert Adam, *Elevation for a Record Office for the Town of Aberdeen* 1772 (Soane Museum)

3.9 Record Office and 1770 tenement blocks (mid 19th century photograph City Library)

3.10 R. Seaton, Castlegate, 1806 (print Aberdeen Art Gallery and Museum Collections)

3.11 Marischal Street, James Burn, Banking Company in Aberdeen and 57 Castle Street (print 1822 City Library)

3.12 Charles Abercrombie, *Plan…Canal from the Harbour of Aberdeen to…Inverury* (sic) (print by J. Cary 1796, City Library)

3.13 Charles Abercrombie, design for a new street and bridge across the Denburn, (part of *Plan and Section of Two New Lines of Road from Aberdeen, to The Two Bridges over the Rivers Dee and Don, together with some further Improvements proposed in that City* print, nd but 1796, National Archive of Scotland)

4 The Designed City

4.1 Charles Abercrombie (*Plan and Section* 1796, National Archive of Scotland)

4.2 Colin Innes, West end of Castlegate and part of New South Entry (drawing, 1798 Aberdeen City Archive)

4.3 David Hamilton, *Design, for the Bridge across the Denburn* 1800 (Aberdeen Art Gallery and Museum Collections)

4.4 James Young, Design for the South Entry of Aberdeen 1800 (Aberdeen Art Gallery and Museum Collections)

4.5 Robert and James Adam, the Adelphi, London from the Thames (Soane Museum)

4.6 Percier and Fontaine, Rue du Rivoli Paris (Pugin 1829)

4.7 A. Shannon, South Entry of Aberdeen from the Denburn Bridge (computer generated image 2008)

4.8 Charles Abercrombie, Aberdeen New Town (detail of Abercrombie, *Plan and Section* 1796, National Archive of Scotland)

4.9 Thomas Fletcher, Aberdeen in 1807 (drawing Aberdeen City Archive)

4.10 John Smith, Design for the Fittie Quarter (detail of *Plan of Aberdeen* 1810 National Archive of Scotland)

4.11 John Smith, Aberdeen west of the Denburn (detail of *Plan of Aberdeen* 1810 National Archive of Scotland)

5 From Classic to Caledonian

5.1 James Henderson, King Street junction with Castlegate (print 1842 Aberdeen Art Gallery

5.2 The Bridewell from the east (print 1822 City Library)

5.3 Assembly Rooms, Union Street (print 1822 City Library)

5.4 Aberdeen from site of Round Table to Justice Port (detail from Ordnance Survey, 1st edition National Library of Scotland)

5.5 Union Buildings, north elevation (drawing City Library)

5.6 Mercat Cross after removal eastward and restoration (drawing, circa 1850 Aberdeen Art Gallery and Museum Collections)

5.7   St Nicholas Kirk and Façade (late 19th-century photograph City Library)

5.8   Market Street in 1840 (print City Library)

5.9   Railway Terminus, Market Street (drawing 1848, probably by James Henderson, Aberdeen Art Gallery and Museum Collections)

5.10   New Trades Hall (print circa 1850 City Library)

5.11   The Triple Kirks and the Denburn Valley (print circa 1850 City Library)

5.12   Union Street East from Bridge (photograph circa 1890 City Library)

5.13   Union Street West (photograph circa 1890 City Library)

5.14   James Elliott, Design for Feuing the Damlands of Rubislaw (drawing circa 1820 Royal Commission on the Ancient and Historical Monuments of Scotland)

5.15   Western Suburbs in the late 19th century (detail from Gibbs' *A Birds-eye View of the City of Aberdeen 1889* Aberdeen Art Gallery and Museum Collections)

5.16   City of Aberdeen Land Association's new streets centred on Queen's Cross 1868 (printed map City Library)

5.17   North western suburbs from Upperkirkgate to Short Loanings in 1866 (detail of printed map Gibbs *Plan of Aberdeen* 1866, Aberdeen Art Gallery and Museum Collections)

5.18   North western suburbs in 1889 (detail from Gibbs *Birds-eye Aberdeen* Art Gallery and Museum Collections)

5.19   Rosemount, design prototype for Compartment, 1880 (drawing Aberdeen City Archive)

5.20   Rosemount Extension and Improvement Plan 1882 (print Aberdeen Art Gallery and Museum Collections)

5.21   Christ's College (print City Library)

5.22   Castlegate, Design for Monumental Gothic Building (drawing Aberdeen Art Gallery and Museum Collections)

5.23   W.S. Percy, New Town House Tower from Broad Street (drawing 1932 City Library)

5.24   Archibald Simpson, Marischal College rebuilt, 1838 (print City Library)

5.25   A. Marshall Mackenzie, Design for extended Marischal College, retaining Greyfriars Kirk 1890s (City Library)

5.26   Schoolhill, Upperkirkgate and Marischal College in 1880s (print City Library)

5.27   Schoolhill, Upperkirkgate and Marischal College with proposed changes (print City Library)

5.28   Schoolhill, Mitchell and Muill's Bakery Block (print City Library)

5.29   Schoolhill and Upperkirkgate in late 19th century (print City Library)

5.30   Schoolhill, and Upperkirkgate improved 1918 (drawing City Library)

6   Architecture for Everyman

6.0   Bungalow Prototype. Mrs Yeats of Auqharneys' house occupied this very prominent site near Holburn junction for most of the 19th century (late 19th-century photograph, Robert Gordon University and City Library)

6.1   *Early Houses*, Scara Brae, Benholm's Lodging, and Provost Skene's House (James Hand)

6.2   Prototype tenement (18th-century drawing Aberdeen Art Gallery and Museum Collections)

6.3   *Urban Houses*, 19–23 Castlegate, Upperkirkgate/Gallowgate corner, 30

Marischal Street, Upperkirkgate Drum's Hospital Lane (James Hand)

6.4   *Trustees Houses*, James Young Union Street and Castlegate, King Street (James Hand)

6.5   *Tenement blocks*, King Street Road, Thomson Street, Forrest Road, Schoolhill at Gordon *square*, Schoolhill (Jameson's House site) ground floor and upper floor (James Hand)

6.6   *Local authority houses*, manse type, modern tenement, cottage, post-war tenement (James Hand)

6.7   Old Rubislaw House, 50 Queen's Road (drawing City Library)

6.8   *National Type*, Brighton Place, King Street Road ground and upper floors, Hamilton Place, 50 Queen's Road (early) (James Hand)

6.9   *Houses*, Granton Lodge, Dalmunzie House, 2 Devanha Gardens ground and upper floors (James Hand)

6.10   Granton Lodge with other early 19th-century suburban pocket-estates, from the first edition Ordnance Survey (National Library of Scotland)

6.11   Old cottage type (detail from Hutton, *Prospect of Aberdeen* Royal Commission of the Ancient and Historical Monuments of Scotland)

6.12   *Cottages*, typical, Broadford Crossover, King Street, Carden Place, and Carden Place at Prince Arthur Street (James Hand)

6.13   Cross-over Cottages at Gilcomston (19th-century photograph City Library)

6.14   Carden Place early 1860s (photograph City Library)

6.15   *Bungalows*, Torphins, Anderson Drive, Garden Kingsgate, Bissett type

6.16   *High flats*, Ashgrove and Kepplestone (James Hand)

7   Granite City

7.1   Hardwierd (19th-century photograph City Library)

7.2   Gallowgate from Upperkirkgate corner (19th-century photograph City Library)

7.3   Gallowgate showing proposed demolitions (drawing circa 1890 Aberdeen City Archive)

7.4   Powis House and Policies (detail from Gibbs *Plan* 1866 Aberdeen Art Gallery and Museum Collections)

7.5   Rosemount Square site plan (Alexander 1939)

7.6   Kincorth Garden City Civic Centre (Alexander 1939)

7.7   M.N. Mason, Market Street looking towards New City Centre (drawing 1949 City Library)

7.8   M.N. Mason, Union Street with the New Castlegate (drawing 1949 City Library)

7.9   Old Aberdeen as University Precinct (City Library)

8   Learning from the City

8.1   Prospect of Aberdeen across the Denburn Valley from the west in 1661 (part of Gordon *Abredoniae* 1661 National Library of Scotland)

8.2   D.E.D. MacClean, Proposed Design for the Junction of Union Bridge and the Denburn Valley at Union Terrace Gardens, Robert Gordon University student project (drawing 1989)

8.3   Union Bridge and the Denburn Valley in the 1830s (drawing Aberdeen Art Gallery and Museum Collections)

8.4   Sebastiano Serlio, Dramatic Modes *Tragedy Comedy* and *Satyr* 1530s

8.5   Union Bridge and Denburn Valley (drawing circa 1835 City Library)

8.6   Union Terrace and Denburn Valley Gardens in 1847 (printed map Aberdeen City Archive)

8.7   Denburn Valley just prior to the Great North of Scotland Railway (detail from Gibbs *Plan* 1866 Aberdeen Art Gallery and Museum Collections)

8.8   James Forbes Beattie, Design for Denburn or Union Terrace Gardens (print 1884 City Library)

8.9   Union Terrace Gardens and Denburn Valley showing Beattie's work (photograph circa 1884 City Library)

8.10   Denburn Valley as proposed by Dobson and Chapman, *Granite City*, City Library

8.11   Proposal to cover the Denburn Valley and Union Terrace Gardens and provide car-parking garage (print, circa 1960 City Library)

8.12   Denburn Valley as proposed by Robert Gordon University students (1996 axonometric drawing from *The Neo-Classical Town*)

8.13   Denburn Valley as proposed by Robert Gordon University students (plan 1996 from *The Neo-Classical Town*)

8.14   Denburn Valley with Union Bridge (early 19th-century drawing Aberdeen Art Gallery and Museum Collections)

Preface

The majority of us now live in cities of some kind, but this is a fairly recent thing. A few generations back those living in cities were a minority, and the cities themselves were still relatively small. Of those an even smaller number had much longevity, and fewer still had claims to having been designed. Cities began to grow quickly from the beginning of the 18th century, when London could claim a million population; many new settlements in colonial America were then in place, though few were cities and others followed elsewhere. Concerns about how cities might be designed can be traced to roughly the same time. We have yet to achieve a satisfactory answer about design, although more are concerned to find such a thing, and even more know what they like, or more usually, what they dislike.

My own interest in cities began early when as a small child I recall a being taken with my father into a coffee shop within a glazed arcade, itself part of the biggest building in a seaport town, the *Virginia Dare Hotel* at ten stories tall the pride of the 'metropolis of the Albemarle' (Bishir 1996: 98). The densely built up downtown was then bustling with all kinds of activity and folk, including, I recall *White Russians* and on three sides it gave way to tree lined streets of closely built tall houses behind front porches called *piazzas*. Such a town as Elizabeth City has since, rightly, became a prototype for what is thought best and most desired in urban living (Calthorpe 1993) not only in the USA, but increasingly throughout our culture. With a population just over ten thousand it was then roughly the size of Aberdeen when James Gordon recorded it for us in his most excellent map and account of 1661. What he described already had a long history, and would cut a figure on the world's stage from the 19th century, when Elizabeth City began its coalescence from tiny Nixonton. It is the purpose of this book to show how Aberdeen, like other successful designed towns can be seen as The Perfect Pattern for a Town.

It, indeed like many cities, despite the palpable sense of excitement felt among those in a train or plane as it approaches the city, takes some knowing before it can be loved. Venice, or Paris, it is not. That is the first lesson: a city may be an excellent one without being at the top of everybody's list of best towns. There is another, more profound lesson here too. That the knowing of a town takes time, and it also takes study if it is to be other than local received wisdom. Curiously such studies are rare, and the present book is the kind I would wish to read about any city but am rarely able to do so, simply because they do not exist.

Aberdeen is old and it has been fortunate not to be destroyed by hostile armies. Its prosperity has been slow of growth but sure. It has kept its records moderately well, and much better than many towns. It has been constructed out of the most durable of materials, and it has not stinted itself foolishly by building cheap. Its topography or landscape is friendly but quirky…just awkward enough to encourage leaving it well alone and so ideal designs have been accommodated to local character. And, of course, the work of earlier citizens is always there to guide, or to form a friendly impediment to change. All these have formed over a long time the way the city is, and the way it looks.

Its citizens have been more adventurous than many, and have travelled much for curiosity or fortune, in business or in service. Whatever was the fashion in whatever hot-spot, there was an Aberdonian to note it, and sometimes to bring it back home where occasionally he was able to convince his neighbours to adopt it. Although it has always been remote it has never been ignorant of current thinking, or provincial in applying it. For its own reasons the city decided to embark on a series of urban improvements in the 18th century, none of which could have been certain of success, and in even the boldest the collateral damage to the town of these improvements was minimized. Apart from being induced to lose one's house, at a good rate, the creation of the new South Entry at the turn of the century was conducted so fastidiously, that most Aberdonians were little troubled by mess and upset. In that decade the town simply continued about its business.

Once it had broken out of its mediaeval form the opportunities to develop became part of the town's business, and at each stage…design, reflection sometimes disputatious, usually allowed a deliberate growth in area and population. Always the principles guiding them were, what is the best pattern or model and how does that suit us as Aberdonians. When affirmation was general then the project went ahead. Rarely was it otherwise, and on those few occasions the mess has still to be sorted. Sadly, our collective memory needs to be tutored and reminded. That is so even in Aberdeen. It cannot be trusted to leaders of politics or business to also have the answers to design matters, and to have mastered the lessons of history. Becoming rich and or powerful is a full time occupation which does not necessarily carry with it wider wisdom.

I have been fortunate in having the job of teaching university students about design and the history of architecture, mostly in Aberdeen (Brogden 2006). From the most fundamental sharing of the works of illustrious masters such as Alberti or Wren we have engaged more locally with Gibbs, Campbell, and Adam. From them, masters and students, I have learned much, and with them we have explored all kinds of conditions and possibilities, about Berlin, Venice or Aberdeen. Aberdeen has been our focus for the last two decades in studies linking history and design, and in those studies the ideas and knowledge in this book have come about. It is great pleasure to acknowledge my debt to my students of architectural history who had no choice, and to those who chose the Honours options, and especially those who joined the Masters Office of Urban Architecture studio.

There are particular kindnesses I have to acknowledge also. Donald Smart and Carol Southee have acted as *constant readers* of the whole, and their reactions and questions from far away New Zealand have made the whole much stronger and palatable. Eamonn Canniffe read an early draft and his positive response is warmly acknowledged. Jim Fiddes has brought his vast knowledge of local history to bear, advantageously, by reading the bulk of the text. Locally James Lamb read early chapters, as did Andrew Carruthers, and commented robustly and pertinently. Sandy Beattie, Brian Evans and Neil Lamb have commented on the latest parts to my advantage. I am grateful to them and to the anonymous publisher's readers for their suggestions, corrections and musings. I have taken their advice on board, and any mistakes still present are my fault entirely.

Former Provost Jim Wyness has provided long term friendly counsel. I am grateful to the City for supporting my work from funds set up by the Scottish Government, and administered through the City Growth Fund by the Chief Executives' Office by Ciaran Mongnahan, Rosalyn Downes, Will Napier, and Fraser Innes.

Various Councillors generously gave me their time for their personal histories and candid thoughts of the city, and I benefited much from Muriel Jaffray, Jill Wisely, Scott Cassie, John Stewart and Kevin Stewart. Officials in the council, Tom Moore; Eileen Smith, Trevor Smith, Sandy Beattie, and Douglas Campbell have been specially helpful.

My debt to the Museums, Libraries, and Universities in Aberdeen is very great and my thanks for their patient responses to countless questions is bound to fall short of their efforts. At Aberdeen Archaeology and History, thanks to Judith Stones, Alison Cameron, and Chris Croly: at the Aberdeen City Archive, thanks to Phil Astley, Martin Hall Fiona Musk, and Ruraidhi Wishart: at Aberdeen City Library thanks to Susan Bell, David Main, Katharine Taylor, and Louisa Costelloe: at the Art Gallery Christine Rew, Jennifer Melville and Emily Hope-Thomson led to me treasures rarely seen. At the Maritime Museum John Edwards as Museum and Galleries Head of Collections was exceptionally helpful, and to him and to Sandra McKay as photographer I am indeed grateful for the provision of excellent images from often difficult subjects. Siobhan Convery and the staff at Aberdeen University Special Collections, as always were superb, as were old friends at Robert Gordon University Library, Jim Fiddes, George Cheyne, and Jane Kidd. Bill Walker of RGU, Design and Print provided critical early help. For kindness on many occasions in sorting out technical problems I am very grateful to Nancy Anderson, Fergus Denoon, Colin Milne, and Darren Norris. Neil Lamb, David MacClean, Lynne Reid and Jonathan Scott have provided support beyond measure.

The staffs at the British Library, National Archives of Scotland, National Library of Scotland, Royal Commission on Ancient and Historical Monuments of Scotland especially Neil Fraser and Sir John Soane's Museum provided much service. To professional colleagues I am grateful for their reminiscences and information about their works: to Charlie Smith, at Jenkins and Marr; Iain Dickson, at Stewart and Watt; Gordon Smith as president of the Aberdeen Chapter of RIAS; Bob Reid, at Halliday Fraser Monro; John Michie of Aberdeen Shire and City Economic Future group; Joseph Sharples of the Pevsner Project; to my old partners John and Marion Donald Castlegate Design Group; to Ian Thomson, lately of Thomson Taylor Craig and Donald; to Mark Chalmers, John Buchan and Mike Gilmour; to Gary Strachan, and Allan Cumming; and to Mary Seth at Ashgrove Court. To Willie Anderson, at Meston and Reid; Trudy Milne of Lyon and McPherson Opticians and Martin Wilson at Dalmunzie many thanks for so kindly showing me their houses and flats. The late Neil Cameron, Royal Commission of the Ancient and Historic Monuments of Scotland; Alan Franchi, Aberdeen Arts Centre; and Ian Shepherd Aberdeenshire Archaeologist are sorely missed but their help remains.

Aisling Shannon and James Hand provided essential assistance in research and preparing drawings for publication. And friends Stuart Cowie, David Kinghorn, Norman Marr, David Paton, Patricia Seligman, Conrad Schaub, John and Judy Tankard shared time and support and bright ideas in so many ways.

I also wish to thank my editors at Ashgate, Val Rose and Celia Barlow, for their patient skilful and cheerful sheperding of this book through all its phases.

A Note on Sources

Since the records of Aberdeen have survived in such good order, it has encouraged later citizens and keepers to continue the good practice. What has survived has been assiduously protected and conserved, and where possible additions have been made. The Art Gallery, founded as Art Gallery and Industrial Museum has continued to add not only fine art subjects to its collections but also infra-structural engineering drawings, topography and maps, and with the establishment of the Maritime Museum this wider remit has continued.

The Town Clerk's Maps forms the nucleus of the city's collection and is housed in the archive in the Town House. These have been extensively used in preparing this book, and examples from the collection appear as illustrations. Although these can be supplemented by other collections, without these sources, not so much illustration, rather as documents in their own right, our knowledge of the earlier city would be significantly poorer. In their time, of course, many of these would have counted as ephemera. Their survival is therefore a blessing.

A similarly ephemeral kind of document is housed in the archive in the northern part of the city at Old Aberdeen. These are the Building Warrant Drawings, and provide architectural drawings for all works in the city for which approval was required. They cover the period 1871 to 1949, and are numbered in the thousands. Although many were consulted a select few are recorded here as references, and they appear in the Bibliography designated by place. These were produced for more than planning permission, which in earlier times was the business of the Police Commissioners, from 1796, working alongside, the fueing system which was the affair of land ownership, rental or feus and sub-feus, and the conditions about what could be built and in what form was set out in these. This system survived until the 1970s, but had been overtaken by Acts of Parliament establishing planning permission, and other acts reinforcing matters of health and safety.

It was as much, indeed more, for these concerns that the Building Warrant drawings were originally made. The earliest ones have less value, as under the Aberdeen Police and Waterworks Act of 1862 only drawings of the intended building outlines and depth of foundations were required. By the 1870s more detail was required by the Police commissioners and their successors, and soon the drawings were copies of full sets of plans showing not only water works and foundations but the construction and details of the plans as well as the exterior designs of the buildings. Such drawings are held in the archive. Not only do they give valuable information about new buildings, but very often, as much work then was remodelling as it is now, they can give the only details we can find about earlier buildings, as these have been subsequently demolished.

Sadly many towns and cities considered these as useless after their jobs were complete and few present the wealth of the Aberdeen collections. The temptation to *liberate* the drawings for important buildings has been impossible to resist, even here, so many buildings, for example His Majesty's Theatre, are missing. Even the more ordinary stock of buildings is not so well served as historians would wish: however, it still provides an extraordinarily strong documentary source for urban architectural history.

The illustrations used in this book are chosen, where possible, from period sources. So generally the image closest to the building's date of design and construction is used. Similarly maps of the period are preferred to later, perhaps more accurate, ones. Topographic paintings and drawings, sometimes of considerable artistic merit, sometimes rather less, have been used where possible, and as close to the period under discussion as possible. Photography in the city was a significant art form and indeed a business conducted on an industrial scale, for example, by G.W. Wilson's enterprise at Queen's Cross. These were taken for sale, and their subjects reflect the 19th century market. However, workaday information of value to us sometimes managed to survive as well.

Prologue

The architecture of cities, or urban architecture, is not so well studied as individual buildings, and many would deny such a thing even exists. And yet all recognize that Paris, or Venice, have physical quality of very significant power, and a moment's reflection will confirm it cannot come about entirely because the merit of Garnier's Opera, or Piano and Rogers' Pompidou Centre. It is the vistas of streets, all different, and yet all the same, with their monumental terminations and open spaces. These establish the readable template which allows the very large city to be easily grasped and used. Without these there would be no Paris (Jordon 1995). And a city, seemingly planned like Paris but only with monuments, and without endless streets of houses and shops would likely resemble parts of Washington, doubtless magnificent, but, somehow inadequate (Caemerrer 1932).

If the power of great cities to move us is accepted then many will deny that similar qualities can be found in smaller or even quite small cities, unless they are historic relicts visited on holiday. Pienze or Bruges are both major works of urban architecture, but they also have the air of the museum, and are perhaps too perfect to be accepted as real. Also as visitors we are apt to assume that what we see has always been, and if the site is historic, then its qualities are assumed to come from its great period. Rome has always been Rome and Venice similarly has been its perfect self for centuries. Although both these have very old beginnings, their set-pieces may not have flowered fully until quite recent times (Howard 1975).

Visitors to the piazza of St Mark's, even learned ones, or professionals in design or history have to be reminded that its status as the most magnificent drawing room in Europe was not only recognized by Bonaparte, but, in effect was made that way in the early 19th century under his direction. Until then there was a second monumental and very important church on its west side, standing opposite St Marks Basilica, with two significant openings to either side: the piazza therefore appeared more like a street, as the piazza San Stefano still does. Bonaparte realized that for the piazza of St Mark's to become a giant room it required to have a sense of closure at the west end. He also wished to have a palace in St Mark's Square. Therefore he transformed

0.1 Camillo Sitte, Piazetta and Piazza of St Mark, Venice

the south side of the square, the old offices, into regal accommodation. He also had the church removed and replaced by a monumental hall (Howard 2004, Canniffe 2008, Fenlon 2009). But he did this within an architecture of arcades with repetitive openings above, in other words, a kind of street architecture. His improvements transformed the great square by contrasting the wall-like north, west and south sides to the monumental east end with palace, basilica and clock-gate, pivoting about the off centre bell tower. So urban architecture is neither instant, nor necessarily as old as it might appear. And it is the result of many communal acts, over time – a kind of civic or social architecture. Much of it is quite recent and the whole effect often comes from repeated experiments in perfecting what was already good (Marder 1991).

The shape and design of towns is of great interest to many citizens, but most will have known that changes, for good or ill, are beyond them as individuals and securing agreement with neighbours to make changes is notoriously fraught with difficulty and is usually best avoided. Therefore developments in urban architecture have come about through the exercise of power, often tyrannical and oppressive whether it is civil or clerical in origin. Developments in Rome to rescue the ruined remaining fragments in the late 16th century were instigated by the Pope exercising newly acquired civil powers: even so, his vision was proscribed, and improvements had to be prolonged and shared before Rome reappeared as the major, and modern, city we all admire. Yet, his concerns and efforts were noticed by others, and they began to be imitated, nearby and far from Rome (MacDonald 1986, Morris 1994).

More typical, and yet equally influential, was the example of Ercole d'Este capo maestro of Ferrara in the 15th century. The city-states of Italy, especially the north, fought each other, formed alliances, and strove to keep their power: they also felt obliged to perform acts of civic virtue and to be seen to be encouraging the arts. D'Este was a patron of L.B. Alberti, the Renaissance polymath whose own circumstances gave him an Italian rather than a parochial point of view, and his own very exceptional qualities as a man were shown in his *De Re Aedificitoria*, the first book of architecture since antiquity (Alberti 1991).

Alberti's observation on straight streets linking to city gateways, what current designers and critics refer to as city clarity, and ease of access, carried a quite different message. Straight streets please a tyrant because it makes it easier for him to keep control, and when necessary, assert his power aggressively. Free citizens prefer a complicated, mazy series of streets where enemies can be confused, and civil power is less easily imposed. The New Town of Ferrara, the first of many we shall encounter was intended to double the size of the town as a whole, make the castle its centre, and, to perfect the geometries of old Ferrara. Thus the new northern half was divided by a broad, straight avenue linking castle and gateway in the extended town wall. Halfway along d'Este built four palazzi on the new renaissance pattern…tall, quadrangular, regular, well built and ornamented with classical architectural allusion. The New Town of Ferrara has yet to be complete after 500 years, that is to say it remains less densely built than the southern half. Yet it has acted as example to any who wish to perfect their own towns.

L.B. Alberti's book was not illustrated, and is not an easy read for those unfamiliar with the subject. Illustrations of architectural ideas are a feature of the following century when Sebastiano Serlio (Hart and Hicks 1996) and Andrea Palladio (Palladio 1997) wrote their own, rather more accessible works on architecture. Plans and views were commissioned to illustrate some of the great new experimental designs, such as the amazing Villa d'Este commissioned for d'Este's great nephew the Cardinal Ippolito II at Tivoli. Although this illustration was done for the King of France, it was engraved and published quickly to act as a guide and inducement for others, although still a very limited few. A little earlier, and for long accessible only to those invited to view them were a series of imaginary, ideal views or cityscapes. (Millon 1994, Krautheimer 233–57) These appear to have been executed in the 1490s, probably as part of the furniture for the study of a Prince, and it has been suggested that Fra Giaconda could be the artist. However private these paintings were, they clearly proposed designs of three sorts of open urban spaces with antique buildings (such as the Coliseum) and modern ones

0.2 Bridge Of Dee, Aberdeen

composed carefully and with great art, and these visions have entered our communal imaginations as exemplars.

How and when this happened is not clear. But theatrical sets, as part of a revived interest in ancient drama, were a relatively easier means to explore and propose an ideal or ancient environment than to build in a city or as a garden. Certainly within a few years Serlio published illustrations of appropriate stage sets for the three modes of drama recognized at the time, *Tragedy*, *Comedy* and *Satire*. His Tragic scenes had public buildings and communal spaces against which issues of the greatest public and communal importance could be enacted, and his vision shows the same kind of ideal urban scene exhibited in the cityscapes of the 1490s. Serlio's books enjoyed a wide circulation from their appearance in the 1530s onwards, and his illustrations, sometimes independent of his text, led lives of their own.

Linking towns to their countryside is another manifestation of urban architecture: initially to make entry and exit easier, and safer, and then these routes become places for expansion, and by implication citizens begin to wonder how also to make the congested cities themselves easier of passage and more regular. As far away as Aberdeen on the north-west edge of Europe a crossing of the Dee, proposed in late 15th century and finished by 1520, had these very effects. In Rome an improved crossing of the Tiber from the Vatican at the Castel S Angelo made the opening up a relatively populous part of the ancient city desirable. The means adopted consisted of a square or gathering place at the bridge end which led to three ways, goose-foot fashion, that is one to left, another to the right and the third straight on. Similar designs were soon adopted at other edges of cities, in Rome at the north end of the Via Flaminia, after many years development in the 16th and 17th centuries perfected as the Piazza del Popolo. In Paris a slightly enlarged version was begun in 1603 where the open space (in that case at a city Gate rather than bridge) was laid out as a semi-circle. That same form was proposed also by Christopher Wren as entry to the city from London Bridge in 1665 (Ballon 1991, Gwynne 1766). By the 17th century there were preferred, even ideal, models for modern buildings in towns, such as the palace block; there were ambitions to lay out New Towns adjacent to old ones; the architecture of these, the ways major spaces and streets were composed was also agreed; and very ambitious and expensive public works were undertaken to construct walls, and then more modern defences, or to construct bridges.

Such knowledge as we have from scholars about urban architecture comes from the big subjects, Rome or London. It was as late as 1966 that the *Making of Classical Edinburgh* (Youngson 1966) appeared, and such studies of smaller cities remain rare. This present work, *A City's Architecture*, seeks to show how a town such as Aberdeen was part of a contemporary and international growth and development of urban architecture. Initially it took, modified, and experimented locally with ideas from elsewhere, and from the mid 18th century it began to contribute forms and types of its own, and to share more equally with its neighbours in Europe and further afield. It is rare, perhaps unique, to find sufficient materials to chart a history of a designed city, from its pre-history to potential metropolis, but such a place is Aberdeen.

Town and country planning, to which urban architecture is related, has been popularly derided in the later 20th century, justifiably since there were many foolish departures from good sense, and plainly bad decisions taken in its name. But it is fair say that it has become also a trope for the less thoughtful journalism, whether print or broadcast, so that it is pretty near impossible to have an enlightened, or even civil, discussion about the subject. Planning appears to be sufficient reason in itself to condemn. There is, however, a fundamental and troubling aspect of planning theory which does need to be considered and changed. We have adopted, especially in America, and in these Islands, one form of ideal living for our habitations, and a quite different one for our work and institutions. Whereas we are content to see roads, infrastructure and places of work planned professionally and with some art, we resist any form of living which departs from single small dwelling houses in gardens, almost invariably on curving streets. While it may be accepted that it is impossible to make a city out of bungalows, only that form of house is acceptable. Therefore we have town for day, suburbs for night, and fraught congestion in between (Hayden 2003).

This cleavage goes back to the beginnings in the earliest Town and Country Planning Acts at the beginning of the last century (Unwin 1917). These grew out of hard thought and justified principles which can be traced back to the Enlightenment of which those of us who live in Scotland are justifiably proud. Patrick Geddes (Welter 2002), born in Aberdeenshire, continues to dominate planning philosophy, just as his ideas informed so much of earlier 20th century practice. That the 'science' of planning wandered into the thicket of 'systems' in the '70s can hardly be blamed on him, or, indeed on the subject: it remains one of the follies to be mended. More worrying is the 'cleavage' issue, and until we can resolve that there can be little progress. Crowded and dirty cities were the source of justified fears of death from disease in the late 19th century. The specific cures, however, were not justified although they are easy to understand. Light, especially bright sunlight was thought healthy in itself; similarly fresh air was known to be a good thing; congestion of streets and houses allowed infections to spread, as did impure water supplies, or contaminated well heads or common sinks of tenements (Welter 1999). Therefore to solve these problems there had to open, airy, sunny, and *detached* dwellings. This was, and remains wrong. Infection, whether from sick individuals, or water borne is the problem. Detachment is irrelevant. All else is innocent.

When issues of public health were being discussed and studied, another related series of thoughts was being perfected by Ebenezer Howard, and other artists and architects of Arts and Crafts philosophical persuasion led by William Morris and John Ruskin. These men and women took as their models the very honourable, if largely idealized, example of honest workmanship, simple unassuming and natural material and forms, and the consequent folk architecture of English country life (Greeves 1975). The Garden City Movement believed that villages and small towns of cottages in gardens with access to factories similarly disposed was the way forward. This aesthetic underlay early planning acts, and consequent practice. British planning was very influential abroad, on the Continent as much as in America or Empire.

The preferred form of houses for city living since the 1400s, and probably as far back as Roman *insulae* (Pevsner 1976) at least is the tenement...a big house on the street containing many and varied private dwellings. This is the type associated with Serlio's Comic stage sets, as comedies were understood to be about homely, personal matters in contrast to public and mighty matters treated in Tragedy. These sets are more informal, less classical but still as urban as his Tragic scenes are. Indeed there are tenements mixed with the antique and modern blocks in the ideal cityscapes of the 1490s. It is with this type that Scottish towns and cities were largely made, and each of the cities is convinced that its form is superior to others as it is characteristic of Edinburgh, or Glasgow, or Aberdeen.

The finest flowering of this type occurred in the late 19th and early 20th centuries. But since tenements were associated with crowded towns and disease, and had already, through our common language become synonymous with the gross over crowding on southern Manhattan, this flexible, innocent, always serviceable and sometimes magnificent form became suspect. In Garden City schemes (Tagliaventi 1994) the ideal was for no more than four houses to be used together, and better were semi-detached or single cottages. When legislation was formed at Westminster the predominant ideas were accepted without thought, and the characteristic form of Scottish cities not so much rejected as ignored. For only those house types which were approved could benefit from the subsidies introduced to encourage city and county councils to build after the World War.

For cities to succeed there has to be a wide range of building types, and when the tenement type is removed in favour of the cottage or bungalow the best urban form that can thrive would be Wallingford at best, or more likely Birmingham. With the City Architect's Office, then Department, under the direction of A.B. Gardner from the late '20s and then George Keith from the '50s, Aberdeen managed to continue, almost unbroken its commitment to urban architecture. (Alexander 1939, Glendinning 1996) There are no other cities whose 'slums' are made of coursed granite under good slate roofs, and exhibit the style and form so loved by the New Urbanists, and if our slums are so intrinsically attractive a little intelligent management of the buildings might make them disappear altogether (Calthorpe 1993).

Other cities have not been so fortunate, and yet any town or city in Scotland, however broken or seemingly unloved, is rich in urban architecture not to be found elsewhere in these Islands. There are lessons to learn, and principles to rediscover, and ample means to overcome the cleavage that has bedevilled our thinking about living and working in cities. When we have charted the development of urban architecture here, we will be in a position to recognize principles that can be used anywhere to advantage. A city's architecture can help to define the architecture of cities.

If any town and county within Britain can count as a *city state* it would be Aberdeen City and Shire (Brogden 1998, Geddes 2001, Shepherd 2006). Of roughly equal population, inextricably joined by history and culture, they are not only protected by geography, but they have no near competitors. It has always been an agriculturally rich area, and is well served by defensible harbours. And being on the north-west edge of Europe, and the north-east shoulder of Britain is has been mostly out of harm's way, and able to nurture its own ways unmolested.

To west and south are uplands. The mountainous Cairngorms begin to slope seawards more as hills within Aberdeenshire, and the southern barrier, the Mounth, is a line of ancient hills of the same range diminishing in height towards the coast along the Highland Line. In geological time these hills are exceptionally old, apparently as old as hills anywhere, and therefore, apart from significant outcrops, rounded and worn with age. The Mounth also marks the edge between the great geological plates of Europe and North America, which we now understand to underlie and determine the shapes the Earth's surface. The higher, or more remarkable hills have ancient names, such as the granite plug of Clach ma'ben near Cairn o' Mount, and to the west these are many, but, the whole of Aberdeenshire is presided over by Bennachie, the 'magic mountain' at the centre of the province, and visible from both north and east coasts and from the Mounth and seems to mark the rolling open plains divided by rivers. These plains were enriched by the scouring of the last glaciation producing fertile soils on bedrock. There are broad bands of *sandilands* along the coasts.

Aberdeenshire has been settled for thousands of years. Its early inhabitants gathered at naturally defensive places rich for hunting or gathering, such as at the confluence of the Ury and Don at the Bass of Inverurie where they left evidence of shell fishing. Agriculture has been practiced as early as the fourth millennium BC. Therefore forests have long been confined to uplands, riversides and marginal ground. Apparently Aberdeenshire has always presented an open, even empty landscape.

There is no history for the period before Christ, and very little in the 1st millennium since, but there are ample remains of human culture, even civilization, throughout this period to require our attention, and to oblige us to make such sense of it as we can. For the earliest dates we have the evidence of Balbridie, near Crathes, but this was excavated only in recent times, where there was a large, sophisticated hall-like timber building, and remains of agriculture on a seeming long settled site. More recently there has been a spectacular find nearby of monumental building at Warrenfield (Murray 2009). For much of these dark ages however we have the barrows, burial cairns and chambers, and hut settlements throughout the region, and, enriching these, seemingly later in the 1st millennium, are powerful artistic remains of the Caledonian people, characterized by Tacitus, and called Picts by Bede at our common history's beginning. It has always been agreed that these later monuments have significance to the landscape in some cultural way. In early references this was thought to be religious, and related to the 'Druids'. Although that is no longer believed, the strong relationship between buildings and landscape is still accepted. What might this relationship and its meanings be?

1

The Landscape

One aspect the peoples of north-west Europe and north-east Britain shared which we now find less easy to accept is the close relation between the land and the sea. We travel very much, over land, and we appreciate distance, and sense of place as elements of land. Since we do much less travelling by sea than earlier people we need to remind ourselves of its importance, and how it can be the missing 'field' in an understanding of Caledonia. To visit Nigg on the North Souttar of the Cromarty Firth, for example and look over towards the north coast of Aberdeenshire the difference in time implied by distance in space between the two places is quite notable and their potential closeness needs no further suggestion. This is even more compelling when considering the Pictish sculpted monolith, Shandwick Stone, on that headland, and reminding oneself of another, Suenno's Stone across the water at Forres, or the ancient church further north from Nigg at Portmahannoch, or, of Nigg Kirk closer at hand with its own sculpted stone depicting the two St Anthonys in the Desert of Sinai (Hendersons 2004).

This difference in attitude is key to understanding the Caledonian landscape. The sea has to be our field of view to give the appropriate sense and strength of landmarks, many of which are not immediately obvious. Bennachie is an endowed landmark, but so too, are apparently others, such as the valley of the Ugie from Peterhead, including New Deer, and Aikey Brae. Coasts, inlets of rivers, valleys, headlands, landmarks, 'places' of importance signified by art…these are the typical major elements of landscapes. One is tempted, perhaps, to add the embellishment provided by surviving woodland in an otherwise open country, as at ancient Greek sites. That carries us away too far, to other tropes, and there is presently little evidence for it.

The significance of landscape is enhanced by monumental art works, the standing stones, singly, in groups, and forming seeming enclosures. These vary in date from 3rd millennium BC to medieval, and there are modern ones for 'cattle rubbing'. Their meaning is unknown but earlier ones appear to be related to burial cairns. There does seem to be a relationship between standing stones of the 1st millennium of our era, the Pictish sculpted stones

1.1 John Logan, 1819 drawing of Pictish Stone, Monymusk

and the mediaeval clerical/political divisions of the later province which had accepted the parish, the last of the elements of Augustinian church government and Rome's delayed but ultimately successful *conquest*.

The earlier relationship has been easy to accept because most believe the later Caledonians had also been followers of Christ. So the relevance of these stones as markers for parish boundaries is attractive. However, large and imposing as they are these stones are not immovable. They were made using monoliths geologically associated with the recession of the last glaciers, so they cannot have place in themselves; they appear to have been moved in the five or six centuries between their making and the establishment of medieval Scotland. (The stone of Nigg was found in the nearby stream, seemingly abandoned, then brought into the kirk and given its own, independent, space. This suggests perhaps a different relationship, maybe a hostile one, between early church and the stones.) But the parishes and the stones are doubtless related in some way. As there are no Caledonian 'churches' to survive the idea of parishes signified by the stones would require argument to convince for which the evidence so far is insufficient (Doig 2009).

When standing stones are used to form circles, it is thought they are related in some way, as perhaps precursors, to the more highly developed, almost architectural complexity of the recumbent stone circles, '…one of the most distinctive categories of megalithic monuments in the British Isles' (RCAHMS 2007). These were thought to be in some way religious sites when first written about in the 15th century. Hector Boece (Boece 1821), an early historian and first principal of King's College, had sought to make a connection between them and the Druids, the obvious thing to do for a late 15th century scholar… put enigmatic local artefact into the context of history. This continued into the 17th century, when James Garden advised John Aubrey on his *Britannia*. That connection began to lose support with the growth of archaeology following the foundation of the Society of Antiquaries in the 18th century. That these sites were of great significance remains accepted by all, but the nature of that significance, moreover their siting in landscape remains to be explained.

What are they? They are open, circular spaces, and vary in size from roughly 10 metres diameter to 30; they are oriented towards the south, in that their raised platform, backed by a kind of dolmen element of three major monoliths, the 'recumbent' centre supported by the two vertical, is always on the south side of the earthen enclosure marked also by the more or less regular widely spaced smaller monoliths lying in the circle. A cairn is sometimes associated at the circle's centre, occasionally impinging on the platform itself. They are sited so as to provide extensive prospect, or, more probably, as objects in landscape to be seen from afar.

Their use is unknown: the most recent account of them suggests their function as funeral pyres, as there is evidence under the cairn element of a flattened and made surface, and also evidence of fire, often repeated. The significance of the three major monoliths, arranged with great art to bring out the colour and textures of the stones, and almost always to be viewed from the south, that is, outside the enclosure, is suggested to be, as it were, a closed doorway between the act of cremation and those still alive. Whatever the use, generally or particularly, the 'numinous' quality of both monument and site remains. The evidence of fire may point also to either bonfires at a later time or bonfires as perhaps the primary reason for being, that is, more to light, or to signal, than to transform corpse to ash. It has to be pointed out also that, as an alternative to enclosed spaces for early Christian fellowship these stone circles would make a very serviceable, even compelling 'kirk', but this has yet to be proposed by any archaeologist. Nearly forty of these monuments survive near Aberdeen, and many others are known to have perished. They were sited not only prominently, but on the best land for cultivation. Once their ceremonial use had faded they would clearly be at risk from harder headed farmers. As they are exceptionally old (these monuments date from the third millennium BC) it is more a marvel that any survive at all, and that fact reinforces the suspicion that they have been reused by the community in relatively recent times.

The circular form for buildings with roofs appears universal in early societies, almost to the point of being *natural*. Even though there were large hall-type buildings (Balbridie, above) in Aberdeenshire, the circular form seems preferred, and its type characteristics can be detected even in quite modern vernacular buildings into the 19th century. At Druidstone near Premnay is a fragmentary example of individual stones, recumbent circle, burial mounds and related hut circles. The design of such a proto-village is a loose assembly of identical forms of varying size distant from its neighbours, roughly, by two to three times its diameter. Similar patterns can be found in other early societies. These groupings, and individual buildings, appear to have been a common rounded almost always circular type. These 'round houses' whether for habitation, storage, or other use were made from both timber and stone, with, doubtless a light roof under thatch (Murrays 2010).

There is aerial photographic evidence of hundreds of these surviving in Aberdeenshire. These appear to date from the 1st millennium BC into the 1st millennium AD. They vary between three and 16 meters, with most seven to 11 meters diameter with walls one to three meters in thickness. Of those that have been excavated are indications of post holes inside. At Greenbogs near Monymusk are more oval houses, one with a centre square of three meters defined by posts, with a further ring of posts at one metre intervals. The larger diameters, especially over 20 meters of which there are many, some up to 90 meters diameter, suggest enclosures containing one, two or many houses. No *brochs* have been identified in Aberdeenshire. Souterrains are common however, and relate to round houses here as they do to brochs on Orkney or Shetland. These very well built but mysterious buildings are said to be for storage, perhaps for communication also, but it is difficult to imagine just how they could be used, and why they were built.

Somewhat easier for us to comprehend are the fortified places of Aberdeenshire. Three of these are very prominent indeed, and they appear in early history. Bennachie itself bears evidence of its fortification at the Mither Tap, and also possessed a citadel among the outcrop of great stones. Almost as prominent is the fort of Tap o' Noth northwest in Strathbogie. Here the summit of a conical great hill was levelled and fortified, and at some time parts of its fortifications were fused by fire, vitrified. Both these fortifications are small in terms of providing refuge, but their potency as symbol, and military power is manifest. They are clearly ancient but specific dating has not been possible thus far. However, most recent investigation reports that these forts were destroyed in the latter centuries of the 1st millennium BC, and they were subsequently quarried to build castles in the Middle Ages. Tacitus (Tacitus 98), the 1st century Roman historian, wrote in his biography of Agricola of the great battle of Mons Graupius, which is associated with Bennachie and Tap O' Noth, and gave the name to the Grampian Hills. The remains of a camp nearby at Logie Durno have been identified as Agricola's base camp for his famous confrontation, and defeat of Calcagus.

The third major fortress is Dunottar, which has continued its active role into modern times. Dunottar is fortified by its site on rocky prominences technically peninsular but really unassailable by sea or land. It is an important place in histories of post-Roman Britain (Bede 731) and was a major stronghold of Pictland. There are also a number of smaller fortified places, less fearsome, more accessible, and offering potential for greater refuge, and some of these such as Barra (east of Inverurie) may have served also in a sense as towns, and might therefore be associated with the larger enclosures of round houses.

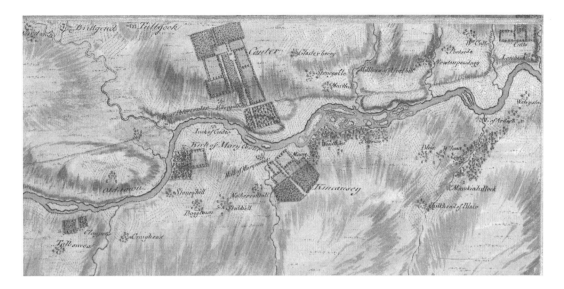

1.2 Peterculter with Culter House and Grounds in the centre, and the site of the Roman Marching Camp to the left at Oldtown

However, no settlement sustained into modern times confirms such an idea. Further excavations may well provide that confirmation. Without that we can be no more precise about any disposition within such a settlement, other than the scant evidence such as Druidstone supplies.

Apart from Agricola's base camp north of Inverurie, there is other evidence of Roman presence in Aberdeenshire. For example, Normandykes lies west of the settlement of Oldtown, just outside the present city boundaries on the north bank of the Dee, and is what remains of one of the marching camps associated with punitive forays into Caledonia from the secure frontiers further south. It appears to belong to the earliest of these, Agricola's decisive campaign for Domitian of 82–3 AD (Tacitus). Normandykes is related to others of these camps a day's march away such as Raedykes near Stonehaven, and at Kintore which has been recently investigated. Some 180 field ovens scattered throughout the site have been identified and 60 rubbish dumps. These investigations show occupation at various dates between 330 and 610 AD. Normandykes has not yet been excavated (RCAHMS 98, 9–10). It occupies a ridge site above the Dee and is an orthogonally laid out rectangle of about 1300 meters, east-west, by 70 meters, that is, comparable to the size, shape and siting of the 1st New Town of Edinburgh.

Retrieving a landscape of such antiquity is bound to be sketchy and incomplete or even problematic. There is much we would wish to know. But this much is clear. Aberdeenshire has been part of a civilization for at least the two millennia before and since Christ, and apart from our inability to 'speak' with the Picts, without significant breaks. It still presents the character of an open landscape with an architecture which ranges through type from sophisticated monument, to the widespread and ordinary in which we can discern the features common in western culture prior to architecture. This landscape is one of meaning, or meanings, which have been long recognized, if not elucidated. The last two millennia of the province's civilization sees the creation and growth of Aberdeen from one of upwards of a hundred other urban clusters into the complex city it presents today, and that growth and development has been, and remains, part of the long term development of the landscape.

The landscape specific to Aberdeen is separated from the Bennachie prominent plain of the province by Tyrebagger Hill which seems to embrace the current city on the west side, as the broad expanse of Aberdeen Bay forms its east side, from the headland at the mouth of the Dee northwards to Peterhead (Roy 2008). The south side is formed by The Mounth which ends in cliffs south of Nigg Bay. Within that are the Dee, the Don and the Denburn, and many lesser streams. The numerous low hills do not detract from an impression of a large crescent shaped plain sloping to the east. The heart of the city, and for a long time the town proper, lies on Schoolhill, St Katharine's Hill, Castle Hill, and Porthill, but there were many other places which might have been the city's centre, and they retained their territorial distinction into the 20th century, and can still be recognized. This appears to be characteristic of Aberdeenshire as a whole at the turn of the 1st millennium AD; in other words it was consistently settled by groups of towns, townships, and hamlets.

Thus 20 potential towns may be said to represent types suggested by their mature forms in the 18th century. There are three *kirk towns*, Dyce, Aberdon, and the Evens quarter of Aberdeen; *roadside* describes three others Hardwierd, Cuparston, and the Fittie quarter of Aberdeen, which could also count amongst the *coastal* types with Torry and Dee Village. There are three *milltowns*, Culter, Gilcomston and Woodside. There are three *planned* towns, the Odds quarter of the city, Woodside and 'new' Aberdon. Finally there are a group of five *Y-types*, a sufficiently complex form to be a town, and to support growth: these are: The Green quarter of the city, Old Aberdeen (Aberdon plus 'new' Aberdon), Hardgate, Ruthrieston, and Gilcomston South.

Apart from the types supporting specific functions there are towns elsewhere in Aberdeenshire where these types have all grown up, as it were, and which support populations up the 20,000 or thereby, comparable to the population of Aberdeen when it began to be expanded. Inverurie and Kintore are Y-types; Kincardine O' Neil is a roadside type; Stonehaven is coastal, and with its new town, modern planned; and Oldmeldrum is planned also, but rather earlier.

We have an established European culture, its own potential transition from ancient folk architecture of the round houses (already with hints of a move to rectangular forms), and evidence of a beginning stone built infrastructure in the souterrains. To this the medieval period, in Aberdeenshire as elsewhere in these islands and the continent, saw the coalescence of kingdoms such as Pictland into larger ones, and after the Conqueror under Norman influence. There are estates, with parishes, which give the landscape forms which are still with us, however much they were likely simply transitions from earlier Pictish modes. And there are towns. These are largely contemporary with kings, knights, castles, monks, parishes and bishops. Some, such as Aberdeen,

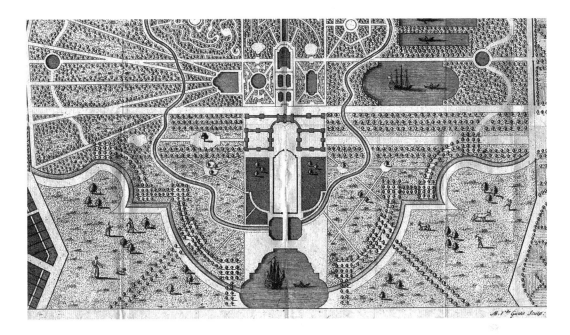

1.3 Stephen Switzer, part of a *Forest or Rural Garden*

appear to be somewhat earlier, but as 'system' towns begin to thrive from the 11th century and many more are established after that time.

We have no surviving evidence of the forms of agriculture from earlier times. It is assumed that the system in place until the 18th century was itself the pattern which had developed without revolution over the millennia. This was based on the rig, or run-rig, and both are related to the burghal plot. The name is first recorded in early 15th century Scotland, although its roots come from the continental sources of our language. It derives from the ploughed furrow, the run, and the resulting ridges between. These patterns can still be seen in many parts of Aberdeenshire, for example, across Barra Fort (above). The widths were between five and seven meters in both agricultural and urban settings. These long narrow 'fields' insured that good land, and less fertile land, could be fairly distributed among tenants by landlords. Changes to the countryside, such as drainage, enclosures, and redistributions on any but the smallest scale was difficult, and effectively, impossible. There were, of course, meadows, ancient forests and some of these were imparked and set aside for hunting, but the characteristic design form or feature was the linear pattern of cultivation. This, with very frequent mosses, or bogs, was the covering of the ground of Aberdeenshire.

From the 17th century, but especially following the Treaty of Union of Parliaments, there is a revolution in agricultural theory and practice. This has transformed our landscape so thoroughly that it is difficult to imagine alternatives. That revolution was carried on as a community effort. It was neither imposed from government, since 1707 established at Westminster, nor even dreamt of by that government. Although it used elements from the Act of Union, and was led by aristocratic landowners, it was also the equal concern

1.4 Monymusk, showing Grant's improvements

of professionals – lawyers, clerics, or surveyors. This transformation of landscape occurs along side, and as a significant part of, the Enlightenment, and it includes not only philosophical discourse about agriculture, but also estate planning, town and village design, roads, canals, harbour works, and also improved building...a melding of local best practice with the Vitruvian (McEwen 2003).

Indication of this revolutionary community effort is to be seen in the *Transactions of the Honourable the Society of Improvers in the Knowledge of Agriculture in Scotland* published in 1742. Familiarly known as The Scotch Improvers these were a corresponding group of the like minded who shared their ideas, their practice, and their knowledge, presumably informally, and these fragments were drawn together and printed by the Society's secretary Robert Maxwell of Arkland (Maxwell 1742). Included were the very great, such as the Duke of Atholl, the moderately great like Clerk of Penicuik, and the professional such as James Boutcher of Comely Bank Edinburgh. One of the most effective and energetic of the Improvers was Archibald Grant of Monymusk. Grant, a lawyer, had acquired an old Forbes property on the Don just below Bennachie at the beginning of the 18th century. He enclosed his lands into parks (as fields in Scotland were known henceforth), planted shelter belts of forest trees to protect them from winds, and used his parks for cultivation and pasture.

He also planted prodigiously for profit, believing with John Evelyn and others that forests were a prudent long term investment for the good of the country, as well as family. Like other improvers Grant planted for the pleasure of it, and his gardens and walks were part of his agriculture, as his canals for draining boggy ground were equally decorative elements in landscape. One of Grant's fellow Improvers, and the only Englishman in this group of Improvers, was Stephen Switzer whose *Ichnographia Rustica* was the first theory of landscape making (Switzer 1718). In it Switzer wrote of his friend's account of Bennachie and its impact on the quality of landscape nearby. And Grant produced *Paradise* at The Lord's Throat, a detached pleasure garden/woodland or the kind described and advocated by Switzer from his experience at Castle Howard. Indeed Grant's Monymusk was for all intents and purpose an example of Switzer's *Ferme Ornee*. Atholl's Blair, and Clerk's Penicuik, similarly were early exercises in landscape gardening, and the idea of perfecting landscape, for profit and pleasure, and in pious imitation of Creation runs through the Improvers' concerns.

An aspect of Grant's improvements at Monymusk was the design of the village (Nuttgens 1996). The Kirk of Monymusk is 13th century and therefore one of the oldest kirks in the county, and Grant used the church's axis to establish a square (originally simply a holding pen for cattle), with pairs of houses forming a kind of gateway to churchyard, and in due course rows of regular houses defined the sides of the square. Similar exercises were carried out throughout the north-east, and well into the 19th century. He had also improved his own agricultural buildings, and the old House of Monymusk, making both as regular as he could. Monymusk was designed as a tall house, like others in Aberdeenshire of the 16th and earlier 17th centuries, with significant rooms for reflection and study high in the building, and commanding views of the Don, its valley, and Bennachie. To this the Grants added pairs of lower wings to east and south, regularly fenestrated, harled and with slated roofs.

These wings were some four meters in depth, two stories with usable roof space, warmed and ventilated by mural fireplaces and well lit. In profile and construction Grant used the same design to build his stables, storehouses, and cottages. Under the old form of agriculture with its short duration tenancies houses were not substantial, nor was it thought an advantage for them to be 'permanent', a tenant could take his roof 'couple' (a sort of cruck) away with him as part of his household goods after his tenancy was finished. Consistent with the archaeological evidence farm houses were still built of low stone walls dug into the ground with turfed roofs over, apart from the cruck, light timber supports. It was to Grant's advantage to have longer tenancies in houses he owned and let. This applied to all improving landlords.

None of Grant's work at Monymusk can be called classical, and yet, in its regularity, and in its modern construction it is Vitruvian as much as Serlio's or Palladio's designs for houses of the 1550s. It is the orthogonal building that makes it Vitruvian. Classical ornament can be applied within the canon, but it need not be. Most of the 18th century building in Aberdeenshire will be like Grant's – regular, modern, and plain (Roy 2008). And planting, enclosure and layouts, will be similar as well, whether as estate, or village, or to embellish the town of Aberdeen. Within the present boundaries of the city are a number of estates planned by men such as Grant. Some of these exist in their original form, and for others, such as Hazelhead, or Sheddocksley their forms have been translated from landscape into townscape as part of the later 20th century improvements to the city. In the earlier ones we can trace the experimentation in design programme and pattern and which was used in earlier urban improvements.

Culter House is contemporary with Monymusk, but it presents a perfect new design rather than a modification to old work. It is regular and plain in the way Monymusk is, but it is a sophisticated and stylish exercise in the French or even Italian manner of composition and landscape making. The design is oriented conventionally north-south. There is a formal squarish garden on the south side of the composition enclosed by woodland, and ornamented with two square doo'cots under regular pyramid roofs, and disposed on either side of the north-south axis. Next comes the house itself, tall narrow, of three rows of seven windows, the top row square, under a slated roof with four prominent chimney stacks. The entrances are, of course, at the centre on axis. To the north of the main body of the house are two wings, since 1900 two stories high, originally lower. These form a courtyard, or square, as entrance space. The axis is continued northwards as a parade, a broad straight space the width of the house with wings. This appears to be the entrance way, but as is the case with very many continental and other British examples the actual entrance is from the east, and forms a cross axis for the composition, and is ornamented by a gateway, which, with the door case to the house form the entire 'classical' elements.

Another designed estate within the present city is perhaps as indicative of how the city was designed. Grandhome is on the east bank of the Don opposite Dyce and like most big houses in Aberdeenshire it has an early core, but it too was significantly enlarged in the 18th century, and its grounds were laid out then, and retain their original form. These are a series of rectangular parks defined by shelter belts of forest trees, with an avenue running north-eastwards towards the sea. The parks are large, the design regular, but there is no particular composition to observe: pure practicality seems to have been the organizing principle. Whereas Grandhome and Culter appear on General Roy's military survey of 1746–55 as exceptional – both as large as the city itself, and extraordinary – within a very few years most of the rest of the area around the town had been similarly enclosed, and organized into rectangular parks. These parks became the mute infrastructure of landscape, and in due course gave form to the developing city whether in the Skene estate, the Mastrick estate, or the Pitfodels estate.

Agricultural improvement was the most noticeable change to the landscape of Aberdeenshire, but there were two other activities of design which were of equal significance, the system of paved roads and the Aberdeenshire Canal (Abercrombie 1796), both undertaken towards the end of the century. These too appear to have been community lead, although there was considerable funding to be had from government at Westminster. And they derive from similar desire to improve and the perceived needs for quicker and safer movement of goods and people. Their forms come about from the application of good sense of an engineering kind to the variations and difficulties of topography, and while regularity remains the guiding principle, hierarchy, variation or other more architectural forms of composition do not yet figure. The Canal became a sort of civilized Don. The falls in that river nearer the city gave opportunity for developing water driven industries, and these were seized quickly, but navigation was impossible. From its Inverurie end the Canal accompanies the Don, and nearer the city it took its own course to join the Dee (or more properly Aberdeen harbour just above the Dee) at Waterloo Quay. The heart of an improved Aberdeenshire was thus opened to the world.

In two generations there had developed a desire to improve. There had been enough experience to carry out improvement schemes effectively, and that experience had suggested forms and styles which became established as best practice. Success in various kinds of improvement encouraged other fields to explore. The successful experience of improvers in Aberdeenshire as elsewhere in Scotland was contributing to the development of an aesthetics of improvement: regular, clearly man made, but responsive to place, if for no other reason than economy (itself another invention of the age), and above all responsive to hard thought, to history, and to imagination. There were philosophers working on these issues – Richardson at Glasgow, Alison in Edinburgh, or Reid in Aberdeen, but none is quite so accessible, or as broad in his understanding as Henry Home, better known for his legal title Lord Kames (Kames 1762).

Like most improvers Kames was a man of parts, a lawyer, farmer, aesthetician and critic, and none of these to the exclusion of others. As a farmer, about which he wrote, he persuaded his tenants to clear the huge moss of Stirling by promising them ten years free tenancy if they cleared the three meters depth of peat covering it to get down to the rich soils beneath. His more enduring claim to our attention is his *Elements of Criticism* that made him a famous author in his own time. For Kames regularity was the hallmark of beauty and appropriate to small or medium sized things. In this he was a man of his time. But for the larger scale he proposed a new means of assessment, and of design. As alternative to even larger regular forms he proposed recourse to the association of ideas – a manipulation of elements, objects, spaces and plants to conjure a sensual response – of pleasure, of melancholy, even terror, independent of form or convention. Kames also proposed that buildings could be similarly broken down to identify which elements had power to trigger an association of ideas. These ideas had been forming in the earlier 18th century and had inspired a revival of interest in the gothic forms, as Switzer had proposed building subsidiary structures in his extended gardens/landscapes in the form of 'some antiquated place' so as to bring forth beneficial ideas of gloom. With Walter Scott in the next generation such ideas are attached to places, to scenery, to remote countryside, even to history itself. An aesthetic appeal inherent in the Highlands would have been met with derision before 1750 – not so since Kames, Byron or Scott (Kelly 2010).

As part of the new appreciation of improved landscape there was a developing curiosity about the surviving monuments, and speculation about their meaning, and about those who had built them and used them. Remains of Roman times were especially evocative because of the close study of ancient authors that classical education entailed. Clerk of Penicuik was so appalled at the needless destruction of a Roman Temple at Cramond near Edinburgh that he had it rebuilt as part of his stables. Reference by his friend Roger Gale to the similarity of parts of the landscape at Penicuik to the countryside south of Rome, and particularly to the Sybil's Cave near Naples at Cumae was most agreeable to him. Roman remains in Aberdeenshire were noted by Gen.

1.5 Alexander Milne, *A Plan of the City of Aberdeen with all the Inclosures surrounding the Town to the adjacent Country*

William Roy in his military survey, and a few years later Normandykes was drawn and published. Antiquities became the study of proto-archaeologists, and the Society of Antiquaries of London was founded in 1750 by Gale and William Stukely (Piggott 1985). The Society of Antiquaries of Scotland followed a few years later. Gale and Stukely had pioneered the serious study of British antiquities from early in the 18th century, especially Stonehenge and other remains in south-west England. Interest in related monuments in Scotland, particularly the north-east, followed shortly. To Stukely and his friend Stephen Switzer the association of historic or dimly known figures from pre-history with specific sites and the use of that knowledge to give extra significance to a feature of a designed landscape also occurs very early in the century and was likely enriched by correspondence such as that with Archibald Grant of Monymusk. By the turn of the 18th and 19th century volumes on Scottish antiquities had been published, and tourism in search of the Picturesque, scenery with antiquities, had become the fashion.

With knowledge about Agricola and his engagement at Mons Graupius naturally a classically educated Aberdonian would want to know something of his opponents there, about whom Tacitus had drawn such an admirable character. The Normans had rather annexed the Roman occupation of Britain for their own purposes and in Geoffrey of Monmouth's 13th century account of the foundation of Britain Brutus had fled Troy and found his way, in due course, to these islands, settled here, and named them. The Normans had simply taken over by conquest, and reasserted this ancient claim.

In an argument about whether there should be a province of the Church for Scotland separately from the rest of Britain, this was the justification put forward against the idea by the Normans. The Scots, however, had an alternative foundation story, and relied on their ancient kings-list to assert it. Their story called in evidence familiar from the other major source of history, The Bible that an exiled daughter of Pharaoh with a Scythian warrior settled here and founded the dynasty, whose names and descent the Scots were able and willing to recite. The Pope believed the Scottish story (Thom 1811, Boece 1821).

James Macpherson, a Morayshire cleric of antiquarian interests, collected in the Gaelic speaking Highlands fragments of stories, and ballads about these times, and began to publish them in 1762 (Ossian 2006). Both Fingal and Ossian had figured in the king-lists before the first recognizably *Scottish* king Kenneth MacAlpin, and Macpherson's translations into English gave them character and histories, and reality. His *Fingal: An Ancient Epic Poem*, and the *Poems of Ossian* provided a believable prehistory, and an accessible story of the culture of the north of Britain in the early 1st millennium, equivalent in power and interest to the culture of the Roman invaders. Naturally enough it proved to be a sensation, and became immensely important in north Europe, especially the German states and Scandinavia. It spurred ethnographic study, and became a foundation for the Romantic Movement. Macpherson was accused of duplicity by both English and Irish critics, and as he could not validate his claims his reputation suffered. Sadly for Aberdeenshire Macpherson's stories, whether true or otherwise, leave the Picts who did stand up to Agricola but who were not Gaelic, as enigmatic as ever. However, Ossian and Fingal remain.

As M-A. Laugier observed in his seminal *Essai sur l'architecture* of 1753, to design a city is easy as all one needs to do is to consult the design of gardens, where walks can become streets, courts become squares, and the conventional hierarchies of main house, and subsidiary and decorative or monumental buildings can be assigned appropriate analogous roles in the city scheme. This was true then, and was doubtless acted upon in France. Hints of such an approach are to be seen in the projects for the New Town of Edinburgh (Cruft 1995), and in some aspects of John Gwynn's proposals to improve London (Gwynne 1766). But if it is a relatively simple thing to see a connection between garden design and town design, it is quite another to alter the complex thing an old town has become, and improvements when they are introduced, are tentative, even timid, and perhaps advisedly so.

But there had also begun a revolution in garden design itself not in France but in Britain, and Kames was very aware of this. The landscape or informal style as it came to be called in England, and also on the continent when practiced there, had already begun to develop into its imitation of pastoral and gentle landscape, and to exercise a profound change in the way we perceive and design our environment. Like similar developments in Scotland by the Improvers early landscape design in England owed much to the annexing of agriculture to the fashionable modes of the time, such as for example Culter House, but with a necessary simplification, almost to abstraction, and an enlargement of forms. These developments do impinge on the design of towns, or parts of towns, but yet not directly and not necessarily as one might have predicted. An aesthetic based on regularity, order and best practice, judged against some agreed needs can be accepted by a community and get carried out as civic action. The sharper, more colourful edges can be explored in literature, theatre or gardens long before they can be used by the community for civic purposes.

So just when the citizens of Aberdeen and Aberdeenshire began their adventures in town design the aesthetic and intellectual forces which encouraged them, and guided them were on the point of very significant change. Whereas all projects were undertaken in the most level headed manner, with engineers and architects being consulted (in that order) on the basis of their recent performance, and their designs examined in public by the citizens, against principles of regularity, and a template prepared by a roads engineer, their discussions were coloured by expressions such as *picturesque*, within a landscape already rich with the gloom of antiquity as much as the clarity of the Enlightenment.

2

The Legacy of the Mediaeval Town

Aberdeen appears in history (Dennison 2002, Thom 1811, Boece 1821) at the turn of the 1st millennium when it is laid waste by seaborne foes. How long it had existed we cannot know at present, but its vulnerability to attack from the sea suggests it was in some sense already a trading town established near the North Sea, and that makes it a different kind of settlement from the other sites within the present boundaries of the city such as Dyce for example where the present Kirk dates from the 1100s or at the south-west corner at Peterculter (which answers to Ptolemy's reference to a major town of the Caledonians) where there was not only a ford of the Dee but a suitably defensive and well-provisioned site for a successful settlement, or what is now called Old Aberdeen which did develop its own urban character as an ecclesiastical settlement. But it is the confluence of the Denburn and the Dee roughly a mile inland from the sea which on present evidence is the origin of the City. This is south and west facing, at the foot of the slope of Schoolhill northwards. It is here that the church was established but when is unknown (Doig 2009, Bede 731, Boece 1821). St Katharine's Hill is to the east (and the natural place for a 'castle'), and, beyond the Denburn to the west a large plateau. There was a loch to the north, and various streams flowing from that to provide power for mills. The Dee was navigable for the suitably skilled, but perilous, and shifting, which makes it ideal for defence. There was plenty of water and a series of other settlements close by in a region of settled civilization.

If trade appears to have been an impetus for growth beyond its immediate neighbours, new arrangements in government were also significant. As the power of the kings grew, Aberdeen was favoured, and after the Normans had invaded southern Britain. Although they failed to conquer Scotland, their influence, of feudal structures, and the church as arm of state, is felt throughout the island, and certainly in Aberdeen. Apart from the site itself, the first determinants of form come with big churches. Within sight of the Dee and the Denburn St Nicholas is enlarged on Schoolhill, whereas more than two miles to the north, on an escarpment overlooking the Don, St Machar's becomes the locus of the bishopric with canons in preference to a former site in Morayshire. Religious houses are established – the Dominicans just north of St Nicholas,

2.1 St Nicholas Kirk

and the Carmelites south of the earliest market place, The Green. There is the Castle to the east of Aberdeen, and at least one further religious house, the Trinitarians, between Castle and town. With these elements in place there are the forces of government, and site, around which Aberdeen will grow.

Not surprisingly the history of both churches in Aberdeen begins in the 12th century. St Machar's structure dates from its complete rebuilding from the 1370s, and its foundation is asserted to be very early indeed (see below). The founding of St Nicholas is unknown, but the earliest part of the building is the north part of the transept, the Collison Aisle, of the 1190s. Its crossing was marked by a simple apse the width of the nave, as at old St Peter's Rome. This was replaced by a choir. A Lady Chapel was added (or rebuilt) two centuries later on severely sloping ground. So it can be assumed that the five bay choir, transept and a five bay nave were of roughly the length we see today, making it an exceptionally large church. There is so little of these dates with which we might compare these churches, and they are all smaller: Monymusk remains complete. Dyce does not. Only St Cuthbert's Dalmeny, west of Edinburgh possesses still the sophistication that the remaining parts of St Nicholas, and its size, suggest it also had. The Mither Kirk, like its town, is testament to age, ambition, and grandeur. But as both churches are exceptionally well lived in, repaired, renewed, and show the signs of responses to new fashions, this testament may be hard to recognize at first (Campbell 1995).

Even harder to pin down is the Castle of Aberdeen. It has always been assumed to be on the Castle Hill at the east end of the town. For such a potent and long-lived element of Aberdeen the Castle seems to have had a remarkably short life. With the failure of natural succession following the death of Alexander III the lineage of the Canmores the lineage of List Kings of Picts and Scots ceased, and the period of contention that failure brought about coincided with the keen aggression of Edward of England. The Castle first mentioned in history only a few years before, was occupied by Balliol and his adherents. The town had suffered, and the Castle was attacked and taken by the citizens for Robert de Bruce, in due course King Robert I. Soon afterwards the Castle was razed. These events at the turn of 13th century have left us, apart from St Ninian's chapel said to be incorporated into parts of Cromwell's bastions at the south-east end, with no physical evidence, but with great history; and it left to Aberdeen the peace, stability, and government that allowed it to grow – and grow without significant hindrance since.

To these somewhat external forces evidence of urban growth is attested by early ways…paths, then streets (Cameron and Stones 2001). The earliest way in the town was *Vicus Fraxini* which is probably Kirkgate (gate, not to be confused with port, but rather derived from *path*'s linguistic cousin, *gatan*, still in use in northern Europe for *street*, also of Scandinavian linguistic origin). More critical even than ways are the divisions of ground on which the town is built, the burghal plot, known as *feus*. As its name suggests this is the fundamental unit of the feudalism established earlier but perfected here by David I's time. These plots are the first acts of design in the town. They vary between eight and twelve meters in width, and they run (usually orthogonally) unimpeded until they encounter a stream, river or other natural boundary. On these plots houses were built on the street edge, with garden ground, subsidiary buildings, and pens for stock to the rear.

What had been, we may assume, somewhat informal areas (in terms of shape) of 'ownership' adjacent to earlier individual dwellings, are now not only structured but over time regularized to be practically identical. Before the 13th century houses appear to have been of light-weight construction, based on the often enforced requirement that they be removed as a penalty for civic infringement. Such lightly built houses existed into the 14th century, but substantial stone houses had appeared equally early, and as the 14th century progressed stone houses became standard. The very earliest of these may not have shared actual party walls, but rather built as closely together as practicable (this almost touching can be still observed in places like Dingwall or Cromarty). Contiguous building along streets soon becomes the defining feature of Aberdeen, as of other towns, making the public side clear, in contrast to the private areas behind. But by about 1350 the town in that form was 'full', and the division of the long rigs into fore, middle and back began, with the vennels, courts or lanes running along the side of the feus beginning to act as streets in themselves

It was not only citizens who inhabited the early town. There are rare references to visits by monarchs; the churchmen lived in the friaries and functioned in the town; but more local powerful men also had houses there in addition to their bases of power and wealth in the country – such as the Earls of Buchan, and Huntly, or the lairds of Pitfodels and Benholm; and we may assume also that citizens had interests in farms, estates or other enterprises in Aberdeenshire. The five ports of the town were lightly defended, and the town was never walled as continental cities commonly were: rather each *feuar* or tenement holder was obliged to make his feu or rig dyke secure where it formed a boundary of the town. Gilcomston and Old Aberdeen and the other settlements, and the suburbs of the town, such as Shorelands and Fittie were quite undefended. So the character of Aberdeen and district was likely more open than defensive or forbidding.

There is archaeological or documentary evidence of habitation in all parts of the mediaeval town and district by the later 12th century. That layout first surveyed and published by James Gordon in 1661 (Gordon 1661) remains the pattern of the heart of Aberdeen today. This compact town was buttressed by the Carmelite Friary at the Denburn Bridge, the Dee estuary along the southern edge, the Castle in the east, the Greyfriars on the north-east side leaving the area between the Castle and St Nicholas and the Blackfriars on the north-west edge free to develop as far as the Loch of Aberdeen. This occurred in the manner typical of small cities in Europe. The extreme limit of this urban area is 1000 meters between Castle and Church, and some 800 meters between the wharf and the Gallowgate Port near Mounthooley. Other old towns of similar dimensions are Bologna (the Roman heart and Lombard extensions), Padua, Munich, and Edinburgh (excluding the Canongate).

Over the ensuing seven centuries Aberdeen grew slowly to a population of near 25,000 at the turn of the 18th and 19th centuries, and that increase was one of the factors that persuaded the city that radical expansion of the town's area was required. However, population within the old heart of Aberdeen continued to grow well into the 20th century. Despite expansion, and subsequent 'surgery' to the core of Aberdeen, most of the mediaeval heart still exists and can be experienced. It remains the functioning centre of the city in terms of daily commerce, government, the law, religion, education, and transport. But most curiously its essentially mediaeval nature, and age, appears to be entirely unrecognized by both citizen and visitor.

Its most ancient street is indicative of the whole and a good place to start as it is 'broken' in two by Marks and Spencer's emporium, the current centre of town. The Via Fraxis of 1212 – within a century Kirkgate, and from 1382 Netherkirkgate – traces its serpentine way from St Mary's Chapel of St Nicholas Kirk to the south end of the Broadgate, the virtual 'centre' of Aberdeen for much of its history. Note that the centre of Aberdeen has moved no more than 100 meters to the west in its 800 years of documented history. The Netherkirkgate forms the northern part of the arc of streets which lined the military crest of St Katharine's Hill and this ring of streets is clearly evident in Gordon's plan of the town of 1661, and apart from the section lying under Market Street (1840s) the ring still functions. Only the feus of these very early buildings' survive. From its few surviving fragments supplemented with archival and archaeological evidence, the nature of early Aberdeen will be clear. A small measure of imagination may also prove helpful as significant parts of this still existing ring are obscured by later attempts to regularize the levels of a town built on hills. A visitor may begin to explore this part of

THE LEGACY OF THE MEDIAEVAL TOWN 21

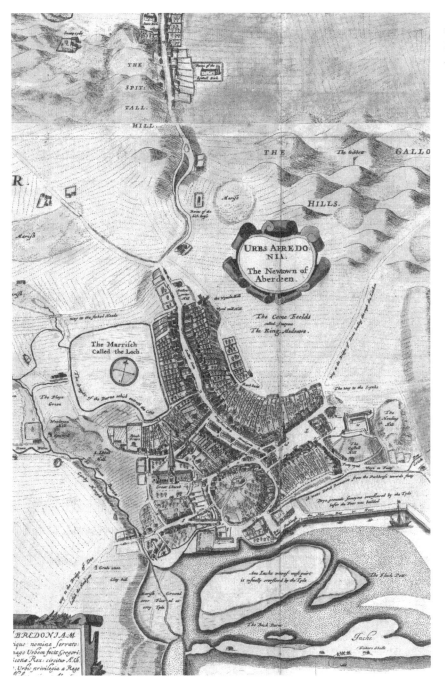

2.2 James Gordon, *The Newtown of Aberdeen*

2.3 Benholm's Lodging, Netherkirkgate

Aberdeen at the entrance to Marks and Spencer where to the right, that is east, a seeming raised walkway leads quickly to the junction of Netherkirkgate and Carnegie's Brae. And at this precise point was Benholms' Lodging, also known as the Wallace Tower, and a familiar landmark of the city; so familiar that when the local authorities were persuaded that it had to be demolished to make way for an expanded Marks and Spencer store, relatively an easy argument to put and win in the 1960s, it was painstakingly surveyed (Netherkirkgate 1), taken down and rebuilt in a park in Old Aberdeen, where it can be seen.

It represents a mature, if small, version of a type seen in both town and country, and often called a castle (McKean 2001, Quiney 2003). The type appears a tall building, even towering, and is sometimes called a Tower House. Early studies of this characteristic Scottish building form classify such houses by reference to their plan forms, or specifically, the disposition of staircase towers, or small 'wings', as the body of these houses is almost invariably a short rectangle of one large room. Thus Benholm's Lodging is a 'Z Plan' since there are extensions on opposite diagonal corners (Macgibbon and Ross 1887). One of these corners formed the sharp junction of Carnegie's Brae and Netherkirkgate, and made the building a landmark. It also marked the gentle slope of Netherkirkgate towards St Nicholas, and the steep decline of Carnegie's Brae towards Putachieside (from the lodging of Forbes of Putachie, a name probably Pictish in origin although Forbes is Norman).

Benholm's Lodging was a rebuilding of about 1610 for the laird of Benholm Castle near Iverbervie; with Niven's Wing it was enlarged along Carnegie's Brae in 1785, thus making a suite of three principle rooms per floor, each with fireplace, with minor rooms including the round one in the corner tower element. This arrangement as *apartments* made for comfortable accommodation for letting as *flats* or as town quarters for landed gentry. All floors were accessed by a turn stair in the south-west tower. When it was relocated it served as public house, with flats above; and by that time all windows were enlarged sash and case. Originally they would have been somewhat smaller, with opening casements and shutters. Its stone built walls were plastered with a lime washed harl, under a steeply sloped slated roof, and this was typical. Not typical was the likeness of a nameless knight, probably removed from a tomb cover, which lived in a niche facing up Netherkirkgate, and which contributed mightily to the house's importance, as it became known as no less than William Wallace himself, and hence Wallace's Corner. There were at least seven other houses of this kind in the town, probably rather more. But, as the antiquarians Macgibbon and Ross complained these had already disappeared without record by the end of the 19th century.

The south side of Netherkirkgate (TCP U 8, Fletcher 1807) eastward from here is largely intact. The actual buildings are replacements of the 18th to the very early 20th centuries. McCombies remains the earliest, perhaps mid 18th century. It was of three full stories with a large tympanum gable element making the third floor habitable, and was very likely an early form of tenement. These upper floors were removed in the late 1970s. At this point there was one of the Ports of the city (Gordon 1661). Two small 18th or early 19th century buildings follow, with a low run of three houses, one of which was the Post Office in 1800. The old centre of town known as the Round Table at the corner with St Katharine's Wynd (until the early 19th century when it became buried under the new South Entry) is flanked by two splendid Edwardian blocks by R.G. Wilson, until recently Esslemont and Macintosh's department store.

The north side of Netherkirkgate, including the site of Benholm's Lodging is occupied by Marks and Spencer up to the corner with Flour Mill Lane. There were three (at least) rebuildings in this row such as James Fyffe's of 1881 by Mackenzie and McMillan (Netherkirkgate 1 and 2). This provided improved commercial premises and possessed good open plans with 'fireproof' columns for at least two floors of trading, with large plate glass show windows in the relatively narrow frontage provided by the ancient burghal plot. The upper floors were separated and had their own entry from the street. Graham Tissot's shop remains as typical of these. The Donald's blocks, 16–18 Netherkirkgate, which follow to Guestrow, are more complex. These were rebuilt in the later 19th century as loft-like blocks for the manufacture and sale of paints; hence *Potty Donald's* which continued trading until recent times, when the buildings were converted to flats. The lower building at the corner, 2–6 Guestrow contains business premises and flats, and was built as such.

Embracing these blocks is the Illicit Still pub, and behind these blocks archaeological investigations of importance were conducted and recently reported (Cameron and Stones 2001). From these comes evidence of how the back-lands were used in the mediaeval to early modern period. There was a continuous sequence of building from the 13th century, and as this evidence comes from some six to nine meters back from the frontage it is assumed they constitute backland developments of what becomes Guestrow from about 1415. These were of light construction with posts and wattle walls in the early period, and by the turn of the 14th century more robust timber framed buildings, followed in the late 1400s by a stone building.

As noted above the block of buildings between Netherkirkgate, Rotten Row (a southerly extension of the Guestrow) and St Katharine's Wynd was known as the Round Table: all these were swept away with the building of Union Street, and our only knowledge of them comes from early maps and incidentally in the negotiations to acquire these properties for demolition. From that evidence it is clear that they were amongst the most desirable and expensive properties in the town. Immediately south of the Round Table is the beginning of Shiprow, and this ancient street picks up the arc of development around St Katharine's Hill and continues it to the south end of Putachieside, now lost under the south springing of Market Street, and the consequent reconfiguration of streets following the removal of the Guild Hall. With Shore Brae Shiprow was also the connection of the town to the quayside. Its maritime nature and neighbouring workaday Aberdeen as well as its proximity to the market square meant that Shiprow was crowded, much visited, and perhaps a little rowdy at times: towards the end of the 19th century it was deemed a slum and was one of the earliest sites of civic clearance under newly conceived ideas of the relationships between old buildings, crowding and disease. As a result of this many of the buildings lining the street were removed: nearly two thirds of the south side, and as much as a quarter of the north side. Yet, what was allowed to remain carried on the street's character, and it has recently been rebuilt following its ancient pattern.

The feus in Shiprow follow the same pattern as elsewhere in the town, but they are exceptionally deep, and converge towards the top of St Katharine's Hill (as did those properties on the south side of the Netherkirkgate). This elevated space disappeared with the building of the Adelphi at the beginning of the 19th century, and with it any archaeological remains. It had been reserved by the town, and was never feued out to individuals: there appears to have been two footways leading to it, and these made a convenient shortcut from Exchequer Wynd (now Row) to the Green, adding to the obvious attraction of the spot as a place to view the estuary of the Dee and surrounding country. The short-cut remains although the eastern arm is currently blocked the western half is maintained as Adelphi Wynd. To what extent the top of St Katharine's Hill was a sort of civic garden is tantalizing: Gordon's Plan shows it as a flattened and embanked area with a regular walk around it, and although no plants are indicated the gardens below were well wooded. Various local histories note efforts to keep this spot genteel, and for a time it was gated and reserved for keyholders only.

Gordon's plan, confirmed by others, shows some 17 separate gardens around St Katharine's Hill, of varying widths, and this would presumably

2.4 Shiprow with Provost Ross' House, looking south-west

demarcate the original burghal plots. These were subdivided along both Netherkirkgate and Shiprow to give upwards of 30 separate feus, most of which indicate the backland developments common elsewhere in the town from about 1350. Some fragments of these subdivisions survive.

A fragment of an early stone wall fronting the street, with arched opening, and somewhat gothic seeming slit, survives towards the west end of Shiprow, but nothing is known of its superstructure, or use. However, just to the east two substantial houses survive from 1593 and the early 18th century. The earlier house is to the east and is associated with Provost Ross. (The Lord Provost was the senior civic office, drawn by election from amongst the Baillies, and whose two year tenure was largely ceremonial.) Both houses were for civic gentry, and had their pleasure gardens rising northwards towards St Katharine's enclosed hill top. These houses have been incorporated into the Maritime Museum since 1995. Both houses are of three stories, stone built and lime washed over harl originally but with dressed stone ornamentation. The earlier house is set back two meters and has a prominent off-centre tower: there is an entry to the tower from the east side, which may indicate that it originally was a room of business, perhaps an early purpose made shop. The larger set back to the west leads to a more conventional doorway into the body of the rectangular plan which provided for apartments of four substantial rooms per floor. The eccentric tower gives a somewhat castle-like quality to the house as could be expected from a house contemporary with Benholm's Lodging but it is rather more urban in its mien. Its internal fittings date from the early 18th century.

The house next door is roughly a century later, and presents a more regular façade. Unusually it has a two bay arcade set into its ground floor at its east end. This seems to have led into a hall-like reception room, from which the other ground floor rooms were reached. It provided access to the staircase, the ghosts of whose windows can be seen on the front. There would have been four or five rooms in each of the upper floors. The arcade likely provided entrance, but it may well have been enclosed booth-fashion to make a semi-permanent 'shop' (Clark 2000). No other house in Aberdeen is known to have possessed such a feature. Some do exist in Elgin, and slightly earlier in Edinburgh in the Lawnmarket at Gladstone's Land (Foyster and Whatley 2001, 62). Both of the Shiprow houses were in a most parlous state and due to be demolished in 1952 but for timely lobbying by the National Trust, or properly by telephoning to Birkhall for Royal support.

Setting back the line of house front is most unusual, as the more common desire to encroach into the public domain was especially prevalent in this part of the town. One of the preoccupations of the early Police Commissioners (precursor to Planning Committee established under authority from Westminster in the late 18th century) was the removal of often substantial, and usually timber, structures attached to earlier buildings, but in the public way (Harrison 1998, Bell 1999 and 2004). In Aberdeen these were rarely more than forestairs (but see Gordon 1892) and in the Netherkirkgate, the Guestrow, or Exchequer Wynd where the street width was little more than five meters it is difficult to see how even these could be managed. In other towns, such as Perth and Edinburgh, more significant constructions were habitually attached to the more secure stone fronts.

The typical buildings in the Shiprow were somewhat narrower than these two, but equally tall, stone built and with developments behind. There was at least one timber building surviving at the end of the 18th century, and presumably because of its great age, was deemed to be in danger of collapse. This was at the north end near the entry to Exchequer Wynd. The feus opposite, just south of the centre of the city at the old Round Table were among the most densely developed parts of the mediaeval town. At the turn of the 19th century they contained, as well as living accommodation along the street front, places of public resort in the backlands. The occupation of these sites was complicated: the feus just south of Union Street had shops and living accommodation in the forelands, as elsewhere, and tucked close behind the shallow feus facing the new street were a series of halls – missions, for meeting, for billiards, other entertainments, and finally for the cinema. (Shiprow 1) The

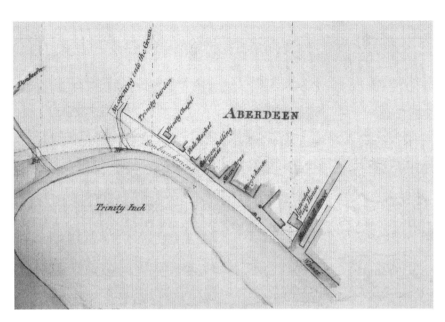

2.5 Wharf, drawing by George Taylor

clearances here and elsewhere in Shiprow took some 20 to 50 years, and these were doubtless longed for, and encouraged by the council and magistrates, by then splendidly established in the new Town House less than a hundred feet away. In 1878, for example, a typical three story foreland house was rebuilt internally to contain a Mission Hall on the top floor, a tea room serving the entertainment hall behind, with a chip shop at ground level, and a new, and lowered entry for the ancient way to the top of St Katharine's Hill, then designated as 'St Catherine's Court'. This then disappeared under first one, then the next cinema, The Regal, in best art deco dress, and representing the planning manners typical of 20th century modernity its ancient street front replaced by a carpark. The street line of this side of the Shiprow has only very recently been recovered.

West of the Maritime Museum the Shiprow continues its short run to Market Street; there is apparently one earlier building surviving and the rest are replacements on ancient feus of the 19th century. Due south of the Maritime Museum the short and steep Shore Brae leads to the quay and harbour, whose mediaeval form can be appreciated even now. Then simply called The Wharf or Pier, the broad paved quayside stretched from Weighhouse Square its effective centre, and now the site of the Harbour Offices, westward to the Trades Hall which lay south-east of Trinity Church, still in existence as a building at the corner of Guild Street and Hadden Street (Taylor 1793). Unlike deep water ports such as Stavanger or Lubeck, shipping in and out of Aberdeen had to be accomplished by lighters, small vessels of various kinds, which transferred goods to and from sea-going ships which had to lie in the deeper water of the Dee. Thus there was the public Pier rather than an effectively private quayside lined by merchant houses as was typical of Hanse towns. Goods to and from the Pier were distributed to merchants in the town

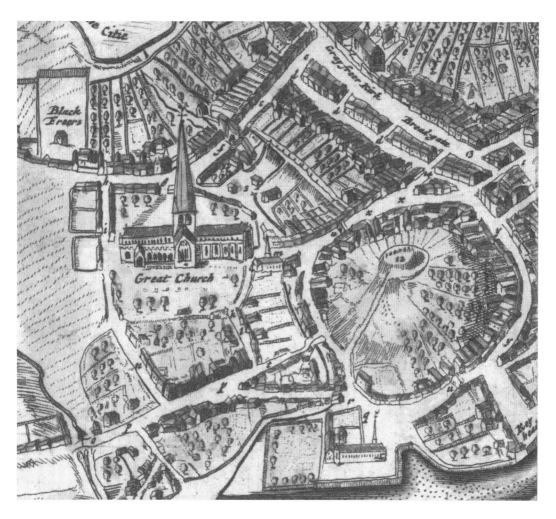

2.6 The Odds Quarter and the Green Quarter

by porters, who formed themselves into a continuing, self-governing society as early as 1498. The Weighhouse acted as a warehouse, and also the customs house well into the 18th century. Gordon, writing in 1661, noted the remains of an early stone pier further to the southwest in the estuary, and this was noted on later maps before the great improvements of the harbour of the turn of the 18th century. He also thought he detected remains of King William's 12th century palace. It is now thought any remains here are associated with the early pier. Gordon also asserted that the Tolbooth originally was sited here before its move to the Castlegate: no remains have been found, and to site such a building in a place subject to flooding seems not only unlikely but unwise. Weighhouse Square (Weigh House Square 1) disappeared in the 1880s to make way for the Harbour Board, but the current gap site now to its west, is of equivalent size.

Shiprow joined Putachieside just west of the present Market Street and then led north-westward to the Green (or the Green Well as it was also known) passed the ancient grounds of the Carmelites, referred to in the earlier 19th century still as the Carmelites' Garden. The north end of this area abutting the Green had been inhabited, and became part of the general manufacturing nature of this end of the town, led by the large Leys Masson works, and Haddens, both producing textiles. These two would disappear within the 19th century, but smaller enterprises can be traced well into the 20th century. The most significant of these was the by no means small Cruickshank and Sellars (later MacIntyre) (Carmelite Street 1) who supplied wholesale a marvellous array of hardware to tradesmen in both town and shire into the 1980s. The work of James Barron a civil engineer with offices in Bon Accord Street, Cruickshank and Sellars occupied several feus between Carmelite Street and Carmelite Lane. Goods were dispatched from the former from a generous warehouse where, from a very long counter, manned individually by assistants in charge of the stacked bins of hardware ranked behind them, parcels were made up for delivery, either by van, or by the nearby railway stations. There were individual shops let out on the other side facing Carmelite Lane at ground floor, and between these the two generous stairs, for Town and Shire customers, led up tenement fashion to the first floor show rooms. The bulk of the building held offices and merchandise. It survives on the east side as the front for a parking garage, whereas the west part is open parking for the new flats which occupy most of the block.

Rather smarter in appearance if not quite so august as an institution were warehouses for Ogilvies (Carmelite Street 2) at 49 Carmelite Street designed by Ellis and Wilson in 1883, where the corner, facing diagonally towards the railway stations is given exceptional prominence, even though it is not the actual entrance. It survives as offices for The Offshore Workers Executive. Smaller establishments for, for example, printers flourished in the area in premises often developed in stages from quite modest cottages, into tenement-like blocks before becoming more loft-like, within the same feu, and exploiting original construction. Blocks of purpose built tenements replaced earlier cottages in the 1870s, such as a pair designed by John McCann for Peter Garioch of Broadford House (the Broadford Works were a very large manufactory to the north of the town, and rather longer lived than their counterparts in The Green). One of the earliest purpose-built hotels in Aberdeen backs onto to Carmelite Lane. The Imperial whose entrance is in Stirling Street is still in business as a more boutique establishment than when opened at the beginning of the 20th century. By then newer streets had been laid out parallel to Market Street making the ground plan of the hotel a triangle. Supplementary accommodation, probably for staff, soon became sought and by bridging across Carmelite Lane the upper floors of tenements were colonized.

In The Green proper a run of replacement buildings of the later 18th and 19th centuries along the south side recalls the original pattern of cottage, warehouse, and often colossal but short-lived factories. Andrew Aedie's house at the Back Wynd corner of The Green survived into the 20th century:

2.7 Bow Brig and The Green, looking east

the ghostly fragment of its roof and east wall with numerous fireplaces remains in place. It was stone built, long, two stories under a steeply pitched roof, where dormers were soon inserted, and dates from the late 16th century probably contemporary with the extension of Back Wynd down to the Green, when it was known as Aedie's Wynd (Gordon 1661). The rest of the north side was ultimately sacrificed to become north-facing properties, albeit some four floors higher, when Union Street was created. This process took up to 40 years to complete, and some of these properties created new entrances into their attics from bridges to the new street until stopped by the magistrates. At its east end two ways lead into the town, East Green to Carnegie's Brae and Netherkirkgate (both also compromised by the new streets of the 19th century), and Correction Wynd to the east end of the Kirk.

Back Wynd, laid out and feued in 1594, formed the western edge of Aberdeen. It skirted the churchyard of St Nicholas, and in 1661 only its extreme north-west corner, on the west side, and opposite within the churchyard, was built up. Apart from the rear of Aedie's House (by then owned by William Duguid) other property belonging to him, to John Sewell, and to Thomas Davidson on the east side; and on the west side the properties of John Michie, J. Gillespie, James Gibb, J. Sturgeon, and the Banchory Society, were acquired and demolished at the beginning of the 19th century to make way for the vaults adjacent to Union Bridge and the new street. The extensive buildings at the bottom of St Nicholas churchyard belonging to Thomas Davidson, and to John and Alex Cadenhead also disappeared then, and the ground remained empty of building until the Façade along Union Street was erected in 1829 and the churchyard extended (TCP U 1).

From Gaelic Lane northwards there is more surviving to guide us. The east side is taken up by the high wall of the churchyard marked by the gateway into the West kirk; the joint between the newer work to the south opposite the entry to Gaelic Lane is plain to see. The west side appears to have been a row of cottages, of uncertain but earlier date, and evidence of alterations to these occurs in the later 19th century. Thus the public house at the corner of Back Wynd and Gaelic Lane, which still occupies part of this site, had alterations to its plan, and was raised for William Ferris in 1885. It was altered again some ten years later, and extended in 1913, when Mr Ferris was designated as 'hotel keeper of Cults' (Back Wynd 4).

Northwest of this public house is Cameron's Inn. This dates from the mid 18th century originally in its own grounds and attached to Back Wynd by a short lane. Ma Cameron's as it is still known has transformed itself many times and yet the old core remains, and the parlour and bar on the east side retains its 19th century character. In the grounds behind Cameron's, and with its own shop fronting the lane at the corner of Back Wynd was the Aerated Water Manufactory built for J.E. Strachan in 1899. Further north was the passage to a warehouse for James Asher & Son by James Rust of 1880; another house, and then an early insertion of a glazed shop front in 1877; then Jackson & Son's Bookbinding establishment, expanded into the backlands in 1907 (Back Wynd 3); the West Church Hall of St Nicholas, opposite its Gate; Sinclair & Company's wholesale druggist, enlarged by Brown and Watt in 1898 (Back Wynd 2); and finally at 37 Back Wynd premises for William Garey, 'Photographer and Artist', including a lofty new studio in 1882. Of buildings on the east side of Back Wynd we have only their footprint and the sketchy indication from 1661, from which we can conclude that they too were of cottage type – stone built, probably tile roofed, and of two or three stories – the same kind of modest urban building found on the west side. However, the use of these buildings was far from modest: this was the site of the famous Sang School. The same can be observed of the buildings facing into Schoolhill. Of these there is at least a photograph during their demolition (Morgan 2004).

By 1754 Gordon's Hospital, which was begun on site of the Blackfriars some 20 years before, was ready to accept scholars. The new building for the Grammar School was built just outside its gates. Gordon's Map shows a wide and shallow courtyard facing south which suggests that the 18th century Grammar School was built on old foundations, having been early established by the Blackfriars. The Grammar School and the Sang School across the way are the reasons for Schoolhill. As a street it has always been a short one with the Back Wynd entry well towards its west end; from there it was straight for a short run to the north gate of the Kirk, then it forked to its junction with Upperkirkgate at the Port, and south-east to a large open area outside

2.8 Schoolhill and Upperkirkgate, looking east

the walls of the churchyard. This area became built-up by the 1770s and had been incorporated into St Nicholas Street early in the 19th century. By then the principal entrance to St Nicholas was by way of the classical gateway there. The current trace of this part of Schoolhill has been modified, and the buildings lining it have disappeared.

From roughly the site of the Upperkirkgate Port eastwards the ancient street and its feus on the north side are remarkably intact. (The south side had become built up in the 18th century in what had been garden ground facing into the Guestrow of Broad Street: these were lost in the 1920s.) The building at 42 Upperkirkgate is a very curious 'survival': it dates from the 17th century, and represents the only surviving example in the once common practice of placing the gable end of buildings facing into the street. At two stories and inhabited roof, it is of the scale characteristic of this part of the town in Gordon's time. Its extensive length into its backlands, and indeed, most of itself disappeared in the 1980s, leaving us simply roughly two meters depth of the ancient building. A later tenement masks Drums Lane, and although the details of the house of the Irvines of Drum the fore buildings facing the street are lost, we can follow the development of the backlands in rather more detail through the information supplied in the rare, but happy, survival of a design drawing accompanying the articles of roup of property auctioned in 1798.

This 'Draught of Houses and Ground in Drum's Hospital Close' (ref Everyman 6.2) by James Johnston and William Littlejohn was for seven houses, fronting a 12'- lane extending from Upperkirkgate northwards to The Vennel later re-named St Paul's Street. In 1798 the property contained the old house (41 x 29 feet) then belonging to a Mr Glennie, behind which and reached by a narrow passage was 'Mr Mather's School', the Hospital Houses, and a smaller house, and finally the long garden, ending at the sharp angle of the Vennel and Loch Street at the south-east corner of the Loch of Aberdeen. There were 'privies' sited there for public use, if not the earliest in the town, the earliest we have plans for, and which Messrs Johnstone and Littlejohn proposed to remove.

The seven identical houses were to be regular with doorway at centre and symmetrically arranged windows. Each consisted of three stories, one level sunk, and a habitable roof space. They had four rooms per floor reached by a central staircase and lobby (TCP D 2).

Immediately next door at 24–6 Upperkirkgate is another survival dating from its rebuilding in 1694, and exhibiting a curiosity probably not uncommon in late mediaeval houses in Aberdeen. There are 'lugs' at the ends of the eaves, and these stand about a meter high: the western one still bears its sundial. Originally there would have been a gallery running between these, perhaps open, perhaps glazed and incorporated into the top floor as accommodation. (A similar feature in stonework existed around the corner in a house where Byron lodged as a boy, and in timber at Rolland's Lodging in the Castlegate.) The rest of this house is harled rubble with smooth stone dressings for windows, and three stories below the roof; it probably served as a later 17th century gentry house, initially at least solely occupied by one family.

2.9 Ross' Court looking south to Upperkirkgate

This was the character of the house eastwards passed two 18th century rebuildings. The building at 6 Upperkirkgate, also known as Provost Robertson's House dates now from R.G. Wilson's rebuilding of 1899, but he and his clients (the newly formed Aberdeen University Press) were at unusually great pains to retain the character, and features of the original Lodging of which there is a good contemporary drawing. Robertson's house is four bays wide and three stories tall like its neighbours, but here the eaves carry engaged dormer windows with carved stone panels above (one of which dates from the 17th century; the others remade to match). There is also a 'frontispiece', the piling up of one classical portal feature or window on to of the others, which we associate with late Tudor work in these islands or with Louis XIV on the continent. This may be largely Wilson's gift to the design as the ashlar granite masonry of the façade is. There is the characteristic passage at the side leading to the backland developments, and an entry from it, and the corbelled turn-stair, was recast by Wilson using original material (Upperkirkgate 1).

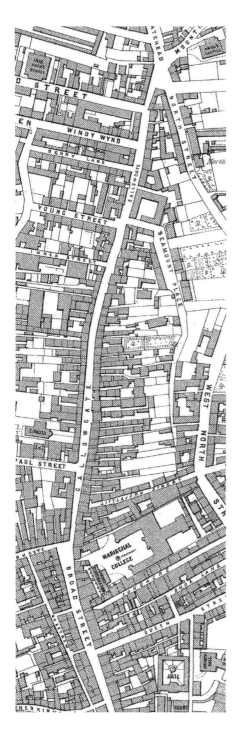

2.10 Gallowgate and Broadgate, the Spine of the Mediaeval Town; Odds Quarter to west, Evens Quarter to east

There was one last feu in Upperkirkgate before it intersected with the Gallowgate. This, and its neighbour, had been rebuilt during the earier 18th century to judge from the steepness of its roof. In the 1870s it was to be recast by James Souttar as a new kind of business, nominally as Gray's Draper's, soon to blossom as a department store, and this part of Aberdeen is where these businesses developed, and thrived, and to which the whole city resorted. Its shorter elevation was to Upperkirkgate, its much longer one, stretching towards St Paul's Street, faced onto the Gallowgate, the most prominent, longest and most populous of the streets based on ancient pathways.

Gallowgate is one of those streets which can be traced back to the 12th century, and it stretches along the ridge leading to Porthill with sloping ground to the west towards the Loch of Aberdeen, and rather more steeply to the east, making a kind of narrow peninsula fit for building on. At Porthill the way slopes down towards the north, and the extreme edge, or, end of the mediaeval town. This part of Aberdeen presents one of the classic formal types of early town design, the naturally straight-ish way on either side of which are narrow but long burghal plots: one thinks of Edinburgh and its High Street for comparison. It, too, became tightly built up by the 17th century, and remained thus well into the 20th century, finally losing its last substantial evidence of its mediaeval origins as late as the 1970s. Its form, character, and its buildings are fairly well documented.

The original pattern of the Gallowgate remains at its south end where Gray's preferred design by Duncan McMillan has been transformed over time into the Aberdeen University Students' Union, and is presently returned to commerce, and beyond it northwards towards St Paul's Street are a series of early 20th century rebuildings on ancient sites, whereas opposite north of Littlejohn Street, itself a 'new' street of the late 18th century made from an old close, are the sad remnants only of the early Board School by James Matthews, the Provost-architect. At the crest of the Gallowgate parts remain on both sides as rather tantalizing reminders of its heyday.

At 117 Gallowgate are the old headquarters of Messrs Ogston and Tennant whose massive soap-works occupied at least three burghal plots on the street, and the middle and backlands of many more sloping west to Loch Street. *Soapy Ogston*, the firm's founder was a well-known character, and fond of building. Norwood and Ardoe in Aberdeen, and the douce Edwardian (as in son of the Queen) manor house and Japanese gardens which include the restored ruins of Edwardian (associated as it is with Edward Ist of England's campaign and occupation) Kildrummy Castle, on Donside, we owe to his fortune and passion. The Aberdeen office building (Gallowgate 6) is 20th century, not built of granite, nor Aberdonian or even remotely Scottish, and yet it has lived happily in the Gallowgate since 1927 unrecognized as the ambassador of American-British capitalism – the Lever Brothers had acquired the soap business, and the offices were designed in the new firm's drawing offices in Port Sunlight, near Liverpool. Its one storey classic composition is clad in white faience blocks occupies three ancient feus, set back slightly and with a sunk lower floor. Next door to it are further remnants of the Ogston empire in which the Blue Lamp public house (as famous as the soap-works) remains as tenant, and there is a remnant, also, of another great local institution the *Co'py*, now part of the Blue Lamp.

The Northern Cooperative Society had its premises in Loch Street where thousands of Aberdeen children came to get fitted with school clothes at least once a year. Its arcade occupied one of the old burghal plots, and its destruction in the late 1980s was lamented. One of its warehouses remains at 144 Gallowgate. It presents two stories to the street, but the sloping ground allows four full floors at its west end. The interior is simple, fire-proof construction (as it was known at the time) and loft-like and is the work of Brown and Watt's office of 1900. Like the Ogston HQ it has always fitted in without trying to do so. Presumably following the ancient pattern of building in the mediaeval street was sufficient.

So, too, did the many tenements, very often combined with shops at ground level, and businesses in the backlands. They were crowded, and often the accommodation bordered on the sub-standard. In 1875 at Findlay's Court (Gallowgate 1) toward the south end of the Gallowgate an early work of William Coutts illustrates marginal house design. Superficially similar to the Drum's Lane houses of 1792, these are designed 'back-to-back' with one half facing north to one close, the other narrow half facing south into Rhind's Court. At the north end where Gallowgate and East North Street joined, beyond the old Port, Alexander Mavor proposed in 1907 to build, for the Northern Cooperative Society no less, an extremely dense scheme of shops and tenements with negligible outside space – enough only for passage to the privies. (Gallowgate 3) Already in the 1890s a very large scheme to open up these neighbourhoods to light and air was being drawn up.

There were religious missions as well, such as St Margaret's in the Gallowgate (1867) which was sited with the knowledge of and in anticipation of these clearances beginning. The Episcopalians led in these efforts, and established

2.11 John Slezer
Old Aberdeen

here an outpost in the very heart of crowded city. St Margaret's still exists, as do enough of the neighbouring buildings to give a good sense of its original siting, at the far backland of an ancient plot opposite Ogston's soap-works. This now looks grandly down over park-like open space onto West North Street. Not so when it was built, or more properly, converted from an existing hall (1889). Admirable as the mission was, the resulting chapel undertaken as a very early work by John Ninian Comper (1864–1960 son of the missionary-priest the Rev John Comper). Already established in practice in London, J.N. Comper designed the very simple extension and internal improvements to the clergy house (1906 & 1908) in partnership with George Irvine whose studio was 231 Union Street (Gallowgate 4 and 5). There are glimpses of the finesse and skill which later made Comper such a very distinguished church architect in this project. The broad hall that had become the chapel was made even broader. The entrance was shifted to the south, not so uncommon in England, but here the 'porch', being open to the old hall, is treated more like an extension to the whole. As the site only allowed a long and narrow room, it reads almost as if it were a very early church building itself, somehow magically surviving the centuries and now pressed into serving the larger congregation as entrance. Its simple, but pointed gothic windows, and, his use of clay tiles for the roof instead of slates, adds to this pleasing subterfuge. In this architectural work, in the context of his father's mission, and the newly reconfigured neighbourhood plan in which they were likely involved, Comper shows sympathy and doubtless contact, with Patrick Geddes then working in the Old Town of Edinburgh on similar regeneration projects. In Edinburgh more of the ancient fabric remained, whereas in Aberdeen almost all of the Gallowgate was sacrificed.

Originally the way forked from the Porthill end of the Gallowgate towards the hamlets and countryside of Aberdeenshire, and to the old Brig o' Balgownie beyond Old Aberdeen. With the Castlegate the Aultoun is the least changed part of the city. Since the 16th century it has been known as Old Aberdeen, in contrast to the rest of the city which was called New Aberdeen well in to the 19th century. This is an attractive myth that retains its adherents, of which Gordon of Rothiemay was certainly one, if a trifle wobbly, as his Commentary shows. It is the earliest part of the city for which a legacy from the past was recognized and celebrated through the efforts of our first historian Hector Boece. For him the story of St Machar's mission to the Picts, his crook, and admonition to found a church on a site to match, was sufficient evidence for a claim of a 5th century foundation for the church here. However, the new-old Aberdeen issue appears to have grown up as a confusion of the two parts of the Aultoun, the Chanonry, and the new town anticipated to grow about the new parish established in 1500 and attached to King's College.

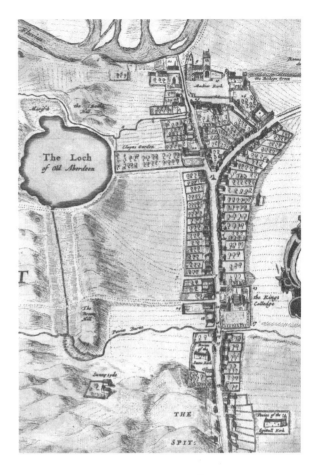

2.12 Old Aberdeen

A comparison of Gordon's plan with the first edition of ordnance survey or even a modern map shows very little change to Old Aberdeen. At the north end is St Machar's, a cathedral before the Reformation, as long as St Nicholas until its choir, perhaps still unfinished was destroyed by the collapse of the transept tower in the mid 17th century. Apart from a brief spell of episcopalian government before 1689 it has remained, as Gordon notes, the Machar Kirk, whose parish was very large and included everything beyond the city's edge. The kirk, consisting now of nave, west front and towers is a venerated and much visited site. It is mostly the work commissioned by Bishop Leighton's rebuilding of the old church which had 'worn out with age'. So St Machar is Aberdeen's example of 15th century architecture, robust, even severe, in red granite; it has little to do with the gothic work to be found elsewhere in these islands. The stout towers on the west are decidedly of the same culture as the contemporary tall manor houses so often called castles. Their spires, built under Gavin Dunbar's bishopric, are rather more classical in profile, but the church remains mediaeval, whereas the same bishop's Bridge of Dee is a true monument of the Renaissance.

The churchyard is walled, as are the streets which make up its 'toun' – the Chanonry, though it presents as three distinct streets, forms with Don Street a squarish block with an urban cast. This part of Old Aberdeen contains manses – originally for the canons – with a bishop's palace at the north-east angle long ago demolished, and the Chaplain's Court, of which fragments survive. The urban pattern here is of a series of large and somewhat smaller courtyards behind high stone walls. Don Street and the Chanonry joined together again at the south to form a point with the High Street, and that point has since the early 18th century been marked by the Town House, the present one being a rebuilding of 1788. The wider space in front of the Town House was the market place, with its cross, and the urban form of this part of Old Aberdeen is very typical of the 16th century burgh seen also for example at Inverurie: both were granted Burgh status by Queen Mary. The High Street southwards remains as Gordon's map shows it, although the feus he depicts contain later rebuildings. These, too, are mostly manse-like houses in their own grounds, but there are runs of cottage like foreland buildings, with extensive inner and backland developments as could be found in various parts of Aberdeen. There are also rows of more modest cottages arranged at right angles to the high street. These are unique to this quarter. Old Aberdeen has been repaired, to a degree restored also, and then conserved during much of the 20th century through a laudable policy of confining new university buildings to the more open ground to the east and the west.

At the south end of Old Aberdeen is King's College, founded in 1498. It forms a quadrangle, as it always has. Three sides of this have been rebuilt and now present 19th century work, although 17th century towers survive on the south east (Round) and north east (Cromwell's) corners, whereas the earliest part, the Chapel survives largely as built. This is a long hall-like building whose east end is fitted out for worship with period woodwork which includes the screen which marked the part for schooling at the west end. A square tower adjoins and is topped by a truly grand crown supporting an aedicule-like spire that was rebuilt in 1633, after a storm, with funds granted by King Charles I.

Originally, and throughout the 18th century, King's was separated from the High Street by high walls and fore buildings including a grammar school and a short terrace of these survives. So this part of the Aulton like the Chanonry was characterized by high largely plain walls. To the southwest is the walled enclosure all that is left of the Snow Kirk – St Mary ad Nives was originally the parish church of this 'new' town. Since Gordon's time the way southwards has developed into College Bounds which joins to the Spital, and with King's Terrace nearly reaches the city at the Gallowgatehead.

2.13 Prospect of Aberdeen looking south from the Spital

At the other, the southern end of the Gallowgate we come to the middle of Aberdeen – the bazaar, the Broadgate. Its origin lies in the pre-historic path or trace running from Old Aberdeen to the heart of the city (Ref 2.9). But it also has characteristics which suggest a design, a more purposeful act than the adoption of the existing state and making adaptive changes to it. Until the beginning of the 20th century the east side showed the inflection of the trace to be expected of an ancient way. However, it is on the west side that a quite different kind of street is encountered. Here is an almost perfectly straight run from Upperkirkgate to the Netherkirkgate, and the intersections to these streets are regular, that is at right angles as in grid plans. That plus the great width of the Broadgate inclines one to the suspicion that we are observing a designed street, or even, a designed quarter. Yet no documentation confirms this suspicion, apart from the evidence recorded by Gordon in his plan. There is a further issue about this part of town and that is the Guestrow, a long very shallow urban block that appeared suddenly in the 15th century. Gordon is the first to comment upon its derivation, for him and for subsequent commentators this has revolved around its name – signifying either Guests or Ghosts (*ghaists* in 15th century Aberdonian).

The hypothesis arises when we explore the notion that the Broadgate was a conscious act of street making by mediaeval Aberdonians. In concert with the creation of the Castlegate it bears unmistakable evidence of design. Perhaps its great width, seen merely as empty space, was encroached upon and regularized on the west side, and accepted reluctantly on the east? Market behaviour in ancient times (as indeed much later) was conducted from single traders, to mats, then carts, and more permanent, yet still occasional, stands (as illustrated by Gordon in the Castlegate). It does not require excessive imagination to consider that these occasional or guest-structures became so habitual as to gain *squatter's rights*, and would then become the row of houses called the Guestrow. Such supposition is not at odds with the evidence we have at present. If this might be accepted then the Broadgate was originally indeed broad, not quite as broad as the present Broad Street, but comparable. It would have occupied the large space between the feus on the east side, and the modified or designed areas on the west. Thus it was twice as broad at the north end as at the south end where it meets Netherkirkgate and the series of narrower ways connecting ultimately into the Castlegate. Two open spaces within a mediaeval town to accommodate commerce is in no way exceptional, and for Aberdeen would make sense of an otherwise puzzling arrangement.

This part of the town was its heart in that it was very dense, very busy and in the middle of things enjoying a sustained active life of nearly seven centuries. Although it was destroyed in two bouts of 20th century urban surgery, yet, apart from its Anglicized name of Broad Street much of it remains to influence later development and gives very significant clues for future development. Some understanding of its form and nature is necessary to understand Aberdeen today. A few characteristic sites for which we have good evidence can give greater substance to the map and visual remains.

At the north end of the Broadgate and facing into its larger part was the site of William Gray's new warehouses. For the conversions Gray first consulted James Souttar who had recently returned to Aberdeen after practicing in Gothenburg, Stockholm and Helsinki. The severely simple plate glass show windows with Souttar's signature quadrant curved finish, to be inserted into the 18th century rebuilding on the feus at the corner of Upperkirkgate and the Gallowgate would have been perfectly adequate, even forward looking for 1870. But apparently Gray wanted something more memorable, more romantic, and almost mediaeval perhaps, so he consulted another architect William Coutts who produced for him the first of several variations on

2.14 Broadgate with gateway to Marischal College left and Cistern in centre

2.15 Byron's House Broad Street

2.16 Broadgate, west side, also known as Guestrow

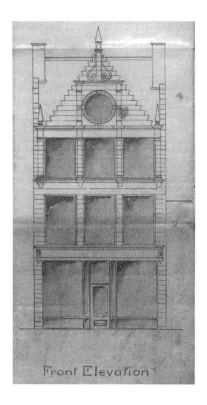

2.17 85 Broad Street, Grant's Emporium for Tea

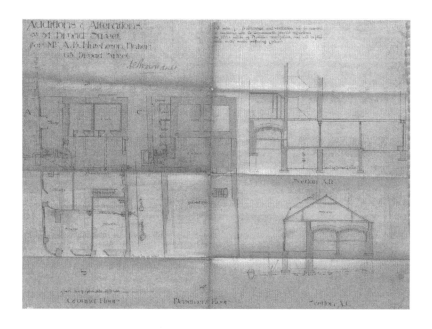

2.18 34 Broad Street at Queen Street, Hutcheson's Bakery

mediaeval themes that that particular site has enjoyed. The plate glass show windows remain as also the closely spaced large sashes above, but at roof level he introduced rather spiky peaked dormer windows and he celebrated the very prominent corner with bay windows rising into a turret wearing a very steep witches-hat. That feature was toned down to a simpler dome when the premises passed to Aberdeen University as the students' union but otherwise the building remained, and remains, as the visual termination for Broad Street, and a reminder of its role as hinge for the two halves of Aberdeen's major shopping street.

The Guestrow of the Broadgate has entirely gone, leaving only the odd address on the extreme original west side. So even its putative ghostliness has to be conjured up. The Guestrow consisted mostly of plots built up entirely and in single ownership. Some of the feus had been subdivided giving larger plots facing into the Broadgate, and smaller ones forming the west face of the Guestrow. J.L. Grant of Richmonhill's Emporium of Tea sited on one of these shallow feus facing into the Broadgate had spectacular show-windows, and Matthew's and Mackenzie's design (Broadgate 2) repeated these in the warehouses on the upper floors. The bright shop occupied the front half of the ground floor only, with a more discreet top lit 'saloon' towards the rear (presumably for drinking tea) guarded by an elegant curved open staircase partnered by a similarly shaped glazed office opposite. The exterior was equally well thought through, and the huge windows were held in place by granite stonework with a crow-stepped and steep gable sporting a big circular window at top.

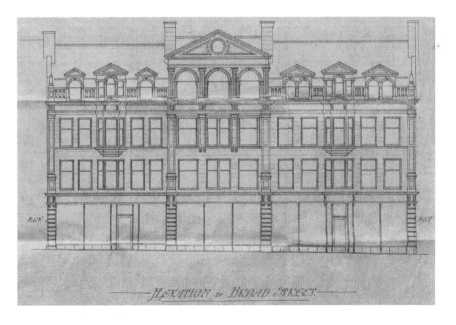

2.19   73–5 Broad Street Proposal for Henry Gray's 2nd premises

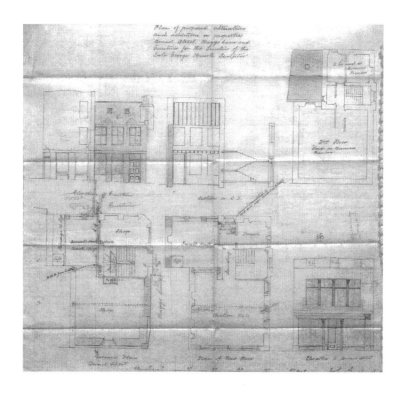
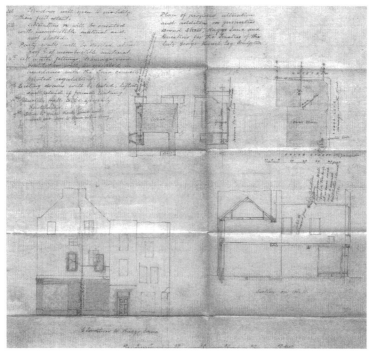

2.20 & 2.21   Guestrow, Ragg's Lane and Broad Street

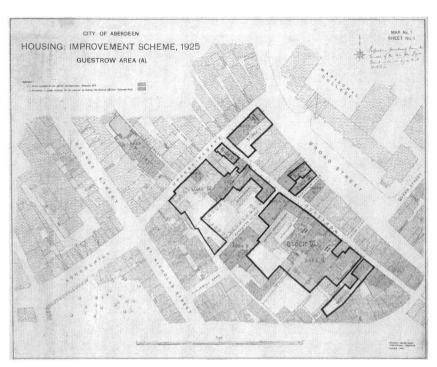

2.22 Guestrow showing parts to be demolished 1926

2.23 Provost Skene's House

Slightly further south at 71–3 on a site occupying three burghal 'guest' plots was Henry Gray's second premises to which he moved at the beginning of the new century. For this project he chose William Gauld (Broadgate 8) and rather than a recollection of mediaeval work they produced a grand classical and in many ways a typically confident Edwardian emporium suggestive of a palace. As the three existing houses were of different widths the architect used all the skills at his command to disguise the discrepancy, and doubtless few, if any, passers-by would have noticed. They would certainly have admired the ten large show windows to tempt them inside from the Broadgate. There was also the handsome roofline of the new work – the raised and arcaded pediment flanked by prominent if slightly asymmetrical compositions of pedimented dormer windows. Only the flanking structural walls defining the feus remained inside from earlier work. That the much larger internal opening was between

72 and 73 suggests that the preferred entrance, and therefore the centre of attraction for the Broadgate still lay towards the north end. Although his plots gave him the option to open also into the Guestrow, Gray rather chose to rely on a Broadgate frontage entirely: after all one of his closest neighbours to the west was the Victoria Lodging House, despite its august history hardly the kind of customer a canny warehouseman would have sought.

Sadly this formerly very desirable address had fallen in esteem during the 19th century and indeed had begun to appear with similarly rundown houses in publications as 'artistically interesting slum properties'. These help us to know something of the district. So little has survived the wholesale demolitions and the dearth of documentary reference, in itself indicative of the meagre rebuilding or repair works taken on in this part of town since 1870. Ironically we must rely on the evidence of the Victoria Lodging House. From these, now known as Provost Skene's House, we will have to generalize somewhat to get a character of the dense populous series of very deep feus between the Guestrow and Flourmill Lane (note that the street currently called by that name is roughly thirty meters further east).

Cumberland House, as the properties became known, occupies two plots as middle and back land developments: the foreland pair of houses were relatively shallow in their plan and are otherwise unknown. Entrance to the inland houses was by way of a pend next to the southern house facing the Guestrow. Between 1733 and 1830 the two inland houses were joined together as one and this is doubtless the high point of their grandeur. It made them the obvious choice as the residence for the Royal Duke of Cumberland in his pursuit of the rebel supporters of Prince Charles Edward Stuart. The earlier of the pair lies at the back, and now faces onto the 'new' Flourmill Lane. It was built in 1545, and has an 'L' shaped plan with turn stair in the angle giving access to the three rooms per floor. The upper apartment was converted into a gallery in the 1670s and its suite of paintings (on panels) survives. At some stage, probably 1733, the eastern arm of the L has been raised two more stories.

The middle house was also raised by one full floor with leaded flat roof, hence the rather tall unfinished appearance. Internally however it is very spacious. Its shallow steps in a series of stairs and landings makes an open square, leading to the suites of comfortable early 18th century rooms: on the first floor are two large reception rooms (three, counting the one added from the house next door), whereas on the upper floors there are suites of three rooms. The rather raw stone work and mortar of the exterior is a response to early 20th century taste: the building for the rest of its very long life was decently covered in lime wash and harl. These two houses not counting the houses facing Upperkirkgate or Netherkirkgate were among nearly seventy others between the Guestrow and Flourmill Lane.

The Guestrow was crossed by a number of wynds and courts and by two lanes. Ragg's Lane, to the south of Provost Skene's House, was the site of a more modest and perhaps more characteristic development. Here three small properties belonging to the trustees of 'the late Geo. Russell' were improved in

1898 to provide two or three shops accessed from the Broadgate and Guestrow (Broadgate 6). Provision upstairs for two Halls and living accommodation was reached by a broad new staircase opening off Ragg's Lane.

Slightly further south was an institution whose entries from both the Broadgate and the Guestrow needed to be entirely clear yet discreetly managed. At 27–30 was the four storey five-bay regular block refitted by John Rust for the New Loan Company. Like its neighbours it boasted large plate glass show windows onto the Broadgate; on the upper floors were a series of secured storage pens where valuables awaiting redemption could be safely kept in pawn. Also at first floor level were a series of ten small counters enjoying light from the street outside. Safe from being seen, they were equally secure from their neighbouring miniature offices. Here Aberdonians who required ready money could carry out their negotiations discretely and with some dignity. If they were bolder they might enter from the centre street door off Broadgate, but if discretion were needed…and how many ladies of Carden Place, King Street or Marischal Street would relish being seen by their friends coming from such a place perhaps on their way to tea at Grants or shopping at Grays? For these there was an entry, decent certainly and safe, also discreet, opening from a quiet part of the Guestrow a short step north of the Netherkirkgate or south from Ragg's Lane. This led also to the first floor landing opposite the stair from the Broadgate, and thus to business.

A few doors south of the New Loan Company was another Aberdeen institution only recently closed. At 23 Broadgate at the corner with the Netherkirkgate, the firm of Esslemont and Macintosh entered into Henry Gray's line of business as Drapers in smart new premises built to the designs of the talented Robert Gordon Wilson (Broadgate 7). With the slightly broader frontage onto Netherkirkgate and narrower ones to the other streets, Wilson made a virtue out of the small site allotted to him by emphasizing the tower and the slightly toy-like quality of his design. The building,

2.24 Ragg's Lane

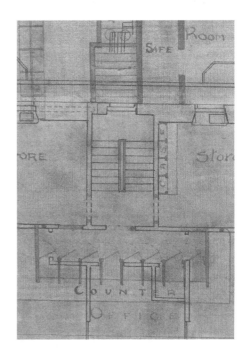

2.25 New Loan Company 29 Broad Street, detail of plan

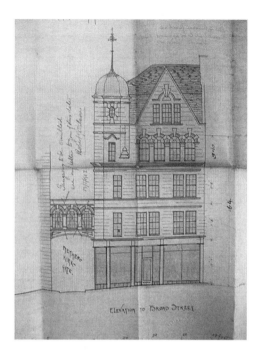

2.26 Design for Esslemont and Macintosh's store

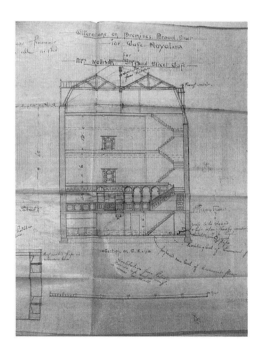

2.27 Café Royal, section

entirely glazed at streets level to encourage the craze for window shopping even after dark with the new electric lights, then becomes stone clad above and distinctly castle-like boasting corner turret with dome and weather vane, and high peaked gable to the Broadgate; his ornaments are what the period called Scots-renaissance. The firm also had interests in the two plain buildings south of Netherkirkgate toward the junction with Union Street, and wished to connect their shop to these by way of a bridge for which Wilson provided a douce design based loosely on the Bridge of Sighs connecting the Doges' Palace and Prison in Venice. The magistrates wisely realized that Drapers are not Doges and declined to approve the application. However, nearly a century later the equivalent authorities were foolishly persuaded by the same firm of drapers to allow them to bridge between the two halves of their store.

Just south of these plain buildings, at 19 Broadgate, Mrs Mollison of St Paul's Street wished to set up in business as the mistress of a splendid establishment to be called the 'Café Royal' (Broadgate 5). This entailed gutting the old building, re-arranging and redesigning the windows to provide three full floors of restaurant at ground level, with serviced large rooms for private parties plus ample and comfortable cloak rooms above. The restaurant was provided with long communal tables, with a separate table screened from the main body of the restaurant by a richly carved wood and glass arcade reserved for ladies. Her plans, provided by Duncan Hodge, were scrutinized very closely indeed. Various changes had to be provided for in the basement for the good of the staff, and only when the magistrates were convinced that the Café Royal was to 'be used as business premises only; locked up all night' did they allow it to go ahead.

The east side of the Broadgate had an equally adventurous and distinguished history but the changes came with significant and often brutal finality for the east side was the side of government, the press, an ancient monastery and a university.

When the New Town House was built, much larger than the old Tolbooth that it replaced, the demolition entailed the removal of the last of the early buildings – a tall somewhat regular house, but with corner turret and steeply pitched roof and probably of the 17th century. Already most of the feus in the southern part of the Broadgate had been rebuilt by the Georgians. The closely packed closes behind – Concert Court and Cruden's Court carried on, and in Chronicle Court the city's newspapers continued to be produced well into the 1970s.

However the section north of the 'new' Queen Street survived in its mediaeval form until it was replaced by a new front to Marischal College (Broadgate 4) at the beginning of the 20th century. This is an extraordinary story better told elsewhere but it made for us a real 'ghaist row' whose haunting is not yet finished. Most of the growth of Marischal College has been entirely laudable. However, the sacrificing of the east side of Broadgate with these twelve houses with the ancient church may not be included among them; its reasons are perfectly clear and consistent with the age. For this part of the story about the legacy of the mediaeval town it will be sufficient to note these twelve buildings, and give some measure of their quality.

2.28 Entry to Broadgate from Union Street

As the third entry north of Queen Street to Longacre attested these were very long burghal plots indeed and reached down as far as the King's Meadow, occupied since the 18th century by North Street. Little evidence, sadly, survives for this densely populated district, and most of the Broadgate feus appear to have been rebuilt in Georgian times. An inland house of the mid 17th century, Patrick Christie's House caught Gordon Burr's eye, and was recorded in his 'Old Landmarks of Aberdeen'. This stood at the end of Jopp's Lane, the second entry north of Queen Street. It was a four storey block with a short 'L' taken up by a square stair tower which led up to the first floor, and then a turn stair, expressed outside as a turret, served the upper floors. Its accommodation would have been of the standard and size of the inland house of Skene's mansion across the Broadgate west of Guestrow. Up past the entry to Longacre was another 17th century house whose roof level gallery we have already noted. This appears to be double fronted but was in fact two houses, with a turret at the north corner of the street front running upwards from the first floor to the eaves level gallery where the air and the view over the street

2.29 Longacre being demolished for further extensions to Marischal College

and town could be enjoyed. These high level open galleries or porches are features of Italian town houses of the same period. They may well have been less rare here than we would suppose. Rooms in this house were occupied by Catherine Byron and son George in the 1790s. Next door to this pair was the Town Reservoir, a rusticated two story building with a prominent pediment and blind windows externally, possibly the work of William Adam. Above the firehouse at ground floor level was the iron cistern fed from far off Fountainhall west of Gilcomston. Beyond this was a pair of Georgian double fronted houses with the handsome arched gateway of 1633 between, leading on to Marischal College.

This was also the site of the last of the religious houses in the city. It had been established in the 15th century and occupied the inner and backs of roughly eight feus. Following the Reformation the Greyfriars site was acquired from the council by the Earl Marischal who, with help from church funds, founded the college for philosophy which bears his title. Gordon's map, curiously, does not show the old monastic buildings which from later evidence appears to have been a tall rectangular block in the north east corner of the court with a turret stair leading to the six floors. Later in the 17th century the roof was raised into a platform to carry an observatory. Also sometime in the 17th century a slightly lower wing was built opposite the gate and finally William Adam provided the third side to the courtyard in the 1730s.

The pride of Greyfriars, and of Marischal, was the Chapel or Greyfriars Kirk. Like its contemporary at King's College, and likely by the same architect, Greyfriars was a simple long rectangular hall with large windows on the west

2.30 Marischal College

side, originally facing onto the Broadgate as well as showy windows in both north and south gables. Neither college nor seemingly the town cared over much for the kirk building, and in the early 17th century it was neglected, vandalized and houses built in front of it, along the Broadgate. However, good sense prevailed at last and it was repaired, and enjoyed a long life…until 1900. A scheme to re-front the College, at national expense, had acquired public and press approbation. This led to civic murmurs about the old church being in bad condition, so that it would require great sums to put right. Matthews and Mackenzie's office had calculated that nearly £3,000 was needed, as far back as 1889. Dr William Kelly produced a less costly alternative but by 1902 the ancient church was gone, as indeed were the houses fronting the Broadgate.

At the south end of the Broadgate were a series of ways – courts, lanes, wynds, rows – acting like capillaries between the more major of the streets – Broadgate, Netherkirkgate, the Shiprow and the great market place of Castlegate. Many of these disappeared with the coming of Union Street, and Huxter Row carried on until the Town House extension. Exchequer Row survives, but at twice its original width, and apart from the 18th century rebuilding at its corner with Shiprow and marking its north side, nothing survives of the buildings, although there remains a ghostly shadow where the south row met the Castlegate.

Its name and location might lead us to think it started as a kind of castle esplanade seen elsewhere, such as Edinburgh or Stirling. As its earliest documented addresses refer to properties 'Castleside' it seems clear that it was the large rectangular enclosed space for essentially civic use from its

2.31 The Castle-gate in 1661

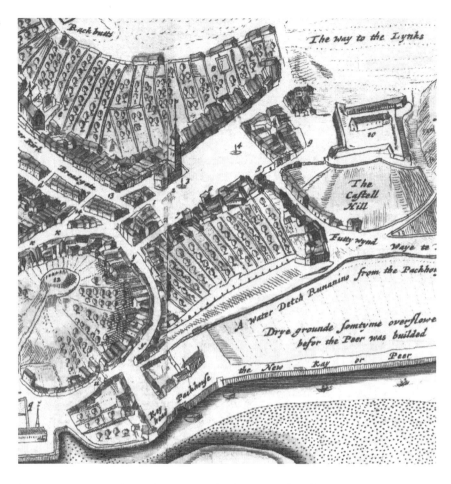

beginning; not a military forecourt. The form Gordon shows had been in place since the 1390s when the Tolbooth was built, perhaps re-built, in its north west corner, and according to him of double square form: 'One Hundred walking paces in breadth and twice as many in lengthe'. The axis tilted somewhat south of east west with the two main entries from the rest of the town, Huxter Row and Exchequer Row with Narrow Wynd continuing the frontage of the Tolbooth to the Round Table. The Justice Port lay just beyond its north east end, and the Fittie Port at its south east corner. For the rest it has always been ringed by houses, many belonging to the great families, with inland and backland development. Its role as market is signified by the Cross towards the west, with another, the Flesher's Cross towards the east. It was significantly airier than anywhere in the town, and sunnier, as well as sufficiently protected from winds, and these qualities were enhanced by the enclosed regular form, so it became the preferred place to live. It is the earliest act of urban design in Aberdeen, and perhaps not surprisingly remained the focus for urban improvements well into the 19th century.

The Castlegate appears to be a generator of the burghal plots surrounding it; a curious exception being towards the northeast quarter. Here there is a definite deflection in the inland and back land parts of the feus that regularly front the square, as if there were some older or more powerful property to influence them (King Street follows one of these deflections). Gordon reported that there were remains of an ancient monastery in this quarter which he ascribed to the Trinitarians. Others have disputed this and proposed the Templars as an alternative. A substantial lodging belonging to the Earl of Buchan may have exerted an influence in some way, as well as pressing early urban growth further west before it moved northwards. Whatever it was, it remained an influence and an emptiness, until the Roman Catholics built St Peter's Chapel in 1803. But apart from this aberration the Castlegate is as regular and as geometric a piece of urban space as one can expect to find in any mediaeval town, including planted or bastide (fortified) ones which Aberdeen very clearly was not.

One ancient house survived into the 20th century, Rolland's Lodging, itself a rebuilding of the 16th century and reworked about 1630. It presented gables to the Castlegate, with irregularly placed windows. Entry to the lodgings was by way of the pend to St John's Court. When it was demolished in 1937 parts of the interior were re-used at Templar's Park, Maryculter. For the rest of the square the buildings surrounding it are all replacements but on ancient feus; most are of the 18th century. The backland developments on the north side were distinctly urban in character and quite as extensive as those in lower Broad Street. Albion Court, Smith's Court, and Peacocks Close survive sufficiently to give good flavour and there is supplementary documentary and archival evidence to add depth to what was typical of the Castlegate as a whole.

Albion Court is accessed by the pend under 17 Castle Street where two early inland cottages were demolished and rebuilt, and this opportunity allowed for archaeological investigations of their site. The further development of this feu towards its back lands were encroached upon by 19th century work onwards and behind the new King Street, such as the school hall for St Andrew's Episcopal Cathedral, and additions to the cathedral itself. The next-door feu of 19–20 Castle Street was less interrupted although the site including foreland buildings were renewed in 1770; parts including a rear wing overlies earlier rebuilding in Smith's Court of a cottage similar in size to those of Albion Court. In this the older work became the basement and ground floors, and perhaps part of the first floor as well of the newer work: dated lintel stones from the early 18th century and other aspects of this Seton brick-built structure are visible from the public way. The further inland site exists as a walled enclosure now used as a power sub-station, whereas early buildings further north have been subsumed into early 19th century replacement work in King Street.

The next feu eastwards which contains also the other half of the rebuilt foreland of 19–20 also visible from and now entered from Smith's Court, is not so clearly founded on old work. Nor are its extensions northwards, the two long parts of the cathedral school, before that feu also was itself terminated, by extensions from King Street. With Peacocks Close that runs between this feu and those of St Peter's Chapel, there is an almost complete run of foreland, inland and backland development of this long plot. There is documentary evidence of its completed nature. A petition was put to the Police Commissioners from Thomas Ramsay who owned these last two buildings in Peacock's Close wishing to improve the Close and his own street frontage to North Street by arching over the close, making it into a pend as it was at the Castlegate-Justice Street end. Their response was, that as crooked as the close was and as hopeless of improving it into more than a passage for pedestrians they were unable to grant such permission; 'unless all the proprietors agreed to the measure then no one of them had powers to make the least alteration'. Notwithstanding this, a subsequent meeting learned that Mr Ramsay's stair which was a cause of the crookedness of that part of Peacock's Close, '…that was now given and would at some future period enable the Board to make the east side of the close a straight line from the Roman Catholic Chapel to North Street' (Police Commissioners Minutes 487 & 492).

The ground occupied by the Roman Catholics begins with the foreland buildings, a double fronted tenement of the 1830s. A somewhat monumental entry leads by a pend to the courtyard. This ancient section was further interrupted in the 1930s to provide an alternative market stance. The location and size of this, often called simply but erroneously the *Timmer Market*, corresponds to the Earl of Buchan's establishment of the early middle ages. Until the 19th century this marked also the north eastern boundary of the town.

The top of the Castlegate has been occupied by the Salvation Army Citadel building for over a century. It had a much more varied usage in the periods prior to that. In Gordon's time its backlands were considerably denser than those of the north side of the square, even more so toward the end of the 18th century. It is only with the 19th century that we can have a true idea of just how dense and complex such areas could be. An undated plan circa 1850 shows Justice Street before it was widened beyond its former twenty feet. The Record Office, and 'front house and shops' occupied the hundred foot width of the Castlegate (TCP C). Behind them was an open court entered from Justice Street by a passage between two houses. This led to a stable and to Mr Combies 'old house' beyond which, going eastwards, was a wood yard, and a cabinet maker's shop, both of which fronted also on to Sinclairs Court (itself separating the Barracks as successor to the Castle, from the civilians). Behind the houses fronting the Castlegate lay another passage entered by a pend which led to Lobban's Court beyond a pair of substantial houses.

This passage was near to the Fittie Port and the south side of the Castlegate, and appears to have had a somewhat different character. It indicates that the owners of these deep plots did not always forgo the pleasures of fine gardens especially when they lay on such a handsome southerly slope overlooking both the harbour and the river. Although this side of the square also saw development in the backlands of the feus, and their longitudinal subdivisions, recent archaeological evidence has uncovered work of the 15th and 16th centuries: stone steps, garden features and terracing of the ground in both the inland and backland sections at the south east side of the square (Cameron and Stones 2001). This had been hinted at in descriptions of the grand houses further west – such as the Earl Marischal's House built around a courtyard with gardens to the south, or Pitfodel's Lodging next door. Now here is further evidence to help us recover the town's garden history to some extent.

A rare glimpse can been had about minor works of re-fitting or building occasionally. From the voluminous and still uncatalogued Moncoffer papers the painstaking efforts of Patrick Duff can be followed. Duff was a relation of the Duke of Fife and he built a new wing to his town house in the 1750s at the south east corner of the Castlegate, on part of his gardens. He employed an Edinburgh architect, and ordered his furniture from London and well as more local sources for his principal reception room which also overlooked the river across Fittie's Wynd. Also on the southern slope behind Castle Street much backland building or re-building of good and substantial houses took place in the 18th and earlier part of the 19th century. By the time of the first edition of the Ordnance Survey the details of these, and in some cases their function can be seen. These were reached both by closes from the market place, while some also enjoyed access from Fittie's Wynd (now Castle Terrace), of and yet just beyond the town. These houses occupied the back feus and a spacious courtyard occupied the inland feu, with one of the smarter new houses associated with Adam shortly to occupying the Castlegate frontage. The southern houses were more extensive than those on the east or north sides and all these will have extended at least to what was becoming Virginia Street at the edge of the Shorelands, beyond which lay the still not fully tamed estuary. Therefore there were the inner and outer courtyards, mansion houses and three or perhaps four terraces laid out as gardens. These had become Bank houses by the 1860s.

New streets have obliterated much of the rest of the Castlegate backlands. Important foreland buildings such as the New Inn have been replaced without adequate record. Fortunately there are paintings and drawings and the old Tolbooth has been the subject of investigations into its earlier history and form. Surprisingly much of this still remains within the rebuilt and much enlarged Municipal Buildings of the 1860s. The late fourteenth century Tolbooth of Aberdeen, illustrated by Gordon consisted of two parts, the Townhouse a longish rectangular and two story high block towards the west end of the square, with a Tower of some six stories and a spire to the east. It was an island building with the Huxter Row part of the Castlegate running behind its north side. The tower held not only the town records and other valuables but its upper floors also served as the prison. The council chambers were accommodated within the Town House block, over the vaulted ground level rooms some of which were let.

The Town House in Gordon's illustration may be the original tolbooth, soon to be repaired, then in the early 18th century rebuilt. The Tower was largely

2.32 South Prospect of Aberdeen

rebuilt by Thomas Watson in 1615 (RCAHMS 1996), with a belfry and spire added a few years later. It still exists, somewhat obscured by later additions to the front. Its original form and setting can be sensed in the Musselburgh tolbooth, and a similar composition was used for the Stirling tolbooth as late as 1700. With the finishing of the tower Aberdeen acquired the skyline it retained for another two hundred years – St Nicholas' spire in the west balanced, if not matched, by the Tolbooth spire in the east. (Mariners were advised to align the two towers to ensure safe passage into the mouth of the Dee.) The densely built-up townscape also remained characteristic as indeed did the apparent extent of the town. Aberdeen already was constructed of mostly stone built houses, largely of three floors or more, with roofs of stone, tile or thatch (Mossman 1756). By 1660 the town had realized itself, in a sense it had perfected its mediaeval form and as the drawings and paintings show, was imageable. Its growth continued, and like elsewhere in Scotland it began to realize new potential with the Union of Parliaments and the eighteenth century. A period of urban improvements, relatively small scale yet significant, begun in the 1680s had by a century later, brought the realization to the town that it had to re-make itself in order to become an important modern city.

Early Improvements

In the later 17th century Aberdeen had endured its last attacks, loss of life, and damage to the town in the battles of the civil wars, specifically of Craibstone. And although there was still some uneasiness about whether there would be Episcopal government of the Kirk this was soon settled in favour of the Presbyterians. Aberdeen was a busy, crowded, and prosperous town of perhaps 10,000 inhabitants. As such its trade with northern Europe brought it into contact potentially with the growing importance of Amsterdam or of Antwerp, both of which were enjoying the benefits of their new metropolitan status, yet there was very little to be seen of architecture here. Despite the civility, even douceness of the town, it was a mediaeval civility where the streets had seemingly grown up by themselves, where the underlying structure of the burghal plots may have been recognized but was hardly celebrated. Indeed even in these newly important metropolitan towns the design of fine building and related open spaces whether imagined or carried out remained exceptional. The new Town Hall (since 1805 the royal Palace) on Dam Square by Van Campen, and the earlier Town House of Antwerp, were themselves extraordinary in their own contexts, and while they might inspire, the only architecture to be seen in Aberdeen was on a much smaller scale. At the gateway to Marischal College for example, certainly in the internal fittings of St Nicholas, Kings and Greyfriars, or the splendid and robust St Machar and apart from the gateway these are all still ecclesiastical monuments, their magnificence is of a different order from what was understood as architecture (Campbell 1995).

Then with the rebuilding of the Mercat Cross of 1686 Aberdeen bids to join those towns whose citizens realized that architectural magnificence is the right, proper, and essential characteristic of cities. Aberdeen does so with the smallest possible monumental building, placed and designed so as to have the greatest possible effect. The Mercat Cross of Aberdeen, in place for hundreds of years as the sign of regality, is in its new form a quite different thing. It is in no sense provincial…its classicism is perfectly understood, crisply executed, and appropriate and would be perfectly at home in an Italian city. Except, of course, Italian towns celebrate their civic squares with fountains, not market

3.1 Castlegate, detail from painting by Hugh Irvine of Drum, 1800

crosses. So it is a very local kind of building but conceived and executed in the classic style. As Giambologna raised the fountain to high art in the Piazza Maggiore of Bologna so John Montgomerie makes the Mercat Cross into a Renaissance expression of the town.

Its design is also a civic act. The specification for the Mercat Cross was very particular, and as well as that, models of the proposals were required so there could be no doubt that what was wanted had been thoroughly thought through beforehand by the magistrates. Its placement, size, shape, ornamentation…its *design* is a genuine expression of the town's collective aspiration. It is doubtless an extraordinary achievement, but why was it designed as it was, and what persuaded Aberdonians to undertake it? Market crosses are ancient and derived from Pictish uses first as assertion of Christian presence, then as official centre and symbol of the burgh, the civic presence and in royal burghs the presence of the crown. The cross of Aberdeen, also known as the Fleshcross was immediately in front of the Tolbooth. Its companion the Fishcross was further east: their early form is shown on Gordon's plan (Gordon 1661). A round slightly raised pavement bore the critical shaft carrying heraldic signs of burgh and regality. However, it was worn out, and the decision was taken to replace it. The cross of

Edinburgh had also been replaced in the 17th century as a drum on which the shaft was placed, and from which proclamations could be made. This may have given a spur to Aberdeen.

The site remained the same as before, not quite on axis with any part of the Tolbooth but nevertheless on the east-west axis of the Castlegate. The Hexagon, also standing on a raised circular pavement, was the preferred plan shape. Its six semi-circular arches support the parapet, and the shaft carrying the white marble Unicorn rises another story high from the centre. For a civic symbol declaring the antiquity of the burgh something clearly old becomes the normal response, but this taste is basically romantic and Scottish, and will come in due course. Compared with the Edinburgh Cross of 1617 (the present one a replica at a smaller scale of the late 19th century) which was quite up to date for its time, the Aberdeen cross is surprisingly modern. It has entirely to do with its simplicity and adherence to plain geometries, classically if profusely decorated. It also is explained by the spatial dominance the Mercat Cross exerts, and this is an affair of urban design, which the 17th century Aberdonians discovered early, and have perfected subsequently.

Urban design (sometimes known as civic design) is a modern term, coined to describe the larger scale compositions of often quite ordinary buildings to form spaces with architectural characteristics. At its simplest, as in the early experiments of Amsterdam and Antwerp where the civic space already existed, the town halls were designed in proportion to them as a rich architectural expression inherent in their shape and size, and also the manifestation of civic pride. This meant buildings vastly bigger than most towns needed, or could pay for. Naturally enough this pleased rich cities all the more. The Continental cloth halls of the late Middle Ages provided an obvious pattern, but something had changed. From the 17th century fine buildings in towns carried with them the expectation of an appropriate corresponding space, from which the building's best qualities could be appreciated, and to which the building served as protector or guardian (Millon 1994). In French theoretical works (and in those times the French adopted theory as if their own) these spaces are called *degagement*. The contemporary design of the last element of the Louvre project in Paris struggled, experimented, and only as late as 1960s finally realized its urban *place* opposite the East Front: these efforts become both theoretical example and best practice (Daufresne 1986). If civic space can be given significance by enclosure with fine building, it can also derive its power from something smaller but centrally placed. The French used equestrian statues of the king for this, throughout the 18th century, with a well-funded centrally directed policy to ornament all French towns. This began at the Place des Victoires in Paris in 1683 (Cleary 1999).

Here the magistrates of Aberdeen hit on a similar idea in their contemporary new Mercat Cross. It is a concentrated and sophisticated little building, demonstrating the correct use of the three major orders of architecture – Doric for the jambs of the arcade, Ionic for the primary structure supporting the parapet, and Corinthian for the central column. Standing on the circular base, and raised three steps above the Castlegate, the six round arches spring from classical jambs and have very good sculptures representing fruits in the arch cheeks. The twelve sided parapet appears to be supported by the Ionic order of columns set at the corners of the hexagon, and above each of these are the gargoyle-like beast's heads which throw the water off the roof. The famous portrait heads of the Stewart monarchs line the parapet framed by foliate roundels. The central column carries the Unicorn, and its shaft is carved to represent tendrils with roses and thistles. The interior of the Cross was divided into booths, initially dedicated to selling wine as way of discharging the costs of construction. It contained a cistern connected to the gargoyles which could be used to supply wine to the citizens on high days, such as coronation days. There is more well-executed and erudite architecture of a reserved simplicity in this little building than there was in the whole town. And it has always sat as the ornament, and guardian of both the Castlegate and Town.

A few years later the old Fishcross was also replaced. This too was a civic monument and built of sandstone, and with its ogee curved 'roof' a rather fashionable one. This was not a building (that is it had no interior) but was the Wellhead from which the Castlegate hereforth drew its water, piped in from the Cardenhaugh west of Gilcomston. The Cistern in the Broadgate was part of this new system which replaced individual or neighbourhood wells. Designed by William Lindsay in 1706 it is a square plan monument effectively of one storey. The ogee top is set off from the rest by a strong cornice. The figure of a boy at the top was originally gilded, and four further figures had been planned.

Architecture is one of the fine arts, a quite distinct and separate matter from building, whether plain or fine. It was also a matter of study rather than practice, associated with the kind of erudition that comes with libraries, reflection, and well directed and modulated leisure (McEwen 2003). It was approached through books, of which there were few in the language of these islands, but that hardly mattered as textual commentary of architecture could almost as easily be followed in a foreign as in a native language. Leon Battista Alberti's *De Re Aedificitoria* remains the best, and is as hard as any. For him the column and its associated parts (like base or cap) was a distillation of the wall. A wall, however plain and ordinary, contains the possibility of being expressed as fine architecture as eloquent as the old Romans had shown. Put another way architectural expression can be like that of poetry, 'what of't was thought but ne'er so well express'd'. With that notion comes the idea of propriety. Some buildings may bear fine expression but they must not be ordinary, and in some way their natures must correspond to their expression. Therefore the Mercat Cross of Aberdeen may be the fanciest in town because it represents the town: all other buildings should be more reserved in their expression, even though they must carry the possibility of it as much as the greatest.

If that is the message there are many and different ways to deliver it. When Sebastiano Serlio (d. 1554) started his illustrated books on architecture in the

1530s the image broke free and began to lead its own and often wayward course (Hart and Hicks 1996). By the 1680s books about architecture were now illustrated, are about reigning in bad style and inappropriate expression: theoretical concerns always have to do with returning to the basics. For a town on the point of becoming a city, well off but hardly rich, one with an inclination to express itself through good building, the turn of the 17th and 18th century was a most wholesome period. One Aberdonian to whom the Mercat Cross spoke was James Gibbs (1682–1754) (Friedman 1984) who passed it daily on his way from the family house in the Fittie quarter through the Castlegate to his studies at Marischal College. After further study and apprenticeship in the Netherlands and Rome he published his own books on architecture, and in his design for the Town's Kirk (St Nicholas West) brought Alberti's message home in stone (Roberts 1991).

Having begun so well with the rebuilt Mercat Cross the town soon turned its collective attention to the Tolbooth itself. As has been observed already, when this was built and when the Wardhouse was raised into the tower, the theory which guided its design (and indeed design elsewhere in the town) sought mainly to demonstrate robust strength. It required a good standard of workmanship, apparently only a decent nod towards any regularity and very little decorative work. With the 18th century new ideas especially about regularity become established and guide ideas about even larger projects as well as buildings. These were concerns also encountered by the Italian towns whose leaders to whom the earlier commentaries were dedicated, sought ways to bring their own buildings and their towns into architecture. To start ways had to be found to show how old buildings could be made to demonstrate regularity and once that is achieved, the more decorative expressions of architecture allied to propriety could follow. Without regularity nothing will be right: so how do we make an ancient Tolbooth regular?

There was certainly no rush to build on the advanced taste the Mercat Cross suggested. Early 18th century work was done, but to the Wardhouse only, and very much out of sight (RCAHMS 1996). William Adam was in town in the early '30s to work for Robert Gordon, for the principals of both Kings and Marischal colleges and, in the country for the Urquharts of Craigston. He also provided a design for the Tolbooth's extension as a new council chamber was needed with an easier, lighter, less martial-seeming staircase. But his design was thought too elaborate and rejected in favour of the modest two bay two story extension to the west. Adam's 'too elaborate' design is lost to us, but we can get some idea from his design for the Dundee Town House of 1732 (Gifford 1989). Robert Gordon's Hospital was begun in the 1730s, and topped out at the very least, but was not fit to receive 'the sons of poor burgesses' until the late '40s. His design for the Tolbooth of Aberdeen will most likely have resembled these buildings in size, expression, and doubtless also of elaboration.

Robert Gordon's Hospital occupies the site of the Blackfriars on the then north-west edge of Aberdeen. It is set well back from Schoolhill and backed onto the Loch of Aberdeen. Adam's design faced onto extensive formal gardens

3.2 William Adam, Robert Gordon's Hospital

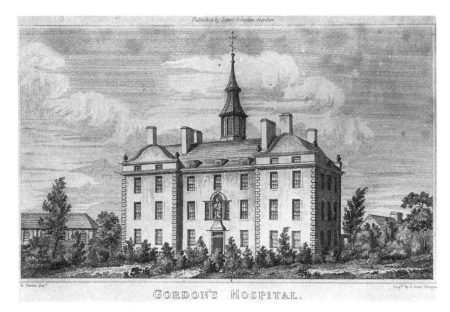

and his hospital had much of the air of a contemporary large country house, if rather less austere than many. It was a broad, three part composition of three stories. The centre three bays were slightly recessed between the prominent two bay wings with their high curved gables balancing the bell turret at the centre of the building. Over the entrance is a Palladian window motif where in the centre is a niche with the statue of the Founder. Otherwise the fenestration was regular and the stonework of ashlar granite, otherwise unrelieved or carrying architectural expression beyond the corner blocks raised as quoins. Gordon's Hospital had (it was modernized by Smith in the 1830s) presence and considerable dignity but was far from profuse which would have been quite contrary to the propriety expected of a charitable institution.

The Dundee Town House had the same kind of character and was roughly of a similar size: it stood at the junction of the four streets of the town and established an appropriate dignified urban centre. Being built directly its qualities will not have gone unnoticed in Aberdeen, as would the new Town House adjacent to the Tolbooth of Glasgow built a very few years later. Only a single drawing remains of the reduced works to the Aberdeen Tolbooth but it shows a handsome typically 18th century panelled room with marble chimneypiece. With this work in hand, the exterior of the Tolbooth remained unchanged and as irregular as ever.

A more critical civic improvement took immediate precedence. The nave of St Nicholas Kirk was dilapidated through age and lack of good maintenance and its state can hardly have been improved by being pressed into service as stables for the Duke of Cumberland who had turned Gordon's Hospital into a sort of temporary castle in his pursuit of the Young Pretender. James Gibb (more often Gibbs) had been raised to the rank of an honorary Burgess in recognition of his birth in Aberdeen and the very considerable esteem which

3.3 Tolbooth, Townhouse, New Inn and Mercat Cross, West end of the Castlegate, early 19th century

his practice as architect in London had brought. In response to this honour he provided the design for rebuilding the nave of St Nicholas Kirk, completed under Thomas Winter's direction in 1752. The footprint remained the same, indeed the foundations were likely pressed into service anew as would any usable parts of the old structure. But Gibbs, like Inigo Jones a century earlier at St Paul's London transformed church Latin into a purer Roman Latin: the space, arrangements, and design were renewed rather than re-designed. The result still strikes us as new, yet classic, and subservient to the building as a whole. It is ashlar, but sandstone and smooth. There are raised quoins at the outer corners like Adam's work across the street and the west door is similarly elaborated but his architraves are much crisper and at the same time there is an exceptional plainness about the design which is especially striking when compared to Gibbs' London churches such as St Mary le Strand, or to his St Martin in the Fields. To be plain can be less costly, but to be plain with this level of quality is in no way cheap, and therefore does not represent a poorer performance. Gibbs knew Rome, indeed he had worked with Fontana at the height of the counter-reformation, he also knew the Church of England, but more to the point he well knew the Kirk of Aberdeen. His design therefore acknowledges its place and his skill went into celebrating that sobriety. His architectural expression is at the edge of what the Kirk took as propriety, not a house of God but a meeting place for sinners seeking the light and redemption; it was also civic as the meeting place between town and kirk.

At the mid-century the Castlegate frontage of the Tolbooth was acknowledged to be defective and if for no other reason much of it was removed; this was keyed into Adam's work to the west and the building was raised to three floors to accommodate the Great Room, a hall for the town's use. This work was done by Patrick Barron (RCAHMS 1996). Within a very few years a Society of Freemasons proposed a very significant partnership. For the whole of its life the entrance to the Tolbooth had been on the east side of the building opening into the larger part of the Castlegate. A forestair was added in the 17th century and although this gave access to the upper floor directly, it remained on the east end but pointed southward. The principal reason the Masons needed a deal with the town was simple...old King Alexander's gift of a site in the Castlegate was for a Tolbooth, not a tenement. Legal minds were no doubt consulted but the projected partnership was allowed to go ahead. Certainly part of the new building was used by the town if a very small part. Doubtless the New Inn, tenants of the larger part of the new building, provided much very useful and stylish accommodation for the councillors, but was not part of the Tolbooth, or *Townshouse* as the building begins to be, and remains, known.

But the joint scheme of 1756 allowed the buildings to become regular and to have an added dignity from that, but also with a greatly increased apparent size. The old Wardhouse becomes the Tower and entrance hall and is reached by a handsome double staircase, a forestair of really civic scale at the centre of the new composition. Furthermore it is now to be marked by a pediment though not quite so handsome as one by Gibbs. That chosen might just have been taken for a decently ornamented gable. The pediment, the top part of the temple front element of architecture, has always denoted the special. In Republican Roman times it was confined to religious buildings only. Its use by others was blasphemous and certainly offended against propriety. Augustus as head of what soon became the Roman empire, became the head of the Roman religion in 12AD, and got special permission to use the pediment on his residence. Of course other great men then followed his example. It retained its symbolic potency well into the 20th century (Watkin 2009).

At the extended Townhouse, to either side of the Tower, were two long wings of identical windows arranged regularly in rows and files. The only exception to this symmetry was the entrance to the close, originally occupied by the Tolbooth forestair, henceforth known as Lodge Walk. The eastern end of the new hybrid had its prominent gable facing into the Castlegate and was provided with another, newly minted but potent architectural form. Named for either of the two great 16th century architect-authors, it is known as a Palladian window or a Serliana. It consists of an arched central window flanked by two identical flat headed servant windows, and here the composition is elaborated further by fragments of architrave suggesting the pediment. All elements of the gable end are arranged as regularly as the long frontage, with the Serliana and chimney-stack punctuating its centre marks this subsidiary but important east end, as the old Wardhouse tower marks the south front.

With each wing having seven regular bays, the central feature based on the old Wardhouse, the Townhouse was now of a scale if hardly of Amsterdam or Antwerp certainly of those of Glasgow or Dundee. In terms of architectural expression it lagged 'behind' in the sense that its dignity comes from its regularity and bulk and not from its architectural ornament, which was minimal. Even so, within a scant seventy years Aberdeen had acquired two pieces of urban architecture which could be counted alongside continental examples. If still somewhat reticently, the Townhouse with the Mercat Cross showed that the town had acquired something truly special.

Each of the wings of the Townhouse when taken separately would reveal that the ordinary house or tenement could also become potentially formalized and regular. Such evidence as we have suggests that this came late, the earliest regular houses in the city date from 1765; there may have been others. Indeed one would have expected it, as there are regular ranges already in houses in the nearby countryside. Visitors such as Daniel Defoe had remarked in his *Tour* on the sash windows of Aberdeen at a time when they had only very recently been introduced from The Hague into London. However it is possible to insert up-to-date windows in old buildings. It appears that the Aberdonians may have contented themselves with their older style of lodgings. The size of the feus of Aberdeen made regular houses rather more difficult to adopt because it normally takes the frontage of two old burghal plots to allow the broad 'double-fronted' style of house which led the fashion in London. In London these had appeared in the new quarters first, and so it was in Aberdeen roughly a century later. Once the full, five bay houses appeared in the city, then the narrower three bay regular façade, albeit with the entry to one side, more suitable to the narrow feu of a mediaeval town, not only appeared but appeared in great number, often as simply a refronting of older work.

3.4 Wharf and Marischal Street with Tolbooth

In the late 1750s the Earl Marischal's Lodging was demolished. It had occupied feus in the middle of the Castlegate opposite the Tolbooth, with southerly open gardens towards the harbour and river. It had a three or four storey high block to the square, but the bulk of it appears to have been a little lower and arranged around a court (no drawing of this survives, and Gordon (Gordon 1661) is the only evidence we have). On the site of this house it was decided to embark on another, much bolder essay in urban architecture;

3.5 W.S. Percy, Marischal Street Bridge with Virginia Street in 1932

to build a 'New Street' connecting the Castlegate and Weighhouse Square, and provide a straight and direct route from the Pier, to supplement the curved and narrow one by Shore Brae, Shiprow and Exchequer Wynd. Because the Castlegate lies high above the river the northern half of the site carries a sloping street at the edge of comfortable steepness. Even so, that half of the new street was two full stories higher than the proposed end near the river. A Bridge with then a series of diminishingly tall smaller 'bridges' masked by houses to either, was needed to finish the way across the flat ground of the Shorelands only recently claimed from the Dee. The purely engineering aspects were daunting, expensive, and entirely untried, but the project was even more ambitious in that it called for a dozen regular, new style, double fronted houses, to be built not only in stone, but in granite, and regularly from identical blocks called ashlar work. And that only went as far as the Bridge, named Bannerman for the current provost. The second half followed on, but with variations in the buildings. Another new street, or more properly road quickly grew up as Virginia Street, passing under Bannerman's Bridge and opening the Shorelands (Brogden 1996).

There is much that is modern about Marischal Street, as it was soon named, and these factors mark the beginning of Aberdeen's transformation from a mediaeval seaport into a modern city, and a city which set a pace, and directions that others had to follow. Firstly it was an act of urban design, a very early one in these islands. John Gwynne (1713–86) had only recently published his *London and Westminster Improved* and the same author had, incidentally, been active in the also recent, and first publication of Wren's and the other architects' proposals for the rebuilding of the City of London after the Great Fire of 1666. The concerns introduced by Gwynne will also occupy the magistrates of Aberdeen for the remainder of the 18th century. They were essentially a way of finding means to make straight, and wider, the narrow and twisting streets of ancient towns, specifically to ease congestion in the capital and in so doing to bring dignity to major buildings and to give something of legibility to London. These ideas are also appearing in French texts with roughly the same concerns, and in Dublin the Wide Streets Commission was shortly to be established in order to achieve precisely those ends (Brady 1802). And the city of Bath, a kind of alternative capital for the later 18th century, had begun introducing regular planning and later urban design to the land newly opened up for expansion. Edinburgh, as we all know, was on the point of establishing the first of its famous New Towns (Youngson 1966, Cruft 1995).

Marischal Street differs from other projects in that although it has the same concerns and might appear to be very similar, it is neither a re-configuration of the old pattern of streets nor is it an expansion on the edge of a built up town. Rather it was intended as an improvement to the very heart of the town and was as much concerned about the harbour as it was about making the town more gracious. Indeed the economic (still yet an idea in Adam Smith's head) and the practical led the design of the project with the architectural advances being the means to achieve them. This kind of thinking remains the generator of all the public works in Aberdeen until the 1840s. If economics and practicality are uppermost, then the purely engineering aspect shapes and carries the design. Essentially a ramp, and on the edge of good practice, Marischal Street is an engineering work joining harbour and Castlegate neatly at its mid point. That it also provides a grand entry or exit, to the town is not its first purpose, although it is immediately recognized and valued as such.

Marischal Street, at the Castlegate being a burghal plot (or two) introduces another new idea to Aberdeen. The *stance*, as it is known in Aberdeen, is the newly designed division, also known as plot, lot, or parcel elsewhere, and shares the characteristic of these in that all are slightly broader and much shorter than the long rigs of the mediaeval town. This change in feu design allows other essentially modern ways of building to be adopted. Each of the Marischal Street houses is double fronted with entry at the centre (Ref Everyman 6.2). The gardens on the west or east sides were not to be built upon, and were seen as a horticultural extension to the house itself; they were smaller and formally related to it. Each of the houses had at least one full basement (a feature hardly known in Aberdeen before) plus the possibility of adjacent vaults: they were more an investment in business than building for residence only. Shop fronts were an integral feature of the design and each house has the possibility of at least two shops with their own entries from the street with two appropriately designed shop windows. Penultimately, but of hardly less importance, each of the house designs were predetermined. Not only are they identical (or almost) but their relation to the sloping street is also regular – each house steps down the slope in a measured predictable and almost dance like manner. At the Castlegate end there is a further sophistication: the terminal houses are treated as pavilions, as though the whole street were indeed two buildings formally addressing one another, rather than a dozen plus houses. This was achieved by exploiting the north houses' gable ends as 'pediments', as the New Inn had recently done on the opposite side of the square, clearly a matter of judgement and design: the last houses could as easily have turned their gable ends to the square itself in which case the Castlegate would have gained a formal gate-like character in its middle. This would have been fine, but hardly necessary. The new street could have come to its end simply because it had run out of room. Its designers chose rather to signify the full stop architecturally. As the first example in Scotland where the street is regarded as a composed piece of building and as *urban architecture*, it remains a feature of Aberdeen and is achieved in a variety of different ways over the following two centuries.

New architectural ideas take time to settle in and often fizzle out before they become established. In Aberdeen the regular house by now was preferably double fronted but also often ornamented by small central gables castigated as a bad taste and wasteful expense (Thom 1811, 187–8), called 'tympanies' as at the Castlegate frontage of Marischal Street. Although that fashion lingers it is quickly overtaken by a preference for an unbroken eaves line. Opposite Gordon's Hospital there was a row of three and of these and one still exists, with a third buried inside a later frontage. All appear to be by William Law and are of the late 1760s: these are slightly broader than those in Marischal Street but do not have integral shops or warehouses and are of an almost suburban nature as this end of the town then was. Each of these is five bays and two stories with a trio of dormer windows in the roof – only the centre one is early, the other two, piended as the fashion was after 1800, can probably be dated from the new windows with lay-lights (horizontal window panes) a brief Regency fashion introduced at about the same time. Ashlar stone work in granite, with quoins at the corners is already a *type* in the making.

Around the corner in Belmont Street newly begun from its north end before 1775 is number 37 built in 1788 as the new lodging for the Menzies of Pitfodels family in replacement for their old one next door to the Earl Marischal's in the Castlegate. This house has the same elements as 61 Schoolhill, except that it is raised a half floor above the pavement (a full floor on the west side overlooking its gardens, and the open Denburn and Corbie Haugh). Otherwise it is identical, if not quite, more a subtle variation on the type; the Aberdeen version of the Georgian house being itself a variation of the same building in Edinburgh or London. The Old Custom House on Regent's Quay, of 1771, is taller, slightly deeper of plan, and decidedly grander, and yet, there is little in it, simply enough: 17 Castle Street, a smaller version of the type also survives. There were examples also in the Gallowgate, Gerard's House of 1787 at number 50 long since demolished, by William Dauney, uncle of Archibald Simpson and designer of at least one of the Marischal Street houses also, in George Street, and notably in Queen Street and the southern end of Broad Street, both lamentably demolished as late as 1973. Queen Street was a natural successor to Marischal Street, and was begun in 1773. Similarly it occupied two ancient feus on the east side of the Broadgate, which were exceptionally long. The new street terminated at the north junction with Lodge Walk.

Queen Street occupied flat ground, so there were no engineering issues, nor were the house designs predetermined as those of Marischal Street had been. They were all of the Aberdeen Georgian type, double fronted as the new arrangement of ground made easier, three storey with habitable roof space, constructed of ashlar granite, and with, at least some integral shop fronts.

3.6 Old Aberdeen Town House and High Street

Generally they had plain roofs with dormers, but some had the tympany, such as 10 Queen Street which was also the north entry to the newspaper offices through Chronicle Court. The junction of Queen Street with Broad Street had another of the curiosities of Aberdeen architecture, the rounded corner. This block, latterly Hutcheson's Bakery may have been the first of these. The last bays of the main and gable fronts are simply constructed as a quarter circle. This allowed a diagonal entry to the ground floor shop, but its purpose was to make it easier, and safer, for wheeled traffic to turn the corners. Its use is a preoccupation with the early planning authority, the Police Commissioners, who constantly refer to the needs to remove forestairs and other obstructions and to 'round the corners' of the streets of the mediaeval town.

Fortunately 81 High Street of 1780, perhaps by George Jaffray, survives. This varies the type, by number of windows and by the treatment of its front. Set back behinds its walled front garden, with pavilions originally at each corner, and a handsome gateway still in place, this three bay house seems bigger, mostly because the bays are broader and impart an air of extra comfort by being less crowded, but that is hardly noticed because the central bay breaks forward under its pediment, which is 'broken' by the arched first floor window rising into it: all else is type – ashlar granite, quoins, plain slated roof, all raised half a floor above ground.

These houses show Aberdeen's development of its own version of the perfected modern urban house type, and in Marischal Street how that could be employed to compose urban architecture. Seemingly simple experiments follow in the later 18th century which confirm a direction and sense of purpose which sets Aberdeen amongst the very few towns which were able to use design to lead and to manage the phenomenal expansion of the 19th century. The critical experiments were in the siting and designing to two civic buildings, the Town House of Old Aberdeen of 1788 and the Town and County Record Office in the Castlegate undertaken the following year. Both use a simple building type sited in the most elementary manner as termination of a vista. Both also have a determining history and context.

The Town House of Old Aberdeen is a rare example of L.B. Alberti's definition of beauty in architecture…a condition where nothing can be added nor taken away which would not diminish the building. Much of its quality derives from its design, by John Jaffray, but as much derives from its setting. Until 1895 Old Aberdeen was an independent burgh, not only the site of King's college, the sometime seat of the bishopric of Aberdeen at St Machar but equally if not more significantly the civic centre of the Parish of Old Machar which remained the much larger of the two parishes of Aberdeen until the 20th century. Its very small tight urban form was perfected as least by the turn of the 16th and 17th centuries, and this has been retained to the present. The Town House is its heart and its centre. As has been observed Old Aberdeen is a 'Y' type town form…its High Street runs from south to north where it widens symmetrically to form a small market place in front of the Town House. This formed a natural *degagement* for Jaffray's strongly symmetrical (it is as tall as it is wide) classic building (Slezer 1691).

Jaffray was charged with rebuilding the early 18th century structure and to incorporate its materials, so his task as much as his success was seen as a perfecting rather than a brand new endeavour. His three bay cube with pyramid roof and clock tower at the centre like other good experiments is so good that everybody assumes that it could not be done otherwise. Mean spirited critics might therefore be tempted to denigrate Jaffray's efforts. Old Aberdeen being the site of an ancient university was naturally bookish and would have been aware of the standard publications about the arts. Indeed so would many of its educated and more fortunate citizens. In fact a very up-to-date scheme to rebuild Kings College was still under consideration, a scheme that would have turned the then dilapidated old buildings into a most respectable and recognizably Roman palazzo (Slade 1991).

As with the other public buildings of Aberdeen built or improved in the 18th century a reticent and understated dress was preferred, not out of ignorance of the fashion of Rome for example, but out of pure preference for what was decent for Aberdeen. Like these this one confines it ornamentation to the quoins marking the ends and centre bay with the simplest of classic profile at the eaves or sills, and relies for its impact on its size, proportion, regularity of fenestration, and fine ashlar façade. The cubic mass of the new building fills the north side of the rather small space of the market place, in the 18th century lined by one and two storey houses, subsequently by only slightly taller ones. To achieve the cube Jaffray raised the Town House to three full floors so that there was always a pleasing sufficiency of space at the burgh's command. The top floor was let to the Mason's lodge, whereas the first floor's three large windows commanded to space to the south. The ground floor had a small gaol with its own entry matched by a further small room to the west side of the central entry.

3.7 Castlegate from Rotten Row

The practical uses of the outside spaces are unaffected by the building…the *streets* carry on as before transformed only by the increased activity of market days of special occasions. Yet its somewhat *theatrical* nature is ever present and was doubtless recognized as such from the beginning. Stage sets have been present in Aberdeen at least since the 17th century and they had come to bear *tropic* significance as indicative of tragedy comedy or satyr. By the later 18th century these would have been part of the education of many if not most of the citizens of Old Machar parish.

In Aberdeen a high level of theatrical portrayal had been introduced by Jamesone the portrait painter. He had studied, along with Van Dyke, in Rubens' studio in Antwerp. On his return to Aberdeen he laid out, and decorated the Playfield at Woolmanhill as a site of theatrical presentations where the Serlian types, suitably modified, would have been part of the town's entertainments. Similar sorts of highly detailed decorative and powerful views in one point perspective had also been the early favourite for the illustrated frontispieces of books. They had also been adopted in the late 17th century for use in confined gardens or in the open as a 'real' view if well managed. Nicholas Hawskmoor while working under Wren in the

Board of Works had experimented with buildings as termination in similar manner in some of his, unexecuted, designs early in the 18th century. Rarely did circumstances arise that made these well known tropes the easy choice to ornament actual places in 18th century Britain, least of all the small market place of a small neighbouring if independent burgh to a small and as yet not important ancient seaport. Jaffray seized his opportunity.

Unusually for mediaeval marketplaces the Castlegate has always been a large regular strongly formed rectangle and so close to 'perfection' as to invite suspicion that it was consciously designed. The original Tolbooth may have been its first ornamentation. By 1686 the replacement of the old Mercat Cross was clearly conceived as a classical urban ornament. The manner of placing Marischal Street is also a significant part of the developing sense that if managed skilfully and carefully the town was capable of serious urban design. There is evidence that the next, and critical, step was to be taken to re-case the Castlegate as a whole, beginning at the top.

At the east end of the Castlegate another civic building, much smaller than the Townhouse, was under consideration which also furthers a comparison with the Roman Forum. To house the Burgh's already considerable accumulation of records an Office to accommodate them outside the Tolbooth itself was contemplated. The details of commission are unknown, but Robert Adam prepared a design for the Town and County Record Office in 1772. Robert was the second of four architect sons of William Adam, and recently returned from his studies in Rome, with his own book of architecture, *The Ruins of Diocletian's Palace at Spalatro* (sic) (1764). As ubiquitous as his father, but with even more energy, and enough brass-neck for them all, Robert Adam is one of those occasional stars that occur with a talent and influence far beyond the expectations of one man's ability (MacInnes 1993).

Just who commissioned the design is unknown. Adam was building a house for a cadet Gordon at Letterfourie nearby and had many jobs in all parts of the United Kingdom. There had been a curious flowering of national standard public buildings for important but still smaller county towns, such as Derby, or Bury St Edmunds. These had the blessing of John Stuart, Earl of Bute, Prime Minister (1762), and Chancellor of Marischal College (1761) who had favoured the young Adam early; equally plausibly the Record Office commission came from other sources, we simply cannot say. The year of his design 1772 is the same as the crash of the banking group led by Aberdonian Alexander Fordyce which had a catastrophic effect on the four brothers' project of the Adelphi. Not only was this an urban design venture of great daring and quality it bode well to make Adam and his brothers comfortably rich (Rowan 2007). One of the consequences of the loss of confidence in the Adelphi project was for the brothers to look to Scotland for commissions. Much very interesting and important work was done by them in Edinburgh and Glasgow in the 1780s. Robert Adam's work in Aberdeen and Edinburgh may foreshadow these efforts.

Adam's design for the Aberdeen Record Office is of at least national standard, and furthermore, at the fancier end of that characterization. It also

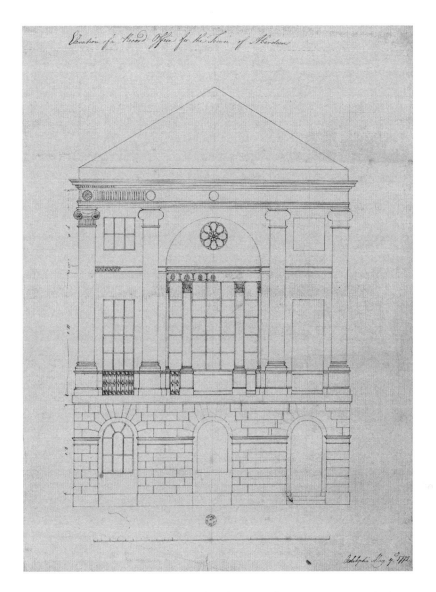

3.8 Robert Adam, *Elevation for a Record Office for the Town of Aberdeen* 1772

employs a full and thorough range of architectural ornamentation. The longest flattest and straightest 'view' in Aberdeen was from the Round Table at the west end of the Narrow Wynd eastwards past the Townhouse, terminated by the ancient feus at the top of Castlegate. These feus were amongst those designated for the new site of the Town and County Record Office. As noted above Jaffray, a few years later had perhaps like Adam exploited the simplest theatrical backdrop rendered in one point perspective. Adam and his fellows in Rome used terminal buildings to be viewed axially in the student competitions of mid-century (Fleming 1962). So whatever was placed on this site had the advantage of being seen *theatrically* by anyone on their way into the Castlegate. Adam, particularly alive to the possibilities of the picturesque at about this

3.9 Record Office and 1770 tenement blocks

time, even before its fashion was established, took the maximum advantage with his design whose west face was tall and narrow best calculated to 'fill' such a view.

If pressed Adam would have further urged his design to Aberdeen by reference to two current and important elements in architectural and urban design theory. Both have to do with propriety and good manners. It had always been accepted that the most complex and decorative of the architectural orders should be used sparingly, and only for very important buildings (such as a royal palace). This idea had recently been further clarified with Adam, at the centre of things in Rome in mid-century. He arrived there from Edinburgh in 1755 when already he and many colleagues had accepted the clarity that Colen Campbell had introduced in his *Vitruvius Britannicus* (Campbell 1966), which promoted the work of those who exemplified the purest yet flexible application of classic architecture to modern practice, such as the Vicenza architect Andrea Palladio (Palladio 1997 and Beltrami 1999). Campbell's books incidentally were almost entirely visual and his drawn examples carried his message. This tendency was known ultimately as the introduction of the *neo-classical*. These revisions to theory come from a new perspective of a widely diverse, self-selected, committed, exceptionally talented and informal group of students of the architecture, landscape and history of Rome and its neighbourhood. They introduced a stricter propriety and a return to embellishing only those parts of a building which had or appeared to have, a structural role.

This new perspective provided a much needed refreshment to the classical canon and was particularly so at the simple end of the spectrum of classical orders where the transition between pure form and the most basic embellishments seen in vernacular or even rustic buildings, excited the imagination of these artists. The discovery and then closer study of Greek architecture reinforced and introduced effectively new potential models. Seeing architectural remains in the contexts of history and landscape encouraged this newly developing branch of architecture. The seemingly accidental accumulation of high quality buildings in ruin from a variety of different periods encouraged experiments in urban design, both as a means of 'restoring' the missing parts and in arrangements for new programmes of building.

These were the differences which enriched later 18th century architecture and Robert Adam led the way. His Castlegate site was narrow fronted and deep, as burghal lots were, so his maximum width was less than ten meters, already an awkwardness for a major public building, never mind one in such a broad space. Without making a direct reference to any model Adam suggests a precious repository – almost a jewel box – in his design. Of course it is tall, not yet a tower but noticeably vertical, and in that sense not an unusual neighbour for Aberdeen. The expression, however, is brand new. His composition is three stories masquerading as two and he uses the Palladian version of a 16th century scheme for urban architecture. This takes a strong base storey made of deeply incised stonework in large blocks with widely spaced, simple openings, characteristics which convey strength. Its elegance adds a civic edge to that strength. Taking the cue for his Ionic order from the Mercat Cross the two floors above are expressed as elegant, even costly, with their finely sculpted full order of pedestal, base, shaft, capital and dosseret, frieze (fully sculpted itself), architrave, and then finally a plain stone band supporting the simple pyramid roof.

The first floor has the four pedestals which support the order, and between them Adam uses finely wrought ornamented iron railings which bow outwards as if they were balconies. These combine with the base storey to provide a comfortable and substantial cushion for the richly elaborated first floor. The central bay here is wider than its neighbours which allows for the big window to dominate the whole building. Adam might well have given this an arched top, but he needed the space above for more accommodation, so instead uses the device of a screen of columns, here Corinthian, to give prominence to the slightly taller, wider central feature. A small but finely carved band of decoration marks the division between first and second floors. He uses an ornamented rose window in the 'storey' above to mark the centre, flanked on either side by plain square ones.

The entrance to the building is by way of a passage to one side, leading to a doorway and staircase in the back part of the feu. There were to be rooms for the archive on the ground floor. The Sheriff Court above faces westward into the Castlegate, with a smaller meeting room behind and three substantial rooms above. As in all his work Adam's internal planning is convenient. He makes maximum good use of the space at hand with the same sort of mastery that the design of the façade and composition suggest.

Adam was not a grudging designer. When commissioned to provide one service he is ever apt to widen his canvas and design things on either side, even across the street…it is clear he sees the specific design as part of the larger assembly enriching either the landscape or townscape. Thus the feint urban design study of about 1774 for the Register House in Edinburgh shows this tendency (Rowan 2004). This major public building, one of the first in the New Town of Edinburgh, and seen on axis from as far away as the College in Nicholson Street. Facing the opposite problem that Jaffray encounters in Old Aberdeen Adam had a most important building with an abundance of emptiness in its context. His square-like *degagement* including the old Shakespeare theatre, terraces of new houses, an appropriate end to the North Bridge, and a suitable frame for his 'own' building, if acted upon would have made a fine addition to the city.

Eventually great sections of London, parts of Bath (Hart 1996), of Glasgow and of Edinburgh were enriched by Robert Adam's urban designs. No similar design by him for Aberdeen has been traced. However, the two blocks which were built on either side of the Record Office site introduce a new style of house to Aberdeen and the timing, their quality and proportional relationship to his design for the Record Office, point to a possible connection. To either side of Adam's site there soon appeared blocks of houses with integrally designed shop fronts that would set the form and create the standard for the major expansion of the town from 1800. The earliest of these blocks occupying the feus between Albion Court and Peacocks Close was constructed (more properly re-constructed on existing work) from 1770.

This four storey composite block of seven bays brings several new qualities to Aberdeen. It is very similar indeed to the then still new north front to Castle Grant in Strathspey. This was built by Robert's brother John Adam five years earlier. Not only is the design identical but so is its character, also breathtakingly stark with only very slightly more decorative elaboration. Both are fronted by smooth jointed ashlar white granite (still a little granular and slightly less 'pure' than the soon available denser stone from Rubislaw). The Castlegate block is severely plain, with no protruding sills, or frames, and without cornice at the eaves level making do with only a simple string course. The fenestration is not only regular but appears to be for the same building whereas it actually serves two tenements. The slated roof, originally lofts without dormer windows, has its ridge parallel to the Castlegate and the ground floor treatment is an arcade or series of round-headed arches serving as shop windows, entrances to shops, entrance also to the passages of Smith's

3.10 R. Seaton, Castlegate, 1806

Court and Peacock's Close, as well as providing entrance to the houses above. The arcade rhythm varies and is unrelated to the register of the windows above and is demarcated from the rest of the façade by a plain string course.

Soon there followed a five bay four-story tenement, immediately south of the Record Office for Charles Clark, an Advocate. The precise dating for this and the neighbouring blocks at the southeast corner is unrecorded. These all show same design features of greater sophistication: there were sill courses connecting the top range of windows and the eaves were raised into a parapet also marked by string courses. Clark's block disappeared with the construction of the Citadel. The surviving pair of house seems to be constructed (as presumably was Clark's block) from the purer Rubislaw granite. Their chimney stacks were also constructed from granite unlike the 1770 block where they are of Seton brickwork. A slightly later date will doubtless be confirmed for these in due course.

Thus the top of the Castlegate was transformed in the last quarter of the 18th century. A new form of urban architecture is perfected by the arcade element, where not only the different floors and uses of the buildings but the proprieties of correct architectural composition are also demonstrated – the civic building (that is Adam's design for the Record Office) is distinguished by a variation of the arcade and the upper floors are given significantly greater embellishment

3.11 Marischal Street, James Burn, Banking Company in Aberdeen and 57 Castle Street

expressive of the building's superior, that is community or public, use. The plan of this new work extended into the north and south sides of the square symmetrically confirming a totality in the design of the group. A most likely identity for this Master of the Castlegate, of course is the Adam family.

It may also have been someone else, or several others. Robert Adam's design for the Record Office was not proceeded with. The alternative design for the Record Office was eventually built by an unknown architect in 1789, perfectly competent but demonstrating a talent inferior to Adam's. As built, the Record Office had nearly twice the width of Adam's and of five bays, but was only two stories only. The centre three bays were given prominence by a pediment. It has always been assumed that the site for both was the same. However it is more likely that Adam made his design for the feu immediately south of the pair of feus actually used, that is the centre of the east end of the Castlegate and on axis with the Mercat Cross and the Wellhead. In which case there was room for two blocks of tenements symmetrically disposed, matching the two further blocks built. By the time the first of these was constructed a wider site was found for the 'centrepiece', and the remaining blocks were built, but in a slightly modified form.

A few years later at the end of the century a variation of these ideas was constructed opposite the Townhouse, on the recently available site (from 1788) of the ancient Pitfodels Lodging. This was the Banking Company in Aberdeen.

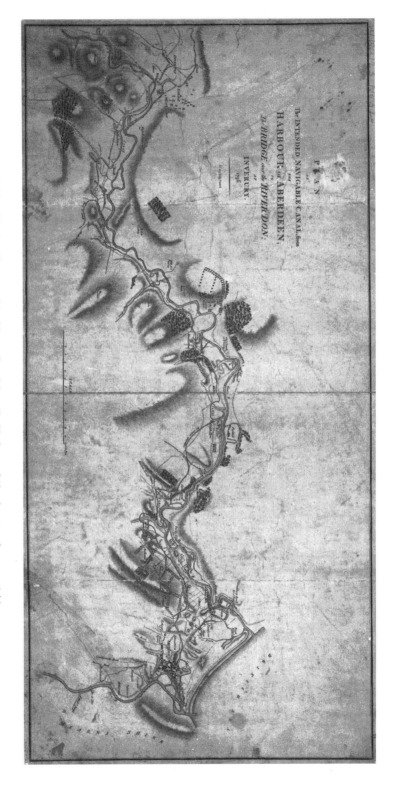

3.12 Charles Abercrombie, Plan...Canal from the Harbour of Aberdeen to...Inverury (sic)

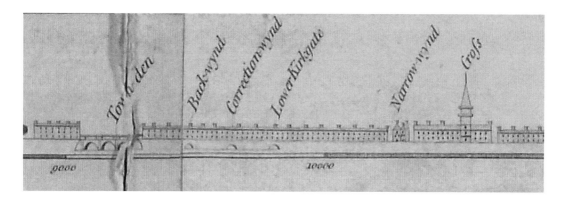

3.13 Charles Abercrombie, design for a new street and bridge across the Denburn

It was designed by James Burn. It too was a piece of urban design as well as urban architecture. This building was under construction at exactly the moment when the competition to design for a new South Entry had been called and Burn's design has uncanny similarities to at least one entry. James Burn, like Archibald Simpson and others afterwards, designed a composite building composed of a 'fancy' block and its plain neighbour – inviting others to add further plain buildings in a similar or best of all identical design to finish the run, (in this case, into Exchequer Row and on to Shiprow). His design proposed a scheme to follow, in the event not taken up, or at least not directly. The 19th century would have had no difficulty whatever in accepting that a bank should have special treatment, and could even be civic. Burn and his commissioning clients were pressing at the edges of architectural decency at the end of the 18th century. However their assertion that a bank should bear a greater architectural embellishment than the civic buildings opposite was carried out, without recorded protest.

The Bank is three expressed stories plus a further one behind the parapet. Like Adam's Record Office and the neighbouring tenement blocks, Burn uses the arcade idea, but the five bays of the ground floor of the Bank are expressed by the seeming strong and channelled coursing of the great granite blocks. The two upper floors are embraced within an order of columns, in fact pilasters that as Alberti would have it, are simply columns, revealing themselves only partially. Here they are Tuscan, the simplest and most robust of the orders and usually indicative of muscular and therefore male strength – perhaps suitable for a bank. These pilasters carry the frieze and architrave which is surmounted by a balustrade on a pedestal element to disguise the inhabited roof. Immediately next door is the plain, slightly lower, and undressed version of the same thing – a three bay three story tenement block with arched passage to one side, shops fronts and an entry to tenement. The Bank, ultimately deriving from Donato Bramante's design for the Palazzo Caprini in Rome is a type of building known as a palace block (from *palazzo*, Italian for tenement block). First given this architectural expression in early 16th century Rome, it was soon modified to provide covered markets in Venice (Howard 1975) and thereafter became the appropriate expression for the big five bay house (Pevsner 1976).

Burn, following Adam, brings it to Aberdeen as part of a composed section of the town carrying regularity and propriety to the city's design.

At the end of the century the Town sought powers from Westminster to establish a Police Commission, whose role was to regulate and where necessary improve the quality of the streets of Aberdeen, particularly to remedy the intrusion of private buildings into the public domain and to regulate existing streets and oversee the making of new ones. By as early as 1783 there had been the proposal to build a new street from Rotten Row to The Green, and in 1794, the engineer Charles Abercrombie had been asked for advice on how the town might best expand itself. He would shortly design and begin the Aberdeenshire Canal connecting the Dee with Inverurie and opening the shire to the sea (Abercrombie 1796). He had also been involved in upgrading the roads leading from the town into Aberdeenshire, and in the creating of new ones with the associated bridge works, embankments and cuttings. His philosophical direction was towards efficient regularity and plainly he was not frightened by a big task, or a long term and very expensive one. Propriety and elegance of building he would leave to others. Indeed in his only architectural suggestions he simply proposed repeating the pattern already established at the eastern end of the Castlegate infinitely (Abercrombie 1796 b). He was, however, able to persuade Aberdonians to take a more strategic view of what they saw rather simply as a need to get a straight and level street into the heart of the town. His Report was an early (and perhaps the first) exercise in regional planning and it made abundantly clear that the powers of the Police Commission were quite inadequate to the challenges Aberdeen's site, its topography and its mediaeval town form posed to its wanted, even required, expansion. Abercrombie answered his commission very well, but he also provided the template for a New Town, and one that could expand far beyond what had been called for.

4

The Designed City

At a population of some 25,000 by the late 18th century Aberdeen was not obliged to expand by design. It could have continued to grow in a natural manner, that is, a slow migration into contiguous but empty ground (Cruikshank 1990). This had already begun north-eastwards in the Evens Quarter and to a degree along the new harbour works of the Fittie Quarter, or northwards towards the Spital and Old Aberdeen. Its closer suburbs, Gilcomston, Broadford, Skene's Square, Hardgate, or empty ground at Ferryhill or Polmuir offered other alternatives – but Aberdeen wished to grow by design. It wished to have an easy and more efficient connection to the west and south by the Bridge of Dee. Perhaps it wished to grow westward, although this was never stated as aim, and that was blocked by the valley of the Denburn. It certainly wanted more fully to join the efforts of Edinburgh whose recent New Town had reached to its west end and the newly begun Charlotte Square with further ground staked for expansion along the roads northwards and halfway to Leith.

Glasgow too had raced ahead, but in a different manner. Its High Street then was similar to Broadgate with the Gallowgate, or to the High Street of Edinburgh between the Castle and World's End, so scope for expansion was very limited. The short street west of the Tron had become the city's effective centre where the Town Hall had been greatly extended as the Tontine Hotel, latterly to the back as coffee rooms with the ground floor arcade forming a spacious and sheltered public place of meeting. Beyond the port Trongate developed as Argyll Street parallel to the river, the Clyde riverside developed quickly and new growth began at the south end near Glasgow Green where a new kirk was built, contemporary with Gibbs' West Kirk of St Nicholas. Here in Glasgow Allan Dreghorn (1706–64) built a handsome version of Gibb's St Martins-in-the-Fields if on a reduced scale. Later in 1787 St Andrews was surrounded by its Square of regular houses by William Hamilton. A decade earlier an even more interesting design had been realized in Charlotte Street, in open ground to the north-east but adjoining the Green where it had its own gateway. Here on both sides of the street were a series of big houses, detached from each other with their coach houses arranged between as if lesser versions of the mansions, with low walls connecting all together to make a pleasing, but suburban, group. Sadly only one of these survives. Its architect is unknown.

The design of the Charlotte Street houses is typical of 18th-century Glasgow where detached mansions in grounds were numerous. These had both a remarkably good pedigree and an equally promising progeny. The Shawfield Mansion of 1712 is the prototype. This was designed by Colen Campbell (Stutchbury 1967), a native of Nairn for a relation. It was the first of a new kind of house, squarish, 'small' yet Augustan and comfortable, derived from both the great 17th-century architect Inigo Jones, and his earlier hero Andrea Palladio. Two stories (on a raised half floor for services) it had two apartments on each level with two reception rooms between a comfortable open square staircase in the middle. The exterior embellishment was concentrated at the central three bays under a pediment, and a simple piended roof enclosed all. It was a design that Campbell – and through his persuasive advocacy British culture – took as the ideal, sometimes larger – with wings, and perhaps pavilions, oftener in smaller versions as a Villa, or even a cottage.

Shawfield stood just west of town on what is now Argyle Street and its planted avenue led southward to the Clyde, to later become Stockwell Street (Foreman 2009). To and from the Clyde was the great trade of the 18th century, tobacco grown and processed by enslaved African labour in the Carolinas and the Chesapeake, transported to Glasgow, and sold on throughout Europe. In these colonies, especially in Virginia and Maryland, houses of the Shawfield kind were as numerous as in Glasgow. Later owners of Shawfield were tobacco factors and with their staff, at least, also slave traders. Shawfield was by then Glassford House, and was demolished in 1791 to turn its garden and grounds to the north into Glassford Street, where a series of four storey houses was built over arcades. The grounds of other mansions on Argyle Street and Trongate were similarly transformed often with terminal buildings on Ingram Street (such as the Ramshorn Kirk) making the old avenue-mansion house unit of plantation and suburb into a unit of urban design, and in this part of Glasgow used to great effect. (P.C. L'Enfant was engaged on his design for Washington, at the top of the Chesapeake at the same time, and also using a similar device, based on Mount Vernon (Berg 2008: 76).

Not only do neighbour's developments increase property values, they can also give prominence and a sense of unity to adjoining schemes: Ingram Street has numerous terminal buildings to benefit its southern neighbours. It too is terminated by the Cunninghame mansion to the west, later augmented into the Royal Exchange and now a museum. This early interlocking of the developments, as it were in competition, also gave visual relief, a sense of place to what became in Glasgow a generalized and as elsewhere a relentless grid. Other parts of the Glasgow New Town were developed in a manner familiar in other towns – St Enoch's Square with church by John Jaffray of 1782 and presumably the surrounding houses: similarly Robert and James Adam built in George Square. They also contributed very handsome and decorative additions to the Trongate and High Street, especially the Professors' Lodgings opposite the College, or the Assembly Rooms whose 'fragment' has adorned the Green for many years as a quite convincing Triumphal Arch (Rowan 2007).

The New Town of Edinburgh is a story so well known as to require little in addition here (Youngson 1966, Cruft 1995). The design of the formal, discrete, gridded scheme won by James Craig in competition in 1767 was nearing completion opposite the Old Town. Of greater interest to Aberdonians, and to the citizens of Edinburgh as well, was the progress of the Capital's entry from the south, threaded through gaps by the Tron Kirk in the High Street, through gardens, over the Cowgate, and past the College to Nicholson Street. To get there, the great vaulted viaduct of South Bridge was a project to envy, and the project to encourage (Fraser 1989). Although Aberdeen had shown the way with Marischal Street, Edinburgh had raised the game very significantly and Aberdeen was up for the challenge.

Like Edinburgh, Aberdeen faced an impediment to growth, especially to the west, from whence a new kind of transport infrastructure was wanting. Roads had begun to be vastly improved in the later 18th century; and were becoming straighter, consolidated and often paved in the modern manner, with many new bridges, and more to follow. Yet, the ways 'to the centrical Parts of the City of Aberdeen…are…narrow, indirect and incommodious' (Act Geo III 1800). With only three uninviting and miserable ways into and out of the town, the bustle of business in the city along narrow and crooked streets meant passage to the Castlegate or the Harbour took more time and created yet more congestion. To alleviate these specific problems, advice was sought from engineer Charles Abercrombie (1750–1817). In providing solutions to these problems he also produced a template which allowed and perhaps even encouraged the five-fold expansion of population within the 19th century, creating a new and designed city.

His remit was to indicate where best to place the two *New Lines of Road extending from Aberdeen to the two Bridges over the Rivers Dee and Don* (Abercrombie 1796a), and in his best professional manner he provided three alternatives for the 'South Entry' as he called it. One of these, and the seemingly most practical, had been proposed by George Taylor in 1793 and remained the obvious solution (Taylor 1793). However it would have made a bad road or at least a road with exceptional difficulties as the main entry was too close to the shifting yet still untamed river Dee. Taylor's route did provide the most obvious and cheapest means to join the Bridge of Dee to the Castlegate and to the Harbour. It would also be an easy connection across the square to the line of the proposed new North Entry. This part of Abercrombie's scheme was presented without alternative as it would occupy the two or three feus of the Castlegate east of the New Inn: the only impediment on that side of the town was these few houses

Abercrombie's second alternative was to construct a new Dee bridge and causeways to connect directly south of Aberdeen at Torry. This would have been handsome grand and present the town to the best advantage as visitors approached along the stately straight thoroughfare to the heart of the town.

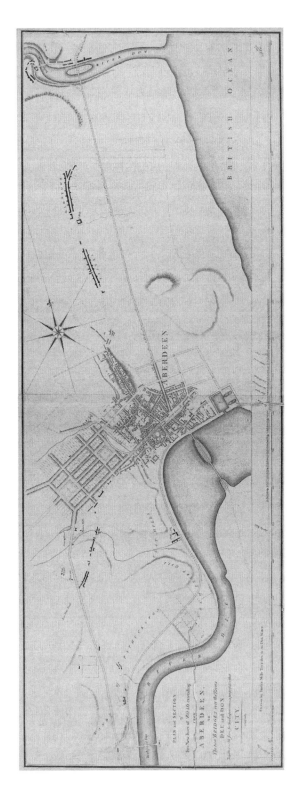

4.1 Charles Abercrombie, *Plan and Section* 1796

It would also been very costly, and given the nature of the broad Dee estuary, least likely to find ready acceptance.

The impediments in the way of his third alternative for the South Entry were also daunting: numerous houses, a warren of congested streets, and St Katherine's Hill to acquire and clear. On top of these he had to bridge over Putachieside, the Millburn and the Denburn, and, not least, the very considerable valley through which the Denburn passed just west of Aberdeen. Beyond that the road was easy to make, on the safe and high plains largely and invitingly empty, not only to the Bridge of Dee but also westward for miles. In the event the Town preferred this difficult and expensive alternative design (Innes 1798).

There were other ideas for improvement, very much connected and with which Abercrombie was leading as advisor. These were independent ventures but were interconnected, supported by and in a sense designed by a group of citizens representing the community – and of course, themselves. These, the sons and grandsons of the Improvers took the next logical steps to improve both shire and city: major works to improve the harbour, the project to dig a navigable canal to the heart of Aberdeenshire at Inverurie, and numerous schemes to improve, or build anew, turnpike roads. All these projects had the city as their focus; they improved its prospects for enrichment and they applied even more pressure on its layout.

To adopt any of Abercrombie's proposals – to connect the heart of the town with its county and its access to the world – meant a Bill had to be argued at Westminster. This was managed by Town Clerk Carnegie on behalf of the Baillies and Provost. Lord Sidney when time was running short raised issues which might well have killed the project. His objections were profound and put with vigour and showed an extreme, to us, form of reverence for the sanctity of property, and a belief in keeping government out of citizens' affairs which would have warmed the hearts of American founding fathers such as Thomas Jefferson. Briefly Sidney argued it was iniquitous that any kind of government should be allowed to condemn private property, acquire it and remake it in other forms, unless the owner freely consented, and in the case of Aberdeen, that would mean *all* owners (see above for related judgement). Of course that was the nub of the Act and the very purpose of seeking its passage. This aspect, which was duly out voted, represented in those days the acquisition of new powers of an almost revolutionary kind. Shortly the affairs of Aberdeen threw up another new power to seek, namely the power to roll over a debt on its coming due, simply because one of the parties was unable to discharge it: in other words corporations such as Aberdeen would be protected from insolvency. At the beginning of the 19th century this was yet to be ceded, and authorities could spend only those monies they had, or could borrow, and when the debt came due they had to pay up. As these fiscal matters stood it is even more to be wondered at that the town felt so emboldened that it had sought powers to execute such a project, and that more legislators beside Sidney did not stop them.

4.2   Colin Innes, West end of Castlegate and part of New South Entry

The Bill's passage was secured and it was assented to by King George on 4th April 1800. The Act acknowledged the problem and the expediency of the solution proposed. It authorized the magistrates as trustees to manage the acquisition of the already surveyed properties from the named owners or possessors, named procedures in cases of dispute and stipulated that no works could begin until the trustees had 'raised and secured, by subscription, loan, or otherwise, the respective Sums of Money...Fifteen thousand Pounds Sterling before beginning the said South Street or Avenue, and Five thousand pounds Sterling, before beginning the said North Street or Avenue'. These monies were to purchase the properties in the way of the works. The Town immediately granted £20,000 from its funds, and the New Streets' Trustees began their work.

There were over a hundred of these 'Proprietors, Liferenters, Occupiers or Lessees' in the way of the South Street, roughly half as many for the North Street. Of these a number were substantial institutions: the Master and Manager of the Trades Hospital, the Incorporation of Hammermen, the Dean of Guild, and the Society of True Blue Gardeners. Others varied from the very comfortably placed Patrick Milne of Crimonmogate, Baillie William Ritchie of Techmuiry, or Mistress Leys of Glasgoforest, to John Davie Wood, sawyer, John Stewart, stabler, and Widow Clark, residenter. Each and all of these had to be treated with; hopefully by their offering to sell, and reasonably; or agreeing to sell after adjudication; or to a forced sale after the intervention of the sheriff and jury. Once a sale was agreed the property had to be leased back until the works requiring its demolition had actually begun. The properties were then to be dismantled and the fittings and materials sold on for re-use.

Abercrombie's plan focused on the Castlegate supplementing the Marischal Street connection with the harbour, with the major extension northwards on the opposite side of the square just east of the New Inn. This wing with the rest of the extended Townhouse established the base line for the more important South Street, and when the Narrow Wynd was widened to 60 feet its new centre line was the same as that of the market place. Therefore both North and South Streets were to join the Castlegate at its middle so that its short and long axes would extend infinitely into the county. The North Street picking up the angle of the feus on that side of the market place was itself to be the geometric generator of the gridded new quarter to the north east that had in fact already begun to develop. Abercrombie proposed straightening the Shiprow to conform, albeit imperfectly, with his engineer's ideal of a regular intersection of streets at 90 degrees.

The grid was to the 18th century a natural abstraction, a realization of the Platonic ideals which old Burnet had stated in his extreme form a century before. Thomas Burnet a member of the Burnett of Leys family had taken Isaiah as his beginning and had written his *Sacred Theory of Earth* (Burnet 1691) where he asserted that before the Fall of Man the Earth had been perfect, perfectly flat, with no mountains or valleys and when all seas and lakes were perfectly geometrical in their shapes. Wren had taken the related idea that perfect rectangular parcels were the best means of dividing ground as his starting point when re-designing the City of London after the fire. Practically Wren could not always reach this level of perfection, but he came pretty close to it. Abercrombie was simply following Wren whose ideas and plan for the City of London had been published in the late 1740s for the first time. A related Platonic notion was proposed by the garden designer John Reid. As a contemporary of both Wren and Burnet he had advocated in 1693 in his *Scot's Gardener* that when an irregularity is met in nature and cannot be moved, a sensible and regular designer will simply repeat the 'irregularity' mirror-fashion about a new axis to form a perfect symmetry. Thus Abercrombie observes his 'irregular junction' of North Street and Marischal Street with the Castlegate and forms a pleasing repetition of it for the junction of the improved Shiprow and the Broadgate. That this might not be noticed by anyone without training would have hardly concerned him. It would not have escaped the notice of his peers, the professional engineers, architects, and the Improvers who commissioned them. That notice would be sufficient.

If the destination was perfectly clear, if the means to get there were encouraged and sanctioned by authority – the highest to the lowest – a deal of persuasion and shifting of earth and then building was still needed. The two halves of Colin Innes's 1798 survey that accompanied the delegation to Parliament marked each of the properties to be affected and showed the existing lines of the land as well as the ground plans of the areas where the two Streets were to be built. Even a cursory glance conveys the great size of the project and gives some inkling of the dangers inherent in it. The drawings showing all the properties to be acquired demolished and then replaced, stand as a witness to the skills of the surveyor and the vision of the town that undertook its commission and execution. These survey drawings, signed by Innes, countersigned by Charles Abercrombie, then attested as the drawings referred to in the Act by the MP for the city Allardyce of Dunottar, James Thomson, and Town Clerk Carnegie became the model to which the New Streets Trustees initially looked as a sort of talisman to reassure them that the scheme was possible to achieve.

It was some little while before their confidence rose to the task before them. The Trustees asked Colin Innes, their surveyor, to mark out the North Street 'by proper figures and marks upon the houses within the town, and by long stones to be fixed to the Ground after leaving…the town…in the same manner as has already been done along the intended South Street' (TM 5 Nov 1800). Initially they were at a loss as to how to find and appoint 'an engineer or architect' to make the designs for the buildings and the necessary infrastructure. They anticipated that an advertisement seeking such advice and offering premiums to the best schemes was the appropriate means, and assumed that their counterparts in Edinburgh and Glasgow would be in a position to give them guidance. In the event they could offer no help: the Edinburgh Town Clerk reported they had no occasion to issue such a notice since they began thinking about the New Town in 1763 and from Glasgow the news came that they had never made such an advertisement but would send a copy of the restrictions and conditions laid down for the 'building in the New Town and St Andrews Square'.

The trustees decided to go ahead as they had intended and placed advertisements in the 'Aberdeen Journal, the Glasgow Courant, two of the Edinburgh papers, the Sun, Star, and Morning Chronicle of London, and the Liverpool paper'. By the meeting of the Trustees in August 1800 numerous enquiries and expressions of interest had come in and by the New Year the Trustees' clerk had received seven designs for the 'Houses Buildings, Bridges Connected with the Work, and also the necessary Number of common Sewers'. There were schemes from two Aberdeen designers, James Littlejohn (who had recently designed the seven houses in Drum's Lane, Upperkirkgate) and John Chisolme; there were others from David Hamilton of Glasgow, two, from James Savage and James Young of London, and two also from Edinburgh supplied by Robert Reid and Richard Crichton (Colvin 1978). These were all young men just setting out on their careers and although only one of the designs survives, it is still possible to gain an idea of the kinds of design the Trustees had to choose from.

John Chisolme was Aberdonian and scarcely 20 years of age when he competed. He had graduated from Marischal College but we know nothing of any prior practice; nor indeed sadly do we have any idea of the quality of his entry. His proposal for the Bridge over the Denburn, the first to suggest a single arch, was subsequently adopted. He went on to be a pupil then assistant to James Rennie in London and is credited with the design for the entrance to the East India Docks. He also exhibited designs at the Royal Academy for a wooden bridge over the Don elsewhere in Aberdeenshire, and a design for the Assembly Rooms in Aberdeen itself in 1808. He had joined James Telford's office and was superintending the new Court House in Carlisle when he died of heart failure at only 28.

James Littlejohn, the other local competitor, is known to us more as a builder, or contractor, than as either architect or engineer. His designs for the seven houses north of the Upperkirkgate in Drum's Lane are on a rather smaller scale than what would have served for the New Avenues, but they are regular and well planned. Littlejohn Street is associated with him, probably as its speculative builder.

Robert Reid and Richard Crichton had just embarked in practice in Edinburgh and their design for the Bank of Scotland at the top of the Mound begun in 1803 is their only work together and incidentally the only work ascribed to Crichton. Reid, became a very prolific and important architect and rose to official prominence as the Government's architect in Scotland, one of his works being the well known, Parliament Square by St Giles in Edinburgh. This was built from 1804 and extended to include the Signet Library in 1810–12. Reid worked formerly in the Adam Brothers firm and it is their, specifically Robert's, mature urban style that Reid carries on. By the turn of the century this had become refined, almost into type, but its main features are interestingly the same as for Robert Adam's projected design for the Record Office in the Castlegate of 1773. All is made masterly by the 1790s when Adam designed the north side of Charlotte Square as a composed block where seven houses and blocks of flats are made to read as one building. At Gayfield Place at the other end of expanding Edinburgh, James Baxter makes a similar design but entirely of flats (Youngson 1966).

Reid carries this paradigm forward. A rusticated ground floor supports two further floors in smooth ashlar, either astylar or with pilasters, engaged or free standing columns depending on whether a centre-piece or pavilion termination or even a modulating feature was required. All these are used, and eloquently, in Parliament Square in the Old Town, and more extensively in his design for the Second New Town from 1803 where his drawing for Heriot Row could have been taken straight from his proposal for the Aberdeen Streets.

James Savage and James Young entered the competition from Young's address in Great Shire Lane, London. Perhaps Savage provided slightly more of engineering skill; it would appear that it was the bridge element that attracted him as in 1805 he won the important competition for the Ormonde Bridge in Dublin, and although that was not proceeded with, three years later he was awarded the commission for the Richmond Bridge, also over the Liffey. He produced a design for the replacement London Bridge (Rennie's design however was marginally favoured) and designed a further project in 1825 for the South Bank of the Thames but this was far in advance of its time. He was a City of London man, and much in demand giving evidence in legal cases. About James Young we know nothing further than the design ascribed to him alone.

Of all the entrants David Hamilton (1768–1843) was the most experienced and at 32, the eldest. He first presents himself as 'Engineer', and later as 'Architect'. Both were true, and as such precisely what the Trustees wanted. Hamilton's training was as a mason and his connection with the Adam firm a most beneficial one for him. The precise nature of that relationship is at present unknown. Probably through his father's connection with the firm, Hamilton had the advantage of knowing many of their schemes from the architects' drawings – for Hamilton the best possible schooling – the joining of his practical experience in building to this exposure, some of the most exciting and diverse ideas about architectural design in response to the requirements of an extensive and varied practice, made his career in Glasgow a distinguished one: indeed he is regarded there as 'Father of the City's Architecture'.

Perhaps for these reasons of which the Trustees would have been aware since the Provost of Glasgow had written a letter of recommendation or more likely because of the presentation itself, his scheme was awarded first premium. At their 7th January 1801 meeting the Trustees noted that seven 'Plans and Designs' had been received by the (slightly extended) closing date. These were to remain on view until the 28th January, 'under the charge of the Trustees Clerk from 11 till 2 of clock every lawful day, in order that the whole of the Trustees who incline may have an opportunity of deliberately

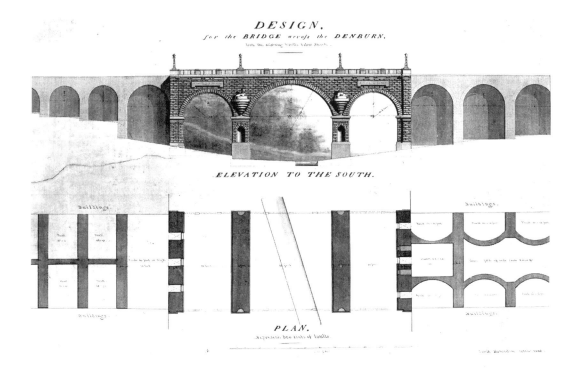

4.3 David Hamilton, *Design for the Bridge across the Denburn* 1800

examining and considering the whole of those plans and their Comparative Merits and fitness to be adopted in the Execution of the proposed Streets' (NST 2 8th Jan 1801). When they met on the 3rd of February the Trustees present, under the presidency of Provost Dingwall, were the four Baillies, the Dean of Guild, Provost Leys, Dr Thomas Black (Principal of Marischal College), Gavin Hadden, Robert Tower, D. Brown, the President of Advocates Mr Lumsden, Captain Storey Shipmaster, Deacon Smith, a Glazier (of the Incorporated Trades), and Convenor Farquhar.

These 14 awarded the 150 guinea premium to David Hamilton's entry as, 'the first in point of Merit and best adapted for the work of the New Streets'; the second premium of 100 guineas went to James Savage. Travel expenses of 2 shillings per mile were awarded to each. The Trustees also decided to authorize further awards to any of the other competitors' work 'as they may consider to be useful and beneficial in the Execution of any Part of the proposed New Streets'. In due course they awarded 20 guineas to James Young for his designs.

Charles Abercrombie (in his proposals) had set a new and an exceptionally difficult design problem. Both New Streets were to be very long, but the South Street bore the larger importance as it would act as principal entry to the town, an opportunity all competitors would cheerfully accept. A symbolic and rather theatrical frontispiece to a city is a recurring preoccupation for architects of the later 18th century. An example: the new customs posts, the *Barrieres* that Claude Nicholas Ledoux (1736–1806) was building on the edges of Paris, acted also

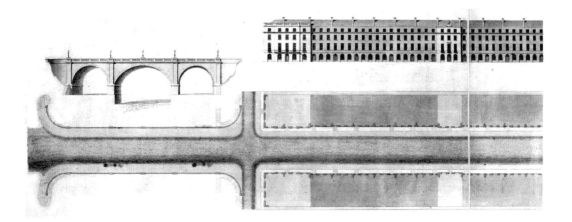

4.4 James Young, Design for the South Entry of Aberdeen

as architectural statements of civic grandeur. The last Ports of Aberdeen had only recently been demolished and would hardly have been missed, though a similar if welcoming gesture is implicit in the Denburn Bridge. Most if not all the competitors and many of the Trustees would have known Robert Adam's recently published designs for the south entry into Edinburgh.

The real difficulty set by Abercrombie was the extreme length of the Terrace he stipulated to be built from the Denburn Bridge to the Castlegate. The composed terrace (or palace block) had appeared in Scotland recently, and would naturally be the type to propose. Charlotte Square in Edinburgh is the equivalent of 14 houses, as is Nicholson's early 19th century Carlton terrace in Glasgow; Reid's later but roughly contemporary scheme for Heriot Row will stretch the design to 23 houses. The South Street of Aberdeen would need at least 33 houses of the biggest sort. All competitors shared the design ideas of the common paradigm of the day. The pair of super-buildings on the north side of the Place de la Concorde (from 1753) in Paris by J.E. Gabriel is among the earliest and is most prominent. It was recommended to C.P. L'Enfant by Thomas Jefferson as best model for the design of the new federal city, Washington (Berg 2008). In the United Kingdom the similar composed terrace block had been largely perfected but not invented by Robert Adam, but by the late 18th century the form was the accepted means of composing long rows of houses. What Abercrombie's problem posed for architects through the Trustees, their Act of Parliament and advertisement, was an appropriate resolution to this extreme case. Like many architectural problems from the late 18th century onwards it required intelligent imagination more than any other quality as there was no ready precedent that any could adopt. Each had to invent his own and this is where Hamilton must have shown himself ahead.

David Hamilton's design for the Denburn Bridge shows how he united the rustic and polite; seemingly a small matter but his rendering of the Corbie Haugh, since the early 19th century part of Union Terrace Gardens, seen through the western arch and part of the principal span, established nature as one pole of his architectural imagination. Similarly the water of the

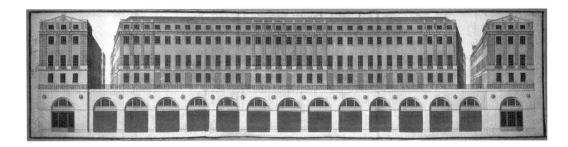

4.5 Robert and James Adam, the Adelphi, London from the Thames

Denburn is the foundation of it. Hence are established the quality of forms and compositions appropriate to each level, from the most basic to the most refined, from nature to civil and commercial government, and all within the common vocabulary of the time. The Bridge, composed into three parts like a triumphal arch where the centre is greatest was to be constructed of rusticated stone work. Savage's design which also follows this standard scheme has a delicacy about it which is in part owing to the designer's metropolitan desire for elegance, failing perhaps to make a proper distinction between the architectural propriety of the two major parts of the work – the Bridge and the Street – and this is exactly where Hamilton scores. His rusticated blocks are very deeply cut, expressive of an extreme elemental structure placed in contrast to nature, a quality that is picked up by the elaboration of the decorative parts of the central span. Here two Sphinxes gaze at one another from the tops of extraordinary elements from Hamilton's imagination. Like two enormous inverted hives, five increasingly large bull nosed stone discs seem to grow out of the rustication to provide the resting place for the beasts' plinths. Below these, flanking the Denburn itself, are two niches standing on – of all things – perfectly plain giant pedestals. It is as if his design is a commentary on the most primitive, lying somewhere between the ancient water spirits and modern roads. The parapets in contrast are as agreeably modern and pedestrian friendly as could be.

From that basis the design of Hamilton's houses intended to line the great Street could follow the pattern of the parts of a 'classical' column – rusticated base acting as a kind of pedestal, upper floors as shaft finishing with eaves and roof (the capitals and entablature). Hamilton had already provided the new but nevertheless appropriate basis for all this in his Bridge design. How he composed the Street's length can only be guessed at, by reference to his other contemporary work. It does not appear that the ensemble which would be expected for the New Streets, the designs in Glasgow of Hutcheson Street and the arcaded row of building immediately south of Hamilton's Hospital was actually designed by him. Indeed the new Hospital was built in 1840 by another architect. Not surprisingly Hamilton's architectural vocabulary and syntax were shared by the other competitors, and owed much to the Adam firm's work in the accepted Palladian ideal. One might expect Hamilton also to borrow from his father William Hamilton's work at St Andrew Square, Glasgow (1786) – only recently built answering similar requirements. Hamilton's design

4.6 Percier and Fontaine, Rue du Rivoli Paris

for the Hutcheson Hospital employs the rusticated base and higher contrasting second stage, of pilaster, columns, tall windows and niches with statues, under prominent entablature and balustrade. The tower and steeple characteristic of Glasgow would not have been appropriate to Aberdeen. Already Hamilton's architecture is lighter than for example Robert Reid's, and more elegant without in any way being less robust. It has been compared to French (Kaufmann 1966) work of the period but does not possess the clarity, the attenuation and the lean look so admired in Charles Percier (1763–1838) and Pierre Fontaine's (1762–1853) work, or in that of JNL Durand whose classism is even more abstract (Villari 1990). All seem to share in an admiration for Jacques Germain Soufflot (1709–90), probably the only contemporary rival to Robert Adam's mastery. David Hamilton's terminal features for the corners of the balustrade of the Hospital design, on one side shown as a fluted drum, on the other as a square base with a distinctly neo-classical garland recall the facade of St Sulpice in Paris by Giovanni Niccolo Servandoni (1695–1766). Possibly Hamilton's lost design for the Streets had a rather French character (Cleary 1999, Picon 1992).

In any case the only remotely comparable contemporary works are Charles Percier and Pierre Fontaine's tenement blocks at the west end of the Rue de Rivoli opposite the Tuilleries gardens in Paris. This Paris project originally consisted of the equivalent of some thirty houses roughly the same size as the South Street. It is raised on a tallish arcade of identical arches, with three floors of regularly spaced windows above and a habitable roof (with rows of later dormers added). The composition of the whole, without any vertical articulation apart from a number of minor streets that intersect the Rue de Rivoli, the total effect creates a compelling, diagrammatic super-urban presence, enhanced by the quality of the detail. The arcades are finely carved and elaborated and there are continuous balconies supported on entablatures at the first and third floors, with the first floor windows bearing individual

4.7 A. Shannon, South Entry of Aberdeen from the Denburn Bridge

architraves, while those above on the third floor are joined by sill courses. All these elements would seem destined to bore by repetition but in fact the decorative elements make a series of horizontal lines in the urban wall which eloquently balance the gardens opposite, laid out by Andre Le Notre (1613–1700). Clearly it is a very high game which Percier and Fontaine manage with success. Their skill makes the absence of Hamilton's design for an almost identical run of houses especially regrettable.

James Young's design although his manner is more a London-metropolitan response to Adam than a French one, does show a similar grandeur and it is difficult to see how anyone could do less given the very great length of the South Street. Young proposes long terraces on either side of the Street, each of thirty-three houses of mansion size. They are articulated by a broad nine bay centrepiece of three houses with terminal pavilions, and two further 'relieving' blocks: these elements are rendered to indicate an especially smooth ashlar, whereas the other twenty four houses have a rougher texture. The whole terrace is five full stories plus roof (where no dormers are indicated). The ground floor is arcaded with major doors under fan-lights recalling the style of London, Dublin and Edinburgh houses with the sunken basements lit by courts at the front. The first floor windows of the special blocks are full length and reach down to the floors with balconies, whereas the others do not. The stories above are regular diminishing in size towards the eaves.

The centrepiece breaks forward twice with the centre three bays supporting a pediment and the flanking pairs a balustrade. Balustrades also ornament the terminal pavilions at the Castlegate and Denburn ends: these also break forward twice but the centre carries the balustrade through in lieu of the pediment. The pair of special blocks between the long runs of identical terrace houses breaks forward, but instead of balustrade they are ornamented by a low block pediment raised over the centre window bearing a further block with swag, which also carries an urn. The house at the centre of the composition is ornamented further still by having its door case in the middle, an entablature over the first floor window, and floral sculpture supporting a roundel in the pediment.

The arcade at Street level is simply presented without embellishment but carries a continuous stringcourse above. The first floor windows similarly carry a sill course the entire length, relieved by the balconies, short at the pavilions, as singles in the mid-blocks and as continuous in the middle trio of mansions. Young does not indicate any floors below the level of the Street apart from the sunk basement with its lower court leading to cellars under the street. There would be very considerable vaults west of Putachieside and especially west of Correction Wynd.

The Trustees must have been very pleased with their project. With the excellent designs in hand, they set about the business of continuing to secure the ground needed for the project that had started well but needed monitoring. Hardly anyone was willing to bid, never mind show his hand. They were aware that they needed to find a superintendent to act on their behalf and not just for this project but also to oversee the works in the harbour. As they wished to begin the Bridges immediately finding the resident engineer was critical. It was noted by the Trustees Minutes of 3 July 1801 that Thomas Fletcher should be approached to take the job – for three years, at a salary of £250 a year. He was then in Lancaster and as the former superintendent of the Aberdeenshire Canal project was clearly knowledgeable about local affairs and attitudes as well as professionally competent. In their keenness to secure his services a copy of their call was sent to John Rennie asking for his good offices in contacting Fletcher. He duly arrived later that month to take up his duties and the effective work on the project began. In September two local masons were contracted to begin the works on the Denburn Bridge but by the end of a slow winter season it was clear the task was beyond their skills. They had asked to be relieved of their obligations.

More positively the Streets hitherto known as North and South Entry, Avenue or Street, were renamed becoming, from 4th July 1801, Union Street and King Street. This was in deference to the King and in recognition of the Union of the Westminster and Dublin Parliaments. Negotiations to acquire the properties required for Union Street were led, enthusiastically, by Provost Dingwall himself. They got off to a very promising start, and by year's end twenty-three sales totalling nearly ten thousand pounds had been agreed, and early in the New Year a further twenty were concluded, these at rather more, £15,225. A number of intractable heritors had been identified whose properties were to be assessed by the two adjudicators, or to be referred to the Sheriff for a more formal investigation and a decision with a Jury. For these cases the same sum was set aside. Therefore, in the first year of the project, nearly twice the stipulated minimum sum had been allocated to purchase property. These continued to be occupied by their residents who, after all had been formally concluded, would pay rental. When the properties actually came to be removed (the first of these in Shiprow and Narrow Wynd in March of 1806) the tenants had to move out.

The buildings here were to be taken down methodically and their materials sold at public roup. In many cases the return on those sales balanced the prices paid to acquire them. Their methodical removal was also required so as not to interfere with the normal life of the most crowded part of the town, enabling the establishment of the new street with the connections to the old streets improved. Sales of the new divisions of ground, from now on called stances as opposed to rigs as the burghal plots had previously been known, were also exposed to roup and a private offer at twenty shillings per foot of frontage for feu duty went for nearly double that when the bidding concluded. That 'duty' would be paid in perpetuity into the Town's Treasury account, more specifically into the New Streets Trustees account opened with the Banking Company in Aberdeen. The principal feuar of that ground could then build and assign the feu duties to the new building or, more likely, to parts as tenements. These also were to be paid in perpetuity and were so, until late into the 20th century when the system was dismantled. The Town had become a major dealer in land. The payment for the improvements to the city would arise from these transactions and the income they produced.

These arrangements for holding land were peculiar to Scotland. The sharing and management of the political power was related to the feu-duty system. It had the advantage of spreading decisions and accounting for them fairly widely within the local community. The appropriate property values had to be agreed individually. Arrangements for changing the street intersections similarly were negotiated between the Police Commissioners and the New Streets Trustees. It appeared from their espousal of the duties imposed on them by the particular institutions that while both bodies were drawn from the same backgrounds, they took quite different attitudes to the exercise of the powers granted to them through Acts of Parliament by their constituents. The elaborate politeness with which these debates about small matters were conducted, especially towards the end of the project, have a comic quality common to town-hall politics. However, it meant that no extreme or even consistent plan could be carried out without community agreement.

One of the earliest auguries of this was the seeming laudable notion to connect Tannery Street, latterly George Street with the new South Street. In the later 18th century it had been opened northwards from the Upperkirkgate. The Act became law in April, and by August the advertisement to competitors had been published nationally. Enquires from architects had begun to arrive on which they would base their designs and in consequence the future of the town. Already by October changes in the nature of the New South Street were being discussed and the Trustees agreed to employ Colin Innes to 'examine and ascertain the Line that communicates in a straight direction from George Street…as being an important and valuable communication betwixt those two parts of the Town, and which may be accomplished at a comparatively small expense' (New Streets Trustees 1, 14).

One of the principal consequences of this undoubtedly imminently sensible decision was going to compromise the whole project unless the very greatest care was taken about levels and the kind of junctions required. Not only would Union Street need to be significantly lower to meet an extended George Street at Putachieside, it would then be too low to pass over an arched Correction Wynd and it could never be carried on to a level from the Castlegate to any Bridge over the Denburn. It was a year later at the Trustees' first meeting with David Hamilton that this arose as a principal matter for discussion, and it was unresolved at that meeting. They departed with the Trustees' rather feeble hope 'that within fourteen days after the Levels, one or more, are fixed on, he would be able to furnish these "revised" plans'.

None of the Trustees, nor anyone else for that matter, would have wished to make a radical departure from their understanding of the Abercrombie proposals of 1796 nor the designs they would choose the following February. Naturally they would take a lively and particular interest in various improvements that might be made from time to time but it is precisely by these means that radical departures can occur, especially in the absence of an experienced professional voice, to guide the course of these seeming sensible departures or amendments to a design. The Trustees as a group or institution could see no difficulty whether, for example, Back Wynd should meet Union Street at a level or whether, 'an arch should be thrown over it' or the folly in having to dig Correction Wynd into a lower course so as to allow it sufficient headroom to pass under Union Street. While they were genuinely inclined to accept any proposed alteration on its apparent merits, it can cause difficulties to a designer whose balanced scheme was based on other, possibly contrary, assumptions. It can pose real problems for contractors: a plan on paper is easy to change as is a cross section, but the spatial design that these drawings describe is much less easily grasped and the consequences of minor changes cannot be foreseen. The alteration of a partly or even half finished building project makes the same kind of sense as altering a recipe while a dish is cooking.

Hamilton's appointment that should have gone so well and brought forth such good work was a short affair with disappointment on both sides. He was new to independent practice in far away Glasgow, where potential clients could easily reach him, and where concerns expressed through the post could be set aside in favour of seemingly more pressing matters. There were issues on the part of the Trustees and these also had to do with a lack of experience. As distinguished as these men were and as sharp as they were in business, in managing the Act through Parliament, and in framing the competition – all of which they performed with great skill and sense – none of them had experience in seeing such a great project through. They met frequently, kept good records of their deliberations and behaved well. They took it as read that all decisions had to be referred to them. However the decisions became demanding and had to be made not only quickly, but could have adverse effect on decisions already made, and with their architect and engineer so far away, the precision of their requirements had to be made manifest, the monitoring of the work had to be checked against them, the Act, and the contracts. They realized sooner than many in their position the necessity of having an agent working between them and the architect and contractors: Fletcher as choice cannot be faulted. Had their chosen architect been a local man, perhaps his guidance would have been sufficient. By the time issues to do with the design of the individual houses become a matter of dispute, any possible remedy by the Trustees had long since passed. The level of the Union Street, and the consequences the designs based on it carried, become matters of flexibility at just the moment they should have been established and codified.

The level of the top of the Castlegate remains at just under 20 meters above sea level. The level of the Denburn Bridge at its west end is the same, and has always been designed to be the same. The competitors would have taken this as their datum and made their designs on the basis of a terrace to connect these two major elements, and to contain the houses, sewers, roadway and pavements, supported by cut and fill, and by constructed vaults and, perhaps, a causeway. What is the first thing that the Trustees adopt for discussion with their newly appointed architect and engineer? Shall Union Street be level, or otherwise? We know not whether it was the architect, naturally wishing to please his new and very important clients but without the experience to know how to guide such a group, or perhaps the Trustees themselves had proposed the review. By early March 1801, Hamilton, 'after making repeated Examinations and Surveys of the proposed Line of that Street, had made out a Sketch and Design of three different levels…' thus he offered three alternative means of delivery of the project.

His observations based on the assumption on which he, and all the competitors, had prepared designs were strong, sensible, and on the face of it irrefutable…'The Design for laying the Street on Vaults and making it all in one Line would have a magnificent Effect to the Traveller of Taste in making his Entry to the city, would look exceedingly picturesque when viewed in the distance, especially from the South on Account of the Shelves formed with the new Buildings, hovering over that of the present Old Part of the City, and would likewise give elegant Situations, Views &c more especially on the South Side of the Principal Rooms in the Lodgings that may be built; And I have no doubt, but in a very short time the vaulting would…pay the Extra Expense…' (New Streets Trustees 1).

Two aspects of his account would have struck political Aberdonians: that a cheaper way might exist spoke directly to the canny and the magnificence within their grasp nurtured also pawkiness never too far from the surface. To spend extra money to please a 'traveller of taste and to give rich citizens 'elegant Situations' will usually meet with a positively negative response in the north-east of Scotland. Hamilton went on to observe that it would be possible to build the Street with two levels, the first sloping downwards from the Townhouse end of the Castlegate to the Bridge over Correction Wynd, the other sloping upwards from there to the Denburn Bridge. It would then be cheaper particularly for those building the new houses to either side, as there would be less 'of the dead Work, which must unavoidably be below the Street'.

These observations were to deliver the telling blow to any alternatives before the Trustees. His final characterization of the 'two level' scheme as being natural and simple and his parting remark that as he could 'only give you as my opinion from the Little Observations I have made in these kinds of things, that the two Lines will have a very good Effect' left it to the 'consideration and good Taste' of the Trustees to make the right decision. Considering that to build the street and bridges as originally conceived on a single level was estimated at just under £15,000 (notwithstanding that they had recently agreed to pay twenty of their fellow citizens more than that amount to buy their houses) and that the alternative would cost only £5,475, and further, to have vaults only on the east and west sides, and 'filling the Middle with Earth, Rubbish &c' would save another £1,000…their taste allowed them to readily concur. They then went on to record that until Hamilton could produce drawings for the new levels he had proposed that nothing could go forward. However in Provost Dingwall's phrase he 'hoped that within fourteen days after the Levels, one or more are fixed on, (Hamilton) would be able to furnish' new plans.

Although the Trustees were slow to realize it, these decisions put paid to any regular and uniform terrace from the Castlegate to the Denburn. Their complacent acquiescence in altering fundamentals as they proceeded weakened rather than strengthened their position. The question of levels also led to Hamilton's premature departure. Although his new plans were timeously and duly furnished and the works begun on the Bridges at Putachieside, Correction Wynd and the Denburn, within the year problems arose, initially with the contractors, then with the performance of David Hamilton himself.

There is no specific evidence of any dissatisfaction between the Trustees and architect, but within three months the tone of the Trustees' clerk Carnegie indicates a serious diminution in common civility: he rudely berates the architect for taking his drawings with him back to Glasgow. Carnegie had wanted to show them to the newly arrived Thomas Fletcher. However until a project is completed the drawings are the sole prerogative of the architect, and even afterwards a special commission for an 'as built' set needs to be agreed: Carnegie might not have known this, but his ticking off of Hamilton for removing what was his own property cannot have made relations between the architect and Trustees easier. The reason why the contractors were unable, or unwilling, to show the Trustees' clerk and the recently appointed superintendent drawings of the work can only be imagined but it would have been a personal embarrassment to Carnegie and Fletcher, and could indicate all was not well, never mind amicable.

The contractors, Mitchell and Cameron had been appointed in September 1800 but had given up the work by mutual agreement, by the following spring. They had made significant progress even in that normally slow building season, completing the piers for the Putachieside and the Denburn Bridges. With their departure Thomas Fletcher, as Trustees' Superintendent, measured the work: some recompense for the unfinished job would be in order and its assessment would be based on how much had been done, and with how much material. In doing that Fletcher discovered what appeared to be mistakes in the levels of the Denburn and Putachieside Bridges. Carnegie wrote to Hamilton enclosing Fletcher's letter where he wrote, 'I am inclined to believe that you have drawn them too high to Correspond with the declivities of the Streets, and as the Work is now considerably advanced it is proper to have the difference Accounted for immediately, which I suppose You will easily be able to by referring to your Plans & papers relative to the same…'. Since it was Hamilton who had fixed these levels in the first place and since he was architect for the two bridges, he might well have considered himself at liberty to depart from them for operational or any other reasons, and responded to Fletcher accordingly. But, a less than respectful letter from a clerk aside, this may well have indicated to him that his position in Aberdeen really was not a sustainable one. He had just begun the Hutchinson Hospital in Glasgow and may have concluded it was best simply to leave the job. From secondary sources it has always been stated that he and the Trustees parted by mutual agreement over a matter of levels. However the documentary evidence only has Carnegie's querulous follow-up letter a month later. There is then a long gap in time in the Trustees' Letter Book of some nine months.

The Trustees' Minutes provide further interesting detail indicating an increasing confidence in the Trustees to take their own decisions that as a sub committee were reported at the general meeting of 22 May 1802 for confirmation. Provost Hadden reported the mistake in Hamilton's levels, which he characterizes as 'very substantial', and goes on to report that the angles of declivity are now to be changed from 1/50 as Hamilton had indicated to 1/52 'or thereby' for the eastern end, and 1/40 'or thereby' for the western leg. The Street is now to be seventy feet wide, the Denburn Bridge to be reduced in width to fifty feet. These changes were unanimously accepted and the sub-committee was further empowered to 'take such measures as they think most expeditious and effectual…and, for that purpose to employ such persons as they may judge most proper to make out the necessary Plans and Sections…' (New Streets Trustees 1).

Clearly Hamilton was no longer wanted and henceforth the design of the city of Aberdeen becomes a local matter. The design of the Denburn Bridge was reviewed in the summer, and various consultations made with engineers and architects; their alternatives assessed in early winter. That by Thomas Fletcher was preferred. His design, as most of the consultants had suggested, was for a single arch spanning between the two abutments already in place. By December a new contract to finish the Bridge was signed. Its completion in 1805, with both designer and superintendent not only resident but also being the same man, is not surprisingly uneventful. Except, that in 1804, the Trustees' clerk, by then a Mr Hardie, wrote directly to the contractor working on the Denburn Bridge parapet, and informed him that they had decided to use 'Ballustres in place of the Gothic parapet shewn in the plan made out by Mr Fletcher' (New Streets Trustees 2 18th Feb 1804).

The design of the houses had been taken up by the Trustees immediately. Provost Hadden sought the advice of James Burn, the architect of the Banking Company and Athenaeum next door in the Castlegate. Burn had requested the plan of King Street and sought more particular guidance about what was required of him. Although the Trustees wanted a regular street 'yet it does not appear to be their Opinion that it should be strictly uniform by obliging every feuar to build to a Plan, but rather leave that to his own Mind & only bind him up to build in a Line & to some kind of height of Wall that there may not be any Deformity on one House being very low and another very high...' (TM March 1803). Burn's own thoughts are solicited with a plan or two to indicate the sort of house that would attract a feuar to 'pay a price for Ground to build on'. Provost Hadden confirms a city centre/suburban split in that the buildings south of North Street will have shops on the ground floors: those northwards of that junction would likely be lower and for the use of one family only. He then notes, with a little regret, it 'may be rather unlucky for Uniformity's sake that the Ground falls that way...' (that is towards the north). The falls of level here, or in the Castlegate, are not noticeable, as if the regularity of the whole diminishes such conditions. Of course the Provost wanted the plan as soon as possible because they meant to begin feuing the stances very soon, and 'must come to a Determination of the plan of building'. The Trustees had their elevation for the King Street frontage in September. Rather crossly they observed that since it did not include the floor plans they would defer decision. In the event the floor plans never materialized. Burn's plan, however, for a regular but not uniform terrace, was adopted for guidance although the Trustees would never be so bold as to accept it as policy. Burn grouped the higher houses at the ends as pavilions, or at the centre with rather cunningly cast two long wings as the same size and same height, but indicating that the internal subdivisions into individual houses could vary: and the whole would have appeared as a uniform palace block, despite the slope from south to north.

This design, of the type stretched to extreme length by James Young, was used in the feuing of King Street the following year and the first stances were sold in the February of 1804. In a fussy addendum it was decided the disposition of the windows and doors ought to be left to the individual owners: fortunately no one in the King Street terrace took this liberty. Later it was sensibly dropped. Among the conditions of feu were: the whole feu front must be built upon, the fronts to be built of granite stone 'dressed as well as the Athenaeum' (56–9 Castle Street); the feuars responsible for laying the pavements and be responsible for a proportionate charge for the common sewers and side drains; have privilege of entry and use of the back lanes; and in return the Trustees promised to remove the 'Slaughter shops' on the west side of King Street by 1806. The first condition of the feu is the most obscure:

one third of the annual feu duty to be paid in perpetuity was to be 'converted into such quantity as shall correspond thereto at the rate of sixteen shilling per Boll…' with the rest paid in money. This importation from agricultural Scotland was soon seen to be anachronistic and charters were changed so that the whole feu duty was to be paid in sterling.

In fulfilling his commission of 1794 Charles Abercrombie included 'Further Improvements' such as the reordered Shiprow and Broad Street already noted. He also indicated (at a very small scale, and perhaps missed by many) the design of regular houses of the kind observed in the Castlegate, such as the Athenaeum. His major 'Further Improvement' in his report is the planning of the ground west of the Denburn, where he proposed a New Town. The plain beyond the Denburn gave Abercrombie legitimate scope for rational design of this kind and his response to that opportunity was doubtless one of the inducements for Aberdeen to accept his difficult and expensive third option. Throughout the 19th century, and well into the 1930s, all new streets laid out on this very large plain sloping gently to the south conform to Abercrombie's basic idea: indeed its rationality remained the best inducement planners could put forward until the 20th century (Unwin 1917).

In his design the South Avenue west of the bridge becomes the south side of a very large rectangle of streets and regular open spaces similar not only to the New Town of Edinburgh but to many regular towns ~ such as Jacques Lemercier's design for Richelieu's own ideal town of the 1630s (characterized by La Fontaine as the most beautiful village in the Universe). To an engineer of the Enlightenment such as Abercrombie Alberti's late 15th-century scheme for d'Este's New Town of Ferrara, any of the earlier Bastide towns of France, or even, Vitruvius' layouts for Augustus' armies, the design of whose encampment at Normandykes just west of the city had recently been drawn, clearly demonstrated the good sense and antiquity of his design. If pressed Abercrombie might well have pointed to these projects as indicative of the right way to conduct these matters: but he was not pressed, as everyone was perfectly content with the design.

Beginning on its east side Abercrombie's New Town consisted of a shallow crescent embracing the west slope of the Denburn that remains as a seeming canal but its park like attributes (picked up by Hamilton) are more fully exploited: the crescent is intersected by two symmetrically arranged 'L'shaped urban blocks which frame the views to and from the first of the squares of the New Town, incidentally framing the same view published by Gordon nearly a century and half before (see below 8.1) (Gordon 1661). From that first square there would have been that view, perfectly framed by regular building, of the ancient Kirk of St Nicholas and the ancient city. Behind that square, towards the west, were to be three slightly narrower streets (than the South Avenue and its northern counterpart) the middle of which aligned with the centre lines of the squares. Although the western square is larger, since it is not connected to the Denburn 'park' the discrepancy is minor. On the western edge of the New Town Abercrombie sets up the possibility, or

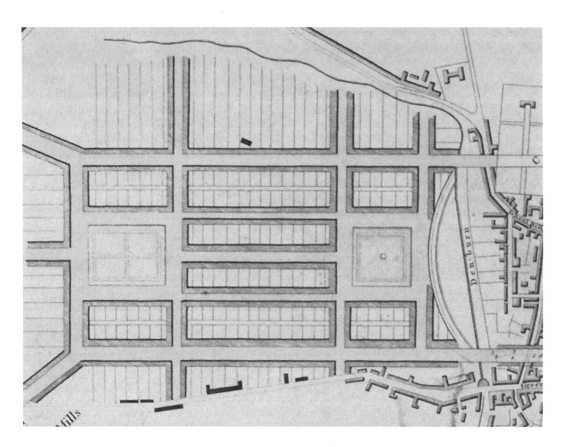

4.8 Charles Abercrombie, Aberden New Town

expectation, of a further New Town extended and based around a central east-west street with two roughly symmetrically splayed ones, the old goose-foot employed from the 15th century onward (Lowery 1996). In the event none of Abercrombie's designs was executed precisely as shown, and yet, at the same time all were executed in due course, and in the fashions of their days.

From 1803 the Second New Town of Edinburgh, roughly contemporary with this proposed New Town and of very similar design, gives a good idea of what Reid's scheme might have offered Aberdeen, had he won the competition. It begins with Heriot's Row, then a crescent Abercromby Place. Robert Reid and his partner William Sibbald produce a slightly ungainly yet novel pair of long but curved blocks based on the now familiar scheme: plain houses of identical design with an emphasis at the centre and pavilion-like buildings at the ends. These face equally into two lesser streets of housing purpose made as blocks of mansion flats. Without changing their pattern Reid and Sibbald gain in confidence as they work northwards. By Great King Street, the major axis of the district connecting Drummond Place and Royal Circus, the typical best of the New Towns, is in place. Refinements here include a pairing of identical houses with pilasters and an extra storey, the introduction of lunette windows (half rounds) into the tops of the pavilion ends and an extra vigorous treatment to the stones facing the sunken areas to visually support the rustication above; and a new way of living ~ the main door flat (Youngson 1966).

The main door flat: these could be as big as a three storey house and as both part of a greater whole with its own grand entrance and address at pavement level that also expressed a comfortable New Town gentility. In this second New Town the type occurs initially as part of the pavilion ends of the major blocks – later it will become more common. Reid and Sibbald catered for a variety of residence from the houses (four or more stories) the mansion flats in pavilion ends and tenement blocks mixing large and smaller flats with shops and store rooms; usually these are in the cross streets. The designers manage to weld these diverse types into a genuinely urban architecture where the street, block or corner is noticed and celebrated but the visual effect of the house itself is moulded into that of the terrace. All kinds and conditions of folk can, and did, live in the same neighbourhood, even the same 'building'. The residents' situation being clear to their neighbours certainly, but the district itself having a designed propriety modulated between 'important' and linking, and work-a-day. All this is within a four/five story masonry architectural framework whose vertical module is almost invariably that of ten feet (about 3 meters).

Although the ground plan of the Second New Town in Edinburgh had been adjusted and clarified, it still retained in its building the original features and general composition; this was to a degree true also in the Aberdeen transpontine New Town. However, the scale of buildings there were never to be as great as those in the old town, nor as those in the capital: three stories, often two, were to be sufficient for this suburb of a smaller city. In the more urban section east of the Denburn where buildings approached the same scale, the mixture of shops at ground floor with lodgings above militated against the adoption of Reid's Edinburgh new proto-type, the main door flat. The balance of ownership of the ground was also different. In Edinburgh the Heriot's Hospital Trustees were the sole owner: whereas in Aberdeen it was shared by the Hammermen, Marischal College, and the New Streets' Trustees, who continued reluctant to lay down strict conditions for the houses to be built.

The Provost having written to Deacon Roger of the Hammermen Incorporation about restrictions on the plan of building to be adopted repeated the opinion that they should be as few as possible. But that each row of houses between the cross streets to be made out from time to time should make a uniform 'compartment' where the walls are the same height, the pitch of roofs likewise the same, the whole built of well dressed granite, and with an iron railed sunk area in front. He also reminded the Hammermen of their original agreement in May 1799, 'it was conditioned that the houses to be built thereon should correspond with any General Plan to be adopted by the Trustees', but by 23 March 1803 no such general plan had yet been issued. The Trustees clearly had thought about the issue, and had drawn up the feu restrictions for King Street, but this guidance to the Hammermen, although the first the Trustees issued has about it an air of too little too late.

The sales of the stances in King Street were agreeable to the Trustees but no building had yet occurred. For all the activity, and three years into the project, life in Aberdeen carried on as before. Apart from the specific sites of work the town retained its old form so even these stances on King Street although marked out by stones were still essentially imaginary. The plain beyond the Denburn valley was empty. It was from that quarter that the Trustees got unpleasant news that spring. Their painstaking 'design' for the King Street blocks had been specific to that location and they had abandoned any design guidance implicit in either Young's competition entry or any of the alternatives Hamilton may have had to offer. Indeed, technically the competition was only for the town part of the New Streets. Other than the advice to the Hammermen (NTS 2 23rd March 1804) the Trustees had given no guidance about that part of the project. They expected everyone would wait until they had given instructions.

With the good news in April that the Putachieside Vaults were ready to let came the news that building was underway west of the Denburn: on ground belonging to Marischal College and of course Dr Brown, the principal, was one of the Trustees. The College had sold a piece of ground fronting the line of Union Street to Patrick Milne of Crimonmogate, whose house in Putachieside had been lately sold to the Trustees. Milne was proceeding to build on it and without any reference to anyone. The Trustees reacted by sending a long letter to their legal agent in Edinburgh seeking to have the Act suspended while the dispute with Marischal College continued. Their complaint was that his large house 'if not soon prevented by some legal Authority will spoil the Symmetry and regularity of one of the finest Streets in Scotland, by his counteracting & refusing to comply with the general plan laid down by the Trustees for that part of the Streets' (NTS 2 12th April 1804). They sought an application to the Court of Session for an 'Interdict against Mr Milne as well as against his authors The Principal and Professors of Marischal College'. The Trustees had already petitioned the Sheriff in those terms but he had declared it incompetent 'although most of us here are of a different Opinion'. The application to the Court of Session also failed. Had the Trustees' had an agreement like the one they had with the Hammermen, then doubtless they would have referred to it. It would have given the Sheriff or the Court of Session the evidence of competence they required. The Provost might have had in mind the 'Further Improvements' Abercrombie's Report but it is difficult to see what he could have done. So how such a 'general plan' could be said to exist? While they had assumed great executive powers and appropriately, they had neglected to follow through from the designs they had commissioned into precise instructions. Milne had discovered and exploited the loop-hole: the Trustees had only themselves to blame.

What Milne of Crimonmogate wished to do and went on to complete, was to build an urban version of a large and comfortable house, but essentially a country houses of the kind Smith soon built at Manar, near Inverurie, or Phesdo in Kincardineshire (Miller 2007: 41 and 53). Others had built similarly rural, or suburban, comfortable houses on the edges of cities such as on the *Champs Elysses*. Still that Crimonmogates' architect was John Smith, shortly to be proposed by the Trustees as successor to Fletcher, is ironic. The Trustees had no objection to the type. In fact it became a favourite form in early 19th-century Aberdeen. His design was simply for them in the wrong place, not where they wished it to be and spoiled their vision of Union Street West. It was against their 'general plan'. The result of the dispute was that they were forced to declare a policy. Having preferred to adjust the plans they had commissioned as it suited them, they found that others could play a similar game and when they finally came to issue instruction it was against a background of relative weakness.

Even so it is only in 1806 that guidance from them is given and then for the Town side of Union Street only. Building of the smaller bridges had carried on despite the hiatus at the Denburn; by April 1804 vaults adjacent to Putachieside were let to the textile manufacturers Masson and Leys for storage: the causeway which supports Union Street on either side of Correction Wynd Bridge is a much slower affair and is only really finished in 1805. In April the corner southeast of Putachieside (now Market Street) was the first available ground in Union Street for sale. Although there was an offer for twenty shillings per foot frontage for a part of this parcel the Trustees' were bound to offer all the properties for sale by public roup, and they were pretty confident they would achieve a better price as well. At issue was one hundred and seventy one feet frontage running from the Bridge eastward towards the Castlegate and it was the east most part of this that was wanted immediately. This stance, very near to what had been the summit of St Katharine's Hill and site of the present west side of the Adelphi entrance, fetched nearly double its upset price.

With the sale of the stance in Union Street imminent then the Trustees drew up the feu dispositions to apply to both sides of Union Street between Castle Street and the Denburn. 'Houses should not exceed four stories high; the Front Walls, Chimney Tops and every part of the Building fronting any of the public Streets to be built of Granite Stone dress'd at least as well as the Front Walls of the Athenaeum; the Front Walls to be of one uniform heighth, and not less than forty two feet nor more than forty six feet in height from the Level of the side Pavement; the roofs to be covered with Slates or Lead and not to exceed in heighth one third of their breadth' (1 Feb 1806). No construction of any of these houses in Union Street occurs until after 1810 but for half the street's full length at least there is finally strong, if flexible, guidance. The same is in place for King Street but here there is a neo-classical design for the composition as well, what in Aberdeen is now called a 'compartment'. For the open areas northwards in King Street there is the anticipated preference for lower, single family houses. In Union Street West the idea of regular compartments, set back behind sunken forecourts becomes common: their design is also 'uniform' but without guidance from the Trustees.

There is a further statement of the layout designs for the extended city and a planned suburban extension to consider. Thomas Fletcher declared the

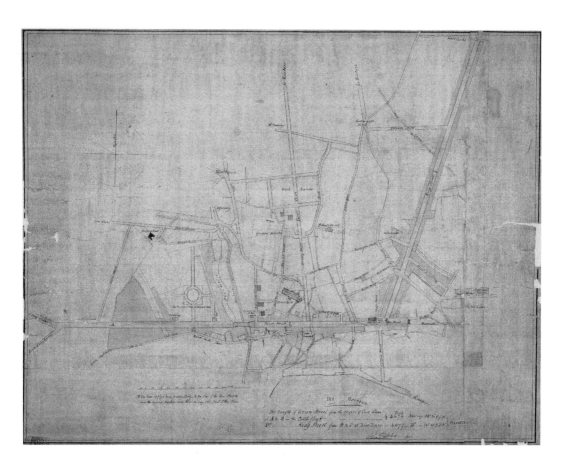

4.9 Thomas Fletcher, Aberdeen in 1807

Denburn Bridge, now called Union Bridge, complete in the autumn of 1805, and in September he retired. His replacement is John Smith, an Aberdonian, both architect and surveyor. Smith becomes the superintendent for the Trustees with responsibility also for the harbour works. As these grow in scope the roles are divided and John Gibb looks after the harbour operations with Smith in charge of developments otherwise. In due course Smith becomes the City Architect. Already his practice has developed in the county, for example Keith Hall, Inverurie and it is Smith who designs Patrick Milne's controversial house on rather than in, in both senses, Union Street West. In 1810 Smith produces his *Plan of the City of Aberdeen with Its Improvements*, a resume of the city's design with his own revisions. Of course the recent harbour improvements are shown but north and eastwards of these Smith also proposes improvements for the old Fittie Quarter of the city.

This part of the town beginning at the southeast corner of the Castlegate stretched along the north side of the Dee to the ancient settlement of Fittie around the old church of St Fittick's. Its character was of a loose grouping or straggling of buildings of various times in no particular pattern. At the mouth of the Dee was the Blockhouse intended for defence but fortunately never severely tested as such. This site was chosen for the Fisher-town, that is, river

THE DESIGNED CITY 111

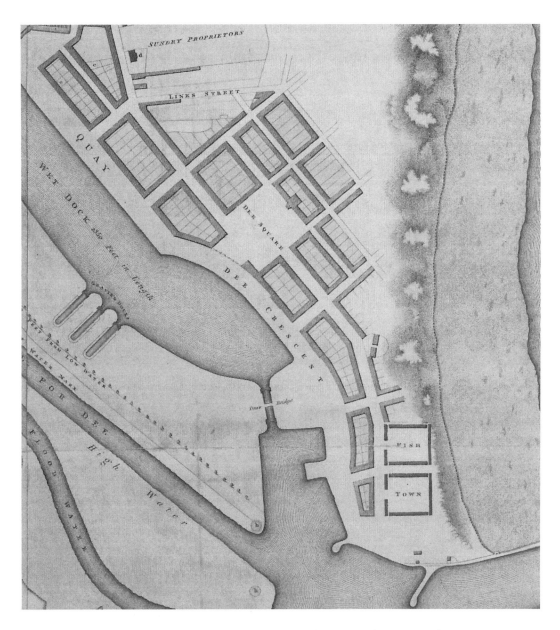

fishing for salmon. Trawl fishery is another story entirely. Curiously it is one of the first actually realized parts of the new Aberdeen. The two almost identical squares of Fittie were defined by rows of single storey houses of granite and of regular design. This pattern was to become very widespread indeed as with many local variations it was adopted in the planning of the improved villages of Aberdeenshire that begin to receive mature growth in the early decades of the new century. The city water supply was piped to this remote edge of town from the Gilcomston reservoirs by way the Broad Street cistern. It would be only in 1831 that water was piped to Footdee (PC IV 468). Since then Fittie has

4.10 John Smith, Design for the Fittie Quarter

thrived, with some of the houses growing upwards as much as three stories yet never loosing its character and strong sense of place. For the extensive areas between the Fisher-town and the rest of the city Smith proposed a series of composed streets containing over two hundred houses and arranged about Dee Square, with a new Kirk opened and linked to a broad and curving compartment called Dee Crescent facing the new Wet Dock.

On the western side of the town Smith indicates the beginnings of Abercrombie's trans-pontine New Town. At the southeast corner by Union Bridge, Hay of Lumsden who had to move out of Shiprow in 1807 had acquired a site for his new house: he was soon joined by three neighbours to make the beginning of the Denburn Terrace as the Crescent was initially called. It was levelled and made fit for building early 1808. Smith shows the Terrace in its completed form of Union Terrace although its northern section is a long time coming. He also shows the Hammermen's projected Golden Square, faintly indicated but with the parts named as the first of Abercrombie's squares. Union Street West with part of the Streets to run parallel to Union Street are also indicated. Apart from Crimonmogate the earliest house, or houses, were built at the corner of Diamond Street, and these survive in a much altered form. Northwards of where the second of Abercrombie's squares was to be built Smith shows the recently built Bridewell standing slightly north of its centre. This prominent building was by James Burn, and became a significant landmark in this part of the town. It was the prison: typically for its time it declared its nature as a large rather brooding castle-like building. There were also groups of dwellings especially south of the Gilcomston Chapel of Ease and along the extreme end of Union Street which when rebuilt beyond the Trustee's remit as Union Place has littler coherence. Further south was the old settlement of Justice Mills, and much open ground. Even so with the Bridewell, Milne's new house and the foundations of the group going up at the corner of Union Terrace, there were only the very beginnings of the New Town.

With the actual construction of the houses in King Street and Union Street beginning, the role of the New Street Trustees came to an end (at the beginning of 1811) and planning authority devolves to the Police Commissioners in the management of streets, sewers, lighting and (small to medium scale) public works. Smith and Gibb retain their roles as superintendents. However the more significant directors of development will be the owners of the particular sites on which houses or new streets may be built. These continue, through the feu charters, to set restraints on the new buildings – the heights of walls, standards and materials of construction and types of building to make their projected compartments. Within these, many different builders contrive to fit varieties of uses, and conform to the different situations presented to them. They are house-wrights, projectors, established and junior builders, and also architects. These latter are led by Smith who is soon joined by his younger colleague Archibald Simpson (Miller 2006 and 2007). Simpson an Aberdonian and son of clothiers in the Guestrow, like Smith, had family also in building. His uncle William Dauney had built in Marischal Street. However Simpson

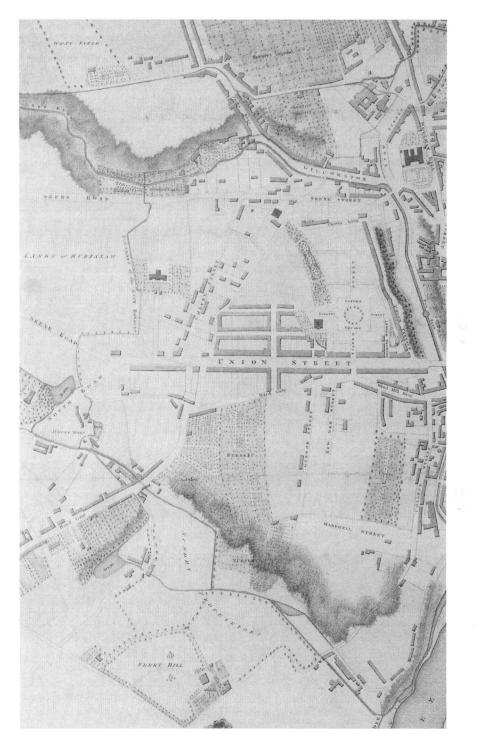

4.11   John Smith, Aberdeen west of the Denburn

enjoyed personal exposure to London where he worked as apprentice, and also foreign travel. To these two leaders devolved the tasks of turning the templates of urban design, using the building blocks established by the feudal charters into not only a town with the Handsomest Street in Scotland, but also a City of Empire.

From Classic to Caledonian

In 1810 Aberdeen was ready to realize its design for the two New Streets, Union Street and King Street by actually building houses (Fletcher 1807). The only requirements for the design of the individual houses were those contained in the feuing conditions, effectively to emulate 55–8 Castle Street, and to observe regularity in the compartments. All houses in Union Street and elsewhere followed suit, beginning with 57–65: often, as at the new junction of Union Street and Shiprow the houses add the curved-corner so loved by the Police Commissioners otherwise following the Athenaeum pattern. In King Street there was the added guidance of the composed block where half of the southern pavilion, also fronting the Castlegate, was already in place and its southern neighbour was under construction. Even here the pattern is followed and so in due course the other houses of the terrace. The memory of that design and the desire for a composed block (never mind a merely regular compartment) was a very strong one, and is a recurring theme in the building of the street throughout the 19th century. There seems also to have been the conscious desire in Aberdeen as a whole to make Union Street the Finest in Scotland by delivering as much of the Young scheme as possible. The dip in the level is ameliorated in the execution of the many different projects during the early 19th century so as almost to be unrecognizable. As the street dips, the building to either side grows taller to make up the apparent difference in level overall. In Union Street West the houses of the regular compartments were lower, often by two stories. The tension between plain houses and those dressed in the classical orders adds surprising interest; this was not called for, nor excluded, by the Trustees, but soon there are calls (if somewhat partial) for more architecturally elaborate designs (Wilson 1822).

In 1811 John Morrison of Auchintoul commissioned 40–44 Union Street from Archibald Simpson, then working as a pupil architect in London. This originally consisted of a large mansion house of (seemingly) five bays, full architectural expression and the obligatory four stories. Next door was a plain smaller house: Simpson following precisely the pattern established by Burn for the Bank-Athenaeum blocks, and, in a more modest way, from Burn's and Fletcher's design for the beginnings of King Street in Brebner's corner and

5.1 James Henderson, King Street junction with Castlegate

Catto's continuation. Indeed, Simpson and Auchintoul had James Young's designs for the east end of Union Street in mind. Their division of 40–44 Union Street into two houses is surprising. Although it is somewhat confused by alterations early in its life to form a bank, it is clear that the mansion 'half' has a rusticated base with three segmental arched windows of two storey height in the 'centre', flanked by two monumental portals in the slightly advanced terminal bays. The western of these terminal bays is in fact the eastern bay of the otherwise severely plain second house on the Athenaeum pattern. So the mansion and its neighbour are elided so as to suggest the beginning of the composed terrace as designed here by Young a decade before.

In 1805 Smith's entry to the city's architecture with his design for the Crimonmogate townhouse/country house in Union Street West raised the architectural game the Trustees had thought they were playing. His young rival does the same with his debut piece for Auchintoul. The Crimonmogate House was almost big enough to count as a compartment in itself. Its composition is forward looking and ambitious, taking the parts of the house and spreading them laterally to make a series of discreet elements that have both a picturesque aspect and also reflect Lord Kames' call (Kames 1762) for the parts of buildings to *speak* and to have powers to raise poetic associations of ideas. As we have seen in Glasgow Green, or at Greenwich near London

5.2 The Bridewell from the east

(Bonwit 1987) this gives rise to houses linked to others, but also with subsidiary elements celebrated, or even at Pall Mall in Altona near Hamburg (Hedinger 2000) with closely grouped cubic mansions by C.F. Hansen seeming to make a stately formal dance on a large green terrace. For Crimonmogate Smith simply uses two monumental and rusticated gateways to either side the broad five bay composition of the house; it is a truly urban gesture, just not necessarily the appropriate one. It would appear that the original architectural idea for Crimonmogate House, perhaps in response to the Trustee's unhappiness, was to repeat on the west side the three storey house actually built to the east: clearly also to Smith's design it repeats decorative and compositional details of the main house: instead of the central bay coming forward, in the eastern block it is recessed and the framed block of the dwarf parapet mimicked and reduced in size. With the hypothetical companion to the west, Crimonmogate House would have produced a regular compartment of some subtlety.

Despite having the Principal as integral Trustee for the New Streets Marischal College, as landlords of the grounds north of Union Street and west of the Hammermen's estate, had shown no reluctance in pursuing an independent course in selling feus. Equally their Huntly Street was one of the early departures from Abercrombie's design. Although there was a cross street already in the hamlet by the Chapel of Ease it did not extend south-eastwards. By 1807 it appears joined to Union Street at an obtuse angle west of Crimonmogate's western monumental gateway. This is contrary not only to Abercrombie's plan, and on Smith's (Smith 1810) revision it is shown regularized; clearly that did not occur in fact. The existing hamlets in the possession of the College were sufficient inducement for them to ignore any plans for development and to press on with their clearly advantageous alternative.

Simpson's Assembly Rooms follows as magnificent and monumental stop to this 'troublesome' interlude of design exploration in another fifteen years and marks the heart of a game of point and counter-point Smith and

5.3 Assembly Rooms, Union Street

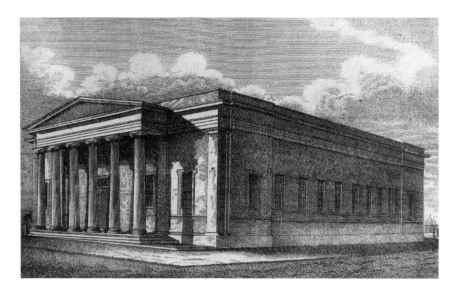

Simpson played giving each other new problems to address, and to which each responded with vigour and skill. Within the modest strictures laid down by the Trustees and given the consistency that the granite construction brings, this 'to and fro' contributed liveliness to the city that would have been denied had the neo-classical ideals as the Trustees had anticipated them been followed. At this early stage in both their careers it would have probably surprised the young architects themselves.

A radical departure from the Burn scheme for King Street was instituted by Simpson as early as 1816 for clients who commissioned him to build St Andrew's Chapel (Episcopal). They chose the centre feus that were intended to carry a pedimented trio of houses (Burn 1800). Instead, Simpson built a sandstone, Gothic revival, rather English looking building with open passages to either side. Although as Aberdonian as any of their neighbours the Episcopalians sang from a quite different hymn sheet and were rather proud to be seen to be doing it. How the Trustees reacted is not recorded, as their time and office were finished. Perhaps they were not unhappy to be rid of such disputes. This act of going their own way however could have ruined King Street putting an end to the regular building. It did not. Later in the '20s, Smith for other clients built further regular houses on either side of the 'interloper' with the final pavilion at the corner of North Street coming as late as 1840. So Burn's composed terrace has its centre though not quite the one he had in mind – the balance between it and the long rows with terminals to either side troubles no one.

In 1798 the Medico-Chirurgical Society was founded by twelve medical students led by the future Sir James McGrigor and in 1818 when rooms were built opposite to St Andrew's Chapel on the western side of King Street, the group of recently educated medics, with Simpson, set an even more devious architectural scheme for Smith. A new building was designated to house their

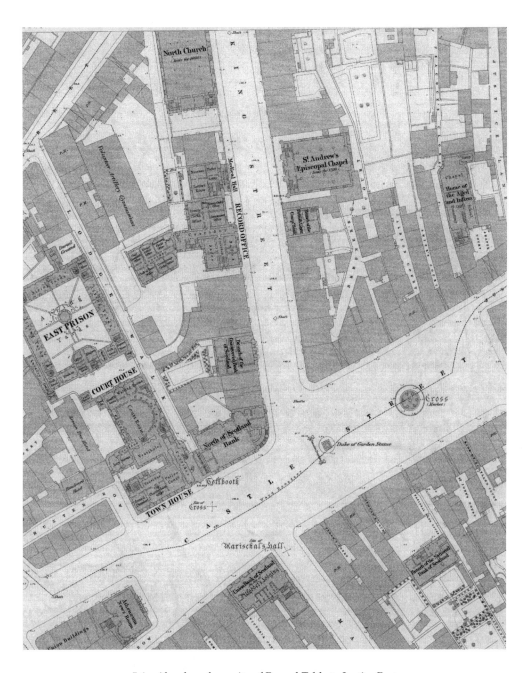

5.4 Aberdeen from site of Round Table to Justice Port

valuable library and a meeting place. The block was composite: its centre recessed and provided with a splendid classical porch of the Ionic order, the first such in the town. Its northern wing (built many years later) is subservient to this consisting of a further three bays. The feuing disposition required that a southern wing was to be built to match. So when Smith was commissioned to build there the replacement for the troubled Record Office in the Castlegate, begun in 1832, he had to fit in. Doubtless he would have wished to fit in any case but he chose to make a virtue of the requirement by adding a seven bay building, of which three follow and echo Simpson's design. Then – with a stroke of Mozartian surprise – comes a seeming one story and reticent entry introducing the other 'half' of his building, a pavilion capped by a balustrade and framed by broad pilasters. This unbalanced the game again, positing a companion to the north. What would come next?

That came from Smith himself with the North Kirk; designed in 1828 and completed by 1831. It too is of the Ionic order but faces in three directions. The eastern elevation begins after a gap north of the Medico-Chirurgical block: the body of the new parish church is composed of five two storied bays on a raised base, marked by the same Ionic pilasters that Smith uses on the southern end of this Record Office. This run is bracketed by two recessed arched windows at the ends, and the eaves line which is higher than its neighbours and is marked by 'parapetade' rather than balustrade. The Ionic porch, whose side only is seen in the King Street elevation, carries its balustrade instead of pediment chosen by Simpson for his porch nearby. The western terrace of King Street was further completed by two later Smith houses (TCP K 20), for James McHardy and Mrs Edwards. These are built according to the Trustees' standards: they remain unaltered and are of the highest quality: Mrs Edward's house is four bays wide, its neighbour just three, yet they present as a regular pair just as Burn had known they would. The three buildings south of these are a different matter being built as late as 1839; their characters and aspirations are Victorian rather than Georgian.

The Commercial Bank immediately south of the McHardy house was built by the Edinburgh architect James Gillespie. Gillespie (who added his wife's surname of Graham to his own) saw himself very much as a national architect. He entered the competition for the new Houses of Parliament at Westminster and it was he who first had the bright idea of employing A.W.N. Pugin (1812–52) as assistant to work out the Gothic detail; but Charles Barry also employed Pugin, and won the commission. Gillespie Graham may have visited Aberdeen before producing his design. If so, he took no notice of his context. His design of an engaged three bay temple front between two flanking windows makes his building too big for its site. It was also thought to be too high and is quite narrow for the site – acting on Simpson's complaint he lowered it. Had another plain house gone on that site as the Burn template had indicated Simpson's premises for the North of Scotland Fire and Life Insurance Company at 1–4 would have made the appropriate termination to King Street. By 1837 with the succession of the new Queen, King Street itself was changing: it had become the home of the banks. The British Linen Bank was opposite, although still within the designs of a plain house. The Commercial Bank however had broken the mould and henceforth the banks identified themselves with grand and even opulent buildings.

These joint essays into the design of the King Street terraces started as a straightforward realization of Burn's version of the palace-block idea. By its finish four decades later it had become a quite different and modern street. Although it maintained the notion of regularity it had introduced a changeful, almost playful, assembly of related blocks varying their forms in response to each other. As it developed, Smith and Simpson began to appreciate the pictorial qualities a regular street might have where the 'movement' of its discreet elements was exploited. This quality in architecture had been recognized in the work of Sir John Vanbrugh (1664–1726) and called to professionals' attention by Sir Joshua Reynolds in his Royal Academy lectures. Vanbrugh had been rather dismissed by the later neo-classical architects as being too coarse, talented yes, but somehow 'untrained'. They preferred the kind of designs that, for instance, James Young had produced for Union Street, not just regular, but clearly and thoroughly regular, even elegant. But King Street ushers in a new appreciation that streets, like individual buildings, may be designed to be best viewed in perspective rather than elevation. And as it lay open at an angle from the heart of the Castlegate where better was there to demonstrate the idea? The results were captured in *King Street in 1840*, one of a suite of drawings made for publication.

Union Street had not yet become the centre of attention or yet the major thoroughfare of the city. Before roughly 1840 it too was the scene of experiments in how best to realize its original neo-classical ideals. The buildings along its length came in no particular order and dutifully, even cheerfully, subscribed to the requirement laid down by their feu charters. There were also conscious efforts to make a whole compartment into a regular block. This was noticeable in Union Street West where from the junctions of Crown Street and Diamond Street westwards in houses of the 1820s and '30s there is an almost perfect repetition of the three or two storey house built according to the rules. At the west end in what was beyond the trustee's powers, called Union Place, the north side appears both disparate and distinctly early, whereas the south block was rubble granite with harled finish, though regular and of the same height. Subsequent replacements with often the addition of further stories have somewhat confused the earlier attention to regularity. West of Crown street these were all houses set behind iron railed and sunken forecourts and were really suburban as were the houses in King Street northwards from Frederick Street to the Aberdeenshire Canal.

There is also the already noticed curious and apparently undirected design intention apparent in the street as a whole. Somehow the architects with their commissioning clients desired to recover the level of Union Street, abandoned so whimsically by the Trustees and Hamilton. Eastward of Correction Wynd the houses are up to the four storey maximum set by the Trustees with

5.5 Union Buildings, north elevation

integral arcaded shop spaces at ground level. From Correction Wynd to the Bridge, they are of three stories also with shops; from the Bridge to Dee Street are three storey houses behind sunken forecourts and then similar two storey houses to Union Place where there were a curious hybrid of three full stories, but rising from the basement. The resultant eaves line of Union Street is near level, while the pavement drops from Castlegate to St Nicholas Street and then rises again. Of course, this gives scope for departures from canon in terms of elaboration and a higher register of ornamentation in individual buildings: these are seized from the 1820s.

The corner blocks were either 'rounded' as at Shiprow, St Nicolas Street, Correction Wynd, and Union Terrace, or they tried to emulate the pavilions explicit in the early designs for the street as a whole. Simpson seems the keener in this regard. At the northwest where Union Street joined the Bridge he built the Aberdeen Hotel block in 1817 as an only slightly smaller version of James Young's proposed terminal pavilion. Because Belmont Street wished to join with Union Street instead of dipping under through an arch, his building has three sides: Union Street at three stories, the Belmont Street side slopes downwards almost the four, whereas the Denburn side is seven. The Denburn elevation is managed as Adam had proposed in his similar terminal block for Edinburgh at South Bridge with a series of increasingly rough rusticated blocks from the Bridge level downwards springing from three large arches at the bottom.

At the other end where Union Street joins the Castlegate Simpson's Union Buildings make a suitable eastern termination not quite in the Young manner but in an appropriately Aberdonian one. This was a hybrid block started at its west end in 1819 with a house at the junction with Shiprow for a connection of Simpson's, Baillie Galen. This Trustees style house had three very broad bays to the Union Street side, perhaps in anticipation of the larger composition for the later new Athenaeum Rooms. These had outgrown their first quarters nearby in the Castlegate, and no doubt Aberdeen also wished to possess a public building with something of the style and ease of Glasgow's Coffee Rooms in the Tontine Hotel entered through the arcade under the old Town Hall.

A building for Public Rooms had been proposed for this site in the first decade of the century, and with the Simpson additions of 1823 the Athenaeum began its long tenure, flourishing latterly in the 19th century as Jimmy Hay's Café (then Restaurant) until burnt out in 1973. The whole is composed of a pairing block at the east end (minus the rounded corner) with a slightly advanced centre block of some five bays width. In his design drawing this called for the first floor windows to be taller than all the others with architectural frames and in the spaces left above bas-relief sculptures in panels. These were dispensed with in favour of the lower windows still in place. There is some difference of texture called for with the centre block smoother and whiter. As the granite overall is worked most smoothly in conformity with the Old Athenaeum it is hard to know what the architect might have had in mind.

His Coade Stone decorations to the tops of the block pediments on this side, and the Castlegate end remain extraordinarily white even after the fire. But even Soane who loved the material never used such a vast quantity of the expensively manufactured Coade Stone. The Castlegate end is the *piece de resistance* of the whole, and has the three giant first floor windows embraced by an Ionic screen, doubtless in imitation, emulation more likely, of Robert Adam's device for his unbuilt design for the Record Office opposite. As the town end for the new street Simpson's Union Buildings as the whole was called could hardly be bettered, and achieves the same kind of magnificence that Young had envisioned for the street. The original ground floor arcades survive, except for a couple of replacements at Baillie Galen's end which should be restored.

Simpson contributed much to Union Street, especially in his consistent concern to carry on the prominence of terminal blocks. Perhaps he considered the Castlegate to be quite different matter architecturally, and in fairness it needs to be observed that the buildings westwards from the Townhouse were regular enough, but hardly part of any composition, and by 1840 the majesty of the Townhouse and its companion the Mason's Lodge block must have seemed a bit shabby without being yet antique. There had been discussion with Simpson about rebuilding the Mason's Block with the Lemon Tree as new hotel, when the North of Scotland Bank acquired the site and conducted a competition to find the best design for their new building. This is very much facing into Castle Street, but its east end also 'completed'' King Street while facing also into the eastern part of the Castlegate at a good angle. This made for a very difficult design problem to resolve. Most of the designs expressed the conventional preference to face the superior address by concentrating their designs towards the Castlegate in line with the Townhouse. Already Barron had shown himself more subtle than that in the 1750s. Simpson followed suit, but clearly in imitation of Smith's recent Advocates' Hall (see below) chose to treat the building as a kind of great *hinge*, also as his old master Soane had done at the corner of Threadneedle Street in London for the Bank

5.6 Mercat Cross after removal eastward and restoration

of England. His engaged Corinthian order porch occupies the obtuse angle between Castlegate and King Street, and also contrives to give the building prominence in the market place as a whole that its nature as a bank hardly merited. The body of the building facing Castlegate and King Street is made of rusticated blocks of white granite under a dentil frieze with short third floor above, itself carrying a balustrade: a coloured sculpture of Ceres (by Simpson's friend James Giles) completes the composition at the corner.

What he may not have realized, and could hardly have altered in any case, was that in recognizing the hinge nature of his site where the two new streets joined, he made the old city form effectively redundant. What had been a series of complex and small streets joining a few major open spaces of great urban significance, from 1840 onwards is seen as a street corner, of metropolitan scale no doubt, but still a street corner. Already there had been grumblings about traffic and congestion. The market uses of the Castlegate and been confined to its eastern end beyond the junctions with Marischal Street and King Street. And even the grand steps leading up the Town House from the market place had begun to be seen as a hazardous nuisance. Soon the Mercat Cross itself was at risk, with calls to take it down and to rebuild it.

The Magistrates resisted that for many years, and spiritedly. They had given in over the issue of the staircase earlier, and it had come down. With some reluctance they finally agreed to re-site the Mercat Cross. Not only was its age more than beginning to show...at well over 150 years old its sandstone would have been pretty shabby, and its life literally in the centre of a very busy and congested city had occasioned various knocks. This project fell to John Smith, and he removed the Wellhead with its *Mannie* statue to the Green, so that he had room to resite the Mercat Cross in the wider part of Castlegate but still on axis. He also removed the remains of the booths and recent Post Office, and opened the spaces behind the arches thus giving the Mercat Cross its truer nature – a classical circular pavilion. To spare it damage he surrounded the building with an iron fence, and substituted a large round pavement in place of the old Plainstanes, whose purpose as exclusive meeting place for the magistrates had long since vanished, having been replaced as a favoured haunt of sailors (Kennedy 1818). With this the Castlegate took another step in its long design history. The New Streets while still incomplete now at least joined the heart of the town in a finished state.

And two long term consequential problems had recently been resolved. These were in what manner Back Wynd should join, or pass under, Union Street, and the related issue of St Nicholas Kirkyard. Had Back Wynd not joined Union Street at grade the alternative canvassed and preferred was to carry a lane along the southern end of the Kirkyard to join Correction Wynd. This would have added another large compartment for Union Street, westward at least to Belmont Street. But in 1819 it had been decided to add this ground to the Kirkyard whose biers were many times over-inhabited. St Nicholas had always been entered from the town at the east, north and west sides, so opening the great Kirk to the new street was a new idea. It also gave the means of *perfecting* the relationship of the city's parts. The Kirk and Marketplace had always acted as the two poles of the town, and as we have seen a street or way connecting the two seems to have been the city's first act of design. With the additional ground to the south of the Kirkyard a handsome formal and more direct connection to the Castlegate was now possible. Had it been an axial connection as well all would have been thought ideal (Simpson's imagination was exercised in these years about the idea of an axial connection between St Nicholas Kirk spire and Marischal College, and his *Simpson Line* became a preoccupation of the town imagination well into the 20th century, see below). In the absence of the early 19th century's ideal, it fell to Smith to offer a workable alternative.

He proposed the notion of a transparent compartment or facade to carry on Union Street, which would also act as monumental gateway and screen for the Kirk and Kirkyard. It needed to be sufficiently bold to actually link the major elements of the old city, and yet reticent enough to allow Union Street its own character. His arched gateway and screen of Ionic colonnades of 1829 has always been known as The Façade. This allowed the Kirkyard to be both open and still protected, with the old church to be through it to the north. Soon monumental

5.7 St Nicholas and Façade

grave architecture began to ornament this end, such as Smith's very severe Tuscan columns and solemn urn which mark the Hamilton Monument of 1843, seen just beyond the contrasting slender columns of the Façade.

When Back Wynd was brought up to the level of Union Street the stance from Gaelic Lane formed the newly available prominent corner site. This presented a suitable new quasi-civic home for the Society of Advocates who commissioned John Smith to design their new premises in 1836. The issue of 'circular corners' had worried Police Commissioners since the late 18th century; they seemed curiously preoccupied by it, and seemed to think it was the solution to all planning problems. The curved bay at the diagonal between two major fronts appeared as the very first piece of street architecture where the new North Entry joined the Castlegate at Brebner's block. And it had been used by Simpson at Galen's House (subsumed shortly into the Union Buildings) and recently to resolve the corner of the compartment of Union Street east of Correction Wynd, the eastern frame to Smith's new site. Smith chose to make that element a monumental one, so that it becomes the seeming object of his design rather than a means of resolving a problem. He naturally placed the entrance at the corner celebrating that element of the composition as a strongly rusticated drum seeming to support a circular temple-like form above. Simpson varied that same idea a few years later. The Back Wynd front is the longer wing and is given a pedimented centrepiece with single bays at either end. The southern of these is then 'taken round the corner' by a curving portion of the engaged colonnade which dresses the shorter Union Street frontage. Both these elements were raised on the rusticated ground floor with deep set openings. The mannerist picture-frame surrounds to the blind windows seem out of place: in some early views they are omitted (Morgan

5.8 Market Street in 1840

2004), and yet William Smith, then on his grand tour was assiduously taken by such *mannerist* features as his sketches show (Kelly papers) so perhaps he can be credited with them. In any case less than half a century later the advocates moved back east to Concert Court and these buildings began their transformation first to public hall, and then cinema with shops below; the traces of these changes can be discerned in the stonework.

With Belmont Street and Back Wynd joining Union Street the route preferred by John Smith (and apparently a not inconsiderable faction of in the town who wanted the harbour to be brought further westward) for a wide and more proper connection to the Harbour area was cut off. In 1840 a private consortium engaged Archibald Simpson to design a new street, and it chose, simply and perhaps sensibly, to strike from the south side of the Millburn Bridge across empty space. The early decison to allow St Nicholas Street to join Union Street had left an awkward prospect of the old and shabby streets of Putachieside visible from the bridge. By a series of arched vaults of diminishing size Simpson's design cut through what was left of the western slopes of St Katharine's Hill with an inclined plane of a new street to join the natural ground level just north of the old Wharf at the fish market. The few buildings at that end were to be demolished to create the open access needed to reach the Harbour.

At the Union Street end Simpson remodelled the earliest house in Union Street, which had become part of Royal's Hotel. There he introduced a real arcade where the ground floor had been, and returned it along the new street. Opposite he built a replica on vaults and partly on the existing bridge. Simpson provided the designs for other buildings on the new street, not least of which was the great enclosed Market building itself. The form eventually chosen for this new type of building was a long rectangle with a semi-circular finish at the end facing the old Green. The lofty Market had a broad gallery surrounding the hall proper, with storage and service from below. At its east end and facing Market Street he designed a monumental and severe frontage of almost Egyptian scale.

Another new street, Hadden Street, runs parallel with the south side of the Market to the Green, where it joined the other old streets, Carmelite, and Rennies Wynd. Further new streets parallel to Market Street completed this small new quarter. An unrealized design for the in-town terminal of the railway from the south designed a little later gives a good idea of the monumental scale envisaged for this part of the town, and the ready adoption of new building types associated with the Victorians. Quickly large blocks for business, banking, and public service followed as if waiting for the suitable site to build, adopting Market Street as the missing piece, the busy claustrum (or cross street every schoolboy knew to be essential to a Roman planned town) to Union Street's civically serene decumanus. So an old Pictish town whose market place had been compared to the Forum, could now appear is if planned by Roman soldiers. Market Street also provided a kind of triumph for the old Tannery Row, now grown magnificent, and through the 19th century and well into the 20th which was to be the superior axis Union Street or Market Street, remained in contention.

From the pairs of arcaded buildings facing into both streets at the north end, Simpson introduced another pair of buildings in contrast – delightful, small and bridge like single storey blocks. On the west side this has for many years been a green grocer's shop, but may originally have been intended to be an arcaded bridge between Union Street and the Market, as it backs onto old Putachieside, henceforth called East Green. Its pair opposite was a Tobacconist's Shop until it was demolished in the 1980s. This small pair introduced the Market 'pylon' and the purpose built new Post Office, a five bay three storey block, with slightly advanced end bays. This too is gone. A four bay severe block of the Trustee type joined this on the east side, and to its south, one of Simpson's masterpieces, and his last work, the Mechanic's Institute building of 1845. As Hadden Street opens opposite the exceptionally handsome façade can be appreciated from a greater distance. Although of three full stories, the third is taken up a wall without window openings. Instead its frieze is supplemented below by a further decorative band while the window heads below carry cornices on top, and at the centre, a pediment. All this gives the building extra mass and gravitas. Its function was the education of tradesmen and artists and both Simpson and Smith taught there. It was the precursor of Gray's School of Arts and Sciences founded some thirty years later.

The southwest compartment of Market Street was intended to be the home of the Railway Station for passengers. The goods station had been already constructed further south partly on the site of the old Trades Hall but mostly as built up ground in the estuary. This has only recently been demolished. It

5.9 Railway Terminus, Market Sreet

conformed to the architecture of railway and river in that it terminated the long and gentle curve appropriate to the natures of both, halfway between its north-south and east-west axes. The design for the passenger terminal, of course, attempted to resolve railway travel with the more orthogonal nature of this part of the city. Its splendidly monumental facades included mixed commercial premises facing Market Street in palace blocks in imitation of the Royal end of Regent's Street, and, a great Triumphal Arch marked the entry to Hadden Street, from which the station proper by arcades on either side of another great gateway gave access to the rest of the UK. Thought to be by James Henderson it would have been extraordinarily grand.

South of Hadden Street Market Street is on the ground rather than vaults, and it is lined with further five bay blocks for the public and for business, mixed with plainer blocks of the Trustees type. Next door to the Mechanics Institute is the old Union Club building at 18–22, by James Matthews, who carried on Simpson's practice, and opposite a branch of the ill fated City of Glasgow Bank of 1858, by William Smith, who as son of John Smith also carried on the practice. In the rapidly expanding city it had become necessary by 1870 for Robert Matheson, the Government's architect in Scotland, to provide the broad and ample newer Post Office building at the fish market corner of Market Street and Regent's Quay as the ancient Wharf became known.

The early phase of Union Street and King Street begins to adapt to a more recognizably Victorian manner during the 1840s. As has been observed with the bank buildings in and near the Castlegate, the styles these institutions thought appropriate for their businesses were increasingly public, therefore grander and more ornamented. They wished to be seen as pillars of the community, although their histories should not have encouraged such a character amongst

5.10 New Trades Hall

the public. By repetition it soon became the accepted norm. In terms of the architecture of Union Street this posed a new problem in realizing the design. If corner sites were taken and only terrace sites remained then the type of house called for was the reticent and plain sort. This unspoken propriety was broken first by Simpson in his design for this newer type. It has to be said it was done in the most understated way possible, and it came early. This was Simpson's five bay block for the Town and County Bank of 1826 built just west of of the junction with Market Street. This is an even more sober version of Burn's Castlegate bank. Its arcaded ground floor was rusticated deeply, and as those who saw its sad demolition in the 1970s realized that the blocks of which it was made were genuinely cyclopean. The stages above this were dressed by a very shallow and broad row of Tuscan pilasters. The two blocks westward of this are also five bays, but are otherwise plain almost to Trustees' standard.

It was John Smith who had the opportunity to complete Union Street by making the final move in building on the stance at the southeast end of Union Bridge opposite Simpson's Aberdeen Hotel. All had seen this ceremonial entry in terms of Robert Adam's scheme for South Bridge in Edinburgh, which although unrealized at least appeared in an appropriate if somewhat bargain basement version. There was no such impediment in Aberdeen.

Smith's commissioners were the Trades Incorporation wishing to vacate their 16th-century hall near the Wharf. What brought him to build here in a gothic style, albeit a Tudor version, instead of the Neo-classical one he normally used? It may have been his clients who demanded it, but this is very doubtful. He might have nursed a resentment that Simpson had, apparently equally whimsically, chosen to build St Andrew's Chapel in King Street, in a gothic style. A church in the gothic style was at least looking back to a model steeped with historical precedent and allusion. That, of course, presented two distinct problems for the culture of Scotland: such models were papist, and being anything less than decently plain, light filled and conducive to receiving the Word was not to be tolerated. The Episcopalians were happy to demur on at the least first point.

And by 1840 it was not only the Episcopalians who could entertain such ideas about church building. The Kirk had the Word as its core, and since its establishment the duty of each soul to strive for its salvation through knowledge and good works had been made abundantly clear. Church government was, and often, brought under scrutiny. It had become established that ministers for parishes were appointed by great men or by institutions if they were also landlords. This system came to a head at the General Assembly of 1843 when its principle was upheld. In righteous disgust the parishes of St Nicholas, with many others throughout Scotland, 'walked out' of their church building. The congregation was the Church, not the building, nor the institution. Very soon new church buildings appeared in which these congregations could shelter. The most spectacular of these were the Triple Kirks, built by Archibald Simpson from 1843 at the corner of Schoolhill and Belmont Street for the disaffected parishes. Its plan is in the form of three large halls arranged pinwheel fashion about a central tower and spire. The halls were broad, light, and as ordinary as a Methodist or Quaker Meeting House. The tower and spire, and even more critically the composition of the four elements is down to Simpson, and to his response to the picturesque nature of his site. *The Picturesque*, as Payne Knight's book had been called, had become a capital letter idea; indeed, it had done by the time David Hamilton had observed to the Trustees that the improved city of Aberdeen would have that specific quality. With the potential of populating the plain west of town, but especially with the frame and focus the new Bridge provided, old Aberdeen's taller buildings against its mass in landscape became objects to inspire a painter, the primary test of the picturesque. And of course, St Nicholas with its tower and spire, were nearest to see. In assertion of their continuing of the Kirk the disaffected congregations would welcome the restatement of the main element from their Mither Kirk. Simpson provides this. He provides it in colour as well. For a city now priding itself on its white sparkling granite, the contrast of the Seton brickwork cladding the granite tower and spire, and the use of that material to cheaply form the construction of the halls carries not only the obvious contrast of light to shade – rendered as dark red against white, and of rough texture against smooth. It carries other messages.

5.11 The Triple Kirks and the Denburn Valley

The picturesque is about qualities relating to pictures. Aesthetics, a pioneering aspect of the Enlightenment (Daiches 1986), pursued since the 1720s by philosophers in Glasgow, Edinburgh and Aberdeen, had extra issues and depths. They derive from the same source. But these Scottish buildings exemplified other reasons for their forms. As regularity, clarity, and embodied good sense drove Enlightenment thinking about almost all things, there was growing up at the same time an equally interesting and necessary series of balancing ideas, which had come form the notion of Association of Ideas. Addison, Switzer, and Kames had developed these ideas and made them widely accessible. If a ruin, or a gloomy place, could bring forth beneficial reflections of sympathy, or even charity from a suitably receptive soul, then perhaps those kinds of form and arrangements might be used by architects and designers to heighten aspects of a building or of a landscape. Adam, and others, especially Walter Scott (Kelly 2010) had appreciated the strength of such ideas. That explains why Robert Adam's Castle style in Scotland was one of his favourite modes, and one for which his talents were very well suited. Scott, initially with the very upright William Stark as his architect, soon William Atkinson and then Edward Blore, had been experimenting at his country place on the Tweed since the very early 19th century with such forms, allusions, and consequent appreciation of rugged, rather than beautiful, terrain. He further extended that taste to include fragments of old building overlaid and given life by both association of ideas, and as part of a storied past. He made it very widely accessible, indeed fashionable, through his poetry and novels.

Therefore, it is not just the look of the Triple Kirks, or even St Andrew, or the Trinity Hall that accounts for their appeal to Aberdonians; rather it is their silent messages about form, ideas, history, and great deeds. So the new premises for an ancient, honourable society such as the Trades Incorporation, dressed in the form and ornamentation associated with its beginnings had immense appeal, and not least to John Smith, sometime nicknamed Tudor Johnny. The modern character of the entry into Aberdeen from the west with these two new monuments mixing local antiquated with the ancient was a huge success.

Prince Albert was especially taken with the Trades Hall when he and the Queen first saw it, and he recommended to Queen Victoria that they use its architect for their works at Balmoral. The new Trades Hall remains a splendid and much loved landmark. Indeed so does the remaining block and the Tower and Spire of the Triple Kirks, even if small minds have yet to understand it, and long for a neat tidy and lucrative modern replacement. Smith's and Simpson's final touches finished the Union Street project. And soon replacement buildings started to go up, more and more churches, and of course more banks, bigger and fancier than their predecessors, and their commissioners and architects were happy to use any embellishments and inducements to Association of Ideas which came their way.

Typical of these is the Bank (now Clydesdale) by James Matthews of 1862. This stands at the corner with St Nicholas Place opposite the entry to Market Steet. The site then still overlooked the descent into Putachieside of Carnegie's Brae. It is twenty years younger than the first departures from the Trustees' strict canon, and although it still observes that decorum it does so with bells on. Of five bays and three stories in height it the end bays are advanced, and there is the appropriate regular movement up the building. But the order of the pilasters, not surprisingly, is the richest, Corinthian. As if to live up this there is rustication, and added ornament, and there are two elaborate balustrades, one marking the first floor, and another along the top, itself with block stops at each bay, crowned by floriated pots. On the Union Street front the end bays have three different sorts of window – double and arched on the ground; treble, arched, with the centre arched raised, and demarcated by coloured granite Ionic columns; and, above the deep dentil frieze marking the division between first and second floors all round, are simple flat headed windows, trebled at the Union Street end bays. The centre bays are less elaborate, but they carry the Corinthian caps, and at the top, ornamenting the balustrade is a block pediment. The front to St Nicholas Place seems slightly more subdued. Its bays are narrower, but carry pediments at the first floor ends, which, with the Corinthian caps, seem to give this front its just share of business. As it faces in two directions its impact is at least doubled, and probably more. That kind of rich building is what Victorian Aberdeen, as Victorian everywhere else is henceforth all about.

5.12 Union Street East from Bridge

West of Union Bridge the stricter interpretation of the Trustees house type is employed to its fullest variation in smart terrace compartments along Union Street, and, new to Aberdeen when laid out after 1810 they are deployed around a garden square. This had been called for by Charles Abercrombie and was carried on by the landlords, the Incorporation of Hammermen. Each side of the square has six three bay houses with opening for streets at the centres. The garden enclosure forms a circle of iron railings, which are also used to mark the sunk courts in from of each house. Golden Square forms the perfect, if provincial, Georgian residential square. Related to it are houses not specifically called for by the Trustees. In Silver Street, and probably also Lindsay Street but this has been rebuilt, and towards the northwest in Crimon Place are two storey granite buildings, whose stonework is of lesser finesse, and whose doorways tend to be pressed into a corner rather than expressing a full bay. These look

5.13 Union Street West

like houses, but whether they are for one family, or more, depends entirely on the requirements of the original builders, and subsequent usage.

As has been observed the area west and north of Crimonmogate's House departs radically from Abercrombie's plan. A road already ran southwest from the Chapel of Ease to Hardgate, and crossed the line of what became Union Street at its official end, where Union Place began to be built, beyond the Trustee's remit. This hamlet or scattering of houses already existed when the New Streets were begun. A junction south of the Chapel of Ease formed the north end of another irregular street running southeast to Union Street just west of the site of Crimonmogate House. All this ground belonged to Marischal College, who after the ill feeling and abortive High Court case brought by the Trustees over the management of their feus appear to have gone an independent way, sanctioning this irregular street, and feuing out many plots for these smaller decidedly secondary but essential houses. In Edinburgh such houses were forbidden in the New Towns or tidied into secondary streets such as Jamaica (finally pulled down in the '60s). In Aberdeen the similar streets are Summer, Huntly, Rose, and Thistle Streets north of Union Street. Southwards are Dee, Gordon, and Bon Accord Streets. These smaller houses were built and occupied by those whose means would not stretch to the small mansions of Golden Square or Union Street, and it remains a remarkable occurrence that so very many large and expensive houses were constructed in the 19th century. The last stance in Union Street, number 248 was built upon in 1868.

The Bon Accord quarter was designed to be both mansions and slightly smaller houses but still superior to the second rate was planned as early as 1823 by Archibald Simpson for the Incorporation of Tailors. This includes the west side of Bon Accord Street, a short connection then to Bon Accord Square, in fact a rectangle, a further short connecting street, and then, overlooking the valley and rising ground opposite Hardgate to the southwest the curving terrace of Bon Accord Terrace, subsequently called Crescent. All these houses are of the Trustee type. They are two storeys, three bays wide, with the sunken court at front.

Simpson is credited with the design, but his clients with whom he fell out after a couple of years had the good sense to follow his layout for most of the quarter, as the individual houses would have been arranged by house wrights or builders to suit individuals in accordance with the feus repeating the old Trustees' requirements. The layout is skilfully managed, tight, efficient, and friendly to its landscape. There is one unhappy discontinuity at its southwest corner, and this may have to do with the Incorporation of Tailors, or perhaps more likely, inefficiently pursued negotiations with owners of ground at the south end of Bon Accord Street. Springbank Terrace is the first, or nearly so, of a terrace of tenements, interspersed as it is with one broad cottage. This long row of severely plain Trustee type buildings runs due east and west, and overlooks the valley between here and Ferryhill. It appears to be clearly designed to join the south end of Bon Accord Crescent, which had become straight for a short section for this very purpose. From the Hardgate, or the newly made up alternative Holburn Street the completed Bon Accord quarter with its ribbon of white granite riding the ridge opposite would have made, in Hamilton's phrase, a most picturesque show to the discerning visitor.

A resident of Edinburgh and good friend of Sir Walter Scott was James Skene of Rubislaw. He was also an antiquary interested in the lore, history and artefacts not so much of the ancient world of the Mediterranean, but of Scotland and especially the northeast. His collections and his sketches of old buildings and landscape then surviving remain invaluable. He was also an astute landowner whose ground in Aberdeen stretched westward from a line from Justice Mills, passed the Bridewell up to the Denburn with the old Skene Road as its axis. He had observed at first hand the growth of the capital: his lodgings there were in Albyn Place just north of the first and west of second New Towns. He engaged James Elliott to make a plan of the eastern parts of this estate as another New Town for Aberdeen. Elliott had only recently designed the third of the Edinburgh New Towns, including Shandwick Place and Rutland Square, adjacent to the west end.

When designed in 1819 this project was not explicitly an alternative to the second half of Abercrombie's New Town immediately to its east, but implicitly it was. Elliot indicates new buildings already occupying that area, including Skene's part of it. Elliott's design was also distinctly suburban in some of its cast, and as realized could be seen also as this first of what is characteristic of the 19th century worldwide, the garden suburb. There were similar, unrealized projects for Edinburgh and of course the grand scheme of Regent's Park north of London (Summerson 1977) Although several villas

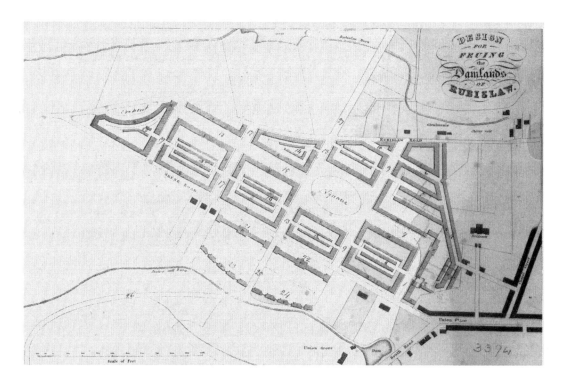

5.14 James Elliott, Design for Feuing the Damlands of Rubislaw

were shown as already in place (and one of these by Simpson at 9 Albyn Place is dated from 1820) Skene's project called for composed compartments on this south side, but significantly set back from the street, and at the extreme edge of his ground the mill race course of the Holburn is mimicked in a crescent of linked villas. The rest of the Albyn estate is made of urban blocks in a mixture of Edinburgh prototypes and Aberdeen ones arranged about a large square marked by a railed oval garden ground. The curving course of the old Skene Road along the northern edge is transformed into to a long curved terrace, with a place called The Crescent at the extreme northwest end.

The Albyn project was a long time in being realized, and was revised by Simpson and then his successor Matthews, but it never lost its essential character, and carried on some of the types proposed by Elliott long past their abandonment elsewhere The villas were the first type to be built and they occupy the whole south side of the scheme. Indeed this type occupied the whole of this suburban side of Aberdeen. The large garden square becomes Rubislaw Terrace from 1852, and the proposed compartments in palace-like five part compositions hang on in memory in more castellated from in Albyn Terrace, of the 1880s, and at Queen's Gardens of the early 20th century.

As interesting as these are it is the earlier transitional types at the east end of the scheme that taxed Simpson as Skene struggled to exploit his assets. The earliest of 'urban' buildings appears to be the short terrace of seven houses set back behind their front gardens at the town end of the scheme and opposite 9 Albyn Place. These were designed perhaps as early as 1828 in Simpson's revision of Elliott's scheme, and were only one quarter of the intended scheme. In his revision Simpson appears to substitute what looks like private gardens for the garden square proposed by Elliott in four blocks separated by streets. The scheme, a reduction of the original by two thirds is finished by a crescent facing south into a communal garden and with its back to the Skene Road. At the east side are what appear to be three existing houses, and the first in the southern section of the street soon to be opened as Victoria Street West. This scheme went no further, although few years later two of the houses of Albyn Place were built and the rest in the late 1840s, their architecture is still based on the Trustee's design, but as realized they have the admirable clarity, even severity associated with Simpson. At this time the overall scheme had changed to include a street at the end of this compartment running northwards. Called Rubislaw Place these houses while keeping to the severe style just noted, but at two bays only they are closer to the type with suppressed doorway and flexible internal arrangements noted in the neighbouring lesser streets off Union Street, but, they have also the superior ashlar granite work demanded of the Union Street houses.

While James Skene was waiting for the market to catch up with his aspirations the Incorporation of Shoemakers began a similar venture on land overlooking the Dee at Craiglug nearly a mile south the city at Ferryhill. This was to become a proper suburb, almost like a small neighbouring hamlet or village near a big town. Its elevation and wooded grounds of the larger houses also gave it an extra attraction. It was in sight of the Bon Accord quarter just beginning, and at the end of Crown Street, by the 1830s largely built up from Union Street West to Dee Village, an industrial hamlet at the foot of Ferryhill. It appears that the district started on the hill's flattish summit just south of Ferryhill House. Here at Rotunda Place, of undocumented date but about 1835, Simpson built an earlier version of the Rubislaw Place houses, a slightly more unified compartment of four, which was sufficient to give them the unity lacking in the Rubislaw group. Simpson also augmented the chimney stacks at either end into a composition of a kind of blocked gable carrying the chimney stacks and with a small, very smoothly finished scroll element at eaves level. These two end elevations are even more composed than that along the 'front'.

Around the corner at the same time in Ferryhill Place Simpson introduces a very necessary type of house, commodious, with plenty of garden ground, yet less severe than any of his previous designs, and economically somewhere between the type common in the lesser streets nearby, but less urban and smart than their close neighbours at Rotunda Place. He began a row of half-cottage houses, that is, two bays, with doorway to one side. Above in the ample roof space was room for three good bedrooms and closets. On the raised ground floor a big square reception room to the front, and two further rooms at the back. The kitchen and other services were in the sunk basement. These houses have simple base course, door cases and window cases of smooth granite which are contrasted to the rougher unpolished finish of the walls. Although

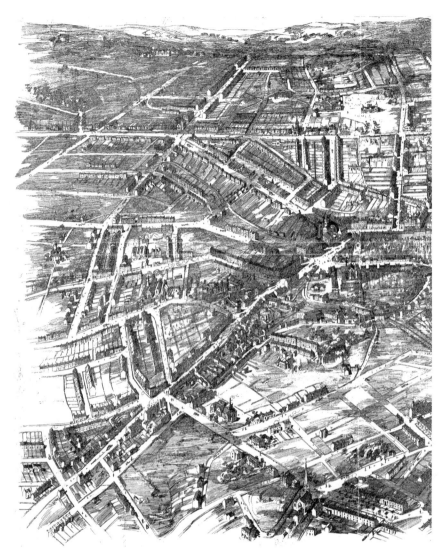

5.15 Western Suburbs in the late 19th Century

they have a rustic air, it is clearly a suburban one with enough implied culture to allow the family to keep their heads well up. This type will become the favoured kind of building for large parts of suburban Aberdeen. After a short break Simpson uses the type to form a new kind of compartment at the east end of Ferryhill Place and overlooking its small shared garden green.

Built in 1837 Marine Place is made up of six houses, still with their original horizontally stressed glazing bars. These are slightly smaller than the houses in Ferryhill Place, but as a group they carry the same kind of dignity already seen in Rotunda Place which comes entirely from siting and repetition of elements within the compartment. Also in 1837 Simpson and the Shoemakers try an even bolder new type – the mansion house as cottage. Originally known as Belvidere Place this handsome terrace of paved carriageway, on formed ground with its own railed joint garden sweeping down the slope towards the Dee, was designed to accommodate eleven mansions, each of three broad bays and three stories. Only two are by Simpson but all are true to his design. The granite is of Trustee standard, the sunk courts in front are very ample, the parapets disguising, just, the piended windows in the roof, where there are four full double bedrooms. The hall and stair of one of the Simpson built houses has the refined minimalism of Soane, whereas the rear elevations showing that the roofs on that side are flat have the same severity of the early modernists such as Loos.

The final design for Skene's project was at last resolved in 1849 (TCP R 3). By this time several streets were in place, and begun, and apart from detail changes to the north end of Rubislaw Place it is the definitive one. Aberdeen, and indeed the country and the continent, were passing from a period of economic depression and unrest when there had been little building, and from this period Skene's project will lead the suburban expansion of Aberdeen and as the premier location it becomes synonymous with the West End. The 14 plots for villas occupying the south side of Albyn Place are complete with a variety of handsome detached houses, and towards the centre is Mrs Emslies Institution for the education of girls, by Archibald Simpson, and in the form a classical villa. The Free Kirk College is indicated at the end of Union Street, and within little more than decade the Grammar School will have moved from its ancient site in Schoolhill to anchor the northeast section of the neighbourhood.

The two new streets bear the names of the new Queen and Prince Consort. Victoria Street (for many years known as Victoria Street West in deference to the earlier homage off Crown Street) introduces the perfected version of another favourite type of Aberdeen design, one unique to the town. The East side of Victoria Street, by 1849 with more than half the feus disposed, is a row of two storey linked houses with habitable roof space, but no sunk courts to the front. The row is set back behind modest gardens. Taking a lead from his Ferryhill Place treatment of the stonework of these buildings is rough ashlar with smooth and raised eaves, window and door cases. Some of the houses were designed internally by Simpson, whereas others were executed by other architects or house wrights. Most of these houses were built as flats.

Opposite, and in the section to the south, are linked cottage houses, of varying breadths, both full and half cottages. Later, beginning in the 1840s and carried on by Matthews and Mackenzie, Albert Terrace uses the same composition, but the houses row to the east is rendered in the severe Trustees style of granite ashlar, as are the cottages opposite. Both rows carry a parapet, and have small sunk courts to the fronts. Albert Terrace, as Rubislaw Crescent becomes, uses the Ferryhill Hill type of cottage, specified in the feu charter, using the suck court at front for those at the east end. Two pairs of specially designed houses occupy and resolve the imprecise geometries where Rubislaw Crescent had been intended. A pair of semi-detached houses set back into ample gardens, and with curved asymmetrically placed gables, are probably by Thomas Mackenzie. Opposite, another pair of houses, set at ninety degrees is cunningly joined together by a conservatory. One final addition to the original scheme is the treatment of the old Skene Road, now called Carden Place, where rows of closely packed individual houses set back behind ample garden grounds are indicated westwards. Four of these are built by 1849, and a further seven are roughly indicated as under way. This street becomes the axis of aspiration and in the 1860s onwards it becomes the home of professional men of substance, later carried on in the same line as Queens Road, where apart from the urban terrace of Queens Gardens, houses of increasing size, grandeur, and expression of individual fortune are built.

From 1850 onwards urban design becomes the business of the lawyers, and using the form set out in the layout plan and the feu charters a very large part of the city is begun and carried on by this means well into the 20th century. The building types are well understood and owe their origins to accomplished architects, the tropes of neighbourhood making – the urban terrace, the terrace and cottage row, the rows of cottages, and the single house in grounds, are also taken from proven models. Similarly the template or field derives from the Trustees competition and the revisions by Smith and Abercrombie: the plan of the New Town on the plain west of the city has become, effectively, vernacular. In the city the Police Commissioners still had a certain power, and in the suburban areas landowners through layout and feu charter were certain of orderly and often handsome developments. When town planning did not exist in these islands or in its cultural family abroad, there was a very workable model in Aberdeen.

To some of the types there were developments and changes of style, to others relatively little and where a design had begun and after a pause begun again changes in fashions were ignored. Houses in Ferryhill continue to be built to the original design throughout the century. A significant change does come in the detail design of Rubislaw Terrace from 1852. These large three bay houses with sunk courts to front, now have the two bays elided into one with a large oriel window, also commonly called a bay window. This feature allows much more of the outside to come into the house, and also the new 'room' half octagonal in shape can be a private yet very sunny adjunct to a major reception room. The bay feature also gives the design of the façade a bias, and this is further exploited by James Matthews and his partner Thomas Mackenzie, by their raising a gable over the bays, and giving it a crow-step finish – not only is the design asymmetrical, but also Scottish, or perhaps Scott-ish as so much of Skene's project shows his affection for Sir Walter's works, literary in the naming of his streets, now architectural in this quotation from Abbotsford.

A more castellated urban block was built in the 1880s at the west end of the long square like garden fronting Rubislaw and Queens Terrace effectively an urban park, and open to view by all citizens from the tram, or in promenade. Pairs of great round towers of rusticated granite ashlar with prominent conical roofs make the western enclosure to the gardens and introduce the new block with a Chambord like air. This block, also set back from the road by a strip

5.16 City of Aberdeen Land Association's new streets centred on Queen's Cross 1868

of garden and carriageway is made up of large three storey houses with half sunk basements. The three bays per house are treated conventionally, relying on the large terminal towers to carry the stylistic message. This block is attributed to Russell Mackenzie, as is the last of the urban blocks in the city, the slightly later Queen's Gardens where the same arrangements apply to the siting and parts, but the architecture is late 19th century classical of a kind found in the western suburbs of London in plastered brick or of Paris in stone. The three storey conventionally designed houses have continuous balconies at first floor level and employ segmental headed dormers and Mansard roof giving it a more Parisian mien.

In the 1860s the Skene estate passed to the City Of Aberdeen Land Association, more familiarly CALA, who add the plains westward and lay out long east west oriented streets with only a few curves. Their designer, James Forbes Beatie's notable stroke for CALA is to incorporate the grounds of the older Georgian house and grounds, specially the wooded glen of the Denburn near its source, and to propose plots for houses to either side. Rubislawden becomes the most aspirational part of the West End, beginning with a very large and rambling house for the printer Cornwall at the beginning of the 20th century. Each of the houses built there becomes an individual expression. In the rest of the CALA additions to the West End more conventional houses of great comfort are constructed in the prime-ministerial streets – Beaconsfield,

Gladstone, or Devonshire, and these large three story asymmetrical houses set in large gardens are both Aberdonian, and national in their similarities to houses in other parts of Britain (see below 6.8) (City Lib CALA 1895).

Rows of cottages were built in the near north of the old Skene project, such as Osborne Place. These have bay windows, and often an added small window to the hall-reception room, and sometimes have further elaboration to mark their superiority. North of these, and interspersed between the pocket estates of Woodhill, Forresterhill, Westburn and Cornhill, was another suburb and new parish Rosemount. This was built along the old Midstocket Road and joins the city at its eastern end in the industrial districts of Gilcomston and Broadford. This ridge had attracted smaller, individual houses such as the one that gave the area its name, Rosemount of 1810, a two storey three broad bays and wings composition perhaps by John Smith. In the 1870s the nature of the district begins to change and become not only urban, but with the beginnings of a village life of its own.

The addition of Victoria Park and its layout as a public garden (TCP V 1 and 2) helped spur the growth of the district and is indicative of its rising importance, as was the building of a parish church at the east end in 1875 just north of an old hamlet called Skene Square. The triangle with Kirk, linked villas of a Simpson style, and a row of linked cottages retains even now its suburban village quality that attracted residents. A row of half cottages on the north side of the Stocket Road called Rosemount Place is the beginning of the urban growth, and is soon augmented from the 1870s by a series of streets with three storey rows of houses on the east sides, and rows of usually half cottages on the west, picking up Simpson's idea, and its augmentation by Matthews in Ferryhill at Caledonian Place in the 1860s. The difference that Rosemount introduces is the six flat tenement style of lodging into what had been houses of no more than three flats before. Also the cottage houses are often pairs of flats with their own purpose built and separate entries. Caledonian Place had already begun to see such a subdivision of the cottage house, so clearly there was a growing demand for smaller flats.

Thomson Street, Watson Street, Loanhead Terrace and Mount Street all employ this trope with the individual houses designed to reflect variations of taste and fashion of the builders. One of these was John Morgan, a young builder who modified the end half cottage overlooking Victoria Park for his own young family by adding a further sitting room beyond the staircase half landing in an otherwise conventional arrangement, to take advantage of the view. The lodgings provided in Thomson Street, as in the other streets whether in the tall blocks or in cottage rows have three apartments, one of which is the kitchen. There are shared lavatories on the half landings of the tall blocks, and at the backs of the cottage type accessed from the garden. Occasional provision for shops occurs at corners at, or towards the north ends of the streets, suggesting that already in the 1870s there was provision on Rosemount Place. The tall blocks of lodgings built there from roughly the same time have greater provision, usually for the entire ground floors to be shops.

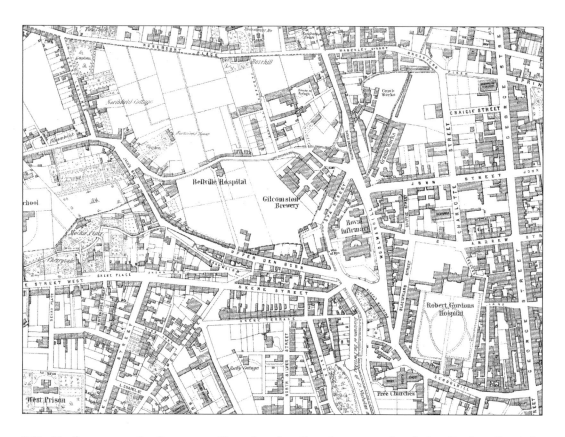

5.17 North western suburbs from Upperkirkgate to Short Loanings in 1866

In the succeeding decades the slopes south of the Stocket Road in Rosemount become the site for more streets laid out by its owners CALA of the simple blocks of lodgings, usually still severely plain. These slopes were the sites of springs and reservoirs, and had been the source of the city's water supply before Provost Anderson's leadership had secured the healthy supply from Glen Dye to reservoirs west of Banchory and thence, over 20 miles into the city. With the expansion of the town into Skene's projects in the West End and the resiting of the Grammar School there, these hitherto light industrial areas became sites for new streets and houses, such as Esslemont Avenue (TCP E 8 and 9), laid out in a lazy curve to connect Rosemount and the eastern extension of Carden Place. The type of building lining Esslemont Avenue, and the Wallfields and Richmond and Loanhead, was the identical plain blocks of tenements with six lodgings each.

Industry in Aberdeen had occupied the lower ground at the Green, to either side of North Street, near the old Loch of Aberdeen particularly northwards where at Broadford advanced textile factories were built at the turn of the 18th and 19th centuries which have only recently been vacated as such. From Broadford south and west along Gilcoms Burn to where it joined the Denburn was the centre of the densest and longest established industrial suburbs Gilcomston, Jacks Brae, Hardwierd losing themselves in the southern slopes below Rosemount (TCP G 1, 2 and 3). These activities had continued along the

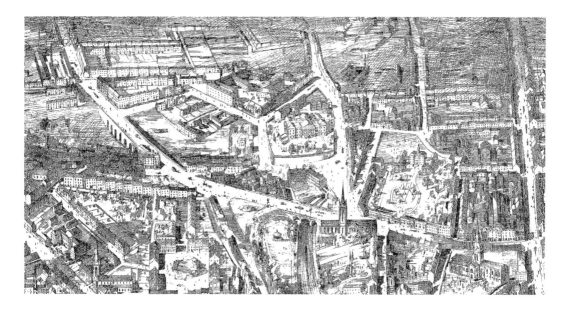

5.18 North western suburbs in 1899

Denburn itself as far as the harbour, completing the circle of industry around, and after the 1830s increasingly through the city. What had been cheerfully accepted as evidence of growth, wealth and development becomes increasingly a matter of regret and of affront to the wealthier Victorian Aberdonian.

The railway had come to Aberdeen to a station at opposite Craiglug and south of Ferryhill, then into the city to the bottom of Market Street. The other line, northwards, arrived by the line of the Aberdeenshire Canal, converted for the railway, at Waterloo Quay. Various projects to establish a Joint Station resulted in the decision to carry both lines along the Denburn (TCP D 10) itself, placing that ancient river in a culvert and altering its junction with the Dee. These improvements solved one series of problem and raised others which still reverberate. Railways, like other early evidence of industry had a novelty value to ensure their welcome as much as the convenience and wealth they brought. The noise, smoke and contamination, especially in crowded districts, soon outweighed the initial attractions. The Denburn Valley has always had contrary characteristics: industrial and, increasingly, squalid to the north, industrial and messy to the south, contrasted mightily with the handsome Union Bridge and the still smart Belmont Street, and the up and coming smartness of Union Terrace. Even Crown Terrace and its picturesque St John's Church nodded towards the Triple Kirks, and slightly masking Gilcomston Simpson's extremely handsome Infirmary added to the interesting, but for the later 19th century an increasingly troubling scene.

A relationship between crowded districts, however picturesque, with disease, coupled with the evidence that contaminated water, poor hygiene and lack of exercise and sunlight contributed to poor health at a time when population was increasing spurred many in Aberdeen to consider what to do to alleviate such problems. The Denburn Valley is an early demonstration of these concerns, and the response to these concerns brings the last major element in the design of a new city begun a century before. The first action is the transformation of the Denburn Valley between the Bridge and Gilcomston into a public garden. Already the trees known as the Corbie Haugh had been planted as part of the earth moving when the Bridge was constructed, and the further levelling to make Union Terrace which followed. This was extended to the whole valley, and further plantations of trees, grass and limited horticultural display, with a foot-bridge connecting the two sides towards the north was the first effort, to be followed by the creation of an arcade to support a widened Union Terrace, and to allow shelter while the gardens were enjoyed in wet weather. The design of this arcade shows an early and admirable evidence of a spirit of conservation. The Old Bow Brig had been the only way into Aberdeen before Union Bridge. It was finally removed when the railway came, but rather than simply demolish it the old Brig was resited as the template arch for the new arcade with the others made to match. The result of all this was a vast improvement as a piece of civic pride instead of shame was created. Still there were the fragments of the extreme east end of the Skene Road, such as Skene Place, which had newer building, not to Trustee standards admittedly, but the standards were superior all the same. These buildings slightly masked the view of the Infirmary building at the north and west ends, as Blacks Buildings led the eye from the Triple Kirks on the north east side.

To realize Abercrombie's northern entry the Town decided also to add a new entry from the now populous Rosemount at the same time. To do this they would reprise the methods used a century earlier, and screen much of the visible industrial 'squalor'. South Mount Street was chosen as the staring point, and Schoolhill its destination, a difference in level of only 50 feet. There remained the Denburn Valley to cross to achieve even this improvement. Otherwise from the junction of Short Loanings and Rosemount to the foot of Jack's Brae at Upper Denburn is 73 feet, and then a climb back up to Schoolhill, and this was really impossible to improve. Although a long and gentle slope was a possibility to navigate with horse drawn vehicles, much engineering of bridges and viaducts had to be designed first. Thomas Boulton achieved this with a delicacy that has made the project seem a natural fact rather than a designed one since. So many do not realize just how bold and successful the idea and its performance were. On a plan of the area his piers for the Bridges which were built first simply occupy the empty spaces available to him (Maritime Museum Boulton 1880). With that part of the project accomplished parts of Skene Street and the end of Union Terrace were cleared and viaducts constructed and embanked into the existing gardens to disguise the join. Thus was provided the gently sloping roadway following an equally gentle curve through a quarter circle and South Mount Street and Schoolhill were duly joined together. The benefit of the additional space in Union Terrace gardens was exploited to provide a place for Stevenson's monumental effigy of William Wallace to stand, and make a foreground for three new civic buildings: the Library, then St Mark's

5.19 Rosemount, design prototype for Compartment, 1880

Kirk, and finally, His Majesty's Theatre. These took the place of the less than civic remnants of old Skene Street left when the gardens had been initially made. Further civic buildings were added at the northern end of Union Terrace Gardens: William Kelly's Trustee Savings Bank of 1896, further commercial blocks by A. Marshall Mackenzie of 1887, and 1896, and then the County Office Building of 1906 by A.G. Sidney Mitchell and Wilson. Within a scant ten years there are seven new buildings of monumental mien, and Edwardian swagger and undoubted individual quality. And in the new century Gray's School of Arts and Sciences and the Art Gallery is joined by the new Central School, and after the Great War by the Memorial and the Cowdray Hall. Thus the north end of Union Terrace Gardens had become the city's cultural heart.

Its frame, the New Street itself, is no less impressive. Called Rosemount Viaduct from South Mount Street to Schoolhill it really ought to be recognized for its full length from Broadgate to Cornhill, from the very heart of urban Aberdeen to one of the many parks to its north. Its scale is, like King Street and Union Street within the city and near west urban, four stories with provision for shops. And like the extending King Street, it pushes this character into the northwest. The compartment issue in this street was addressed by each being built by the same commissioning clients and architects, notwithstanding the trouble taken to commission a prototype compartment design. The architect is not recorded, but his design is an elaborate and suitably Victorian version of earlier proposals in the city. The spirit of the prototype was accepted, but each compartment vied to improve upon it. The underbuilding which seems to have alarmed some at the beginning of the 19th century is cheerfully accepted at the century's end. The aesthetic principles guiding the project are a culmination of thought and practice from the city to itself, but also shared by the contemporary Viennese urban designer and critic Camillo Sitte (Collins's 1986).

The value of using such large blocks to form a street of a character to complement and extend the heart of the city is more demonstrated in Rosemount Viaduct and related streets, or as it was known in its making,

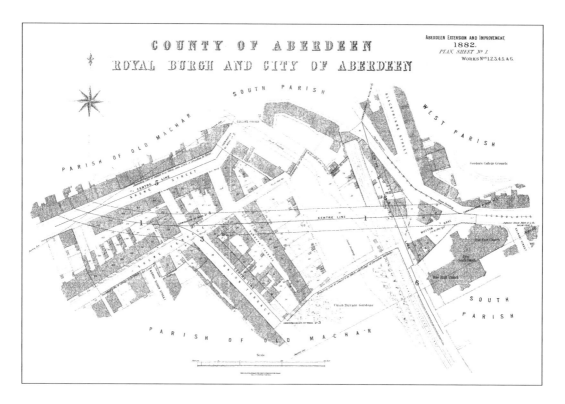

5.20 Rosemount Extension and Improvement Plan 1882

the Rosemount Entry. Abercrombie's proposals always recommended a street parallel to the South Entry to the north, joining the heart of the town at the Gallowgate having passed in front of Gordon's Hospital and ultimately picking up the trace of the old Skene Road. As late as the 1840s Simpson had recommended completing this unfinished part of the plan. At that time even the western sections of Abercrombie's New Town had still to find its market. But these ideas have a way of recurring in Aberdeen until their day arrives. The 1880s was the time to revive, and to carry out this major part of the Abercrombie plan. James Matthews was Lord Provost and having an architect in that post may have helped the idea forward. Perhaps it would have recommended itself in any case. It was adopted in 1886, carried out and finished in a remarkably short time of slightly more than ten years.

Mention has been made to the effects made by the Picturesque and related ideas about judging the arts in the realization of the city's design for the finest street in Scotland and its New Town. This became even more pointed in two projects for terminating Union Street. Placing some monument, or monumental object at the end of a street, or a walk in a great garden, has been the preoccupation of all concerned in these matters since the 16th century, and it guided Aberdeen in both Adam's design for the Record Office and Jaffray's rebuilding of the Town House in Old Aberdeen at the end of the 18th century. That Union Street should terminate at the west end was far from the minds of Abercrombie or the Trustees, and there were schemes to connect to the Deeside

5.21 Christ's College

Turnpike by simply extending it. However, in the 1830s Smith with Simpson concurring, proposed that the new Chapel of Ease to serve Gilcomston should be built at the end of Union Street, and facing down it towards the city. This siting was to be further marked by building a tower and spire at both the new Kirk's centre and on the centre line of Union Street. Had it been carried out then two classical monuments would have marked the ends of the street – the re-sited Mercat Cross in the Castlegate, and the Chapel of Ease at the West End. In the event another termination took its place, one which performed the same role, but in a decidedly Picturesque rather than classic manner. The break-up of the Church of Scotland required not only new buildings for the congregations but also colleges to house the new seminaries. Christ's College was built in 1850 for this purpose. Its architect was Thomas Mackenzie who had joined Simpson's office in 1835 and brought to it a fresh eye, and an eye and mind very much alive to the opportunities of allusion – of the strength of the association of ideas in framing architectural designs.

The design is essentially a simple one of two parts; a large airy rectangular hall occupies the first floor and provided the principle requirements of the

5.22 Castlegate, Design for Monumental Gothic Building

College. These were supplemented by further rooms below, and all was served by central doorway, and stair to the rear. Mackenzie chose to dress the building, as Smith had recently done for the Trades Hall, to underscore its antiquity, specifically its seeming origin in the 16th century. The reason for such a choice is as simple as the buildings' form. He and his commissioners wished to demonstrate the connection between the Free Kirk and the Kirk of the Reformers, underlining the intellectual and spiritual imperatives of the disruption, and removing it from a charge of power politics. Until the architects Macgibbon and Ross had finished their surveys of the domestic, castellated and ecclesiastical architecture of Scotland, actual knowledge of 16th century design, and whether there had been variations in kind in the various parts of these islands, was still unknown and indeed hardly an issue (Macgibbon and Ross 1887). Therefore Smith, and Mackenzie, like Scott simply borrowed from the then available past to fire their imaginations. Thus Christ's College's details are inspired by what we call Tudor examples rather than Aberdonian or wider Scottish ones.

Its composition and the reasons for it are by 1850 both local and universal. As it stands at an angle to Union Street the College is naturally seen in perspective, and perspective rather than face on can bring picturesque effect to an otherwise regular design. And the College is regular once it is reached and entered. The off centre stair and tower to the rear is hardly noticeable in Alford Place. It is very noticeable indeed when viewed from Union Street. From there the other essential of picturesque architecture shows itself. A complex and varied old seeming piling up of elements into a designed, and apparently regular whole, 'entertains the eye' until the observer is close enough to work out what is really going on. The picturesque of Union Street West was further enhanced by a pair of major spires, that of Gilcomston South of 1868 by William Smith, and in the next year James Matthews' for the Langstane Kirk. These two spires combine with the College, and critically the severely plain Neo-classical edges supplied by the compartments of Union Street to provide an almost textbook example of excellent theatrical urban design.

Almost immediately on Christ's College's completion the engineer, John Gibb, proposed a building with similar qualities to be built at the head of the Castlegate, and to 'balance' Mackenzie's termination with its counterpart. As this has to be seen flat on from close up and from far away Gibb employed a similarly 16th-century architectural language for his otherwise mostly regular composition: his two terminal towers are linked by an arcade of five bays, whereas the fenestration of the body of the building set back behind has six bays. The really noticeable element of course is the great tower standing behind, both old seeming and set off to one side to give the exercise its picturesque character. This project had to wait another forty odd years and was realized by James Souttar in his design for the Salvation Army Citadel.

5.23 W.S. Percy, New Townhouse Tower from Broad Street

The Citadel also followed the lead provided by the new Town House project which encased the oldest parts, the actual old Tolbooth, but sacrificed the 18th century additions in extending the city's headquarters westward to Broad Street (TCP T 8 and 9). This new composite building housed not only the Town Hall and the Council's rooms, but also the Commissioners of Supply as the Shire Council was then known, plus the functions of the Sheriff Court. It was built between 1869 and 1874 by the Edinburgh firm of Peddie and Kinnear who won the commission in competition. Their design is the first in the city to employ early Scottish forms in civic work. Their new Tower at the corner of Broad Street acknowledges the Tolbooth tower at the building's other end, and then proceeds to perfect it, and to make it as grand as might have been possible in an earlier time. This was often the attitude taken by Victorian 'restorers'.

5.24 Archibald Simpson, Marischal College, rebuilt 1838

They were actually responding to a new building programme for a building for which there was really no precedents. Like Mackenzie they naturally wished to demonstrate the longevity of the city and its government through their use of Aberdonian and Scottish forms. Although the result was modern, its picturesque aspects were critical to that actual building, but the Tower added a further and dominating picturesque quality to the skyline, and therefore to the city as a whole. Of course, from any part of Union Street this newly built element took its part with St Nicholas' Tower and Spire, itself rebuilt in stone after destruction by fire in 1874, and the other monumental markers of the town's scene.

The Citadel design owes much to Mackenzie and the College and to the new Townhouse: it is also the furthest of the elements of the Rosemount Entry project, whose responses and effects reached this far into the city. Like the termination in the Castlegate the first of the compartments of the new street was provided by James Souttar, recently returned to practice in Aberdeen after a sojourn in practice in Scandinavia. His 96–120 Rosemount Viaduct, 1886, uses Scottish architectural ornaments to mark his three large blocks of tenemental lodgings. The internal arrangements of these provide two three apartment lodgings per floor which has the effect of making a bigger tympany feature to carry the chimneys for these rooms. Souttar uses that to make a broader and more significant element at the centres of his blocks, made wider by adding two castle-like turrets to the ends of tympanies (these were designed to carry conical roofs). The trio of windows is marked by plain granite piers and sill and stringcourse, which also throws the rock-cut ashlar into relief and at its top three pointed arches, reach upward into the chimney stack. Piended dormers in semi-circular plan finish the roof levels of each block. Below are simple, rather severe, doubles of windows, and at ground floor rows of shops with plate glass show windows carried on steel joists.

Three further blocks, by James Mackay, of 1887, employ smoother granite ashlar and the same provision of two and three apartment lodgings over shops. Because of the underbuilding these shops were let to firms who could exploit the volumes of basement, sub-basement and further before reaching ground level at the Denburn. The vaults under the roadway were also exploited for dead storage and warehousing. Brown and Watt's compartment

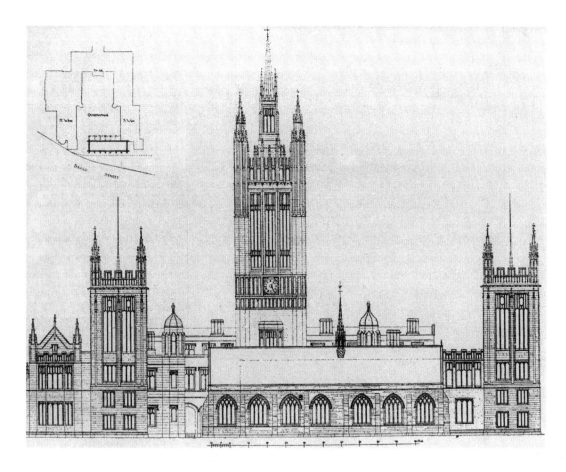

of 1897 where Rosemount Viaduct, Skene Street and Union Terrace join uses the distinct curvature of its Rosemount frontage to advantage. The body of the block is treated almost like a big office building, and articulation of the blocks is confined to the roofscape. Throughout the architects use elements so as to stress their linearity. The sharper of the ends is finished as a stack of bay windows and topped by a turret roof, and has much of the same effect as Burnham's Flatiron Building in Manhattan built a few years later.

At this point in Rosemount Viaduct's sweep there is either a satisfying view of the curving cliff-like compartments of lodgings as the roadway heads north to Rosemount, or, looking towards the city there is the panoply of the old town from the Triple Kirks south with St Nicholas, the South Kirk and the Congregational Church until the eye is stopped by the Bridge and its terminals by Simpson and Smith. Further on and to the left the Library group shows itself, not frontally, but little by little as all street buildings will, but now the architects seem to bargain with that fact to bring more interest to their works. Soon the mass of the town, and over it the Tower of the Townhouse comes into view in the middle of the street's scene as if placed there on purpose.

5.25 A. Marshall Mackenzie, Design for extended Marischal College, retaining Greyfriars Kirk 1890s

154 A CITY'S ARCHITECTURE

5.26 Schoolhill, Upperkirkgate and Marischal College in 1880s

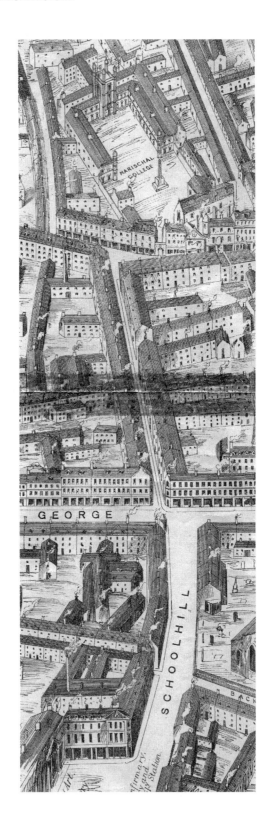

FROM CLASSIC TO CALEDONIAN 155

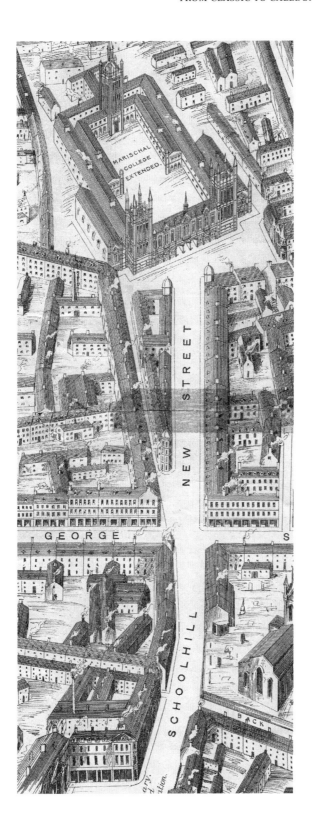

5.27 Schoolhill, Upperkirkgate and Marischal College with proposed changes

5.28 Schoolhill, Mitchell and Muill's Bakery Block

John Gray had acquired the old Grammar School site for his School of Art, and around this Matthews and his architect colleagues began to create a very satisfying exercise in urban design in the oblong open space. This would be a square in any other British town, but here it acts more like a continental open space. To the south side of this is J. Ogg Allan's Central School of 1901, replacing the row of houses before the roadway was widened. The north side is provided by Matthews and Mackenzie's office, and after Matthews' assumption of the Lord Provostship, A. Marshall Mackenzie's, and is an ensemble of the Art Gallery and Industrial Museum of 1883, Gray's building itself of 1884, the linking gateway between which also heralds the entrance to Gordon's Hospital of 1885, and blocks of splendid lodgings for Mitchell and Muill's the Baker from 1886.

All these share the classical, rather flat expression enlivened by pink granite mixed with the grey. The blocks for the gallery and school are both seeming one storey palace like blocks on a high base, with pediments marking their entrances. The gateway, while lower, is baroque in its character, and holds it own, decently – between its neighbours, and of course forms a good frame for the very distinguished Adam Hospital block with wings and additions by Smith. Gordon of Khartoum stands sentinel in front of all this. The block of shops, bakery and lodgings which forms the east wing of this space, also forms a front to Schoolhill. It uses the same architecture, but is much more reticent being composed of ranges of regular flat headed windows over plate glass shop fronts, with dormers enlivening the roof. The flats above are a mixture of lodgings for the workforce of the bakery, and genteel lodgings fit for either the Mitchells or the Muills. These are commodious and comfortable.

5.29 Schoolhill and Upperkirkgate in the late 19th century

Next door is an 1884 reworking and enlargement by John Rust of an earlier building for Shirras and Son's warehouse and showrooms. In 1887 new showrooms were built on the corner also by Rust.

Beyond Harriet Street (which continues the line of old Back Wynd) a five bay two storey Georgian block remained, but the famous house belonging to Jamesone the painter and built by his grandfather was demolished as part of the improvements of the Rosemount Entry. To this there was an almost universal outcry of dismay. Its architectural value, its familiarity and importance to the town, with its acknowledged historic value, plus the press campaign were not sufficient to save it. It then belonged to the Wordies whose business was the lucrative and important livery stables to the rear. Jamesone's House was replaced by an interesting, if fundamentally inferior, group of lodgings. These were provided by Matthews and Mackenzie and above the shops to be expected are the other end of the scale of accommodation. Tiny flats of two rooms, but with all appurtenances are provided on either side of a corridor, hotel fashion. There were two blocks of these, which still exist. The rest of Schoolhill on this side was left untouched, although some of the old buildings in Upperkirkgate were replaced at this time. The south side of Schoolhill where St Nicholas Kirkyard lay beyond it was demolished to make a wider street, and to enhance view of the new works at Marischal College.

A desire to connect the college more formally with the rest of the city had been proposed by Simpson in the 1830s when he rebuilt the old monastery buildings. He then suggested a line of development, after the essential surgery, to visually connect the tower of the College and the spire of St Nicholas. This would have cut through one of the most populous districts, and had little chance of being

5.30 Schoolhill and Upperkirkgate improved 1918

carried out. His successors proposed similar arrangements in the 1880s. The idea had taken hold, and like a slow virus grew in the town's imagination to resurface in the 1920s, later in the Granite City report, and still bedevils thinking about Broad Street. Even with the lamentable demolitions the east end of the Rosemount Entry project presented a most picturesque glimpse of the works then going on at Marischal College (TCP 11 and 5), which was captured by E.B. Mackinnon as late as 1918. This shows the prominent gothic tower at the Broad Street and Gallowgate end of an extended north wing with the Mitchell Tower beyond. Simpson's and Thomas Mackenzie's rather crisp toy-soldier gothic of the 1840s rebuilding of the college, is brought out the street and occupies the range of early Georgian blocks and the original gateway to the college. The new Tower of 1891, and the new entry at the bias united the old, and new parts of the college, and left the ancient Greyfriars Chapel, a companion piece to the chapel at King's, in place The Tower also loomed above the Rosemount Entry at Upperkirkgate, and suitably marks the end of a century of quite exceptional distinction for the city.

That would have been more than sufficient. But the city had been fond of Marischal College for many years, and as the long discussions about uniting Marischal and Kings into one as the University of Aberdeen went on so the association of Marischal as the town's university increased. This feeling seems to have been most intense at the turn of the 20th century. Another aspect which has figured already in the Rosemount Entry story is the value it is right to place on old buildings. Like Jamesone's House Greyfriars Kirk was ancient, and in fair shape, and was to be exposed to the Broadgate after the later buildings west of it were cleared. To many an old building in such a publicly prominent position was not good enough. Rather they wised to have a new building which looked like the old building, or better, looked like the best building it might have been possible to have built in the period of the original.

This had been fundamental to Victorian thinking about restoration. Modern thinking especially by the Arts and Crafts Movement had already begun to question this, but in the 1890s the issue could still go either way. Aberdeen could not resist the grandeur, and on this occasion chose to demolish old Greyfriars and substitute a long frontage of neo-Gothic work as the new ideal *restoration* of Broadgate, with the replacement parish church at the end, built mostly in Queen Street but with its tower and spire finishing the new Marischal College at the south end. Doubtless the built design is a great improvement on the solecism on the earlier proposal for a neo-classical palace block composition but with Gothic details.

Once two important and revered old buildings have been demolished, even if for dubious advantage, a new idea begins to work its influence on Aberdeen. Perhaps the fabric and heart of an ancient city might be similarly removed to be replaced by new and *better* patterns. Of course further demolitions somehow seem easier and can become the tool of partial, or political interests, and even of fashion. These problems will be the banes of 20th century planning and unimaginable to the confident Aberdeen which started the 19th century as an important town of 25,000 intent on joining the world as a serious player, and ended it a city of over 180,000 with interests and renown worldwide. As a city its architecture could confidently compare with any, however grand, without apology.

6

Architecture for Everyman

Any city's architecture has the two fundamental aspects of what is public and what is private (Cornell 1997). The clustered houses of our ancestors came together around what became courtyards in the earliest towns of the Mediterranean where the type survives still and is not uncommon. Clusters of houses are evident also in north-east Scotland, and in Aberdeen their growth into a city has given it a somewhat similar organic character, but instead of revolving around a courtyard for private life the kitchen is the heart of household and links to street and place by way of the door outside or to common stairs. In Aberdeen in the urban realm there is much evidence of the organic (that is curved shapes and ways seeming to conform to habit and ease) always, apparently, tempered by concerns for convenience but expressed in orthogonal arrangement. A similar play and contrast can be observed in the design of the habitations of the town (de Mezieres 1992).

In larger and later towns everywhere the urban block of several stories, in often mixed occupation became typical and it is the kind of building which we find in early Aberdeen. The division between public and private may be startlingly abrupt where streets are treated as both thoroughfare and sewer and houses are protected by high walls, forbidding gates and no openings (Wallace-Hadrill 1994). But in most western cities facades give clues to what lies behind, whether commercial institutional or residential. In many cities the natures of the private habitations are signalled by their public presentation. Big houses cater for rich and important people, smaller houses for less rich or important and so forth, with variations to do with location. In Scottish cities this does not apply in the same way as in other parts of these islands and in other parts of the world. Often the interiors in which people live privately are surprising – an unprepossessing entry in a crowded street may well lead to lodgings of great comfort and style; a great house clearly presenting itself as such may well be a house for two families, either sharing the front door in common or with a secondary but equally major front door leading to the other half. In Aberdeen lodgings are largely independent of the apparent architectural building type.

Within Scotland some cities have larger lodgings than others. The rooms of Edinburgh, especially the New Towns are on the whole very large, most flats

6.0 Bungalow Prototype. Mrs Yeats of Auquharney's house occupied this very prominent site near Holburn junction for most of the 19th century

and houses have several rooms of the order of 4 to 5 meters by 6 to 8 meters, and in Glasgow similarly: in Aberdeen even one such room is uncommon. Reception rooms or family bedrooms are characteristically smaller. There are other curious differences between the towns for which the reasons remain obscure. Yet they appear consistent through time. The climate and culture of Scotland contribute to a lack of balconies for relief from the heat or as tiny garden spaces, even those houses set in gardens can appear exceptionally cool or sparse, especially to the visitor from England. Life outside the home in Scottish towns is public: this may not be so surprising perhaps in the predominately urban nature of Aberdeen or Edinburgh, but it is evident also in the leafier suburban parts.

About most early forms of habitation we are without reliable evidence and have to rely on guess work and speculation. However, two early examples of urban houses survive in Aberdeen, although one is now part of a museum and the other has been moved northward to parkland at Tillydrone and therefore it is heavily restored, and without context. Benholm's Lodging or Wallace's Neuk, was the heart of the town until it was sacrificed to extend Marks and Spencer's store (Figs 6.1 and 2.3). In its role as town house for the laird of Benholm, a brother of the founder of Marischal College, it presumably was used only by that family. But at that time family would have included staff who likely were cousins, so the lodging within a building of other lodgings was there in principle from the beginning. This, of course, is to speculate. As the survey drawings, made when the building was taken down and removed, indicate, the plan form was then designed in apartment or flat fashion (Netherkirkgate 1). Never a large house Benholm's Lodging appeared as a tiny Z plan castle with towers at the diagonal ends of the rectangular body (Macgibbon and Ross 1887). In the late 18th century it had been almost doubled in size by the addition of the Niven

ARCHITECTURE FOR EVERYMAN 163

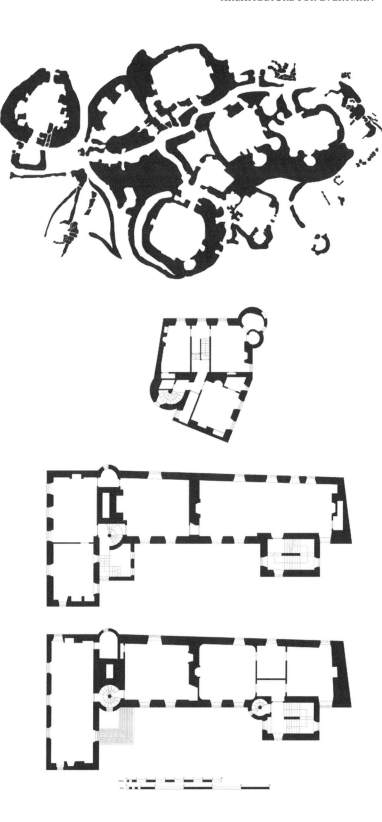

6.1 *Early Houses*, Scara Brae, Benholm's Lodging, and Provost Skene's House

wing to the rear along Carnegie's Brae. At this time the interiors were altered and the staircase and entry changed to accommodate the different floor levels of the old and newer parts. In this form, as a tenement, the building provided two flats per floor: to the north in the original part of the building was the larger apartment and this consisted of two rooms each with a fireplace and one with a round closet just big enough to take a bed. Above this and reached by an 18th century stair was a further flat in the roof space: this could have been let together with the first floor to make a larger apartment. To the back was a smaller chamber, with bed closet and a long service room. Chambers served multiple functions and the notion of a bedroom as such was novel: bed closets often opened off chambers; the chambers themselves would have been supplied with a bed, normally curtained. In its original form Benholm's Lodging would have had only the two large rooms with adjacent closet per floor, this was reached by a pend to the west which led to the turn stair, altered in the Niven work. Throughout its life the ground floor would have been for business and most likely let as a shop.

The two room and closet suite seems somewhat small for a rich and powerful man but if seen as for his use only it was as much as could be expected and indeed marked a development in domestic planning. These private suites, or *apartments*, as they were originally called at for example Chambord were a significant improvement on the guests' accommodation heretofore available even at royal French great houses, where one large room led to another in enfilade and privacy was unknown. Apartment planning allowed for reception room, a private room and the closet, usually occupied by a servant. At Chambord the suites for royal guests or members of the Royal family were slightly larger and had the capability of being joined together. Their use was adopted in the 1530s by James V immediately at Stirling (Dunbar 1999), where he and his queen shared closets but had each a suite of guard room, presence chamber, and private chamber. At Falkland there were also Chambord type apartments for them. Soon these apartments appear in the houses of the North East. In country houses a hall was included for receiving large numbers whereas in towns this was not necessary as meetings in larger groups would occur in the town itself or in hired rooms. The cross-over of such suites of rooms into the domestic planning of lodgings (more generally the early tenements) appears on present evidence to be somewhat later in the third quarter of the 18th century, roughly the same time as Benholm's Lodging was extended.

Evidence for internal arrangements of buildings before the 19th century is slight and sadly patchy (Gow 1992): it is true that Aberdeen and Edinburgh are very fortunate in having the plans prepared by James Gordon recording these cities in the middle of the 17th century. From these we know the patterns of streets and places, the arrangement of buildings and something also of their natures. For more detailed knowledge we may guess or infer, but never be absolutely sure. St Nicholas Kirk and other special buildings, of which there were very few, clearly stand out, as do the market stalls indicated in the Castlegate. Also his rather sketchier (because of the scale of his enterprise rather than his relegation of them) are the other urban buildings…the houses which formed and gave character to the streets and places. The commonest type of these in Aberdeen from at latest the 17th century attested by Gordon was the three to four story houses, to which Defoe adds the information that they were stone-built, with slated roofs and sash windows, the then very recently introduced fashion from the Low Countries which we still employ today.

But how did these buildings work? Where did Aberdonians shop, where did they make or store things to sell to each other, and where and how did they live? Gordon's market stalls (Figs 2.5 and 2.29), clearly visible in his plan shows that these stalls, whether wheeled platforms, or more elaborate covered stalls were where goods were displayed and sold. Perishables and more marginal trade was left to carry on from pallets or cloths laid out on the ground. Some trades would have been carried on from booths, as the stalls were also named, but attached to the fronts of the houses (Clark 2000). These booths sometimes extended into the ground floors of the houses, where there could be workshops. Further workshops might be built in the inland and back parts of the old feus (Cameron and Stones 2001). Remnants of this pattern survive into the 20th century in the house of professionals where the room of business for a law agent, or banker was at the front of house otherwise occupied by his family.

These houses look like the houses elsewhere in these islands whether London, Bristol or Dublin, and were perfected as type by common experience led by the Acts regulating the rebuilding of London after the Great Fire, where regularity, masonry construction and confining the house within a fire-proofed area were introduced. Although there had been convenient and perhaps widespread houses of multiple occupation on the pattern we associate with old colleges, that is, *sets of rooms* opening to either side of a common stairway, these are not encouraged in the new London and are confined to neighbourhoods outside the City, such as Covent Garden (where the sets had already *spread* laterally) or in neighbourhoods like St Giles' where Dickens places Fagin's gang of thieves who run from one house to another like rats. It is only towards the end of the 18th century that designers and builders perfect a modern style of urban buildings containing many 'houses', the tenement. These appear first in Scotland, and a perfected form like the old collegiate one is used in Aberdeen from the middle of the 19th century, when a more efficient stairway leads to two or three of flats on each floor.

Evidence of how even modern houses were actually used in the 18th century is sadly very rare indeed, so it is really fortunate that we have a contemporary drawing of the plan and front of such a house, in multiple occupation, and in Aberdeen. Its rooms' uses are indicated, for otherwise, no-one could have guessed at them, nor be believed it if he had. This drawing shows a large shop on the ground floor opening from the street, and above are lodgings reached by a modest entry lobby (which opens into the shop and back shop also) reached from the city street by a protected but open passage. In the cellar floor (not a common feature of Aberdeen houses) are a brew house, plus other three cellar rooms (one each for three of the floors above) while

166 A CITY'S ARCHITECTURE

6.2 Prototype tenement

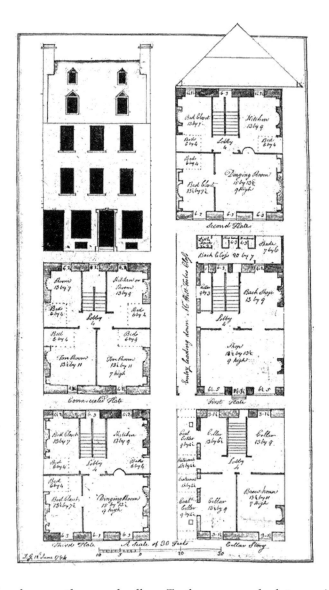

below the close are three coal cellars. To the rear are shed, two privies and 'little house'. There are two lodgings floors indicated, each of four rooms with fireplace: a large reception room *Dinging Room* (sic) with bed chamber adjacent, while the second bed chamber and kitchen are accessed only by way of the common lobby. A niche is shown for both dining rooms in the centre of the rear partition. (In a similar position in the contemporary Marischal Street such a niche survives with shelves to show off good china with architecturally rich surrounds made all of a piece in fibrous plaster). Curiously, there is a further floor with four further heated bedrooms in the *combed plate,* the lower of two loft floors within the roof. Both of these floors are lit by small dormer windows. So two rooms only were seen to be necessarily part of a *private domain*. Presumably the spare bedrooms, perhaps even those on the same floors as the sets of lodgings, could be used or assigned as required. Certainly the chance of meeting a neighbour, or a neighbour's guest on ones way to bed, was not considered a problem.

A large block at the north-east corner of the Castlegate, which may be associated with Robert Adam, was built from 1770 (Figs 6.3 and 3.7). It is at partly on older foundations and the first lower floors of the wings towards the north incorporate 17th or early 18th century inland properties entered from Smith's Court. It is probably this earlier work that gives an irregular cast to the whole building making the stylish Georgian rooms fronting the Castlegate somewhat squint rather than orthogonally pure. The staircase of the western part is built rather as a Georgian version of the old turn stair ubiquitous in Scotland in earlier centuries: here it is an open half ellipse, partly to accommodate the interiors to the squint site condition. The eastern, and larger half, has a more regular but also less grand stair opening off Smith's Court and also (originally) from Castle Street/Justice Street. According to the Register of Sasine, the legal document dealing with the building the site was to contain, 'Ten houses in number all lying on the north side of the Castlegate of Aberdeen near the Justice Port' (Sasines 66 3 Jan 1770). It is possible that the present block contained as many as ten flatted dwellings, as later legally defined, of a large size. The whole site might also have extended slightly further eastward. Whether such a large site became available through a catastrophic fire, or the collapse of an ancient building, is unrecorded, but it is rare.

The plans have been modified but its original may be deduced (Castlegate 1): in each of the present pair there were a series of rooms with fireplaces which open off the common stair. Their arrangements into apartments seem to have been either as pairs of rooms, that is a chamber from which a secondary chamber, presumably for sleeping was reached), so the ten houses can be easily accounted for. Or there could have been larger self-contained flats occupying the whole floor. It is also just conceivable that the part to the west was rather used as a house occupying the three floors and lofts above the shops. Of course each block originally or at some other time might have been divided into smaller suites, catered to by a resident housekeeper with staff who occupied the kitchen and rooms at the rear and acted also as concierge. Water closets were only introduced in the 1890s. At ground level there were arched shopfronts leading to four shops facing the square, and arched entries to the floors above, and into Smith's Court and Peacock's Close which were essentially narrower streets leading to further houses, or blocks of *houses*.

James Burn, essayed a similar design idea when he included 57 Castlegate in his project for the Banking Company next door, but built together, in 1800 (Fig. 3.11). This becomes the standard house type chosen by the Trustees and imitation of its design is stipulated in the feu charters for properties to be built in the New Streets. The house at 57 Castlegate accommodated four entrances within its modest width at ground level: the Close, the entry to the Athenaeum (the reading room to the rear of the property, a shop, and the

168　A CITY'S ARCHITECTURE

6.3 *Urban Houses*, 19–23 Castlegate, Upperkirkgate/ Gallowgate corner, 30 Marischal Street, Upperkirkgate Drum's Hospital Lane

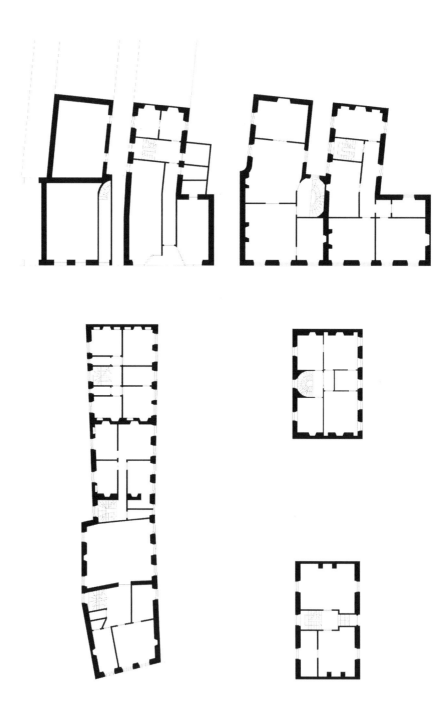

lodgings in the floors above. These are three rooms each: a reception room of two bays like the Dining Room of the 18th century proto-type, with a bed chamber and kitchen. These are served by a grand staircase with pilaster strips articulating the gentle ascent at the curved ends. Whether these flats were used as they are today, or whether the upper floors were allocated as bedrooms for use by whomever we cannot now say. At least there is the possibility of each flat to be used privately: the lobbies lie within each flat and occupy the irregular spaces left over from the orthogonally designed other rooms.

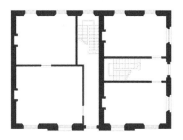

An even larger early house was built for Baillie Galen at the junction of Shiprow with the newly formed Union Street (Miller 2007). This building has a roughly square plan form and it faces two major ways: the ground floor is made of a series of round headed archways (like 19–24 Castlegate), and one of these leads to the staircase and to the house, or houses, above. Like Burn further east Archibald Simpson designs each floor about a curiously formally indeterminate lobby/corridor, which leads from the staircase landing to six big rooms per floor. As these floors are obviously detached by Simpson's design it is probable that Galen's house was always used in tenement fashion (Fig. 5.5).

Galen's house appears to be an Aberdeen variation on the then normal urban house. The houses designed as part of his competition entry in the 1800 contest to choose the architect for the New Streets by James Young indicate conventional houses with very large rooms of the kind one would associate with London or of the New Towns of Edinburgh. A near neighbour, while fulfilling Young's basic designs, is Simpson's mansion house for Morrison of Auchintoul of 1811, intended to be a very large family house for the Morrisons. It became a complex tenement within a few years. Whether these large houses in the New Streets were tenements or simply large houses which may be used by many can only be determined when the history of each can be traced: their exterior forms do not betray their uses.

6.4 *Trustees Houses*, James Young Union Street and Castlegate, King Street

An educated guess would propose that those nearer the heart of town, for example near the Castlegate, or Shiprow and Broad Street would be built as flats: the houses are larger, and as they are central they are easily let. Certainly the block built by John Smith for Mrs. Edwards in the 1830s south of the New Record Office was built as two (perhaps three) separate flats above shops. It remains externally indistinguishable from the buildings opposite, built by the same architect for the British Linen Bank (Figs 5.1 and 5.4). The Edwards block has flats of six rooms each, with water-closets included, with two reception rooms towards King Street (each square and handsomely fitted out) and the main bedroom, all served by a large rectangular reception hall which opens through double doors with fan and side lights from the curving cantilevered stone staircase. The other *half* of the flat also opens from this hall where a lobby leads to the three service rooms (and the second water closet).

For less fortunate families there were flats available, and not all in older rundown less favoured properties. The lesser new streets west of the Bridge, or the renewed sections of the old city, saw much new building at the same time, and here there is a similar dubiety about uses. For example the row of houses built by James Littlejohn in the 1790s on the site of Drum's Hospital (TCP D 2) a close running northwards from Upperkirkgate, were identical and had four floors served by a central staircase. Each floor had two apartments of two rooms each, a kitchen with bed chamber opening off it to the rear. These could well have catered for a smaller family, or a larger one of modest means, or a household with *outlying* bedrooms.

Other small flats of two rooms, sometimes only one, existed in various parts of the town. A block was recorded in Cotton Street (Cotton Street 1) in the Fittie quarter in the late 19th century, seemingly like other tenements but instead of shops at the ground floor there were flats of two small rooms: the first had its sink in the window embrasure to the front, its stove is the fireplace and a press standing close by, exactly the same provision as the 18th century prototype showed. Beyond it was a bed chamber. On the other side of the block was an identical flat. At the centre of the block a passage led through to the back close, which contained not only privies, but also an external stair to landings which gave entrance to the same accommodation, but arranged back to front. In more outlying neighbourhoods such flats would more likely be in small houses, typically as half of a cottage.

For the first half of the 19th century it is difficult to judge the balance of houses in use as tenements or as complete houses. From the 1860s however the tenement block becomes perfected and recognizable. Early forms with the simple two chambers with bed closet plan appear on King Street Road just beyond the Militia Barracks, that is, the very edge of town. Also then at the extreme edges of town are others in Crown Street near Dee Village, and opposite Cornhill on Westburn Road, facing into the parklands of Cornhill, a large block of purpose built flats served by a central staircase was built in 1865. Of four stories, including the roof with its large dormers, there were cellars (sheds) in the enclosed green to the south, and ample open garden ground to the north.

From this period also they appear paired with rows of cottages in the northern suburb of Rosemount. Soon other similar blocks begin to appear further west in newly laid out streets running from Belvidere Terrace (soon to be called Rosemount Place) northwards towards the newly laid out Victoria Park. These streets were built up by individual builders conforming to the cottage/tenement row pioneered by Simpson form the late 1830s but only recently fully realized. The feu charters for these streets laid down the rules: tenement blocks set back behind small gardens on the east side with one storey half cottages in rows opposite, also set back from the street with small gardens.

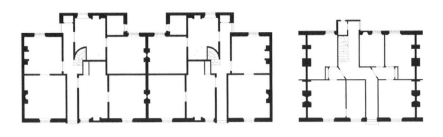

6.5 *Tenement blocks*, King Street Road, Thomson Street, Forrest Road, Schoolhill at Gordon *square*, Schoolhill (Jameson's House site) ground floor and upper floor

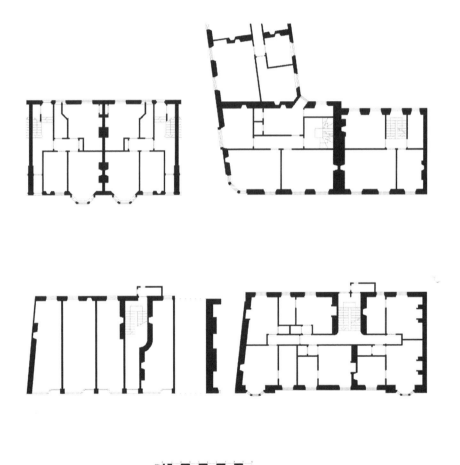

Both rows were to be provided with enclosed back greens and cellars for the east sides and walled individual gardens behind the cottage rows. Lanes served both back gardens and greens. The tenements appear to have been built to let, whereas the cottages were seemingly sold, and of varying plan arrangements, often divided into two houses (of about the same size as the flats opposite), one on the ground floor entered from the font, the other occupying the roof space and entered from the back, where the garden became divided into two, or also characteristically *shared* between the two houses.

Accommodation in these flats consisted of a combination living room and kitchen and chamber, sometimes two. The kitchen had a fireplace of course in which was a fitted range to provide heat for cooking and living. The sink was in the east facing window, as common for at least a century. Some flats in these rows had also a short wing opening off the kitchen which contained a scullery for the wet functions of the flat. A usually curtained bed recess, large enough to take a double bed only, was located on the inside wall. The lobby, now very efficiently designed, connected kitchen with doorway to the staircase, and off it opened the further room with fireplace, facing west, designated chamber or parlour, and perhaps also a smaller bedchamber. Water closets were located on the half-landings of the stairs, and laundry sheds, containing a boiler and little else were provided in the back green. Both these shared facilities were subjects of civil arrangement between the flat-holders, as was the rota for stair cleaning. Tenement blocks individually, and in fact whole streets, acquired personality because of these arrangements. Shopping occurred in the nearby ground floors of Rosemount Place, but towards the ends of the new streets there were occasional shops designed to occupy parts of the ground floor. These streets provided flexible and useful accommodation for those who needed, or wished, to rent conveniently near neighbours in their own small houses, and all within easy walking distance of an early neighbourhood *centre* which shortly also carried a tram route to and from the city centre. At the other end of these streets was the new Park. Not surprisingly it became a most successful venture and has remained so until today.

The *architecture* of these tenement blocks was of the most severe and plain sort. Of rubble walls, with entrances often slightly off centre and fenestration equally plan driven they were relieved by the small gardens between front walls and pavements, and the street trees which have characterized these streets as *avenues* leading from the main streets of Rosemount to the parks. Some blocks are given distinction by the addition of the lingering old Aberdeen favourite the *tympany* at roof level which is the only feature that marks the number of blocks and sets them apart from being pure urban walls. Soon means are discovered to make each block fully symmetrical, by insuring the entrances lie in the middle of the street side, and dividing the block and facade between the smaller (one chamber) and the larger flats, soon to be embellished by providing balancing bay windows. In even minimalist projects, such as the early local authority streets for workmen off King Street smartly detailed tympany and details of the window's astragals are sufficient to bring the form up to the city's standard. Elsewhere string or cill courses and other moderate decorative elements join smarter window and door surrounds leaving the variously ornamented tympany to give distinction and mark the individual blocks. These more mature designs become standard by the 1880s, and are used to develop streets and neighbourhoods in all parts of the city's edges, and in the case of Torry, they become the urban architecture for a little town attached to Aberdeen only by ferry, and then by bridge to Market Street.

The Rosemount entry project was lined entirely by these perfected tenement blocks. These were to be where they also aspire to compartment standard and contribute a sense of more city scale monumentality. One of the earliest drawings associated with the project shows the standards anticipated. A revived palace-block format of four or five stories and of five bays breadth with full ornamentation is produced for guidance (TCP R 8, Fig. 5.19). In the event these were followed, but were stylistically varied from compartment to compartment until it reaches the newly enlarged city park at the top end of Union Terrace. There, the tenement blocks join new office blocks to continue the Terrace and new civic buildings such as the Library and Gray's School of Art. Not only are there variations in the buildings styles of block and compartment, there is also, on the city side of the Rosemount entry project variation in the scales of accommodation the tenement blocks may provide.

The east side of the *place* the unnamed square at Schoolhill defined by Grays, Gordon's and the Art Gallery on one side and the new Town's School on the other, is formed by premises for Mitchell and Muill's Steam Bakery with grand scaled tenement flats above (see Fig. 5.28). These are much larger and consequently more comfortable than any flats built in the city since the early part of the century. Built of both pink and white granites by the same firm who built the educational frontage next door on the north face, Matthews and Mackenzie these flats are clearly meant to carry on the crescendo of the whole scheme and act as appropriate joins to the ancient and soon to be aggrandized approach to and frontage of Marischal College.

Flats in this block were, at the corner with Schoolhill, of three floors with *Drawing Room* taking pride of place and marked by a turret bay at the corner, and dining room and kitchen with bedrooms on the floors above. The planning of the flats to the north are marked as a pair of good sized *Parlours* facing onto the square while across the spine corridor bedrooms face east, and over the roofs of the bakery. Eastward in Upperkirkgate, and passed a pair of smart but otherwise now standard tenement blocks and the emporium for Chivas Laing are flats designed for the other end of the scale. These, also be Matthews and Mackenzie's were built for the Wordie Company whose livery business lay behind. These flats replaced the ancient Jameson's House, one of the grandest and distinguished 15th–16th century houses of Aberdeen, whose demolition, without record, was loudly lamented. The Wordie flats are served by a staircase then a long lobby or corridor running along the spine of the building as flats commonly are when built today. The style of accommodation is more modern as well. There are five apartments per floor. One has the parlour and kitchen with small bed chamber already noted as minimal. The rest are made up by kitchen and bed closet only: the kitchen in these are partly to the front, and are longer than normal and clearly would have been rather more living room than cooking room. The *bed closet* so named but slightly bigger than bed closets in standard tenements was contiguous. Such arrangements are rare in Aberdeen and suggest the serviced flat, in the early 21st century a very common feature of the city's life. Similar serviced flats were being introduced, also experimentally, in late Victorian London in Jermyn Street, Piccadilly.

Flats in London were either Peabody lodgings built usually discreetly out of site for working staff, or the splendid blocks of mansion flats, with which the Mitchell and Muills might be compared. Although much of the western extensions to London near the Albert Hall, or of Battersea, or northwards towards Hampstead were built as these, the English, particularly the professional press, affected to disown these as being rather foreign. Professionals, including particularly the new planners and others who fought for slum clearance, and for the improvement of cities, were committed to the village; the village house, ideally the cottage, was the means to rectify all such problems. They carried the argument, nationally, and soon were backed by the government who were committed to the single family owner-voter as best means not only to solve problems of overcrowding and poor planning, but also the means to avoid revolution and the continuing return of Liberal parliaments.

In the post 1914–18 period tenements and urban developments employed in Aberdeen so successfully were decidedly out of favour. Funding for house building by local authorities was to be sanctioned only if it conformed to national standards, and these standards had been arrived at furth of Scotland and without any cognizance of Scottish developments. If the horrors of modern warfare and the consequences of economic depression following it had not been enough, such direction about house building from central authorities made further tenement building impossible. Cottages in pairs or in short rows were anticipated and encouraged nationally whereas tenements were not. As living in small flats was still deemed desirable by urban Scots a sort of hybrid type was developed, the Manse type. This house form contained four flats, two per floor; the top pair were accessed by a central stair, usually open, and the lower pair at the sides of the block. Fenestration was regular, the chimneys paired, and well related to the slated piended roof. The walls were sometimes of granite, but more often harl on brickwork. The similarity to the 19th century manses built in great numbers all over Scotland was obvious, and yet the distinction between the types was equally clear.

The tenement was revived however under the 'short row of cottages' rule, in Aberdeen by works carried on with Government approval and subsidy by the City Architects Department.

King Street, as a city street had stopped with the Edwardian tenements blocks where Kings Street became King Street Road. Here, opposite the old Militia Barracks and next door to the earlier tenement discussed above, A.B. Gardner's group of designers built their modern version of tenements in the late 1920s. There were differences, and significant ones. These blocks are lower by at least one story; they are set back behind gardens, as those of Rosemount had been, but these gardens are municipal and they slope upwards making certain that their use was severely limited by anybody. Also there was no provision, nor even the possibility of shops being sited

 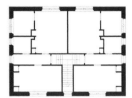

6.6 *Local authority houses*, manse type, modern tenement, cottage, post-war tenement

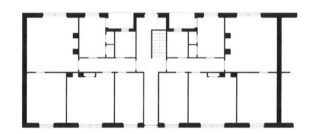

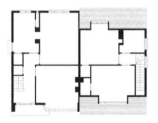 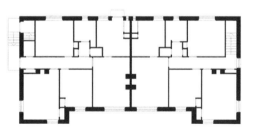

on the ground floors of these buildings. It may have been prohibited for the local authority to engage in commerce; if so they appear to have accepted the burden very cheerfully. The earlier tenements (except for the Urquhart Road ones) had been undertaken by tradesmen, or companies, overseen and scrutinized by the local government: that pattern ceased and was never revived. Sadly when commercial interests started building houses and flats for rent again in the later 20th century they adopted the local authorities recent 'rules' of segregation of shops, gardens, house and flats: the recently built schemes are indistinguishable from their local authority precursors. But, at least the King Street blocks, and those further out at Woodside, and by the river Don at Hayton were designed to make places and to define street edges, and these building are made of good granite, well worked, and simply designed under substantial slated roofs with plenty of open spaces in gardens and parks, and adjacent to good public transport to and from the city. Had they also been designed so that commercial and the other social activities of streets and urban places *could* develop then they might indeed have become *places* their designers sought, and thus able to be part of a living city rather than a residential enclave, and one that despite all its qualities of design, siting, construction and placement has become as close as Aberdeen has to being thought a slum.

As good as public transport was it still has to be paid for, and those living at the edges of the city probably have less to spend simply to get into town. This foolishness in civic policy was well understood in the 1930s (Alexander 1939: 20) when a pamphlet was produced making that very point, and further noting, that residents of the slums recently demolished in the city centre had not only to find the fares to add to all else, but had also to find the means to furnish several rooms from scratch, all within the same meagre income as before. There the building of the super-tenements of the old Morrison's Jam Factory site opposite one of the smart compartments of Rosemount Viaduct was heartily welcomed in 1939.

Conforming to the same constraints the local authority had, or had adopted, Rosemount Square was designed by the City Architects Department using exactly the pattern perfected by the 1880s, the common stair serving two flats per landing, and providing kitchen, living room, bedrooms and scullery, now with drying place and lavatory *en suite.* All this to be built around a communal garden (rather than drying-green/playground) and within *walking distance* of…schools, theatre, shops – big and small, pubs, churches, library, art gallery, university, art school, railway and seaport; what any city resident would wish. Rosemount Square is designed as a continuous ring of tenement blocks distinguished only by the entrances and stairway windows, and formed by the pattern of the existing streets. The ring is resolved into a semi-circle at its south end, the one facing towards the city, where a robust semi-circular arch makes a grand entrance to the interior. Period sculpture here, and horizontally expressed windows and tooled if plain and minimalist granite walls gives the scheme distinction and style. Its similarity of materials, its height and its purpose lets it fit in with its grand and older neighbours without difficulty or apology.

Rosemount Square (Fig. 7.5) is emblematic of its time, however. Apartment buildings any whatever part of the UK were designed to be set back from the streets, and ideally significantly so, such as Berthold Lubetkin's High Point the modernist exercise in Highgate, London. Aberdeen had no Modern Movement buildings and yet it too had subscribed to the modernist programme on the issues of site planning, and of roads. These are the last and most strongly held remnants of the Modern Movement in these islands, and may be permanent. The arrangements to make cooking and laundry separate places as well as activities with the house is also part of the *functionalism* associated with modernism, and the part most eagerly taken up by the British. Kitchens for cooking only were characteristic of post-war houses built to national standard. There remained in Whitehall the worry that if it were made bigger the Scots might continue to have bed spaces in the room government had decided could be for cooking only (Gale 1949). Elaborate utility rooms were sanctioned officially by the Scottish Office as part of late war-time planning for improvements (Scottish Housing Advisory Committee 1945). These were wisely never implemented. Similarly at the urban scale it was the efficacy of traffic flows, and the consequent zoning of like with like, realized as assemblies of detached buildings in their own landscaped grounds that British theorists and practitioners advocated, and to which practically all local authorities subscribed in the period after the Second World War. The *styles* of those buildings, critically important to some even now, are hardly the point. Whether refined classical or ultra modern the urban fabric of mid 20th century Britain was radically changed and was pretty universally welcomed.

Urban houses, and their descendants the modern tenement or apartment blocks, are special kinds of house, and developed along with the two primary kinds, the big house and the cottage. The typology of the great house in North East Scotland owes more to ancestry than to wealth or size. Country houses which head estates still take precedence (Macgibbon and Ross 1887). They continue to have that connection to the last great upheaval in these islands when the Normans arrived and reorganized everything.

In Scotland these houses almost always carry the baronies associated with them, and often they share their names with their owners, whether granted by the Lord Lyon or more likely as common parlance of lairdship. Those surviving in the city are Grandhome from a two storey somewhat irregular beginning augmented into an imposing three wing composition. At a similar date on the other side of Aberdeen is Peterculter (Fig. 1.2). This is larger and more regular, of seven bays with three stories with two story wings embracing the forecourt: its grounds are seemingly more designed as a baroque ensemble. But both are of similar importance and carry the same kind of social weight; not surprisingly both are reputed to have a very early house at their core. Country houses of apparent genuine age, such as Rubislaw were demolished, as were their more urban cousins Jameson's

6.7 Old Rubilsaw House, 50 Queen's Road

house and Marr Castle. 17th century in origin Kingswells shows a curious and interestingly regional type, the Ha'hoose. These are found in the North East as far as Orkney and a much restored example is Raemoir near Banchory. These are compact regular, usually two storey, blocks with characteristic small advanced wings, more closets actually, at either end of the principal front where small oval windows are often found. All these count as proper country houses; however rich and prosperous an Aberdonian may become, aspiring to this type requires something more than funds: funds plus a prudent marriage is usually required.

Between country house and cottage is a type of large mansion tending to the classical before 1840 after which a more Caledonian mode becomes prevalent. A prime example of these can be seen in Pitfodels new lodging in Belmont Street; others can be observed in Carden Place, its extensions westward particularly Queens Road and in their own grounds in the suburbs along the Dee. These are the residence of fortunate merchants, lawyers and other professional men. While it would be grossly unfair to call them 'Hatter's Castles', in social terms they were a big step forward but hardly a destination. Their architecture is inventive even in the more conservative examples and often bears comparison with similar contemporary experiments elsewhere. An exception to this is the survival of one urban mansion of the early kind, the two houses known from the mid 18th century as Cumberland House or Provost Skene's House. These have a somewhat complex history (already noted) and were two houses before 1733. The western of these was a larger version of Benholm's Lodging and of L plan formation where three good chambers per floor were arranged about

ARCHITECTURE FOR EVERYMAN 179

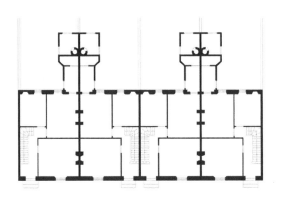

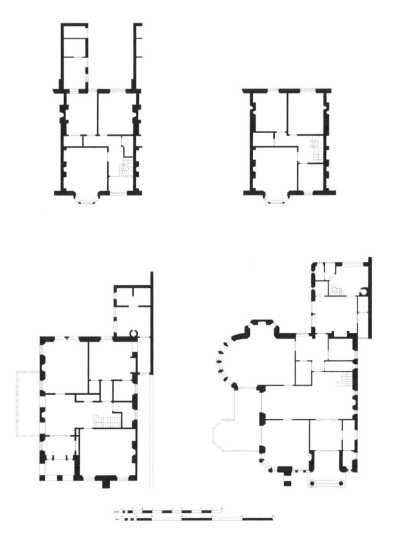

6.8 *National Type*, Brighton Place, King Street Road ground and upper floors, Hamilton Place, 50 Queen's Road (early)

the stair, and where a gallery or upper reception room with excellent painted decorations of the later 17th century survive. Apart from the first floor, where two original chambers were joined to make a large and handsome reception room fit to receive a royal tenant, the eastern half has a similar plan formation. These lodgings, or mansion house, so long as they remained in occupation by one family are of a different order of size and comfort from their neighbours. They also point towards the modern type which appears in the 18th century. The ground floor was occupied by service rooms such as the kitchen with stone vaulted construction. The stair at the southeast corner is a comfortable airy series of steps and landings on a square plan with ample light. From being essentially a vertical corridor this stair has been enlarged into a spatial connection from one floor to another and becomes a chamber of some importance in itself. On each floor are large chambers, lighted from both sides, separated by a bed closet. The original forms were replaced in about 1733 when the house was refitted and enlarged both upwards and latterly by joining it with its western neighbour. Therefore it now presents an 18th century character. However, it would have appeared rather modern even in its earlier arrangement.

With the formation of Marischal Street the apparently very grand and commodious Earl Marischal's Lodging disappeared – sadly without being recorded in any way. Its equally early immediate neighbour to the west was also soon demolished ~ again without trace. Pitfodels Lodging was the smaller, perhaps of the order of Cumberland House east, but fortunately its replacement survives, and is a public building. The Menzies of Pitfodels had their country house within the modern city at Pitfodels where the very early Norman period motte survives: their country house was demolished in the 1840s. Their new town lodgings were in, properly on, Belmont Street at the extreme western edge of Aberdeen overlooking the Denburn valley. There they built almost a replica of the new houses then being built in their own former backlands. Sadly the feu charter which laid down the design, and codified the type of the houses in Marischal Street, has yet to be found. However, it is mentioned when early, and important, builders in that street flexed their political and artistic muscle sufficiently to have them modified. As Provost Young and some of his colleagues observed, '…with equal Anxiety with any persons whatever in having suitable Symmetry adhered to…(Sasines 63 13 March 1770), the cills of the houses would be too low to allow anyone sitting down to properly see out: in consequence their request that the Articles of Roup be varied was agreed. Therefore the cills of the middle floors were dropped by six inches and the heads raised by six inches.

The new Pitfolds Lodging is almost the beau ideal of the 18th century, with sunny gardens terraced down toward the valley overlooked by both the reception rooms and chambers of the well-lighted house. The house at 37 Belmont Street is a squarish block of a building with originally two short dependent wings, of two stories above a slightly raised basement with prominent gable chimneys. Its corners are enriched by quoins and the windows have classic surrounds: the windows are of course regularly placed and in the new manner they are both larger and more numerous than in earlier houses. Service rooms occupied the basement; the ground floor has a new format, but it likely contained a major reception room, probably a dining room, and perhaps also a hall. This is speculation, however. Its lightness and the nature of its architectural treatment can be appreciated even now. The square open staircase is the modern descendent of the one at Cumberland House, notably lighter and made of timber. This rises to the first floor which retains much of its original arrangement. The stair opens first into a square hall, from which the new style pair of reception rooms is reached: this is in L plan with a wide segmental arched opening separating the larger space to the east from the smaller room overlooking the gardens and valley. A more private suite probably occupied the rest of this floor. There would have been chambers for family and staff in the roof space lit with small dormer windows. Probably panelled in its early form, some of the plaster cornicing, and the window and door frames survive in restored form.

There were many houses of this type which survive such as the Old Customs House on Regent Quay while variants showing the tympany or gable feature at the centre are sadly mostly gone, particularly that in the backland of the Castlegate exploiting the sunny aspect above the river. Others such as Friendville, on Great Western Road at Mannofield, survive in a heavily restored manner. Over the succeeding decades there were many more which became more and more refined in their detail; at first sight one of these is 12 Carden Place. This building started its life as a cottage and became a mansion at the turn of the 20th century, under the very skilful management of William Kelly who was beginning his independent career after his time in the last of the Smiths' offices that in a sense he inherited. The basic arrangements 12 Carden Place are the same as the type: service rooms in the raised half basement, reception rooms with the double drawing room now nearing its time of fashion and, now located on the ground floor. The placement of the drawing room in mansion houses is variable in Scotland and in some ways difficult for us to understand. It is often noted as being on the first floor with the bedrooms, but in subsequent usage it becomes another, if best, bedroom. In this house the arrangement is with both conveniently on the raised ground floor and with Edwardian punctilious bourgeois detail suitably demarcated between front and back and behind the dining room, the parlour. All visitors would be acutely aware of the nature of their visit and their intimacy with the family by whom they were received.

Originally there were two big canted bay windows to right and left of the entrance. Kelly enlarges these into larger, rectangular bays in his rebuilding of the front wall of the house and this makes them into something more like the intimate 'best' part of the space, both inside and out, sunny even airy, yet still protected and set apart. On the dining room side this would be used for teas (the evening meal), probably also for breakfasts. On the drawing room side the use would have varied from a place for music to the more intimate lady-like teas. For big parties such variations within the room would be especially welcome. The bedrooms above are large and airy and, typical in later comfortable houses such as this, would have also been reception rooms for special friends, for children, for resident guests to withdraw and for individual family pursuits. A well-planned block for 'wet' services is built with an almost modernist 20th century severity at the back, entered here as in contemporary tenements from the staircase landings.

The exterior materials for the walls, roofs and windows remain the same as at Pitfodels, with their regularity and relationship but 12 Carden Place expresses these in smart early 20th century fashion. The sash windows are large plate glass sections in the lower three quarters of the main floor with the later typical fashion of small square paned section to the tops – in what was called Queen Anne style the British equivalent of the nostalgic recollection of earlier domestic architecture, named 'Wilhelmite' in Germany and Colonial in the USA. Kelly adds a more modern twist in rendering these as even smaller squares of glass in a leaded framework. His entrance door has a large 'art glass' coloured panel. The bedroom windows are linked arcades, plate glass below small panes within the semi-circles. This late Victorian taste derives from a brief Romanesque revival in the late 1830s. The new roof is both piended and gabled: the hipped part is lower than other examples in Aberdeen, at an almost Italianate angle. It carries a wrought iron decorative ridge and decorative iron work at eaves level. The chimneystacks are linked to the main roof by lower gables, expressed also on the side elevations almost as reminders of the original cottage roof.

Although houses within the city are of the same as design as contemporary country houses they sit within feus along streets, and that constraint to urbanity in a way *civilizes* them. For those who had choice another kind of way of living proved increasingly attractive. In the still largely empty land west of the city houses in their own grounds became the fashion in Aberdeen as it had become elsewhere. There were small lairdships, such as Powis House (Fig. 7.4) and its skilfully landscaped grounds west of King's College to emulate. Old farmsteads were transformed into pocket landscapes, and soon, commissioners and their architects began to design houses and grounds together, on purpose (Loudon 1834). Granton Lodge, often ascribed to Archibald Simpson, is an almost textbook case (Figs 6.9 and 6.10). It has always been within walking distance of the city, and yet, its architectural form, addressing three fronts indifferently, and is major reception room as it were bulging out into the adjacent garden is a new way to design the house. It also is more specific, even scientific, in its internal planning (Gallet 1972). The tensions that this form will bring to urban planning do not become apparent in Aberdeen. Almost uniquely the forms and notions of these suburban houses and landscapes are simply absorbed into another form of urbanity by the expanding town.

Dalmunzie House on Deeside is in one of the railway suburbs, Milltimber and was essentially an estate scale suburban house. It is an early work by A Marshall Mackenzie with John Morgan. It is about a mile north of the station in a wooded site with extensive views to the west. Its manner is similar to the slightly earlier romantic cottages, but it is also a *proper house* in the late

ARCHITECTURE FOR EVERYMAN 183

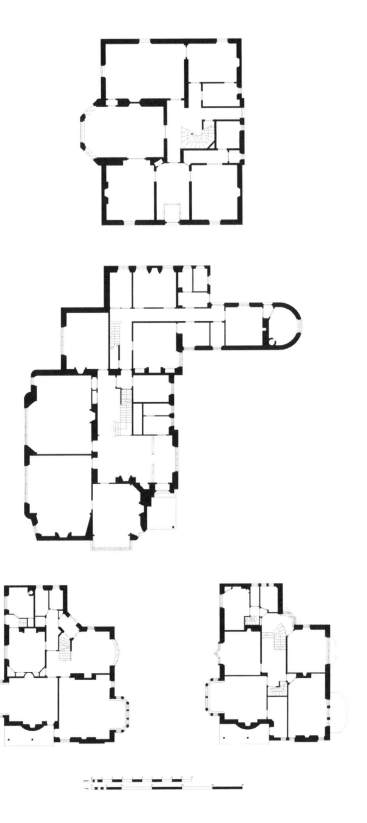

6.9 *Houses*, Granton Lodge, Dalmunzie House, 2 Devanha Gardens ground and upper floors

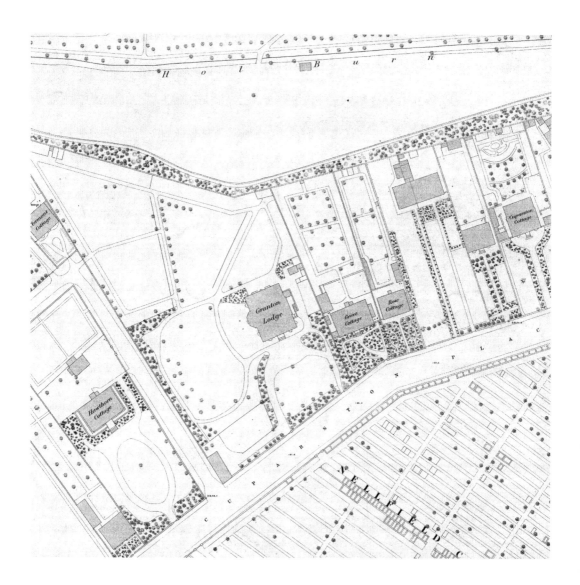

6.10 Granton Lodge with other early 19th century suburban pocket-estates, from the first edition Ordnance Survey

Victorian sense with ample rooms and services. It was commissioned by the Hadden family and appears to be their last contribution to Aberdeen. Provost Hadden was the industrialist whose giant factory dominated the Green in the late 18th century, and who served his time as Trustee for the New Streets and also as Provost. Dalmunzie looks to the 20th century and seems much more modern than its date 1884 would suggest. Its suite of reception rooms is strung out along the west and south fronts, and their individual functions follow the day and sun in an almost text-book like manner. From the cosy, if grand, hall for any up so early, light floods in from the east across a screened lobby. Immediately south is the morning room, by lunch-time the south facing dining room calls, and its neighbour the drawing room would do for afternoon visits. The west facing smoking room is tucked away at the corner with the service wing. All these rooms are fitted out with the same care the architect gives to their placement. Similarly fastidious are the chambers above, used for reading, private musing and sleeping. The service rooms are designed with as much attention as the rest, discreetly detached and yet in full view of the family's coming and goings. Garden grounds lie to the south and west. Dalmunzie represents the *beau ideal* of the comfortable gentleman's house well into the 20th century.

Ross Macmillan's 2 Devanha Gardens West, Ferryhill is the architect's own more Arts and Crafts (Cumming 2006) statement for himself and potential clients of how a more suburban version of Dalmunzie might be designed. It occupies the recently feued-out grounds of Devanha House, and nearly fills it plot. However its Dining Room, and above the family bedroom with adjacent open porch also overlooks the contemporary Bowling Green, leaving the two smaller and more public reception rooms to face conventionally into the street (Nicoll 1908). Despite its comfort and size it is a much smaller affair than Dalmunzie, and its planning therefore has to be tighter and even more ingeniously managed. Evidence of that can be seen specially in the manner of how the entrance serves equally the Reception Hall, the kitchen quarters, and the stair to the family rooms, giving each its appropriate place. The elevations demonstrate a similar ingenuity in including and displaying gables and half timbering and the variety of different roof forms which can be deployed on a rectangular plan.

Littleways at Countesswells was built in 1934 by Leonard Stokes, then working with A.G.R. Mackenzie on the firm's reworking of three feus in Union Street West in their *art deco* Capital Cinema. His own house was, for him, rather more an essay in a sober version of the Modern Movement. Like Dalmunzie and Devanha Gardens the reception rooms are responsive to sun and view, and are combined into one along the west side of the plan with a kitchen (without staff) at the south end and all the paraphernalia of stairs, hall lavatories and corridors efficiently arranged along the east side, thus allowing the bedrooms also to enjoy maximum sunlight and view. The concerns for convenience are the same: however, there is more a whiff of science, and recognition of the value of sunshine and light for health that the Modern Movement wished to see adopted. Also, the simplification is greater here.

Never far from the most urban of Scots is the memory of the country and the farm. Aberdeen uniquely made the cottage into architecture. It employed the type to compose streets in regular compartments while its architects added decoration and elaboration to give greater significance and mansions begin to masquerade as cottages. As the smaller cottages group together, and put on this fancier dress, so the grander houses assume the forms of rural simplicity. The cottage abroad modified itself to reflect India, Australia or America and comes back home as the bungalow in the later 19th century, although the term is specifically used from the '20s and by the Second World War the local version had numbered into the thousands. The cottage is the primary building block of much of suburban Aberdeen. Its form here as in other parts of Scotland was

6.11 Old cottage type

a result of its modernization and improvement in the late 18th century from earlier forms. The type constitutes a rectangular plan, one storey with roof space (sometimes habitable), two rooms with fireplace at either end with a lobby and smaller room (without a fire) in the centre. Its construction is stone with timber linings; the timber roof is clad in stone slates. The elevation to the front is symmetrical with windows either side of the door. The windows are of timber, in sash and case format. A child's drawing of a house is often similar to a Scots cottage. When it has a central door and windows to either side it is known as a cottage; when door is to one side and the window on the other then it is know as a half-cottage. The type is capable of great variation: in plan it can be made deeper by addition of small rooms, or of larger ones, with a consequent enlargement of the roof space. This can be exploited by using it for bedrooms with combed (sloped) ceilings. If the rooms themselves become larger then the same additions begin to make a substantial house and with the addition of a sunken half basement even a mansion in a cottage style is possible, and remarkably, common.

Its lineage is fairly simple to trace. Its rectangular plan form is like the more primitive forbears whose traces can still be found in remoter districts. The Blackhouse/ Whitehouse is its sire. In this type a central entry leads to two divisions, one for beasts, and the other for the family. The family side had a central fire ventilated directly through the roof. In earlier forms the 'gable' ends are still somewhat rounded. The low walls are stone, found rather than worked and are dug into the ground. The roof is light timber carried on a couple, a cruck, or cruck-like member which helps to carry the lighter roof supports. The roof covering was thatch (often heather) and was brought down low over

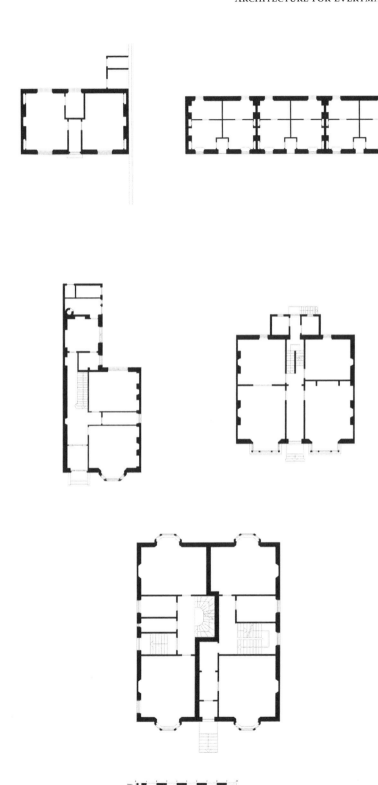

6.12 *Cottages*, typical, Broadford Cross-over, King Street, Carden Place and Carden Place at Prince Arthur Street

6.13 Cross-over Cottages at Gilcomston

the walls and with significant over-hang. The walls were doubled with rubble or rammed earth centres; the insides whitewashed. These buildings were in a real sense alive and if unattended they quickly rotted away. When well used, the constant fire (with its smoke) and the habitation of humans and animals, the wind, rains and damp were all kept in balance. The Whitehouse is of this same kind except there are chimneys, initially hanging lums (timber tubes in the roof) to encourage a draw on the fire and in due course mural fireplaces in what became gable ends. By this time beasts lived in byres, the stonework had become mortared and timber linings with air gaps behind and timber floors appear. In the late 18th century and into the 1830s, slate replaced thatch but was laid to overhang in a somewhat exaggerated manner in imitation. This soon disappeared in favour of the neater, sharper eaves usually with iron gutters to take off the water. Stonework becomes sharper also (lime washed or harled and later in ashlar blocks) with the sash windows regular in form and disposition; thus, the classic type appeared.

With the discovery of the ancient Neolithic houses at Scara Brae, Orkney (Fig. 6.1) it became clear that the pre-history of the Scots cottage was a very long one indeed. These had been buried by sands for millennia when a storm exposed them. What is left are the dug-in stonewalls, with stone framed 'furniture' in the form of protected bed spaces and press-like or cupboard like spaces. These houses presented rounded edges or ends. The roof and its character of course did not survive, but it is easy to imagine the light timber, perhaps supplemented by couples, with a thatch covering like cottages. We also know from recent archaeological discovery near Banchory that large complex buildings of timber superstructure similarly existed in the 2nd millennium BC. Scant evidence has ever been discovered to satisfactorily explain the crossover from these timber supported structures into stone ones, and thus into architecture. In fairness scant evidence has come to light anywhere for such a transition, a fact that has been accepted for some time. That Greek architects built in stone structures developed from earlier timber ones has been always accepted. Apparently it is not uncommon in ancient societies to observe that where a technology changes, the artefacts continue to be made in the old ways, and in response to methods that are now redundant. It is only later that the newer ways start to be reflected in the products. For reasons peculiar to classical Greece, the homes of heroes, the megaron of their mythic past, guides them to translate lighter timber construction into stone sanctuaries for religious observation. These were then refined into the marvellous marble constructions that have been admired ever since.

A possible cross-over has been discovered in Greece at an 8th to 6th century BC series of shrines to Apollo at Eretria, and at Euboia an even earlier hall-like building, apparently also a shrine, show how light timber constructions over a relatively short time, moved progressively from the rounded back end of a sanctuary, open at the other, with rows of posts to hold up a light roof, to first a more rectangular form then to a plan form almost identical to the classical ideal (Spawforth 2006: 22, 50). The same sort of progression can be traced from ancient houses to cottages, so is there the larger scale form from which an architecture might derive? The only type which might be a candidate at present is the enigmatic broch. Although there is ample evidence of a sensibility to the landscape and its design by the Caledonians, and although they too possessed large timber buildings there is no evidence presently of steps towards a monumental architecture of the kind developed in the Mediterranean. However the recent discoveries at Crathes suggest that evidence of such steps may be found (Murrays 2010).

There is much evidence about these house types, much of it of course adduced to show how miserable and poor they were as opposed to the modern forms built to take their places by the Improvers and their successors the stewards and servants of 19th century landlords. Certainly to come upon one of these houses in partial ruin but still recognizable would hardly tempt anyone to consider it habitable. But similarly coming across a corpse would hardly be conducive to imagining it as a cherished companion. The comparison to a live being is much more than a device of argument. Black houses were successful because they were a balance of living by humans and domestic beasts in often stormy and inhospitable environments with a severely limited range of materials with which to build, exacerbated by cultural forces and plain economic forces which discouraged permanence and solidity.

These houses, like their predecessors going back for millennia, were built into the ground, that is, one had to step down by several feet, perhaps as much as metre, into the actual houses from the ground outside. The purpose of that was to conserve heat, and to minimize the amounts of material to build the houses. To us this very feature suggests the primitive and the rising damp we associate with such construction. Similarly the arrangement of the walls, which were a mixture of stones, turf for the exterior, and available rubbish reinforced as possible for the cores, with some kind of relatively smooth human friendly finish to the interiors, also brings to mind extreme discomfort. What is missing, of course, is the life for these houses...the inhabitants and fire.

When heated, to serve the necessary needs of cooking, and any artefact making, and even the simplest kind of farming, then an environment conducive to comfort is more easily imagined. If this state were a permanent one, as it would need to be while these houses were used, then it is easier to see how the balance of habitation with its warmth came to be joined by the repulsion of bad weather and damp from the climate and the earth to make a perfectly good house. We can assume that ventilation took care of itself, and low light levels inside were solved by expectation and behaviour. The major difference between these houses and modern ones has to do with the time it is possible to leave them unattended.

The houses for tenants came to be built similarly. Therefore the early experiments in modernizing the basic house were very much part of the agricultural and landscape Improvements to which we can also trace developments in town design. The proto-type modern cottage was equally at home in the town as in the country, but it is in Aberdeen that the type is made into *urban architecture* as well. No where else is the cottage adopted so whole-heartedly, or managed so skilfully to compose streets and places. The type appears in publications such as Wood's *Architecture*, one of the many pattern books available to house-wrights architects and landowners at the end of the 18th century (Maudlin 79 *et seq*.). In plan these houses all have an entry at the centre of the long front, often by way of a porch with its doorway to the side in country settings. The entry leads to a small lobby, from which two rooms (or suites) are reached. To one side is the living room, also called the kitchen. This will have its own large sash and case window (sometimes two) and substantial fireplace, normally with its iron stove built-in. Adjacent (and sometimes with in the same space) will be a scullery with sink, sometimes also a bath-room, and often a bed chamber. To the other side of the lobby will be the other half of the house, normally a parlour with fireplace and press, and often a further smaller chamber opening off it. Above in the roof space is the loft for sleeping, or storage. This may be reached by a staircase from the lobby. Earth closets, or water closets, are outside, usually to the rear.

In Aberdeen this double fronted type occurs, but the favourite alternative is the half-cottage. The doorway is to one side and leads to a lobby or stair hall, with two rooms, parlour to front and kitchen to rear, and two and three rooms in the roof space above. The roof space in the Aberdeen examples becomes equal even dominant. What had been secondary and somewhat marginal spaces for simple sleeping, lighted if at all by very small gable windows, become full working stories by the 1830s. Early examples of simple dormer windows grow quickly into slightly bowed wider ones, and then into the canted bay three part feature, the piended dormer, almost large enough in itself to count as a *room*. These can be found all over Scotland, but are an urban characteristic in Aberdeen.

In Ferryhill behind its own common garden realized as a tiny village green is an instantly successful and potent new form. Marine Place is a row of identical fronted half cottages. Unlike their superior neighbours whose front stonework is ashlar granite blocks, these houses are in rubble with window and door cases built in worked smooth granite. They are raised slightly to allow for a service floor below, but this is disguised on the north, show front, to further their cottage like manner. This is carried further in the front reception room where the one large window, rather in French window fashion shown by their low sills and the lay light style of glazing bars suggests a more direct access to the outside. At the rear of the row there are the broad sunk courtyards, exactly the reverse of Marine Terrace. Also to the rear are two other rooms, while in the roof space are two to three spacious rooms, lit by the three part piended dormers.

This is the type of dwelling, often paired with taller tenement blocks, which becomes the material for the streets of Victorian Aberdeen, and enjoys significant revival in the 20th century. The materials used in this type of building are masonry walls, often with lime *harled* finish, later in Aberdeen more often in dressed granite. Roofs are slated, and architectural ornamentation varies from minimal at the beginning of the 19th century through various styles mirroring current fashion, such as crow stepped gables, or castle-like features, or in the 1930s *art moderne* elements. Also in the '30s there are experimental steel, timber and concrete forms of wall construction.

The early Aberdeen street of aspiration, its Quality Street equivalent to the ubiquitous Grand, Monument, Sunset or Hillsborough Streets of similar American cities, is Carden Place. Here, it joined the still industrial Gilconstom and the ancient road to Skene and defined the north edge of James Skene's developments. The half cottage is employed in a number of smaller ventures by house wrights to the south whereas on the north side of the Skene Road, as close to the city as is practicable, are individual houses on feus large enough for setbacks, gardens and for space to either side. It is here that the potential buyers for the houses of Marine Terrace choose to settle. The form they choose is not the mansion house, but the cottage, and that remains the preferred form until, rather later in the 19th century after the extension of the Skene Road as Queens Road, the mansion house form takes over.

In their size form and disposition these house are almost identical to Simpson's Marine Terrace. But they are detached from their neighbours, they front a road rather than a place or street, and their gardens are no longer jointly held (even if enclosed by iron-railings and locked) but are individual. Carden Place is where the suburban ideal begins. Seemingly typical of these is at the corner of Prince Arthur Street and Carden Place where there is a large raised double cottage with big piended dormers in the roof. It is rendered in granite blocks and smooth white dressings and stands in its own, if relatively

6.14 Carden Place early 1860s

small, garden ground. While it is not unusual in Aberdeen, anywhere else its true nature would be considered a great fall from grace. Because it is, and always has been, two mansion houses occupying one big cottage (Fig. 6.12).

The *front* door, that is, the one in the centre of the Carden Place frontage leads to a lobby and stair hall as would be expected: it also serves an ample establishment over three full floors. Its neighbour within the same building occupies the smaller half to Carden Place, but is entered from a significantly larger front to Prince Arthur Street, where what might have appeared as the service entry for the whole building is clearly demarcated as of equal status by its size and the signals of its design. Its house also is arranged over three full floors and offers the same kinds of accommodation. It is true that Carden Place responded to the same changing fashions as occurred elsewhere in the world. As has been noted already Kelly had converted one of these large cottage style houses into the more fashionable mansion house mode early in the 20th century; and the earliest of the Carden Place houses at its south east connection with the city, had become first consulting rooms for its medical resident, and later a school and then a series of flats: yet nothing seems to have diminished its, or its neighbours' comfort in their choice of home. As is apparent here and elsewhere the pattern of personal occupation and the pattern of architectural occupation follow different rules in Aberdeen.

The cottage, of course, has a strong appeal to many in Great Britain, where its comfort cosiness and lack of pretention has a long and rich presence especially of a literary kind. Partly in that role it also enjoyed a very bright flowering as a less pretentious mode of good living in the later 18th century. This was mostly carried out in the south, in the West Country of England, and in parts of Ireland near Cork: it also, famously figured in France. The agent of much of that fashion was one of the daughters of the Duke of Gordon, who as Duchess of Bedford built a small if rambling thatched and decidedly informal house in Somerset. It was sufficient for her needs as an occasional residence, and could easily accommodate many guests. But it had no significance as a seat of power and in no sense rivalled any of the family's territorial houses. Yet its appeal was clear and strong: its informality being chief. Her architect John Nash had also built at Blaise near Bristol a modern *hamlet* where the estate staff were accommodated in a series of small individually designed essays on the English cottage style, around an informal village green.

Characters in contemporary fiction, such as in Austen's *Persuasion* give a very convincing voice to its power to charm, echoing in much more fashionable terms the appeal voiced a century earlier in *The Choice*, the most popular daydream poem of the 1700s where modest wealth, peace of mind, tranquillity and simplicity are valued above all else. As early as 1715 in the first edition of his *Vitruvius Britannicus* Colen Campbell had given architectural expression to such ideas in his design for Ebberston Lodge in Yorkshire which is not only the earliest expression of the modern cottage as type, but was also designed in a landscape setting of similar intent and of scale. The cottage, in modern terms or as *pastiche*, had a great deal to recommend itself to builders and residents of early 19th century Aberdeen, and they adopted its modern form with gusto. Both Simpson as we have seen at Ferryhill, and Smith used the cottage form to suggest a villa or small country house. The Cottage for Mrs Yeats of Auquharneys (Miller 2006, Fig. 6.0) stood on Wellington Place (now the corner of Holburn Street and Justice Mill Lane) until it was demolished in the 1890s. It was in many respects a full or double cottage, and had that level of accommodation. Like many others it was raised to allow for a service floor. Its great difference and perhaps the explanation for its special appeal lay in the treatment of the roof. Instead of having living space between the gable ends it dispensed with both, and substituted a low piended roof. This had the effect of making the house individual an effect increased by the comfortable overhang of the roof on all sides. Not only is such a from inappropriate to join to others in a row, it also reinforces the idea of a small and complete work, something like a pavilion to be viewed from several if not all sides. Its finishing in ashlar granite and its precisely detailed openings set it apart as a house of quality.

Smith's essays in this mode, apart from his augmenting of Willowbank for his in-laws the Gibbs, sought to reconcile the needs of a large-ish suburban or country establishment, but reduce its apparent size, and give it the air of cottage simplicity. His St Machar Cottage (now called Tillydrone House) like its more suburban neighbour Balgownie Lodge (Miller 2007) does this by not only by concealing the service rooms in a semi-basement but by enlarging the rectangle of the floor plan to allow for more rooms. Yet all these houses present themselves as cottages and as symbols of all that that designation carried with it.

The stylistic history of bungalows is neither a clear nor a direct one, and there is good reason to doubt even their linguistic lineage. The name was clearly a popular one in the earlier 20th century, and has been defined as a one story house of light construction deriving from India, specifically Bengal. However, there are few if any houses in Bengal which look like bungalows and those which are so called look more like an Aberdeen cottage such as Miss Yule's. For example the Aberdeen firm of Catto's housed some of its senior employees in Bengali bungalows in the period before and after the last war. These are low, one story white houses with low pitched roofs and large openings shaded by louvered shutters. The interiors were lofty, shaded and relatively cool. The disposition of façade and plan was symmetrical and the main reception room was like a lofty internal court, as if Smith had put a roof on his St Machar cottage design.

What is more likely is that 18th century British visitors and residents of Bengal used the same architectural sources and memory they brought with them and accommodated themselves to life on the Hugli accordingly. Calcutta was as civilized and comfortable in these times as anywhere else in the world, and its climatic directives had already been managed by Palladian style houses as the many published views of them in the period attests. So the Catto bungalows of the 1940s were just what they seemed…comfortable cottage style houses adapted to a hot and humid climate. Already in the 1780s William Urquhart had designed a similar climate friendly house for the family plantation of Craigston in the West Indies (Slade 1984). The export of such houses from these islands had occurred as well. When Bonaparte was imprisoned on St Helena his house was designed by William Atkinson, who had been working for Scott at Abbotsford. It was pre-fabricated and shipped abroad for the late Emperor's use. Its form had no crow-steps or other Scottish features; rather the neo-classical cottage style that Smith and Simpson also used was employed. The house was essentially a bungalow, broad low, squareish in plan with large openings shaded by louvered shutters.

Other warm and moist climates brought forth similar kinds of house to make residents comfortable. The Queensland House as it is known in Australia, is a four square raised cottage under a piended roof: similarly on the coast of the Gulf of Mexico there are many Raised Cottages, as they are called there and elsewhere in the American South (Swain 40). These too share the same characteristics. These later buildings are 19th century ones and therefore should be seen as potential products of the growing publication of pattern books, increasingly not only for house-wrights or landowners but becoming genuinely popular. Until the 1830s these were British in origin but also available in America and of course the Empire. From mid century the traffic in these publications becomes international and the UK is as apt to be influenced by them as much as setting the standards it had done hitherto.

In earlier buildings which were more the product of conforming to new climatic and cultural forces using the *vernacular* skills of emigrant tradesmen and occasionally of commissioners of buildings with some education in architecture there are also indications of more rather than less similarity of form. In Louisiana the raised cottage form developed through the 18th century into a recognizable local sub-type. There the service floor was at ground level, not sunken, with reception rooms on the floor above. The plan forms remained the same, as did the American habit of continuing the roof-line to form contiguous sheltered *rooms* outside. These variously were known as *piazzas*, galleries or porches on the Atlantic coast; and *corridores* in Spanish America. The difference in Louisiana was simply that the galleries often went around the entire building, at both levels, and characteristically from a hipped or piended roof, thus giving yet another version of a vernacular bungalow.

However, in terms of the popularity of the bungalow throughout the world in the early 20th century it is the more ordinary colonial American cottage that acts as proto-type and spur. The pattern for American houses was established by the 17th century although very few of these originals have survived. Sometimes these were quite substantial brick built structures like for example the Newbold-White house in the Albemarle section of North Carolina but lighter timber structure were much more common, and these were known in the UK as *Virginia houses*. The forms and plans of these houses were the same as those from whence the immigrant had come, whether embarking from Plymouth, or Stonehaven. These by then old American houses began to be noticed as interesting and antique from the beginning of the 19th century, when their wholesale neglect began to be regretted. Images of these are published in popular and illustrated papers and periodicals.

By that time none of these survivors remained pure to its origin. Early on they began to have *lean-to* simple additions, and these developed into more substantial porches, which in turn were transformed by the addition of *piazza-rooms*. So these buildings were revered for their complex form and ground hugging irregularity. Often the orientation changed so what had been the back became of primary artistic interest. There were houses built to commemorate the *Centennial* in Philadelphia as faithful replicas of colonial houses which nobody of the 18th or the 20th century would recognize. But these old and *impure* proto-types were much admired, and architects and builders began to produce designs for new houses in that style. It is from these that bungalows in the USA derive. These need not be one story and typically were not, always they were roof-dominant in appearance where large shed dormers lighting the roof space become a very prominent feature, and they always had porches (Hodgson 1916: 2061).

Architects and builders in Aberdeen responded to attitudes to similarly picturesque examples of earlier Scottish architecture in the latter part of the 19th century, mostly as aspects of the lessons of John Ruskin, and later of William Morris and his collaborators, and from these thoughtful designers and lovers of buildings everywhere began to appreciate good old work for both its picturesque qualities and for its craftsmanship. John Morgan, the builder of many excellent works in Aberdeen including the new frontage to Marischal College and his own house at 50 Queen's Road was a passionate devotee of Ruskin and fully a member of the Arts and Crafts movement. Morgan knew Canada and admired the timber framed, rambling and picturesque kinds of house he saw there, and built houses in similar vein such as Woodcote at Torphins (Fig. 6.15). Yet while there are elements which are shared with American work in his and other designers there it is not yet direct influence. Apparently somewhat more directly pertinent to the Aberdeen bungalow were the two big proto-types built at the turn of the new century by G. Fordyce, The Bungalow in Dyce and The Chalet on Anderson Drive: but as neither of these produced direct imitators their appeal must have been realized in other ways.

An important periodical which draws many of these strands together was *The Craftsman* published and largely written by Gustave Stickley. This

6.15 *Bungalows, Torphins, Anderson Drive, Garden Kingsgate, Bissett type*

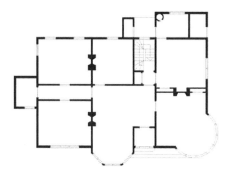
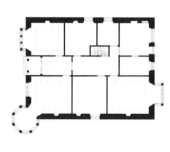

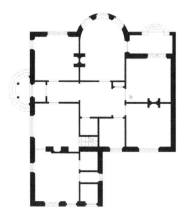

was a curious amalgam of Arts and Crafts theory, camping and a love of the outdoors as John Muir was teaching all to embrace, and examples of the appropriate style of furnishings and buildings for those so persuaded. Craftsman bungalows become a recognized and desirable type, not only for holidays but for year round living as well. Stickley's designs never gained the level of architecture, but two young architects from New England setting up practice in southern California partly for health reasons built a group of houses there which did raise Stickley's type, using Morris' and Ruskin's sanctity of material and craft to a high level of design quality. Their large 'bungalows' were in turn influential on many builders of small houses in Pasadena and Los Angeles and they strove for the kinds of effects that the Greene brothers had achieved, and to such an extent, that what had been an international quest for high style for small houses is realized in the Californian Bungalow. That becomes the marketable type from the 1910s onwards filtered through the studios and publishing houses of Chicago internationally, and incidentally as mute backgrounds in the motion pictures newly settled then in Hollywood (Stevenson and Jandl 1986: 205).

Aberdonians were as prone to these fashions as anyone and the earlier bungalows built at the beginning the 20th century reflect many of the conflicting impulses from international sources. But it did not take long for local concerns to produce an especially Aberdeen version of the bungalow, and that was of course largely the same as it had been when first introduced by Simpson and Smith, but with *mod cons*. The design of the house for J.H. Garden at the then extreme end of Kingsgate in 1922 has some of these characteristics but also exhibits a tendency to a more sober, almost classic, mien which soon becomes the standard again. Although the feu enjoyed an extraordinarily extensive view of Aberdeen bay the house resolutely ignores it, facing, as convention requires towards the street where the drawing room flanked by dining room and bedroom present the face to Aberdeen (Kingsgate 1). The entrance however is in the centre of the west side, with only enough space left for the drive to reach a garage at the back of feu. Slightly larger than the standard plan, and designed for the client by an unknown architect, the house appears to cater for a couple with servants, perhaps recently returned from service abroad. A housekeeper or couple might have occupied the small bedroom in the roof. Certainly the living room kitchen and access to the upper floor form a convenient suite to serve the primary apartments which are arranged as the three rooms fronting Kingsgate plus the lobby, inner hall and a further bedroom and bathroom. The whole plan is almost a square, with only the vestigial *veranda* off the front bedroom and perfectly uselessly facing north onto Kingsgate, and a short service wing to the back departing from it. The plan may well have been produced by the clients from a magazine for building here. But taken altogether it represents a gentleman's residence, if marginally so.

In the interwar period the bungalow is the house type of choice for those able to buy their own houses, and it carried that extra significance then appearing to signify that its residents were just that superior. There were some other types more like the cottages of old or of other parts of the UK such as those built for the Aberdeen Garden City company in part of old Ashley Park: these are essays, by Duncan Macmillan in an Arts and Crafts mode, which though perfectly acclimatized to Aberdeen would not look out of place in the Home Counties.

As was common elsewhere in the early 20th century small individual houses for sale were provided by a series of builders companies (Glendinning and Waters 1999), such as Bissets', who preferred to build in small groups such as those beyond Anderson Drive in the extended Kingsgate designed by E.L. Williamson in 1937 (Kingsgate 2). These are a mixture, and not untypically, of detached and semi-detached houses. They all have set-back gardens to the front, neither large nor small, a minimum distance separates the house from their neighbours, with just enough space for a car to pass, and for access to be gained to the kitchen, called scullery and in fairness of that size. They provided the by then almost universally desirable garden-suburban environments, at a somewhat smaller scale (Greeves 1975 and Harris and Berke 1997). There are two rooms facing the front, both with a shallow bay window. One is the reception room, its opposite the main bedroom. There is a further bedroom at the back, a bathroom and stairs leading up to the loft which in this group contains another bedroom and box rooms. The upper bedroom is lit by a large centrally place dormer window, almost invariably with a flat roof. Heating is supplied by two fireplaces, and sometimes a boiler at the rear, and the chimneys for these are expressed as tall thin granite clad shafts.

Variations by this builder, or others, would include a superior front door in teak, superior timber for the bay windows, occasionally a bay window could be provided in the space of the rear bedroom transforming that into a morning room. Other builders offered overhangs to the front and part-way along the sides only. Into the '50s overhangs become a positive design feature and are quite deep: also in these houses there is extra width, and clearly they were seen to be like the *ranch* houses then in vogue in the USA or Canada. Construction of the bungalows includes granite ashlar, to the front and rubble elsewhere under slated (very occasionally tiled) roofs. Earlier houses were sometimes harled, and were enriched by the local version of half-timbering expressed as a light screen of timbers standing proud of the enriched gable; but these are more a hangover from Edwardian modes into the '20s.

But many such houses were also built by the City Architects Department to let, and the arrangements for allocating these, and establishing rentals was a City function rather than a market one, and therefore to a degree also political. Early schemes such as the Garden City part of Torry by William Kelly use the national that is UK or English type of design, the Westminster parliament had in mind when it allocated funds to local authorities for building house to rent (Hebbelthwiate 1987). By rendering these in white harl Kelly manages to make them Aberdonian. By the 1930s both private builders and the City had hit upon a design for a modern cottage, to type certainly and similar enough to national types to pass, and yet with more than a little Aberdeen in its nature. These can be found at Kaimhill, also in the southern parts of Torry and later near Cults.

Leslie Rollo was in private practice as an architect: he was also Head of the School of Architecture, and seems to have acted as consultant to the City Architects Department. His precise role in the design of Kaimhill is not as clear as we might wish. Certainly the *Master of the Kaimhill cottages* deserves much credit. The design is like many others two rooms and scullery downstairs with two bedrooms and bath upstairs, and yet there are no mistakes, no niggling cuttings of corners, or of letting something just adequate to pass. The trick is in the site planning and the section mostly: here the gable is rendered as a perfect equilateral triangle which gives the whole building a substance and solidity any other angles would deny it. These strong roofs, whether clad in slates or red tiles (and these houses are experimentally rendered in granite, white harl over bricks, or concrete, cedar shakes on timber frame) satisfy the architectural critic, as does the balance of wall to window in the arrangements below. The cottages are arranged in pairs, or short terraces, and often these units are joined by garden walls separating fronts and rears which further help to unify the whole ensemble. The windows are glazed in 1930s fashion as horizontal strips of glass held in place by painted steel. Especially in the use of the design by private builders for sale these windows are also often finished as curves. In the for sale groups the front room of the cottage is called *The Lounge*, whereas in the local authority rented ones the same room is designated as Bedroom.

Housing schemes in the city were composed of cottages, rows of tenements and four apartment blocks, generally in a Garden City configuration. However from 1959, with Ashgrove Court, the tall building is introduced to the city, now aware of LeCorbusier's (since the early '20s the chosen name of the Swiss architect and theoretician Charles Eduard Jeanneret) writings from the '20s, and of Swedish and English experiments of the '50s. As modern as the Modern Movement ever became in Aberdeen Ashgrove exhibits a certain reticence to accept the style fully that was not British (Lettstrom 1950 and Smiley 2001). It was painstakingly designed by Jean Crann working in the city Architects Department and remains exemplary. So too do the first of the city centre high blocks on Castlehill, Virginia and Marischal Courts of the early '60s. These are much more indebted to LeCorbusier's seminal Unite d'Habitation of 1948 where a favourite trope of the times…the complex planning to provide double aspects for the flats, and floor-division between reception rooms and bedrooms; they also have balconies. The most distinguished of the schemes is Hazelhead. This occupies the northern edge of the landscaped grounds of the country house previously on the site. It provides houses and flats with integral shops and services into a composed and thoroughly designed grouping contemporary with and comparable to the famous West End scheme in the Garden City satellite Otoniami near Helsinki.

Following these examples, political forces intervened: and subsequent high flats were versions of one of these excellent prototypes, made progressively cheaper and with limited attention to detail or appropriate landscaping. Yet,

6.16 *High flats,* Ashgrove and Kepplestone

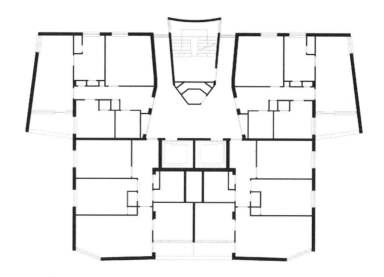

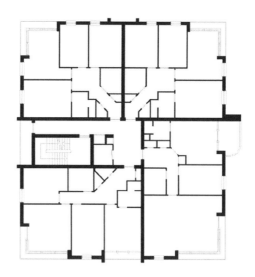

living in these high flats in Aberdeen is not seen as social condemnation as it is in other British cities. A reason for this circumstance may be that in Aberdeen the high flats are mixed into the heart of the town where there are some of the biggest and earliest of the schemes. They are found as well along the northern ridge behind Forrester Hill, at the head of the Kings Links and as later towers in the shopping precincts of earlier Garden Cities like Kincorth and Mastrick. There was an effective maintenance programme for these buildings and a careful manner of allocation of tenants. Movement between schemes was regulated by locally monitored exchange. All these factors are suggestive but in reality it seems to be that Aberdonians, like New Yorkers, have never thought of high flats as a demeaning way to live.

Ashgrove Court was designed as a *tower in landscape* at the extreme northwestern edge of the old Ashgrove estate one of the many small lairdships on the edges of the city, smaller country houses in their extensive grounds, but not yet the fully fledged landed estate of power. The site therefore came not only with a name and a history but also plantation of trees forming parks with the whole set off by stone walls...a *place* rather than a building site. Clearly the City Architects Department thought long and hard about this new departure, the kind of design young architects had been contemplating since the '30s. LeCorbusier, who had proposed the radical reorganization of modern cities based on skyscraper blocks in a Gallic version of the Garden City. His ideas were published in *Vers une Architeture* in 1923 with further elaboration as his *plan Voissin* the first of many and the most influential of ideal schemes for living taking motor transport as determinant. He was hardly alone. In 1933 the architecture show at the Museum of Modern Art in New York, *The International Style* (Hitchcock and Johnson 1966) had included a design by Raymond Hood for *An Apartment Tower in the Country* (Kilham 1973). This provided a proto-type for Ashgrove Court. But where Hood provided a tower of three stepped parts in plan (and with flats occupying two stories) Ashgrove has the three and four room flats common to Aberdeen in an inflected plan: in both cases the plan was arranged to take maximum advantage of aspect and view. There had been experiments of high flats in parkland at Roehampton, near London in the earlier '50s as well as the Highpoint blocks of Highgate (see above) but these like LeCorbusier's were in slab configuration. Jean Crann, working under both A.B. Gardner and his successor George Keith as City Architects produced a tight and elegant plan of four flats per floor in a modified fan arrangement, served by an enclosed staircase and two lifts which opened onto a small yet naturally lit lobby. Each flat had a fitted kitchen lit by the contiguous balcony (both for clothes drying and for leisure use) which opened off the living room. The living rooms had the advantage of views in two directions. A bathroom and one or two bedrooms opened off the lobby leading from the entrance. When finished Ashgrove Court was opened to a curious public who queued down the road as far as Westburn Park waiting for the pleasure of viewing the flats. The block was an instant success and has remained so, and in pristine condition.

When designed Hazelhead lay at the terminus of the tramway, on land acquired by the city, first as recreational grounds, for golf for instance, and for the pleasures of the mature woodlands of the old estate. These had been landscaped in their present form in the 1840s by James Forbes Beattie (TCP H 8 and 9). The north rim of these woods was selected as perfect site for a designed community of houses, flats in tenements and in high blocks, with at least some provision also for shopping. Scandinavian *modernism* exerted an appeal to British politicians and designers, probably largely because it appeared to be less extreme than some other Continental work. Professional exchange visits were commonplace in the post-war period, and it has to be acknowledged Scandinavian designers and reformers had themselves been interested in British garden cities for much of the 20th century. When Helsinki decided to rebuild itself in stone in the 1890s it was to Aberdeen that they came for advice and for ideas (Ringbom 1987). Therefore when Hazelhead was being designed in the early 1960s it seems entirely appropriate that the favour was returned, and that Otoniami, became the model: in the '50s and '60s there was none better.

In Forbes Beattie's reworking of the Hazelhead design he overlaid the earlier Scottish design of rectilinear parks conforming to topography, in favour of a more English and informal landscape style of woodland. The architects working of the housing scheme recombined the rectangles for two groups of linked houses separated by an open clearing with a series of informally placed square towers and mature trees. The rectangular parts contain rows of two story family houses seemingly enclosing short squarish blocks of flats. But none of these enclosures is complete…rather they meander and while giving promise of geometrical resolution of purity it never comes as such, although the regularity does. This seems slightly confusing to visitors but is easily navigated. Accommodation is provided in the standard ways of one and two bedroom flats, with houses sometimes providing for larger families but generally giving typical living spaces. All these provisions would have been calculated on norms and manifest local need.

There is an observable change in architectural expression at Hazelhead, modernist still but less attenuated and elegant than Ashgrove; here more robust and sculptural, almost *butch*. So the bases of the towers are expressed as several times apparently deeper than absolutely necessary, and dormer windows not only break forward from the line of the façade but also protrude into the roof in an expressive and almost graphic contrast. Such aesthetics were the result of local young architects, more mature and with war experience entering into leadership roles in practice. They had admired and studied local traditions of the North East coast, especially the fishing villages where such expressive contrast of form and particularly of colour could be found, and they wished somehow to see these attractive elements become part of new work. Basil Spence (Spence 2007: 41) had shown how this might be done in his additions to Fife fishing villages with local authority houses in the '50s, and James Paul in practice in Dundee, and indeed nearby at the hotel at Mastrick, and Ian Paterson in his painting and teaching in Aberdeen produced work of this kind. And so do the younger designers in the City Architects Office team at Hazelhead.

Since the mid-18th century a Barracks had occupied Castlehill. This was regular and classically Georgian, but purely military without any castle-air. Its shallow U shaped plan faced due south. It was demolished in the 1950s and caused little regret or outcry. The Citadel had long before formed the climactic and theatrical end to the Castlegate and Union Street, and the scenographic possibilities of the prominent empty site to its east were not lost on the City Architects Department who designed the two large slab blocks completed in 1969. These are two of a large group of similarly designed blocks built on various sites on the edges of the ancient city centre during the '60s, and being completed by 1978. The group of four at Gallowhill and Mounthooley at the north end of Gallowagate are perhaps the most LeCorbusier-like and when viewed from north in the park-land which Mounthooley has been transformed into recall his own images of *la ville radieuse*. There too the scale and mass can, as intended, be appreciated while manoeuvring the dual carriageways of the eastern and northern quadrants of a mercifully incompleted ring-road, adjacent to the slums cleared from the slopes from either side of the Gallowgate from the 1890s onward.

On closer inspection, even at middle range for example from the parking area adjacent to the King Street supermarket, wisely sited as an urban building there but on the west side share the aesthetics of simplicity and speed, they appear less oppressive and dystopian…more dynamic and exciting as compositions. Closer still the skills in site planning and the hard and soft landscaping comes into play, and areas of calm, with sunny places to sit outside, and where dramatic views outward over the city are formed. These are especially well done at Castlehill where the old ramparts make a fine raised terrace to view the harbour below, while also forming an enclosed and protected playground and entry *court* for the flats. The modulation of spaces from the east end of Union Street through the Castlegate by Justice Street into the precinct of the flats is very well managed. As places to live these more urban blocks have an *edge* lacking at Ashgrove, but are just as comfortable as residences. The Castlehill blocks have corridors at every third floor with a scissors-like arrangement in section which allows each house to face both north and south, or east and west. The living rooms are at one floor level, and the bedrooms on another mimicking a conventional house, but lodged in the super-block. LeCorbusier had pioneered this scheme at the Unite d'Habitation in Marseilles of 1948; it has to be admitted more elegantly than here. The blocks here are raised up above the terraces at entry level by sculpted *piloitis* the idea being to allow the garden ground to flow under the buildings as well as around them. The chunky texture of the gable ends made up of rough granite stones held in large concrete frames echo a similar aesthetic observed at Hazelhead, here in *beton brut*.

The 1970s saw the end of local authority work in providing houses, and when in the '90s there was significant new work appearing not only had aesthetics changed…the Modern Movement had become despised by the press certainly, and even questioned by the thoughtful… recent contributions to domestic architecture in the city have been tamer, market driven essays in McMansions which are neither one thing or another in terms of style, and there has been a more welcome return to building houses in compartments, though sadly yet without the quality of their forbears. There has also been much reinforcement of the architecture of streets, as for example along the Beach Boulevard and some admirable work in tenement making at Kittybrewster, and the surprising flowering of tall blocks of flats for sale…at Elmhill, along the Dee, and most surprising of all on Queen's Road at Anderson Drive. Here it would appear the Modern Movement is back to stay, at what the taxi-drivers refer to as Tillydrone West.

In terms of *style* the high blocks would pass as modernist, and their placement along the north and east sides of the large site certainly commands attention to them, so that their large areas of glass, and expression as steel framed towers, with busy and angular roof forms put them in a family of easily recognized late 20th century modern buildings. The flats on the top floors, the penthouses, are decidedly metropolitan with double height spaces and gently curved staircases, recalling High Point and numerous films of the 1930s with their *smart* and sophisticated settings. For the rest, indeed even for these, what is on offer are two bedroom apartments, at four units per floor, like the early high flats at Tilllydrone, Kincorth and Mastrick which were the modified versions of Jean Crann's Ashgrove. At Queen's Road extra space is gained by generous areas, and by eliding the living room with the kitchen to make a more generous reception room.

But for the site and project as a whole the designers have sought to bring the best thought about neighbourhood making to bear. The foot print of the towers and their spacing echoes those of their neighbours, the Edwardian to art deco villas nearby, many of which had become apartment blocks themselves. The interior of the site is organized around a central axis which has not only a sense of grand entry, but is spatially modified as it passes into the site, which is composed of rows of town houses in terraces, a crescent and finally a square made up of tenement flats. At the extreme lower edge are the McMansions which border a large group of '30s bungalows. Therefore they achieve a large quantity of new houses in a neighbourhood with its own character which also acknowledges its place in the town and in time, respects the character of the streets, or roads, it fronts, and tries to nestle into the planted landscape left by its predecessors Kepplestone House and the, genuinely if late, Modern Movement School of Domestic Science.

Granite City

At the beginning of the 20th century Great Britain was rich, confident and mistress of a worldwide Empire – acquired by warfare and defeat and by a willing association, a commonwealth of nations before Commonwealth replaced Empire. Aberdeen was comfortably associated with both the Empire, and the Union is built into the city. It too was rich and confident; any problems with its physical structure that lingered could be put right. With naval supremacy there was no empire effectively to challenge Britain's and few cities to ruffle Aberdeen's good sense of itself. Had it not contentedly welcomed the Monarch every summer for over fifty years on her way to her favourite home? Was it not the Silver City by the Silver Sea, the Granite City?

In common with other cities the conditions of living for the poor began to occupy Aberdeen, specifically as civic improvements generally had been seen to. Although Jack's Brae and Gilcomston had been decently masked by the Rosemount Entry project, much of their squalor remained as it did in the Gallowgate, Broadgate and Shiprow, as also in the Shorelands south of Castlegate, and the Barracks neighbourhood to its east. Together with the grubby industrial grounds from North Street toward the sea they were reminders that all might not be so well after all. Containing, and to an extent, masking the dirtier aspects of industry is an important factor behind the Rosemount Project and a similarly straightforward wish to see things in their appropriate places seems to have guided the development of the northern parts of King Street, until the later 19th century still known as King Street Road. In response to growth in the granite trade located in this part of the town blocks of lodgings to house an increasing population begin to appear in the 1880s, continuing, and revising the line of smaller granite houses of the Trustee type built by John Smith and others which had never grown as far north as the Aberdeenshire Canal. These usually two storey houses are replaced by four story blocks, some plain in the style of those near Rosemount, but most showing monumental pretensions as a more uptown kind of architecture appropriate to this, the relatively unfinished of the two New Streets. Immediately adjacent to these new blocks on the old King's Meadow, the large plain between the Gallowhill and King Street were the granite works, and other heavy industrial concerns.

7.1 Hardwierd

Typical of these new blocks is Washington Buildings at 198–212 King Street. (King Street 2) These were built for D. Courage, Spirit Merchant, by the firm of Brown and Watt in the early '90s. Concerns about over development, especially the overprovision of sprits storage caused the initial proposals to be declined, but the tenements were approved in due course. Their internal arrangements are a variation on the then standard type; an anonymous doorway, marked by piers, led to the staircase at the back, with access to the cellars at the rear and to water closets on the landings, and at each floor, four apartment and three apartment lodgings. The northern group presents this slightly different plan from the norm, and is blessed with a corner bay window rising into a turret, and topped by a witches-hat roof. Internally this supplemented the lighting of the room, whether used as parlour or for sleeping is not indicated. There were two bedrooms, the smaller at the rear without fireplace. The main 'living' room was the kitchen, also at the rear, and supplemented with a bed closet. The smaller lodging was arranged with only one bedroom fronting King Street, the same kind of kitchen at the back, plus a further bedroom opening off this in a short wing to the rear: it was also provided with a fireplace. In other blocks such wings are ascribed to sculleries, but apart from the kitchen the actual usage of these spaces varied to suit the tenants.

At the ground floor were a series of plate glass fronted shop premises. The architecture of the street elevation above this now dominant if transparent element is in the somewhat restrained manner of Brown and Watt. The ashlar is channelled to give a distinctly horizontal cast to the group of tenements. The fenestration is regular and enlivened only at the roof level where broad dormers sit under pediments. Typical of these more urban blocks is the gathering of the chimneystacks with window to produce a tympany-like feature. In multiple blocks such as Washington Buildings this further varies the skyline and provides a more complex rhythm. The turret at the north-west corner finishes the composition and is the only non-classical element.

These new blocks of lodgings, known from the '90s as tenement blocks, were built as individual enterprises with the lodgings rented out to tenants, an investment, in the terms of the times 'as safe as houses'. On Urquhart Road, running eastward from King Street towards the new City Hospital was a different kind of enterprise. Equally convenient to the granite yards and other industries along the old canal route and the Town's Links, these very plain dwellings in typical Aberdeen tenement format were initiated by the Aberdeen Building Company in 1886 (BW Urquhart Road). They were subsequently carried on by the Town Council by John Rust who from the late '90s is styled City Architect, a term not recently employed. Provision of houses to rent by the Council is characteristic of the period following the First World War: these are exceptionally early. The earliest are the most severe; three-storey rough granite ashlar. The masonry was admired by a visiting group of architects from Helsinki who called it Aberdeen coursing, large blocks separated by three stacked smaller blocks; in these houses the only relief from the minimalist aesthetic (Ringbom 1987). Windows are arranged regularly with the doorway at centre. There was no enrichment at eaves level, and roofs were utterly plain: what a century before was decent modernity, was now clearly more a commentary on frugality and charity. The internal arrangements were simple: short passage to stair from which are two or three apartment lodgings with kitchens, with bed closets to rear. Water closets were on the landings. No shops were planned, although a small workshop was indicated at the corner block. As Rust took over the project and added further blocks standards of ornamentation and style begin to rise. The secondary bedroom in the three-apartment lodging has a fireplace, and the chimney for this addition is expressed at the centre of the front as a minimal tympany gesture. Later this is given a pair of scrolls and quadrant supporting brackets. The sash windows are divided in Edwardian fashion with small panes above plate glass. A shop is indicated at a corner, but these are clearly still to be seen, as the drawings indicate as Workmens (*sic*) Dwellings.

The *British Medical Council* held a meeting in Aberdeen to address public health, not because the city was in particular need of attention but rather to honour its well deserved and growing reputation in addressing public health issues. Overcrowding and its consequent contagion occupied these medics. To them clean water, fresh and easily circulating air uncontaminated by smoke and coal dust, and sunlight were desirable, but all were impossible to achieve in a densely populated old neighbourhood crowded with traffic. All and sundry were crammed together, where work and living often occupied the same space or were perilously close together. Perhaps it was the overcrowded neighbourhoods that gave rise to sickness. Thus the foundation of modernity was promulgated in Aberdeen, to a population keen to address any lingereing civic ills.

7.2 Gallowgate from Upper-kirkgate corner

A scant fifty years later the city suffered the indignity of demonstrating just how gravely weak that foundation was when a West End butcher's shop which served only the best neighbourhoods poisoned a small city. By then the old neighbourhoods were gone, ruthlessly cleared, usually with little idea in advance of what was to take their places: Broad Street and the Guestrow empty and turned into parking lots; Shiprow empty; Gallowgate shortly to be almost entirely cleared. The benefits an ancient town and its old neighbourhoods brings to its own civilization and contributions to the culture of its neighbours and the world, was realized remarkably as late as the '60s with *The Life and Death of Great American Cities* by Jane Jacobs whose thorough critique of modern planning with its insistence on zoning (keeping house, workplaces, town centres distinct and separate) the primacy of fast transport, and building for the short term. These three fundamental flaws in modernist planning remain with us; while a style of building is almost universally condemned as though it were the cause.

That Aberdeen remains one of the most agreeable cities, with much of its past still in place is more to do with its long-term strengths rather than the

7.3 Gallowgate showing proposed demolitions

decisions it took in response to a modern movement not invented there, at a time when the town's good opinion of itself was undermined by the Great War, followed by the depression and a dawning recognition that the Empire was ephemeral. Its 20th century has now become its past too and there is much that is good about it, but the century came as a somewhat unpleasant surprise to Aberdonians and it is only recently that native confidence has returned.

There were two decisions by Government which struck at the root of Scottish ideas about urban design. Taxation policies of the Liberals, newly in power at the beginning of the century, had a deleterious effect on architectural practises already struck by the economic blow of the failure of the Bank of Glasgow. Whereas small often one-man practices had been common and useful in furthering the design quality of the tenement blocks built from the later 1880s, these dried up as an uneconomical enterprise. The most famous firm to be hit by the changes in taxation was Keppie Henderson and Macintosh in Glasgow, when Mackintosh had to withdraw. The other change was worse and presumably equally unintended; it was only partly governmental and pressed by convinced members of the profession of architecture with the newly established profession of town and country planning. It also had a trans-Atlantic aspect. The Garden City Movement (Tagliaventi 1994) had begun in the late 19th century through the writings of Ebenezer Howard in response to his assessment of the ills facing the English situation. In the Midlands and the North, fast urbanization had taken place with little planning and even without apparent concerns for the well being of the citizens. Various writers recognized these bad conditions but it was for Howard to come up with the simple, elegant and seemingly irrefutable solution. He proposed that a series of New Towns, altogether different from those of Edinburgh or Aberdeen, should be planned near the metropolitan areas of England. They would be distinct, separate, and self-sustaining although connected to the cities by railways. They would have their own industries and these would be planned so as to avoid both the contamination which was obvious and with the dangers of pollution that shortly followed. These settlements would be on the small side, some 40,000 residents, and they would be organized, naturally enough for Howard, on the principles to be seen in old English villages and the smaller market towns. These still existed as examples, although many had been smothered by the northern conurbations.

Howard's ideas attracted a great following. Even a fondness for his diagram which he had been at pains to say was not a plan; soon the diagram found itself becoming just that. Advertisements for the newer suburbs in west London extolled the virtues of a clean, airy, open and safe lifestyle for families while still close enough by railway to the city. The ideals of garden city living permeated not only the relatively few actual new towns but fired the imaginations of many. English garden suburbs, as every one knows, are entirely suitable for England, perhaps also for Denmark where they were imported and to other continental European countries. Something like them was also built into the fabric of American life, soon also into Australia and New Zealand life, based as they were largely on homesteads and small farms. Somehow these essentially English ideas and solutions to problems became part of United Kingdom policy. One of the West Lothian questions this posed was why should solutions suitable to England be thought suitable also in Scotland? When it was proposed that an ordnance workforce be transferred from Kent to Lanarkshire at the beginning of the Great War, a number of these good people objected to having to go and live in the tenements they thought were everywhere in Scotland instead of the villages, to which they aspired but hardly were able to call home, in England.

Tenemental living began to achieve a very bad press indeed (Seiber 1994, Welter 1999). *Meitshauses* in Berlin and elsewhere on the continent and the grossly overcrowded tenements in New York City were held up as examples of bad planning and vicious policy by increasingly convincing writers – both in the political journals, and more widely in novels. Poor housing and bad neighbourhoods also became the stock for motion pictures. 'Tenement' simply became shorthand for bad housing. Urbanity appeared to be almost equally suspect in early 20th century Britain. Both these influences can be followed in the early textbooks about town planning (Unwin 1917) to which can be added the mindless curving of streets. Unwin and all his thoughtful fellow planners conceived a dislike for straight streets as being conducive of boredom, running against any idea of sympathetic working within existing landscape. This was partly a late hangover for the arguments rehearsed back in the 18th century against the formality of the French garden as opposed to the fluid

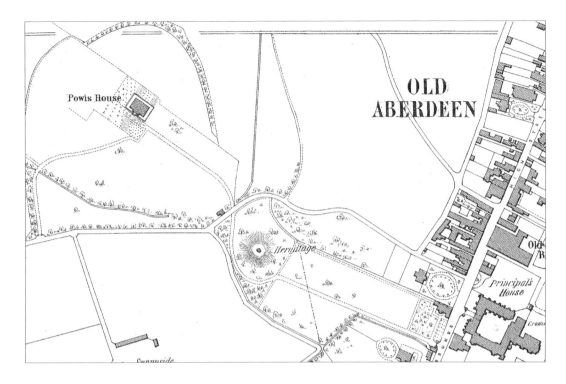

7.4 Powis House and Policies

naturalism of the English landscape gardens as created by Capability Brown and Humphry Repton. In hilly landscapes perhaps also in villages, Unwin had a point but his strictures against straight streets were so successful that these practically disappeared in the designs for extensions to towns. By the 1920s when housing was beginning to be provided by the local authorities, a new set of aesthetic principles surfaced, sanctioned and to a certain degree enforced by the Government (Gale 1949). No longer were streets of tall stone buildings enlivened by churches, schools and other public buildings where mixing shops and entrances to flats supplied the possibility of urban life. Obligatory front gardens, spaces between buildings, curving streets, and increasingly 'zoning' to insure that a section was either for houses or for work, became characteristic of the ideals of the time (Harpmann and Sutcoff 1999). As these were invariably on the edges of towns so they were distant from existing centres and by the very similarity of their designs, impoverished them.

It is remarkable that the 20th century development of Aberdeen was able to continue to thrive in such changed aesthetic circumstances. The slow re-establishment of the City Architect, first as consultancy from Dr William Kelly (Simpson 1949), then as Director of housing and finally with the City Architects Department under the direction of A.B. Gardner; these alien and essentially unsympathetic ideas were managed with great skill and grafted onto the ongoing design of the city. Sensibly, local authority housing was built near to the existing railways, tram and bus routes. Thus it was possible to continue to enjoy an urban life in the new estates although the fares were bitterly complained of and this would have been especially so for the residents of the schemes along the river Don, roughly centred on Woodside, but at least it was sufficiently developed to provide some interest and potential work was close at hand. For example he Faulds Gate bus route called from the city centre first at the suburb of Ferryhill and those who got off and on there were referred to as the 'tuppeny toffs' since it was 5d fare to Kincorth. Early 20th century Stockholm similarly housed its working population on the edges of the city in the belief that as air was fresher and kitchen garden grounds were available for those who could only afford a modest rent, they would be better off. But these good people were obliged to walk into the city to work as there was no alternative transport and the shuffling of the clogs, early every morning, would awaken the residents of the inner suburbs and the city.

Amongst the earliest of this new type of housing was the development at Ruthrieston, then on the edge of the city near the Bridge of Dee. Ruthrieston was an old village with its own parish Kirk and a Board School. To the north of Holburn Street a circular street was laid out and in two concentric rows and Gardner's team built a series of four-flatted blocks as close to the tenement as Anglo-centric directions would allow Scots local authorities to go. In size and design these resemble a manse. They were constructed in a dark red granite with slated piended roofs and the windows regularly arranged about a centre doorway. This 'entrance' in fact led up to the pair of flats on the first floor. Entrance to the ground floor flats was at each side of the block, thus a maximum sense of privacy and 'ownership' of the garden ground was established by design. Each flat had a living room with scullery attached, one large bedroom and a bathroom: as the design was reused elsewhere in the city the large bedroom was often divided into two making a family bedroom and a smaller single one.

Other early local authority schemes used these four-flatted blocks and with the linked houses, two storey usually to a maximum of five, they looked much like their southern neighbours apart from the materials. Very occasionally there were somewhat experimental blocks of flats, such as that built by A.G.R. Mackenzie in the '30s in The Spital: its granite, regularly fenestrated streetside elevation is rendered in a less modernist manner to that of the east side on high ground with views towards the sea. Here Mackenzie employed a series of horizontally expressed concrete walkways from which the flats are entered: this eastern front was close to the style of housing practised by Continental architects and praised in the architectural press of the day. Other brushes with the Modern Movement can be seen in parts of Anderson Drive where the four-flatted Manse block was built occasionally with flat roofs: however, with their symmetrical frontage and regular fenestration they present rather more as Art-deco, than modernist. Three blocks in Rosemount (designed by the City Architects Department in 1935) return to a form of small tenement with seemingly flat roofs though in fact the parapet hides the piended slated roof. The horizontally expressed steel windows and the simplicity of the granite clearly indicate a tendency toward the modern. The most thorough honest and admirable essay in Aberdeen modernism occurs with the local authority housing scheme on the site of Morrison's Jam Factory destroyed by fire in the early '30s and therefore available for building as the last block in the Rosemount Viaduct group of composed compartments from the turn of the previous century.

Here, of four stories, a wall of identical two bedroom flats surrounds the site's edge. Windows are steel with horizontal expression contrasted to the vertical expression of the prominent painted concrete frames to the staircase windows. The wall is curved into a broad semi-circle at the south end facing towards the city and it is here that is found the entry to the interior gardens space, an equally strong semi-circular arch. This motive is repeated on the long flanking elevations. Low relief sculptures grow out the walls of plain but tooled granite above these arches. Designed in 1938 the Rosemount Square flats were finished internally 1945–46. Socially the project is very modernist although that style of architecture was conceived essentially as a Continental response to the First World War and the defeat of recently great empires, where an abstraction of form contrasted to the prevailing over-decorated Wilhelmite form of baroque that had been the fashion since the beginning of the century (Hitchcock and Johnson 1966, Riley 1992). The experimental schemes to provide mass housing quickly, at places like the Stuttgart building fair at Weisenhoff, had used light materials for cheapness and flexibility and, one suspects, for the joy of exploration of a more spatial kind of architecture even for these simple flats: these represented modernity to the young men of the time. The equally ambitious and honourable building programme of for example the Hamburg local authority, during the same period, received no such favourable press (Hipp 1985). It, like the programmes in Aberdeen, used the traditional methods of construction and demonstrated a similar regard for the from of the contiguous city. Since spatial openness is a primary feature of 20th century modernism, building in stone in a chilly climate, and hoping to achieve similar results, was doomed to fail.

Most of the work of the City Architect's Department was good even exceptional. The Kaimhill housing scheme, in association with Leslie Rollo, resulted in a most admirable restatement in modern terms of the Cottage as a building type and experimented with the varieties of construction, in a kind of mute Building Fair way that had earlier been practiced on the Continent. These houses, made of granite, brick, concrete and timber by turns, and these developments guided their work into the '60s. The timber houses, curiously always known as Swedish, have enjoyed good opinion throughout their very long lives and still attract. Their seemingly plainer neighbours are equally admired. None of these houses, nor indeed the Kincorth Project (Alexander 1939) houses put to national competition, designed before the War and largely built afterwards, carried the hallmarks of modernism as seen by the critics and failed to achieve any kind of stardom.

To a list of admirable national characteristics of community actions to plan for better and healthier neighbourhoods, allied to the persisting work ethic

7.5 Rosemount Square site plan

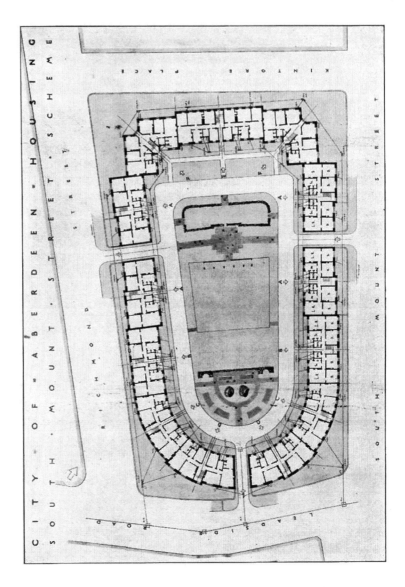

and the veneration for education characteristic in all parts of Scotland, ought to be added the architectural taste for neo-classically minimal buildings. For this, earlier 19th century Aberdeen had been famous and had survived later tastes; it was apparent in the work of William Kelly also in much of A.G.R. Mackenzie's later work and in that of Rollo, also head of the Aberdeen School of Architecture. Teachers of architecture at Edinburgh such as Hurd had recognized the closeness of the vernacular Scottish work from the 17th century to the abstract forms so admired by 20th century modernists. The early esteem accorded to Macintosh and his associates by some of the Viennese modernists at the very beginning of the century, curiously told against him, and them, by later critics and revisionists who found their works somehow both 'formalist'

7.6 Kincorth Garden City Civic Centre

and 'impure', or put more simply not really Modern. The reaction of all Scots architects including Hurd's students, the knighted stars of mid-century British architecture, Basil Spence and Robert Matthew (Glendinning 2008), in the period from 1930 to 1960, was a sort of cowering shame in their own performances, and in the country's, where it ought to have been politely but firmly asserted that they were producing their own form of modernism, from their own rich, cultural past. Few could see this, and simply longed to be more like LeCorbusier. Putting the Kincorth garden city to a national competition is not known to have intended any suggestion of lack of skill by the City Architect's Department, and they were certainly fully stretched with Kaimhill and Rosemount. It cannot have boosted their confidence much, especially when local practises were beaten by a young firm from Liverpool led by James Gardner-Medwin.

No work of significance occurred during the 1940s owing to the War and the dreadful realization of its costs, and the continuing cost that became clear after the restoration of peace. Central direction of the economy and much of the culture also continued in a pinched, miserable manner. That central direction was heartily supported by the election in 1945, driven by attitudes which had grown up during service, mostly service overseas, where occasional terror was separated by long opportunity to reflect, to plan, and to hope for a better world. Many towns and cities had begun to commission reviews of their environment by consultants such as Patrick Abercrombie who showed how both London and Edinburgh might be transformed. These were big pieces of work, and relied much on sound observation and research pulling all these into plans for action. In Plymouth and Coventry it was abundantly plain what was required to be done. But even where there had been little or no damage from bombing raids, there was an earnest longing to see British towns and cities replanned along modernist lines.

Aberdeen, among the last to commission these chose Chapman and Riley, the firm of planning consultants from Macclesfield, near Manchester, in 1948. The *Granite City* appeared in 1952. R. Dobson Chapman was past president of the Royal Town Planning Institute, an architect, a landscape architect and a teacher of these subjects; his younger colleague Charles Riley was a planner and architect and had also taught at Manchester and at Newcastle. Meanwhile their chief of staff in Aberdeen had been appointed Director of Planning and his assistant Tony Colclough remained in that post into the 1980s. The Granite City therefore is the blueprint for the changes in the city in the third quarter of the 20th century. Their report, as published in large format, contained nearly 200 pages of text and many graphs, maps and other illustrations including large folding plans for particular parts. Not only included in the published version but framed and hung within the planning department were the series of fine drawings of various parts of the New Aberdeen for the Post War Era. The principles on which the Granite City was based, and which underpinned all its recommendations were: Zoning, Easy Movement of Traffic, and Modernity within a context of Northeast Scotland…fish, farming and mountains, and, of course, granite.

It may seem ironic but the last workings of the Rubislaw Quarry were also in 1952. Already in the '30s, houses built in Bright Street on the southern edge of Ferryhill were proposing to use artificial granite to save costs. Ten years after the report's publication, Councillors tried to insist on cladding their new office block, St Nicholas House in granite but contented themselves with concrete and tiles which they thought looked close enough to it. There is hardly anything in the report that shows a real respect or fondness for the granite buildings already in place. It is the 'ancient' buildings such as St Machar they point out as valuable while great swathes of Union Street, the Castlegate, Broad Street, King Street, and Schoolhill are to be consigned to demolition. The two interlinked and self supporting reasons for that, was the need to make the streets wider so more traffic could flow easily and quickly through the city and since the city centre was to be the site of the main commercial and shopping areas, and since the old buildings were not fit for these new and modern functions it was thought they ought to be replaced. In any case the lodgings that would be displaced had no business being in the centre in a modern major town anyway and their residents were deemed to be better off in the large areas of the plan coloured yellow for residential use.

7.7 M.N. Mason, Market Street looking towards New City Centre

The heart of Aberdeen from West End to Beach Boulevard and between Springbank and Midstocket Road was to be for business (Blue) and for Civic and Cultural uses (Red) with some residual residential areas along the north edge and behind Golden Square. The effective boundary of this area was to be a dual carriage road with roundabouts. There were to be three New Squares, a large one at the west end of Union Street, another just west of Union Bridge, and finally the Castlegate was to be enlarged and reoriented and the area north as far as St Andrews Cathedral cleared, to make way for a boulevard to run straight to the beach; finally the Citadel was to be replaced with a new Townhouse.

Chapman and Riley saw the main problem of Aberdeen to be its lack of planning and by that they meant that there was hardly any zoning, that residential, shopping, civic and all other functions were mixed up together. That these are the very functions and attractions of city life did not occur to them: they inflated the idea that civic affairs possessed a dignity that required grouping with other buildings having similarly characterized functions. Shopping could be near-by but ought also to be grouped so that shopping and only shopping is what the area should have to offer. They were also concerned about the lack of open spaces. They did not realize that streets are open spaces in Scottish cities, as they are in Continental ones. Chapman and Riley lament the small size of Union Terrace Gardens for instance, and they regretted the lack of broad streets designed for motor traffic; for them the Inner Ring Road was a 'most urgent' matter. The major building groups were a problem for them: Marischal College and the Infirmary group, both far away from their supposed 'natural' neighbours were to be housed in a University Precinct and a Medical Precinct. Even the Townhouse itself was in doubt.

Indicative of their approach and of the course of planning practice in Britain at mid century, were the people living in the city centre. Of tenements they wrote with the disdain that English commentators had for the form, 'The tenement type of dwellings, formerly scattered indiscriminately throughout

7.8 M.N. Mason, Union Street with the New Castlegate

the Central Area, have been removed or replaced by suitably sited multi-storey flats' (Chapman 1952 68). The Granite City proposed to reduce two storey houses by 18 per cent, and tenements by 58 per cent. Educational buildings were only to be reduced by 34 per cent. All 'special industries' and 'amusements' were to be removed from the Central Area. The benefits that these clearances would bring were widened streets, car parks, open space, light and air.

The Industrial Areas such as Tullos followed, and according to their prescriptions, so did the Beachfront amusement park, although it took nearly fifty years and then a concerted effort to carry it off. And of course the Housing Units to the north and west of the city are legacies of the Granite City. In a sense the programme of multi-storey flats we also owe to them. However, apart from the fiercely thorough tidying of like things together and removing the tenements from the heart of the town, many of these developments were already set up and had been planned before the war (Alexander 1939). It is

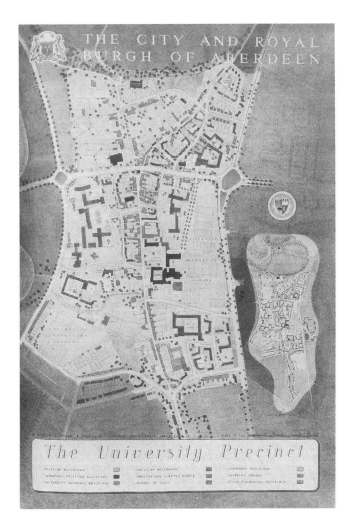

7.9 Old Aberdeen as University Precinct

hard to judge at this distance just how serious the city was about carrying on the ideas offered to them: one suspects they commissioned the study anticipating a congratulatory result. If ever pressed in argument Colclough would always assert that the Granite City had never been adopted as policy, yet the continuing course of the ring road seemed, if not formal policy, then at least sacred: there continues to be evidence in various parts of the city of an influence along its notional route. Even when it was published the bases of the Granite City had been called into question by planners themselves in the one British, and the last of all meetings of CIAM also in 1952 (Mumford 2002). Within ten years both Jane Jacobs' analysis condemning such planning theory had appeared with Ada Louise Huxtable's assault, as architecture correspondent of the *New York Times* on modern architecture as handmaiden of bad planning, and also Rachel Carson's *The Silent Spring*, the implications of which took longer to reach a wide audience.

Had Aberdeen carried out the recommendations of the Granite City it would have soon become a much poorer place, with hardly any of its character remaining. The windswept nature of Broad Street, as it now is, has never found the same favour with Aberdonians as it clearly found with Chapman and Riley who would have had it even bigger, with more such places, where before there had been tenements and people. Stockholm's flirtation with modernist planning was more successful in that it combined business with some living in the city centre, but even there, the planners were soon howled down (City of Stockholm 1959). For any who have visited the similarly sized cities of America will know, the town centres have plenty of light and air and open space, but they lack citizens and they lack character: when shopping trends indicate a downturn all the stores leave for fresher pastures elsewhere within the town or conurbation (Longstreth 1992). Easy enough to get to because of quick roads, paid for by Federal funds, and car parks but then that is often all there is. Not only are the town centres empty of shops or character, they are also soulless, even frightening.

Fortunately these proposals for the city centre were honoured more as aspiration than acted upon so with time for reflection, soon the cultural climate began to change. Cities with character, old buildings and with all kinds and conditions of people and activities, all mixed together, became positively attractive again. With the improvements of central heating and more modern plumbing, the old houses were seen as preferable to the meaner, smaller alternatives. The air is no longer contaminated by coal smoke mixed with inefficiently burnt petrol. The streets and urban open spaces are thought to be quite bracing enough, without encouraging the clearance of yet more acres of open space.

Learning from the City

Over time there have been a number of proposals and designs for improvement that have not been carried into execution: some for several or many years and then appear in greatly modified form while others remain merely on paper. Whether executed, ignored or forgotten they remain as design ideas. When changes are required and agreed on by the majority, they are often also carried forward speedily without thorough investigation into alternatives or alterations. These may be satisfactory but often need revision later; others will be lamented by the thoughtful. Therefore a scheme, whether it is carried out or otherwise, is independent of its merit. The qualities of these abandoned projects invite careful examination, not necessarily in order to resurrect them so much as to discover why and when they were designed in the first place, and what reasons there were for not carrying them out.

All citizens will have an attitude about such proposals, sometimes a very strongly held one. But how can they acquire knowledge about architecture, and how are those who make the proposals qualified? Architecture has been one of the fine arts since the renaissance, and is known also as the mother of the arts. Its theoretical basis is ancient and strong. And yet it is only in recent times that it has been an academic study. Knowledge about it, for intending practitioners was acquired through *pupilage* rather like the old system of apprenticeship, but shorter and less formal. On the Continent there were Schools often related to the military, in France related also to officials for buildings. The famous *Ecole des Beaux Arts* in Paris held sway from the late 19th century, although it was under siege from the '20s . In the UK pupilage was augmented by lectures, often informally arranged as at the Architects Association in London (still known simply as the AA) or at Institutes such as that established in Aberdeen in the 1840s. The Architects Registration Act of 1933 recognized some thirty Schools as fit to examine for qualification. It was only in 1958 that it was decided that such study should be conducted within universities. Slightly different patterns were followed elsewhere, but the universal system is for five years university study, plus three years internship to become qualified as architect (Mallgrave 2005, Brogden 2006).

8.1 Prospect of Aberdeen across the Denburn Valley from the west in 1661

From the informal studies of Adam, Gabriel, Chambers and others in Rome in the mid 18th century, and in the Schools later designs in competition for imaginary monuments related to a city or to landscape became a vehicle for demonstrating skills by would-be architects. Projects similar to these were often proposed for the improvement of cities.

The advantages of design within an academic setting are many, and not least is the very detachment from the particular instructions of a client, which brings objectivity. The disadvantages include lack of maturity in development (by definition) and too close an affiliation with the current educational or professional direction. Students at the ends of their academic careers will have studied for some five years design, history and other core subjects necessary to enter practice and will have acquired significant experience in practice as juniors. Their very youth and lack of maturity can also bring an edge to their ideas. The affinity with current ideals is a problem when those ideals are not universally shared. Projects derived for the academic system of schools and studios perfected in France, specifically Paris, drew students there from all over the world, not least Aberdeen. However, by the 1920s these set pieces, such as a metropolitan railway terminal based on the Baths of Caracalla which could well win the Rome Prize (and was actually constructed in Milan) were seen as stale, even irrelevant, and in the '30s were despised.

More attractive to the students of the '30s and indeed to their communities were projects about urban regeneration and improvement that seemed less elite, addressed problems of poverty and overcrowding, for example, or even of new ways of treating illness. At the schools everywhere these become the choices for both tutors and students. While the system based on the *Ecole des Beaux Arts* lingered into the '60s, the expressions became increasingly Modern. Robert Matthew's winning entry for the Bossom Studentship at the Edinburgh College of Art is typical (Glendinning 2008: 48–9). This called for a series of slab-block high rises to house the cleared slums nearby. He parlayed it into service in the Scottish Office on policy and after war service transferred to the London County Council where he led the team that built the Festival Hall. In his extensive private practice (his firm Robert Matthew Johnson Marshal and Partners has long been familiar as RMJM) he turned his skills to the problems of places like Old Aberdeen, its conservation and its need to house the development of a modern university. His colleague James Galletly (Galletly 1934) at Edinburgh took a different course. Winning the Andrew Grant Travelling Scholarship he studied urban planning in continental Europe and the USA, before taking a teaching post in Aberdeen where his Civic Design course gave many students the opportunity to explore issues of urban architecture within their familiar setting, decades before their professional standing would bring consultation for real. So the projects he and his students proposed for Union Terrace Gardens in 1944 or for housing regeneration ten years later may well have similar merits to those made or proceeded with since.

Clearance of old neighbourhoods had been seen as necessary for health in many cities, and planned from the later 19th century in Aberdeen. Their replacement was to be hygienic and modern housing with initially square-like gardens, to be later replaced with more park-like spaces adjacent, then simply *open spaces*. These ideas were universally welcomed, certainly as aspiration. When old buildings of acknowledged merit, such as Bannerman's Bridge, The Music Hall, or the Asylum for the Blind were also scheduled for demolition or for mutilation, a significant and leading part of the town were all for it. Others argued against it on the grounds that the buildings were sound, of architectural and historic importance and that alternatives to achieve the desired modernity existed. Therefore, that the necessity of a dual carriageway in Virginia Street in the way proposed was far from proven; or to turn the Music Hall into a 'modern' convention centre with attached hotel on the site of the Blind Asylum was a mistake, in any case in the wrong place. Half of these mistakes were thus averted. Similar follies were avoided in Edinburgh where it should have been abundantly clear that they should never have been put forward. To ensure the swift and efficient movement of traffic Queen Street was to have been turned into a motorway with a tunnel under Charlotte Square: this was stopped but in Glasgow even worse mutilation to the city was applauded, and carried forward with zeal (Boyer 1990).

A by-product of these concerns was an increased interest and consequent research into the history of the architecture and design of Scottish cities. These studies found their way into the studios of the schools of architecture. It had been a fundamental principle of the Edinburgh School, initiated by Patrick Geddes, fostered by Robert Rowand Anderson and the Royal Incorporation of Architect in Scotland he revived, and carried on by Matthew when he instituted a second course of architecture at the University of Edinburgh. The principal was that a thorough knowledge of the history and design of a place was essential to understanding its future. This is now so obvious as to be hardly worth stating; however it was far from obvious to professional leaders and Governments in the mid-20th century. Therefore from the '70s schemes for study and experimental design acquired an extra and very important dimension which modified the then dominant 'scientific' systems approach and the fashion for social sciences, with the reintroduction of Geddes' hypothesis about the importance of place, and its history and design. Notions of sustainability of materials, and of processes, and of the costs of the works to be calculated over the lifetimes of the works themselves or at the very least, something further into the future than the then financial standard of thirty odd years, came also to figure, and latterly to direct projects and their assessment.

Aldo Rossi who directed studies of this kind at the Venice School of Architecture invited proposals in competition as part of the Biennale of 1984 (Portoghesi Rossi et al. 1985). Each of the programmes included sound originally researched documentary evidence on the history of the sites and of the various changes made to them over time. Here the invitation was simply to propose – a building, a landscape, a sculpture...whatever. Although various interests had declared for themselves the simple wish of a consortium to demolish part of Venice and rebuild it to their own advantage, that was not in itself sufficient cause to comply, as in those days it appeared to be to similar interests in these Islands. Rather a more disinterested series of design studies would have had the effect of exploring alternatives, suggesting possibilities, all without damage to the actual fabric of the city, its hinterland or culture.

Another influential competition was launched by the civic society of New York. It was used as a graduate studio project in Aberdeen and many other schools worldwide. The Municipal Arts Foundation posed a similarly open examination of the lower West Side of Manhattan from 35th Street to the Battery. In researching this on site by Aberdeen students the disparate desires of the residents of the various neighbourhoods was most striking. Equally informative was the methodology used in the urban architecture studio at the Cooper Union School then led by David Eisenman and using the similar approach of Geddes and Rossi: this included not only cultural archaeology but also a thorough examination of the actual layers of Manhattan Island itself before any design proposals began. It was in the light of these studies that their merits or otherwise were discussed, and it was the design response to these seemingly *extra* issues that secured the first prize to the Aberdeen student group (Arredo Urbana 1988).

These and similar ideas were explored in my graduate studios at the Aberdeen School of Architecture, and in earlier years as well (Donald 1996). The architecture of the street (specifically Union Street) was an early subject for study, initially its design history in the context of Scotland and of similar streets in other parts of the world, before the individual student chose his or her own design project. Initial criticism of that work by both external and internal critics was agreed to derive from the context of the design problem and place differed from what the experienced critics had expected...a complex building design based on a client brief and carried through to details studies. Henceforth examiners were happy to see projects where students were merely set the problem; their researches and explorations determined what the criteria for judgement should be as the nature of the

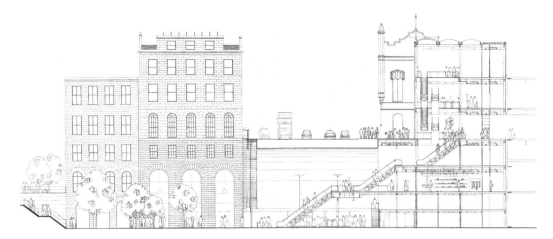

design intervention became clearer to them. Naturally the qualities of these decisions, and the responses they were able to make became the subject of their oral examinations.

The profession and most academics in the '90s wished to see an effective move from tuition (that should be ending at least by the honours degree) into an early evidence of leading from the student architects themselves, in establishing a problem, assessing it in terms of history, context, and theoretical concerns and then demonstrating their abilities to turn these studies into a design proposal. A similar pattern of work was practised in the leading professional offices of those days, such as Ove Arups in London. Specialization was also then encouraged in the hope that some students would proceed to further postgraduate work or seek further professional training in allied fields. The choice by students to work in small units of interest was also encouraged: these might be conservation, large buildings, the place of work or urban studies.

So the Masters course content was transformed. At Aberdeen a short series of projects was introduced at the beginning of each graduate year from which the students chose their preferred tutor and theme. In due course we established a template for such study at a masters level: a research semester with group and joint works; then a design semester where individual (or perhaps small teams) could address a building programme based on the first semester's work; and a third semester when those who wished and were thought competent could prepare a written master's thesis providing an academic argument and conclusion to the three semesters' work. Later this programme of study was established as an alternative degree, with professional recognition, for urban studies and architectural history. A similar route for those interested in the conservation of old buildings was planned, and of course the template would admit a range of related graduate programmes of study.

For this masters group, composed of normally about fifteen to twenty students of whom half were native, the rest made up variously of continental Europeans, Israelis, south east Asians and Americans typically, a theme was proposed. Initially we took the Rosemount Project of the 1880s as the

8.2 D.E.D. MacClean, Proposed Design for the Junction of Union Bridge and the Denburn Valley at Union Terrace Gardens, Robert Gordon University student project

subject of study. Using design drawings from the archives, contemporary prevalent, and emerging, theoretical issues of the later 19th century were explored, through written papers, seminars, drawings, and sketch designs supplemented by study visits to either Berlin or Prague. This was followed by an intensive *charette* or master's class in the Black Isle at the university's study centre in the recently restored Old Brewery at Cromarty. There the idea of making a *new street* from the Castlegate to Footdee was proposed – to pretty near blank incomprehension that turned into a recital of all the good reasons to do something entirely different. However their uneasiness was allayed when they were reminded that Provost Mathews had led such a project in the 1880s and had managed to see it through within ten years, and asked what could be so difficult about a similar gesture a century later? Especially as the recent Tall Ships visit to the city had brought a hundred thousand people cheerfully into what had been considered a dangerous back of harbour scene of dereliction.

There was the further stipulation that the 21st century tenement or shop house was one of the required types to design, with a public building from each student as counterpoint. The clues from the earlier effort in Aberdeen were there for guidance but the principles which carried that project were to be tried, to see if they still had validity. If then they did not, what alternatives were needed to make the project work for the last decade of the 20th century? Basically the design problem, and it is a most taxing one, was how might an architect compose a street? And a long one at that, using the simple means of a single, if flexible, building type and how might such a street be threaded into a complex old town with the added problems of exposure to the North Sea, polluted and contaminated ground, and a very busy working harbour?

Initially some basic problems were identified, mostly to do with the two proposed ends of the New Street on Castle Hill and at Footdee. That Castle Hill was ancient and had been reworked many times over was clear to all from previous experience or study. Footdee to them, as to most Aberdonians, was a mixture of indifferent history, fond expectation and myth. As no sensible proposal to develop or to conserve seemed possible without sound knowledge, some of the researches began there. Related to these, curiously, was one of the glaring problems of using any site at the back of harbour lands for human habitation or work, without special protection owing to the gross contamination at the old gas works and the potential lateral subsoil pollution. The contamination became a subject in its own right and as investigation proceeded the various ways of cleaning up were discussed and the implications for design proposals debated. One of the favoured schemes (and this was the early '90s at about the time of the first conference on global warming at Rio de Janeiro) was to turn the large area into a kind of garden, fenced and suitably contained, to be planted with chemical 'eating' plants whose own ecosystems would cleanse the area, by which time it could be opened for public access, recreation, or in due course, healthy development.

As these discussions progressed, the nature of dune systems as sites for habitation began to contribute its own rules and implications. These would have been obvious to geologists and others rather earlier but student architects must learn in their own far from linear fashion. One of these implications was the potential leaching of contaminants into underground 'streams' of water thereby spreading the concerns about health even more widely throughout the site. An extra subsoil investigation before detailed planning was therefore indicated: it became clear beyond doubt that ancient peoples would never have chosen such a place to begin settled life in a village, as a reliable source of drinking water is the first requisite. The myth of ancient settlement vanished, to be confirmed by evidence from archive sources where it was clear other architects had planned *ancient* Footdee less than two centuries earlier.

A large open and derelict space apart from desultory storage lay in the middle just behind the harbour at Waterloo Quay. It was closed off but appeared to have usable railways. This was, of course, the site of the Aberdeenshire Canal's junction with the Dee latterly the site of the railway northwards and its station: all were subjects of design by engineers and architects in recent historic time. Hence all the parts of the site were investigated in a similar manner and their relationships explored. That all these matters were known to someone, could be discovered without special access to sensitive sources and yet had not been part of the original briefing, began to dawn on the student architects, as did the realization that it was their duty to discover these as part of any response to a commission, from whomsoever it might come. The innocent expectation that any client body with the economic, political and organisational power to put together and manage such a project, would have known such things and would have thought through their implications began to be questioned, and then doubted. It was replaced by a dawning understanding that this is what architects must do. The activity covered about two months by about twenty people. Hardly any firm can justify so many man-hours to research a project before beginning. It is only the largest and most attractive firms such as Foster's in London or Gehry's in Los Angeles that can carry on such design research, and many young architects are prepared to work in such firms for little recompense, or nothing. Some larger firms carry on such design research commercially, that is, the fees pay for the time, and the most distinguished of these was perhaps Arups. These researches are undertaken to enable and better to answer the needs of the clients and to a degree the work must point to that as the goal and therefore should be as professionally and commercially sensitive as necessary (Evans 1996).

The lack of relevant or current research about a particular area could be filled by local authority teams, commonplace in much of continental Europe but impossible in the recent political climate of the United Kingdom. Alternatively, probably in parallel with others it could also have become the role of the schools of architecture. Such a role had been encouraged by luminaries such as Sir Robert Rowand Anderson early in the 20th century and pursued in the various cities of Scotland at various times throughout the century, but apart from rare exceptions, it has yet to become either systematic or core to the thinking of the schools and their host institutions. For any number of reasons architecture as an academic discipline has never established an appropriate body of research. This is despite the fact that of all the arts and sciences it is architecture that enjoys the most robust thorough and ancient bodies of theory. However, the value of that inherited architectural theory was significantly diminished in the 20th century, partly in response to heavy handed tuition based on the *Ecole des Beaux Arts* system, and the consequential shift of practice into the severe abstraction of the Modern Movement. As this movement was seen as a practice based enquiry and response practice has become the dominant side. The ancient body of architectural theory has been *relegated* to history studies. What was the subject's greatest strength was set aside at the very time when university education became not only wider, but subject to concerns about its own theoretical basis. A further disincentive to a settled view has been the attitude that as architecture is about synoptic thinking and is analytical only about various small contributory matters, then advances in the subject are seen to come from best practice. By that is meant practice at a very high level indeed. Any interest in an aspect, be it history, elements of building, science or structural advances, is to the leaders in architectural education the business of specialists. The tension that exists between central direction (its validation of professional practise, with its concerns to reach national standards requiring national goals to be judged externally) and the study and celebration of local material, culture and history, has been typical. Naturally enough even younger students soon see themselves as paler images of those at the top of their profession; and the greater stage naturally appeals.

Still much of value could have been done and should have been done; there is really no excuse for the lack of knowledge in the schools about their place, its history, its contributions and *longuers*: any concerns about architectural matters in a particular locality ought to be addressed to its school, in the certain knowledge that there will be an archive of information, and a museum of students' work and a library enriched by the material – sadly this is rarely so and almost never so consistently. As an aid, an impetus and a means to carry on research, what could be more natural than to set the acquisition of knowledge from primary sources in a progressive and structured manner as part of the student's education? The results can be set aside and stored against the time when it will be useful in answering someone's later questions; and more importantly it will have enlivened the discourse removing it from the reliance on journals and the apparent concerns of stars of the profession.

Research in universities has been graded as are the funds granted to carry it on and that incidentally enrich the universities in all senses; all is dependent on assessment. This assessment is carried out nationally and, occasionally, by boards of experts. Neither the schools of architecture nor their guiding institutes acted on Anderson's (and other's) directions: judgements about research in architecture are made by a board called 'built environment' whose standards are not only very high but very remotely particular and bureaucratized. Work must be of national or international importance to qualify for serious consideration; furthermore it must be amenable to what is called 'scientific method'. Instead of building up collections of local knowledge that could be systematically classified, arranged and presented and in due course compared analytically with another collection or for researching a series of monographs on works and designers, (neither of which attracts research attention), funded-research is steered in other directions less congenial and further away for the subject's core. Of course, collections are deemed expensive to house and care for – sadly it is then rare to find evidence of accumulated work within such a student community.

An investigation into consultants' reports for local authorities, specialist agencies advising on planning matters or the deliberations of Royal Commissions shows these documents to have a short shelf life: perhaps this is a matter of cause and effect as it is only after the passage of time that they can be seen to have any value, mainly because of the form and background to the manner in which the advice was sought. It is far from corrupt but most professional advice is sought in anticipation that actions, judgements and proposals go in a certain direction and will be, after due deliberation, confirmed. The best that comes out then, will be a tidying up and confirmation that the worst errors have been avoided. When the wrong answer occurs, then a new group of consultants is approached.

The issues encountered in the New Street idea were thought to be of a proper kind: taxing enough, quirky enough, yet soluble by students at that stage and clearly bringing forth thoughtful design proposals. Discussions with the external assessors and students about the experiment, its strengths and specially its deficiencies, led to the advice to try the programme again. In framing such a project the need for clarity and focus was stressed and, in its management, more group, team and individual work were encouraged, with their outcomes and varying contributions clear to all students, critics and assessors. These assessors had three distinct roles: they were external examiners appointed by the University; they acted as representatives of the professional body; they also represented Parliamentary oversight through the Architects Registration Act. Therefore the mixture of roles in which the students performed had to be made manifest and clear. Henceforth for over a decade, projects of this kind have been framed, pursued, discussed and assessed within this curious hybrid of academic, professional, and national oversight.The question remains: what is the value of this process of gathering information about the history of the design and development in Aberdeen or elsewhere with parameters about how design projects should be framed, tried and assessed. Can a means which allow student architects to define explore and come to understanding about complex issues of design in public have value for others?

At a distinguished architect's memorial service one of James Morris' friends, the leading merchant banker Ian Noble, made comments that brought an almost audible gasp from the congregation in St Giles' Edinburgh. Reflecting on the benefits of good building and the honourable part architects play in bringing it about, he as a banker naturally wished to point up a direct, causal link between the sustained civic pursuit of quality in design and building and a place's suitability in competition with other places to significantly attract external investment. It was his calm and firmly stated relation from experience that in the late 1960s Aberdeen was chosen to be the most appropriate place from which to exploit the newly discovered oil fields of the North Sea because of its physical attractiveness, and specifically, its architecture. To an audience inured to the notion that economic principles not only exercise power but somehow are naturally endowed to do so and therefore determine serious actions, the assertion that good building and design outweighed those of disinterested prudence came as a real surprise. A few moments' reflection allowed the truth of his story to begin to sink in.

To pursue economics further, a town whose investments in itself (its streets, squares, parks, harbour and other infrastructures with its buildings, even its bungalows) yield continuing growth in value, while at the same time meeting the day to day requirements expected of them. This is surely sustainable in the best sense. That it may occasionally fall from fashion (its buildings certainly will do so from time to time) is everybody's observation and that fashions come and go, hardly make a criterion for judgements about architecture and urban design. Being substantially even splendidly, out of fashion becomes character and can lead to its own attraction in the medium term before the fashion again changes. Certainly Aberdeen could show a good return for the monies it invested in itself and these could with little difficulty be added up, adjusted for the changes in nominal values and then presented as a valuation. If latterly its housekeeping has been foolishly allowed to deteriorate, it is hardly unique in that. Expenditure of capital sums is smiled upon by the Treasury, whereas recurrent spending for maintenance is disallowed. But that becomes politics, not economics. If the error is reversed soon enough the damage can be overcome without too great further expenditure. If left too long, the accumulated values of the city may be put into jeopardy.

Discernment about those things requiring to be done and those which may be desirable for a short time only, is another way of judging a city's sustainability. Sometimes it is circumstance rather than good judgement. Put another way, if pet projects drag on without being realized because they cannot be afforded, there may come a time when also their fundamental lack of value becomes recognized. There has been an observable time lag between projects being proposed and their being realized in Aberdeen. There were twenty years between the idea of 'public rooms' at the west end of the Castlegate and the building of the New Athenaeum, fifty between the idea of a grand, castle-like termination at the east end of the city and the building of the Citadel. Abercrombie's northern street parallel to Union Street to be carried through the grounds of Gordon's Hospital to the Gallowgate, despite Archibald Simpson's raising the idea again, was finally 'achieved' though quite differently, a century later.

At the beginning of the 20th century many architects were convinced that the Garden City ideals provided the perfect pattern for towns: a tendency to sprawl and to simply add many small things together and call them cities soon showed that while these ideals were good for villages and small towns somehow cities required a larger format. LeCorbusier approved of Garden Cities and tried in his influential 'Plan Voissin' of 1925 and in his commentaries such as *Vers Une Architecture* (1923) to extend their principles to the city scale. From him derive the high buildings set in parkland where vertical streets replace horizontal ones, where there is plenty of open space and light and air. Following on from the Second World War, Glasgow is the best example of this approach at city scale, but in all fairness these rather caricature his principles. The suburb of North Antwerp is a fairer, if much smaller essay, and by him: similarly the building fair in the Tiergarten of Berlin in the 1950s shows his ideas to better advantage. But the fundamental flaw of both LeCorbusier's ideal, and of those who prefer a garden city approach, is their seeming common dislike of cities as such. To discover the perfect pattern of a town it is essential to like cities – many theoreticians of ideal cities are like medical men who would propose inventing a new species that does not get sick rather than healing the one before him.

A way to discover the value of such a town is to search for qualities amongst the towns that may be visited. Even the most banal and featureless places have something of their own, and something that may make their residents happy, or at least content to remain. So it is not a question purely of form. Weather, culture and many other human desires and requirements come into it. The most attractive places to visit somehow will not appeal as potential places to live – 'fine for the Venetians, but...' A balance of the range of possibilities may give the clue; optimum accessibility (in and out); a sustainable and decent comfort for all; maximum liberty to become rich; the availability of spiritual and intellectual comfort and stimulation. All of these have been and are part of the recipes for perfection; each is immensely complicated in itself and likely to produce self-cancelling conflicts when attempted.

What are those things that have to be accepted? And what might be altered? The climate is a given: it may not be changed. Aberdeen will never be Padua and anyone who has endured a summer there will be pleased that is so, as will most Paduans that they do not have to endure a *dreich* winter here. Yet there is much we could do to modify the effect of our climate, while much has already been done by ancestors in the arrangement of streets. Visitors to Aberdeen from Naples are amazed the town does not embrace the North Sea as Naples does the Mediterranean. They are far from convinced when it is pointed out that the sea is appreciated well enough, from the inside of a car or a building or when it is fine and mild and good to walk along. But to endure its foul moods without protection? No thank you. In fairness it needs to be pointed out that places like Oslo, Norway manage an outdoor café life, come summer and winter, with a climate hardly milder than north-east Scotland: so do the Danes of Copenhagen.

There are also the given geographical matters that have to be accepted, the obvious one being location. If the northwest edge of Europe is bad, then there are a lot of towns besides Aberdeen that will be emptied. Our dominant culture has taken a long time to settle and establish and those who might find the rather Calvinist conviction that it is our duty to put things right that can be put right, even if it is not an entirely pleasant thing to do, will probably be happier elsewhere. Should they prefer to stay and attempt to put the town's culture to rights they are welcome to try. Other things can be changed, some with difficulty and time. One of these might be the density of population. An economist might say that population should continue to increase to whatever the market level and natural forces dictate. Equally there are those who will have an ideal size in mind. Larger cities will have two major centres, or more, with other lesser and more specialised ones. This is true of both Edinburgh and of Glasgow. Aberdeen has one major centre only and when extensions are proposed to it, the cry goes up... 'what will happen to Union Street?' What effect might another hundred thousand people have on the city and would this increase have the weight to fully exploit Union Street as the varieties of memory would wish it to be? Would their habits further undermine its prominence? With those extra numbers would it be possible to drive from Cults to shop in the city? Even with those extra numbers the destination of Union Street might still make sense but only after the alternative modes of transport have been thought through and their implications understood. On the other hand perhaps a reduction in population might be better. A drop to 150,000 perhaps, at a level when Union Street, George Street and Market Street all had bustling shops and there were still trams to use. Other towns of course would not necessarily become smaller as well with the result that the relative importance of the city would be diminished in the eyes of many.

There exist successful cities which try to limit their population size and Portland in Oregon is one such. In the USA the competitiveness of cities is extreme. All wish to be bigger, richer and more important than they presently are. Any question about population will usually be met with the response that it is growing so fast it cannot be accurately guessed and which includes moving the boundaries to incorporate the metropolitan region and thus add a million or so to an otherwise perfectly ordinary town which does not even have a city centre with stores in it. Not so Portland, that does have a downtown like Aberdeen's, but whose residents might say...it rains a lot, we are quite a small provincial place, nobody ever comes to visit, and the like. Of course, this makes people of sense want to move there all the more.

Population, like weather and culture might be something better left unplanned.

But Ian Noble's remarks about the attractiveness of Aberdeen forty years ago and the effects that had remain relevant. Would they apply now? The schools remain good, the houses also, the general sense of the place as busy and purposeful remain too. It has to be agreed that when the worst neighbourhoods in a city are granite built, with slated roofs, near to public transport, and parks, and shopping, and have all the amenities and qualities that Prince Charles is trying to create in Dorchester, perhaps we are nearer to the perfect pattern for a town than we might care to admit. There are some tiresome aspects to moving about, especially if one chooses to live in Bridge of Don, work in Portlethan and want to shop in Berryden. Should the policy for traffic for a whole city be based on that? It might appear so. These imbalances about car use need to be solved but building a motorway between Portlethan and Ellon is hardly the only answer. Of some use to the few who have business at either end, what kind of alternatives would the expenditure on such a motorway buy? And what changes can be made which do not require big capital sums? Where are the irritations for the majority of Aberdonians? What is being neglected presently that requires tender loving care?

With all these queries, there are currently still undervalued parts of the city of Aberdeen: undervalued in the sense that the quality of environment (judged by architectural merit, historical importance, fondness by citizens, and other factors) and its use by citizens and visitors is plainly disconnected. A telling example is the first block of King Street northwards from the Castlegate. The buildings are in good to very good condition, and cater for a mix of public, arts, religious, residential, official and commercial activities. It lies on a major traffic route with public transport service adjacent to the centre of the city. As the site also of fine artistic effort by two of Aberdeen's most distinguished architects with further contributions by three architects of Scottish and British prominence, it also exhibits important milestones in the history of religion, medical arts and science, and provides current performing arts over a wide spectrum. Plainly this block already answers what any city would wish to achieve if it wanted or felt a need to establish a centre of excellence. Yet apart from the many passing by daily, hardly anyone *uses* it with the pavements normally significantly emptier than those just around the corner. Many would say therefore that it is a failed area. Yet it would take very little to make it the reverse.

A similarly glaring example of this kind of discontinuity can be seen daily in Broad Street and into the Gallowgate. Buildings of merit, one of world class, line it and stand nearby: a major open space was created here a century ago. The warmest of commercial centres is within a stone's throw in one direction with another potentially in the other, augmented by two artistic venues, but, there is little apparent activity from ordinary citizens or visitors.

Concerns have existed for many years about the fear of discontinuity in the fabric of the town between the new Union Square and Union Street, where it appears that citizens and visitors would need to be bribed to walk from one to the other through the Green and related ways or by Bridge Street (slightly more hopeful) or Market Street. Distinguished firms of consultants have been engaged to square this circle, so far without any success. Yet the pavements of Union Street remain clogged and overcrowded, exacerbated by their use as bus stations especially for citizens travelling to the towns and villages to the north. The street itself carries traffic as if it were a highway and not the Finest Street in Scotland: so long as it tries to be both it can never succeed.

Much of the difficulty we perceive in using and enjoying our city (and any other city) has to do less with the design of the town than with its management, its housekeeping, and at the present time the lamentable lack of an establishment of priorities in the uses of public spaces. Partly these concerns might be alleviated by simple changes in the patterns of use, and by other related infra-structural improvements. Suppose that buses do not run on routes across the city but rather that buses run on routes to and from the city centre. Citizens arriving at the city centre would find a bus free, car free, and delivery free series of major streets which could then have much wider pavements for ease of moving about and on Union Street (and others) a series of special trolley-like shuttles running east-west, even connecting to services further afield. Once established, frequent users of the routes would be able to plan connections and minimize their waiting times if they were in a tearing hurry or more profitably do the daily shopping in the heart of the city en route.

So a necessary beginning for improvement would be to change Union Street from a highway (governed by forces far from Aberdeen) back into the Finest Street in Scotland; in the process enliven currently underused areas of merit contiguous to and connected with it. North Street is already of highway standard and could be a means to enliven the heart of the town if used to link to car parking in Broad Street. Large, clean, airy and safe car parks are commonly built underground in continental Europe. The number of cars which could be accommodated under the open space outside Marischal College is phenomenal and would justify the cost of supervision and maintenance; incidentally bringing pedestrians out of their cars into this otherwise underused part of the town would increase its sense of liveliness. The increased number of people passing by would have a good effect on shops and would encourage others to set up in business nearby, thus the architectural qualities of the space would be nearer matched by the numbers frequenting the area. In the absence of restoring, even at least rebuilding Broad Street as the residential and commercial mix it was by its very nature and history for centuries, nothing less can so effectively bring life back there.

The uses of the open spaces which define Aberdeen have not remained constant. We now assume that commerce, in the sense of shopping, is not only natural but enduring. However, it is really a phenomenon of the last couple of centuries. Markets occurred, and were given formal sanction at the beginning of the town's history…indeed were the evidence of history. The Green, and Castlegate and Broadgate is where these occurred. Latterly the Broadgate became the town's shopping street, and remained prominent into the 20th century. The Castlegate also remained the centre of commercial as well as other civic activity.

When the city expanded the Trustees realized that the, by that time, typical mixture of shops at ground floor with living spaces above would be the standard for lower King Street and the new Union Street only as far as Union Bridge. Even then many of the new buildings, such as Auchintoul's House, were built as mansion houses without shops. The new enclosed Market built by Simpson in the 1840s as part of a new quarter connecting Union Street

8.3 Union Bridge and the Denburn Valley in the 1830s

over Putachieside to the harbour struck even at the ancient open markets nearby. To ease traffic, generated by the New Streets, the ceremonial steps into the Townhouse were removed, then the Mercat Cross itself, reluctantly and after much thought, was moved further east. Market activity was shortly afterwards confined to the eastern end of the Castlegate and ultimately dispatched around the corner in the 1930s.

Although such an idea is based on two misreadings of history and logic, there are still those who can only justify public space on the basis of its use, and deem any diminution of activity as evidence of decline. Cities are much more complex than our modernist theorists would allow, and as we have seen the making of public open spaces is a very long term matter. Uses will vary, and citizens and visitors will bring their own individual expectations to such places. These are sometimes to the discomfort of their neighbours, as the drinking habits of a hard core of Aberdonians shows. However, a wide range of behaviours is one of the principal qualities of cities and distinguishes them from tidy villages.

It would still be a great shame, and a great loss to the city to have the Salvation Army Citadel removed. Yet, such was the advice of the *Granite City* report, and for little better reason than that it did not fit the ideals of the 1940s which fervently believed that all had to be functional and modern, and therefore different. That kind of modernism was driven as much by the shock of the recent War and its dismal aftermath as with good sense. The Castlegate was ancient before it finally received its most spectacular and theatrical building, the Salvation Army Citadel. Such a display would have been anathema a century earlier, when, public spaces if graced by *architecture* at all, would have such expressions confined to the Cross, the Townhouse, and the Record Office. All else was subservient, and reticent, and architectural only the sense of exhibiting a decent type of probity and comfort. The Citadel was put there to ornament the city, and especially to give a finish to Union Street: the Castlegate had already received three modern buildings to ruffle its classic probity…the Banking Company, the Old Clydesdale, and the Athenaeum.

Citizens are apt to want to know what is right or what is appropriate, so that they may judge, moan to good purpose and cause change if necessary. These concerns for a normative architecture of cities are ancient. Marcus Vitruvius Pollio drew up such a prescription for the use of Augustus Caesar. Based on his observation of what was best, most useful, and his view most Roman, Vitruvius wrote a summary of how to build well, and his *Ten Books of Architecture* has come down to us as the oldest and many think still the best guide to the subject.

It is to Vitruvius that we owe the idea of probity in architecture, the distinctions to be made about kinds of buildings and their just sorts of ornamentation and how these should be best arranged. And to him and the other old Romans we can trace the dichotomy of how far should his advice be followed. The design of cities to Augustus Caesar was important: it was also important to his generals whether in campaign or in establishing colonial government. And as it was integral to their training it was of great importance to junior officers and other ranks. To literate Romans these matters would have been familiar. To everyone else such matters can rarely be more than of occasional interest. In such times, and when the rare occasions to act occurred, they would refer to him, and to those who followed. In the Renaissance other writers follow Vitruvius' example, and from the 1530s they do so using the then new notion of illustration. Sebastiano Serlio is one of these. Following Vitruvius he illustrated the three modes of stage sets, appropriate to the three kinds of drama recognized in antiquity. These illustrations, in the newly made scientific art of perspective, show idealized scenes demonstrating the qualities associated with Tragedy, Comedy and Satire. These were known also in written description but with these stage sets in one point perspective the scenes came to illustrate also the qualities of actual places. So the stage sets, and the parts of life they illustrated, became connected.

Tragedies were about great men and great actions and great falls from grace, and they were to be illustrated on stage by monuments of a public kind, such as temples and other classical forms of architecture, the whole tending perhaps to symmetry. These were naturally associated with the major open spaces of antiquity like the Forum of Rome or the major market places of other towns, such as the Castlegate. Not only were there the stage sets of Serlio and other commentators, some theatres such as the one in Vicenza employed the ancient *scena frons* and actually constructed the theatrical scene as part of the fabric. Both kinds of representation were well known to many Aberdonians, either through their own books, visits, or perhaps the Playfield at Woolmanhill.

LEARNING FROM THE CITY 237

8.4 Sebastiano Serlio, Dramatic Modes, *Tragedy*, *Comedy* and *Satyr* 1530s

This had been set up, enclosed, and furnished with large painted scenery by George Jamesone in the 1630s. There were also studio paintings on seeming similar themes, now known better as paintings of ideal cities. The design and the placement of the new Mercat Cross here in the late 17th century is clearly part of this collective vision. So, even with its additions from Banks, reading rooms, and aggressively theatrical and redemptive symbol of salvation the Castlegate still maintains its poise as classical scene suitable as stage set for tragedy. More than three centuries of developed design has gone into making the Castlegate with the Union Street approach the clear entrance and heart of the town.

It is rare for a city to have a recognised entrance, rarer still for it to be given architectural prominence. Venice has at least one…the Piazetta of San Marco where visitors land at the heart of the city, or even its more modern equivalent the Piazzalle Roma where the parking garage, buses from the mainland and the railway station gather visitors. Aberdeen also has others, such as St Nicholas' Place, outside Marks and Spencer's. It is rarely so called, and many will not recognize it as such. Yet that is its role. It terminates an axial view from as far away as Victoria Bridge at Market Street which carries traffic from the south, picking up sea-borne visitors from the ferries and the trains and buses nearer the old Wharf, then up the ramp to join Union Street… at St Nicholas Place.

This all had to be made. It came about by design but in parts and without an agreed destination. First by the negligent acquiescence of the Trustees who allowed Tannery Row to join their New Street back in 1800, then a century of the curious mix of two bridges, and an old street disappearing into a hole, marked by the statue of the Queen. Then in the late '50s the Neuk (and Wallace's Tower or Benholm's Lodging), the very heart of workaday Aberdeen shopping, was sacrificed by clearance and Carnegies Brae fully covered and the new space created. In Serlian and Vitruvian terms this the very image of Comedy. For them a Comic scene is about everyday folk, about shopping, about ordinary aspirations and little sins; such a scene should mix houses, shops, although a church must be nearby, in a jumbled and workaday manner. Its architecture should be vernacular and common rather than grand or classical. Despite the fancy Banks framing this stage set (perhaps because of them) St Nicholas Place makes a perfect Comic scene, with its access to the city right and left, and forwards into shopping, pubs handily off to the left and right, salvation when needed also near at hand, the irregular composition has, with flats recently reintroduced, all the characteristics. And it presents itself as a stage, formally approached yet set apart at the crossing of the two major streets of the city. This was consciously designed by the city Architects Department with Planning and Roads, and commercial pressures joining in.

If Tragedy and Comedy have long been recognized as ideals for town design; the third, Satire is curiously less so. However, it can stand very well for the longings of suburban life, whether for good or ill to the city as an idea. Seen by many as an escape only the favoured and wealthy can accomplish, such as an early advertisement for Bedford Park near London (Greeves 1975), where the health and air is contrasted with the dirt and smoke of the city, which Father can reach by rail leaving Mother and children safely behind. In Aberdeen idealized suburban living came earlier and closer into town, and of course its small size makes urban or suburban life still a choice any can make. But that is neither Vitruvius' point, nor would suburaban dwellers in Bedford Park take kindly to any comparison to satirical writing or stage plays.

Vitruvius' satire, or Satyr, is far ruder than douce suburbs can usually live up to. His is about wilderness, loss of control, and even danger. In terms of urban typology it has more to do with the garden or park, in contrast to populous comic or tragic areas. The old civic garden on St Katherine's Hill was too small to have passed as satiric, although it was probably sufficiently rude, the Links are much too exposed and large, and in any case the easy access from the old city to open spaces of various kinds was an easy one, and indeed remains so even today. The contrast between tight urbanity and open scenery within view, and usually easily accessed is a recognized characteristic of Scottish city life, as even the largest city Glasgow shows.

Aberdeen's third dramatic scene is its home ground, The Denburn and has been also an exercise in collective design since Union Bridge was conceived. Its southern end was built up for industry whereas its north side opened into countryside leading to Woolmanhill. This middle part was transformed into Union Terrace Gardens, whose history begins from where the Bow Brig gave entry to Aberdeen and near the circular basin just north finished a canalized Denburn. Its east slopes were already wooded by the gardens of new houses along Belmont Street. A broad Bleaching Green, of use to all citizens, lay along the west side of Denburn and then wooded slopes of the Corbie Haugh. This scene is captured in Thomas Hamilton's prize winning design for Union Bridge of 1800.

There are a variety of views taken in the Denburn in the earlier 19th century and they all show it as a lively open space for resort and still for bleaching laundry, but still its basic nature as 'a piece of countryside' is apparent. Its potential for the picturesque siting of buildings was noted, at least from Hamilton's time, and became the principal manner of composing the Triple Kirks in the early 1840s. Simpson had appreciated these qualities for that site even before, and of course, his manner of siting the Infirmary at Woolmanhill also exploited the distant prospect, partly wooded, partly with other buildings so admired by the landscape painters and theorists of the picturesque. Woolmanhill also carried with it memories of the Playfield and theatrical performance where 'a Wood near Athens' or the 'Forest Of Arden' were easily conjured up. The new residents of Union Terrace enjoyed this still slightly wilder aspect. Their prospect across the valley to the ancient part of the town was an even livelier one than their neighbours in Belmont Street, and had been part of Charles Abercrombie's ideas for the new quarter, as noted before. The north end of the town grew also, and although it too contributed to the picturesque it was less grand, maybe a little squalid

8.5 Union Bridge and the Denburn Valley

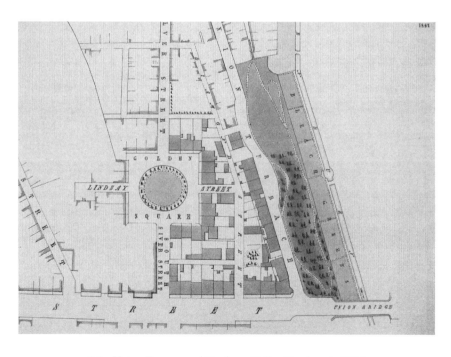

8.6 Union Terrace and Denburn Valley Gardens in 1847

to look upon. When it was decided to route the railway through the Denburn and join the two lines together at a new station it contributed positively rather than otherwise to the scene. There seems to have been no worries about soot and dirt from the train, rather the thrill of speed and progress the new lines brought contributed to the sense that all continued well and progressively.

By the 1840s there are indications of some tidying of the valley. As soon as the railway was built there followed plans to turn the whole valley into gardens, whose new and scientific sewage works, like the railways, was seen as ornament and evidence of forward thinking improvement.

William Forbes Beattie, to whom the city owes so much, was chosen as designer and his scheme was carried out, giving the character the Gardens have enjoyed in the century and a half since. There was significant building also towards the south of the Denburn Valley. First a new station shed, roughly where the Joint Station was later built defined a southern edge for the view form Union Bridge. Shortly afterward Bridge Street made a grand alternative to College Street, and connected the west end of the Bridge, and of course, Union Terrace, into the bustling commercial and industrial life of the improving harbour, and the newly opened Guild Street. In what was really a new quarter were built new very large buildings for business with a High Victorian confidence: these lined the west side of Bridge Street and were big enough to command the whole space across the railway to the old Green. Soon a modern luxurious hotel took pride of place on the southwest corner of Union Bridge and dominated the city for over half a century.

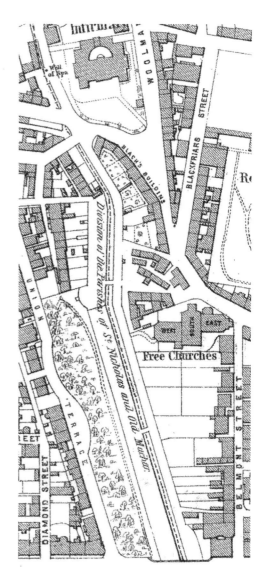

8.7 Denburn Valley just prior to the Great North of Scotland Railway

It was Bridge Street with Union Terrace which signalled successful business in the later 19th century, leaving Union Street West and the suburbs to either side as largely residential. This new north-south axis was splendidly finished when the north end was developed as part of the Rosemount Entry project of the 1880s. The fully ornamented, still classical, thrusting and confident buildings for business were then joined by the Library, a new parish Church, and a new Theatre (on the site of the old Playfield) to usher in a new century. All these celebrated their collective front garden in the Denburn Valley, and it showed off their swagger to best advantage. The topography of the valley,

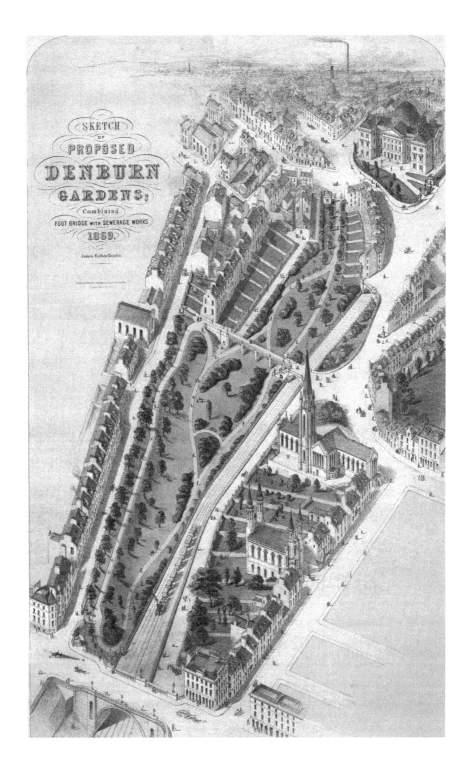

8.8 James Forbes Beattie, Design for Denburn or Union Terrace Gardens

8.9 Union Terrace Gardens and Denburn Valley showing Beattie's work

its treatment of strong landforms with forest trees and walks, occasionally decorated by bedding out of flowers at the north end, being lower than Union Terrace gave the new buildings an extra lift and provided the best kind of setting. The final stroke was to transform the carriageway into a proper terrace by the repetition of the elliptical arch of the old Bow Brig into a vast arcade supporting Union Terrace, and providing shelter for the gardens below. Even the widening of Union Bridge by Boulton and Kelly enhanced the Denburn Valley. Union Terrace Gardens is the sort of civic treasure that other towns, many of them much larger, have good reason to envy.

The early part of the 20th century had brought much railway use, which with the city's contamination from coal dust and smoke, and ill burnt petroleum, together with rogue fly-posting along the Denburn Road had begun somewhat to tarnish the Trainie Park's appeal. One of the major results of the Granite City report was the strengthening of planning as a civic provision. Indeed it became an independent department headed by the consultants' former local man. One of the strongest reasons offered for the need of such provision was the fly-posting and by then, ill kempt nature of the backs of Belmont Street. This aspect became almost a trope, shorthand for the ills brought on by little or no planning. It also contributed to a sense that there might be something basically wrong with Union Terrace Gardens.

As we have noted schemes to modernise the Gardens and cover at least the railway and Denburn Road were produced in the early 1940s. In the dreadful aftermath of the War, when exceptional cold, continued rationing, a democratized Empire, and the insistence by Britain's greatest ally that war debts and loans be repaid in full, sapped the self confidence Aberdeen had enjoyed previously. In the '50s whatever seemed modern, and American, was

8.10 Denburn Valley as proposed by Dobson and Chapman, *Granite City*

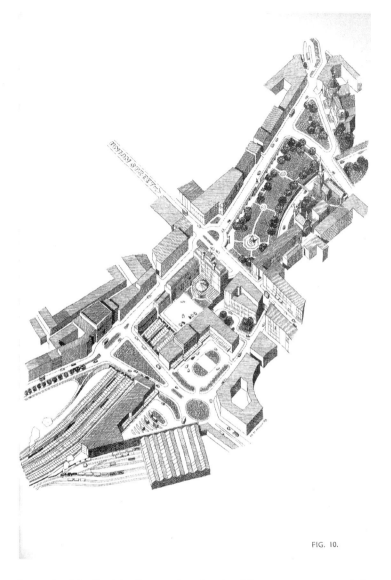

FIG. 10.

thought preferable. In this climate the Granite City report appeared showing how these new ideals could be realized Among the recommendations were very significant reorganisation south of Union Bridge, effectively a rebuilding after demolition from Bridge Street eastward to the Links was proposed. Curiously, significant alteration to Union Terrace Gardens was not among the proposed changes. The Report was the last of the excellent efforts of the 1930s when a motivated and well directed City Architects Department, acting on new planning powers from the 1932 Acts, and more than ably supported by Councillors achieved remarkable advances such as Rosemount Square, the Kaimhill Scheme, the Woodside Schemes, and after national competition selected the design for Kincorth (Alexander 1939).

8.11 Proposal to cover the Denburn Valley and Union Terrace Gardens and provide car-parking garage

Yet, that same desire for modernity in the post War gloom could cheerfully recommended the removal of the Market buildings, and the demolition of a major bank in Union Street and proposed building a multi-storey parking garage in the Denburn Valley in place of Union Terrace Gardens. Its roof was to be used as alternative gardens. That particular scheme withered, but the loss of the Market, for the reason, and only reason, that British Home Stores wished to have a large new store as much as possible on one level, was sanctioned, not by the Council mercifully, but because of the curious bypassing of standard feuing in the 1840s by a Parliamentary Commission (of two MPs!).

It is very hard for us now to understand the attitudes prevailing in those times. Local qualities and history, and the culture of the north-east were held to no account; so indeed were those of Scotland and the rest of these islands. The leadership in design matters, not to mention intellectual leadership more generally exerted by north-east people were entirely forgotten, or set aside as worthless. A collective shock brought on by the terrors of the war, and the exhaustion of the country at its end must be largely to blame.

Design ideas from outside were different. The programme of high-building, the last burst of leadership by the local authority provision of houses for rent is an antidote to the more general malaise. This is not because of the inherent qualities of building high: as is well known many local authorities managed to ruin their cities quite effectively by using such a type. Aberdeen did not. It continued to observe the same good rules of siting and planning with respect to established neighbourhoods and streets as before, and apart from the latest and cheapest, generally speaking its high buildings have been a success. When, in the early 1970s the revisions to modern theories of architecture came to be discussed Aberdeen professionals and councillors were content to listen, and to engage, and to modify official attitudes. Much of those changes in Aberdeen, as elsewhere in Scotland, came not from formal or even social concerns, but in reaction to the contempt of the achievements of Scotland in the previous centuries, and the desire to re-establish links with that tradition.

Significant changes in governmental occurred in the 1980s. There was a diminution of trust by central government in local authorities, much of it generated by party political attitudes, but not entirely. The creation of a new suite of quasi-governmental organizations by the same government, particularly the enterprise agencies, brought about freer and more responsive groups to orthodoxy, hitherto not involved in planning or design matters. These were not only funded, but were courted by government to bring about radical and new ideas. With the enterprise agencies came economic considerations, and there was a time when a business plan was the only kind of plan anyone wished to see, never mind the problem or issue it purported to address. Engaging with these agencies and their professional directors became a means of exploring how to re-establish links with the best of Scottish urban planning of the past, and at the same time stimulate new developments. They had the unusual, for a while unique, capability to see connections between building design and the much larger scales of planning, that is, of urban architecture. Grampian Enterprise funded, for example, the professional validation of graduate students' work on a new future of St Clements to bring the project forward for actual development (Evans 1996).

In reaction to the enterprise companies the local authorities also launched a number of initiatives which were of a scale and aspiration to compare with civic projects begun in the 18th century, and a series of funded studies were proposed, and judged in competition to address such issues. The *Aberdeen Public Realm* study led by Gillespies of Glasgow is typical. Consisting of economists planners traffic and urban design experts it was invited to address the short to medium term future of the city centre and to provide a masterplan for development. Others were asked to address more specific issues, such as the Green, and how best to re-establish its connection to the rest of the city. These reports were competent, often imaginative, and always professional.

Aberdeen Beyond 2000 was a grouping of business leaders interested in the city and its development. They were encouraged by the enterprise company, and became an established and funded agency in themselves. Their biggest project was the idea of transforming Union Terrace Gardens into a civic centre for the city. Important members of the planning department worked closely with them to generate a variety of schemes which were to be funded by the newly established Lottery, and its big projects scheme. The programme of these schemes shared many of the characteristics of the time, especially those of the enterprise agencies. The projects had to be big, they had to be transformative, and they had to generate new and large economic advantages.

Each scheme shared these characteristics, and each was denied funding by the Lottery Commission on design grounds. The projects were thought to be too big, over-developed, and many appeared to have the design qualities of booster American towns. Few found any favour with the citizens of Aberdeen. A funding opportunity for which Union Terrace Gardens was ideally suited, and for which it would doubtless have received big Lottery support was the initiative to restore and bring up to modern standards Victorian urban parks. That was never tried. For the backers of the big scheme that would have been a much too small endeavour. But in all candour that, if anything, was all that was required to answer the stated objectives.

Once a solution to a complex problem has been identified it is especially difficult for its authors to see merit in any alternative. One observes this in students at every level of attainment, also in professional colleagues. It is certainly no less true of committees, or other bodies, established by government as 'trouble-shooters' on the basis of their distinguished public service, or business acumen. Clearly to the *Beyond 2000* group and their professional colleagues bringing the gardens up to pavement level is such a clear, and obvious solution and doubtless to them worthy of comparison with any past achievements of the city. That such a 'solution' ignores many cogent problems such as climate, topography, or the existence of numerous building and monuments listed as being of historic and architectural merit has been thoroughly rehearsed in the public prints. Their proposals have also been offered to the public in professionally organized series of presentations, exhibitions and opinion gathering. The results of these, nearly 60 per cent against to 40 per cent odd in favour, have in no way altered the confident belief of the authors of the idea and their supporters that they are right, and anyone who disagrees is wrong.

There remain three basic kinds of solution to the 'problem' of Union Terrace Gardens. And it is the framing of the statement of intent, or the programme outlining what is to be addressed and its contexts that is always the where a brilliant 'solution' will lie. A basic level of competence could be thus assured, and if artists of exceptional skill respond and are then supported perhaps something great will be the result. An alternative to 'putting a lid on it' is to make the Gardens the site of a public institution, such as a specialist but popular art gallery. Such has been proposed, and the design found favour, not least because its designer showed exceptional skill in seeming to fit a modern building into a public park. However, turning a public park into a building site raises great short-term problems, and brings statutory obligations with it such as issues of health and security, access by ambulance, fire engine, trash collection, police and other security agents. All these have very significant and inimical implications to public gardens in the short and longer term. There

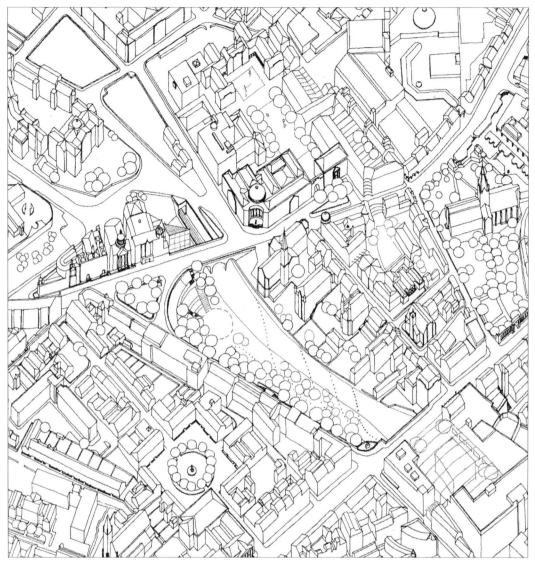

8.12 Denburn Valley as proposed by Robert Gordon University students

are also questions of balance and 'ownership': are the gardens now to be the grounds of an art gallery, or, is the gallery to be another incident within a park?

A class of solution which has been explicitly excluded by the successors to Aberdeen Beyond 2000, the Aberdeen City and Shire Economic Future group, in their international invitation for designers to act as consultants, is simply to improve the gardens while keeping the present topography, and all the listed buildings (Brogden and Lamb 1996). Such an attitude appears to have a majority of support in public opinion, and has formed the basis for Councillors to agree further exporations of alternatives. It has also been found to be prudent and efficacious in a number of studies by architecture students in recent years. One, by a Strathclyde University student won an award from the Royal Incorporation of Architects in Scotland in conference in the city, after it and others had been publicly exhibited in the Bon Accord Shopping Centre: her idea was to connect The Green with Union Terrace Gardens thus opening up new links to the ancient heart of the city and renewing the old, and obvious, link interrupted by the railway. Aberdeen students also have used the opportunities of the extended site to show for example how Belmont Street could be easily integrated with the gardens by way of existing pends, such as Patagonia Court, or new footbridges, or by extended terraces over the road or railway.

Others have explored how the arcade supporting the pavement of the east side of Union terrace could be exploited and connections made under Union Terrace to the lower floors of buildings on its west, allowing them to have direct and new access into the Gardens. By extension these could act as ways from areas further west to access the gardens also. Extensions at lower levels to the north are clear and obvious, and if exploited would allow Woolmanhill, and the rest the Denburn to have joint access in and out of the Union Terrace Gardens: from the Denburn much of the West End and Rosemount could be afforded wooded walks into, and of course, from the city centre.

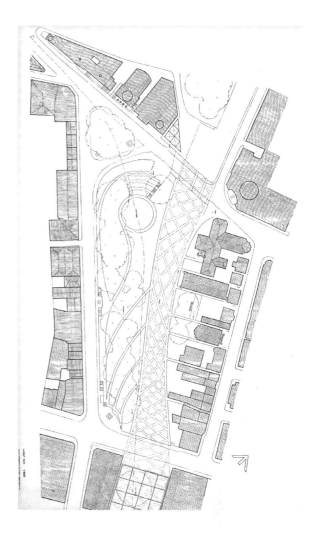

8.13 Denburn Valley as proposed by Robert Gordon University students

A connection to the railway station is also obvious, and yet repeatedly ignored. Re-designing of the spaces presently in place and used either for car-parking, or as waste space used for nothing, could be so arranged as to allow an easy and agreeable means of accessing the Gardens, and form such a route, accessing also the Trinity Shopping Centre and also Union Street itself, either at the Bridge, or by intermediate links to the Green, to Windmill Brae, or the lower floors on the south side of Union Street, and the cavernous spaces of the splendid vaults adjacent to the Bridge under the Street...presently inaccessible. Access between the pavements of Union Street Union Terrace or Belmont Street and all parts of the gardens can be made easy by automatic escalators, which are commonly used in such situations elsewhere: their costs,

8.14 Denburn Valley with Union Bridge

including supervision and maintenance would be considerably less than raising the gardens up to the pavements. Surely it would be better to make it easy for people to move about the gardens, rather than moving the gardens to the pedestrians. Re-imaging the 'problem' in such terms would bring much greater benefit to the whole town, and allow it exploit rather than seeming to regret its natural topography. Although the Council in response to the kind and generous offer from the former chairman of Aberdeen Beyond 2000 has set these very conditions on their acceptance, their resolve remains untested.

There are doubtless other projects which might enhance living, working and visiting the centre of Aberdeen, and whatever they might be, an assessment of their value is relatively easy. Any scheme that diminishes life for the residents there, requires the removal of any building, adversely affects the flow of people about the area on foot, that commandeers rights of way in the name of commercial security or significantly alters the topography of the city centre and its historical patterns of streets and passages, or crowds great numbers into spaces too small for them, should be refused. With such a specification the fine balance of large numbers of people living in the centre, many others working there, many more shopping there, or visiting for pleasure, can be assured a sustainable future. With prudent management of traffic from outside and the removal of merely transiting traffic there could be beneficial growth of population in the centre and its adjoining areas enabling sub-centres to flourish and perhaps encourage specialist businesses.

These are matters of management and could occur independent of any merit in either buildings or urban design, even the furnishings of what is a handsome city. To discuss, determine, and isolate the factors so as to allow an assessment of these values becomes a necessity to propose and define the determinants of value. Once these can be identified, understood and accepted then anything that would threaten or diminish them should be denied. However, there are those issues beyond these absolutely basic ones that often become confused with them. These are of two quite different kinds. They are to do with funding: from time to time, funds set aside from Government to address environmental problems, and invitations to bid for these, in competition, are then assessed before any projects go ahead. Local reactions to these sorts of projects are almost invariably 'to go for them', with every extra and afterthought that could possibly occur included. These invariably fail, because they are too clearly opportunistic. The projects for raising Union Terrace Gardens to the level of the Bridge are an example of this, including almost anything underneath to justify the expense. Had there been a worked out and attractive project that was clearly wanted and needed but for which funding could not be granted locally and that also answered the criteria of the competition, then success would have been forthcoming.

There are two lessons that can be taken from this. Firstly: any projects for public works (and private ones) must answer the basic requirements of good sense, probity, the nature of the place, health and safety and such. It is amazing just how many are deficient in one or other of these areas and yet are taken seriously. Secondly: just because someone else is paying for a project, it does not give them carte blanche to expect their fellow citizens to accept it. The significant corollary to both these lessons is that projects for improvement and/or changes to an old city such as Aberdeen require to demonstrate: homework, pre-planning of the most thorough kind, demonstration of value to the community, evidence of imagination and an idea of costs without being cost driven. These essential characteristics are not naturally bedfellows. Even the most cogent and well argued of projects may encounter opposition and it may be that that opposition is proof to the common sense inherent and already demonstrated. Arguments based on other qualities must then be brought into play, arguments about fundamental qualities of place-making related to history and to best practice in Aberdeen (or in other places).

Despite evidence to the contrary proposers of projects have to be assumed to have done their homework, and thoroughly, and be tested as such. In other words there can be no vagueness about implications, inattention to detail, or downplaying the rights of immediate neighbours and citizens more generally. Their critics need to have an even more thorough understanding of the issues presented and the implications more widely: this is essential also for the officials who will advise the councillors when matters come to them for decision. Citizens at large need not have expert knowledge, nor, apparently do the press, although the power they wield would make knowledge on their part desirable. In our system we cannot expect elected Members to be experts:

their judgements are usually based on advice from officers, but their decisions will also have a very large political component, which may well be swayed by reactions to and from the press, and argument from interested individuals. If they were to pass projects which had not been very thoroughly thought through nor had availed themselves of appropriate advice they would be justly blamed.

In varying measure these have always been the conditions against which issues of design have been debated and decided in Aberdeen. With each of these the city has changed, and whether the decisions were small ones or very large generally they have made the city more complex and richer. Because these decisions were realized in white granite Aberdeen is unusual in wearing its old design decisions as if they were recently made. Since the 18th century the town has prided itself on the happy abundance of this very long-lived material. Therefore at first encounter every building looks equally new or old. Its ancient patterns were renewed and modernized, is old buildings remade on enlightened lines incorporating light and air and comfort within very robust construction whose designs sought to conform to both local ways and the types brought to perfection in various parts of Europe deriving form ancient sources. Having perfected the old city and made it fit for modernity the citizens, like their neighbours elsewhere in these islands and abroad, began to experiment with just what modernity might be, and how it might give Aberdeen new form and growth.

That has been the collective, the social, effort of the town since 1800. As a city it has grown in population at least tenfold and occupied the whole of its hinterland as far as Tyrebagger, the Mounth and far into the northern plain, and significantly further as nucleus of a looser essentially suburban entity of greater Aberdeen.

The urban design of a place like Aberdeen is by nature a very long term project. The lengthy debate, the variety of designs, the intractability of its topography, has given to Aberdeen a very long, sustained vigour as a built environment. Its life force appears to be as strong as ever. Granite is not just a symbol of the town's character and growth, its physicality is also one of a number of characteristics which require to be understood and accepted, perhaps even celebrated if, as many wish, it is to continue to grow and prosper. There are lessons from these observations which may not be immediately as agreeable to those who would wish to run with cities such as Houston. But they need not despair, for it is not only possible for Aberdeen to continue to 'compete' with any town of whatever size it wishes, so long as it follows its own nature, looks to its own history, and forms and manner of doing things, and cherishes itself.

Bibliography

A.

Charles Abercrombie, *Plan and Section of Two New Lines of Road, extending from Aberdeen, to The two Bridges over the rivers Dee and Don; Together with some further Improvements proposed in that City* nd (c. 1796) engraved by J. Cary

Charles Abercrombie, *Plan of intended Navigable Canal from Aberdeen harbour to the bridge of Don at Inverury* Town Clerk's Plans C 1 1796, together with his *Book of Reference*, Town Clerk's Plans C 25 1796

Malcolm Airs, '"Good & Not Expensive…" Lord Harcourt's Nuneham Courtney' in *Architectural History Journal of the Society of Architectural Historians of Great Britain* 44 Leeds Maney 2001

Anna von Ajkay, 'James Souttar in Sweden' in *Architectural Heritage II* Edinburgh EUP 1991

L.B. Alberti, *On the Art of Building in Ten Books*, trans by Rykwert, Leach & Tavenor, Cambridge (USA) and London MIT 1991

Sir Henry Alexander, et al., *City of Aberdeen Housing and Town Planning* Aberdeen Mearns nd (1939)

Stanford Anderson (ed), *On Streets* Cambridge (USA) and London MIT 1991

Arredo Urbano; New York, Wanted A Waterfront, il concorso per il lungofiume del'Hudson nos 27 and 28, Rome 1988

B.

Back Wynd 1. Building Warrant 5310 PB/D Alterations at Ariated (*sic*) Water Manufactory for J.E. Strachan 25 Aug 1898 William Ruxton Architect

Back Wynd 2. Building Warrant 4869 PB/D Additions to Premises for Messrs Sinclair and Co Wholesale Druggists Brown and Watt 17 Union Terrace 15 July 1898

Back Wynd 3. Building Warrant 7450 PB/E Extension of Bookbinding…for Wm Jackson & Sons, Back WyndWilson and Walker, 181a Union Street 30 June 1907; see also 3993 PB/C and 4310 PB/C

Back Wynd 4. Building Warrant 4518 PB/D John Rust 224 Union Street 28 Dec 1897, 9 and 11 Back Wynd; also 8585/F Alterations for Wm Ferris Esq Hotel Keeper Cults, Robert Buchan 488 Holburn Street 7 March 1913

Hilary Ballon, *The Paris of Henri IV; Architecture and Urbanism* Cambridge (USA) and London MIT 1991

Jonathan Barnett, *The Elusive City; Five Centuries of Design Ambition and Miscalculation* London Herbert Press 1986

Anna Barozzi and Gabrielle Tagliaventi, *Il Ritorno alla Citta* Modena Franco Cosimo Panini 1990

Bede, *Historica Ecclesiastica Gentis Anglorum*, 731 (Oxford edition 2008)

Dorothy Bell, 'Seeing and Believing: the case of the misleading evidence' in *Architectural Heritage X* Edinburgh EUP 1999

Dorothy Bell, 'A lost aesthetic: traditional architectural form in wood and its neglect' in *Architectural Heritage XV* Edinburgh EUP 2004

Guido Beltrami et al., *Palladio and Northern Europe, Books Travellers, Architects* Milan Skira 1999

E.H. Bennett and A.W. Crawford, *Plan of Minneapolis* Minneapolis Civic Commission 1917

S.W. Berg, *Grand Avenues; the Story of Pierre L'Enfant* New York Vintage 2008

Like Bijlsma and Jochem Groenland, *The Intermediate Size; A Handbook for Collective Dwellings* Delft SUN nd (c. 2005)

C.W. Bishir and M.T. Southern, *A Guide to the Historic Architecture of Eastern North Carolina* Chapel Hill UNC 1996

Werner Blaser, *Architecture and Nature; the Work of Alfred Caldwell* Basel Birkhauser 1984

Hector Boece, *History and Chronicles of Scotland* (John Bellenden, trans) Edinburgh 1821

M.T. Boatwright, *Hadrian and The City of Rome* Princeton PUP 1987

W. Bonwitt, *Michael Searles; a Georgian Architect and Surveyor* Society of Architectural Historians of Great Britain Monograph 3 Leeds Maney 1987

Franco Borsi, *Leon Battista Alberti; The Complete Works* New York Electa/Rizzoli 1986

M.C. Boyer, *Dreaming the Rational City; the Myth of American City Planning* Cambridge (USA) and London MIT 1990

Joseph Brady (ed), *Extracts from the Minutes of the Commissioners for making Wide and Convenient Ways, Streets, and Passages, in the City Of Dublin* Dublin 1802

Garbrielle Brainard et al., *Grand Tour; Perspecta 41*, esp Robert Manguiran and Mary-Ann Ray 'Re-drawing Hadrain's Villa, Re-wiritng Caochangli Urban Village' and Esra Akcan, 'Reading the Generic City' Cambriidge (USA) and London MIT 2008

Broadford Lane. Building Warrant South Side 2321 PB/B Alterations and Additions to three cottages for Mr Richard Hallgler, Spirit Dealer Dec 29 1890, George H Jolly Architect. 'Walls raised from 5'-0" to c 9'-0"; floor level raised c 2'-0"…original floor to ceiling, 7'-0" raised to 9'-6", with ventilated space under floor; 2 existing cellars converted to WCs, Browns Parfait Flushing out Closet'

Broadgate 1. Building Warrant House at the Top of Broad Street & Gallowgate for H. Gray 27th Dec 1876 W.B. Coutts Architect, also Shops at Broad Street & Gallowgate for Henry Gray Draper 27 Dec 1876

Broadgate 2. Building Warrant Rebuilding at 85 Broad Street for Mr J.L. Grant 12 Dec 1887 deferred, 15 Dec '87, approved 29 Dec 87, Matthews and Mackenzie, countersigned John Morgan co, 'New Building no 85 Broad Street to be erected for John Lyall Grant Esq of Richmondhill, Tea Merchant Aberdeen'

Broadgate 3. Building Warrant 2307 PB 34 Broad Street East Side Additions and Alterations for Mr A.B. Hutcheson Nov 24th 1890 Brown and Watt 17 Union Street

Broadgate 4. Building Warrant (Marischal College) 3619PB/C Broad Street East Side Additions to North Wing Marischal College August 28th 1895 A. Marshall Mackenzie; also BW 4163 Bundle, South side of Marischal College, 1897–1898; 4140 PB/C and 4163 PB/C (Bundle 2, 3 &4) New South Wing for the Aberdeen University Court; and 3081 PB/C Mitchell Tower, Nov 11th 1893.

Broadgate 5. Building Warrant (Café Royal) Broad Street West Side, 4553 PB/D Alterations…for Mrs Mollison 27 Jan '98, Duncan Hodge Architect 176 Skene Street Aberdeen June 1897, with note, 'to be used as business premises locked up all night'

Broadgate 6. Building Warrant Broad Street, Ragg's Lane and Guestrow, 4938 PB/D, Alterations for the Trustees of the late Geo Russell 28th Sept 1898

Broadgate 7. Building Warrant (Esslemont and Macintosh's) 6286 PB/D Broad Street West Side and corner of Netherkirkgate, New Premises for Esslemont and Macintosh July 9th 1902…Robert G. Wilson Architect 181 Union Street. Also 5449 PB/D, 5649 PB/E, and F/9562

Broadgate 8. Building Warrant 73 and 75 Broad Street West Side 6369 PB/D Alterations and Additions for Henry Gray 10 Dec 1902…William G. Gauld Architect 258 Union Street. (3 feus 58 ft south of corner with Upperkirkgate)

Broadgate 9. Building Warrant 27, 29 and 31 Broad Street West Side 6577 PB/E and 6598 PB/E, Alterations and Additions for the New Loan Coy 28 April 1903, Declined 11th June 1903, Amended 23 June 1903, Approved 26 June 1903. (also entered from Guestrow, noted as 12'6" wide)

W.A. Brogden, 'The Bridge/Street in Scottish urban Planning' in *The Neo-Classical Town; Scottish Contributions to Urban Design since 1750* Edinburgh Rutland Press 1996

W.A. Brogden and N.A. Lamb, 'The Denburn, Aberdeen's Past and Aberdeen's Future' in *The Neo-Classical Town; Scottish Contributions to Urban Design since 1750* Edinburgh Rutland Press 1996

W.A. Brogden, *Aberdeen, An Illustrated Architectural Guide* Edinburgh Rutland Press 1998 new edition in press

W.A. Brogden, 'An Education in Architecture: 1956 and All That' in *Architectural Heritage XVII* Edinburgh EUP 2006

E. Brown, *Rubislaw/Skene estate* Town Clerk's Plans R 2 1803

I.G. Brown, *Elegance & Entertainment in the New Town of Edinburgh* Edinburgh Rutland 2002

Thomas Burnet, *Sacred Theory of the Earth*, 1691 (London Centaur 1965)

C.

H.P. Caemmerer, *Washington, The National Capitol* Washington US Government Printing Office 1932

Peter Calthorpe, *The Next American Metropolis* New York Princeton Architectural Press 1993

Colen Campbell, et al., *Vitruvius Britannicus* New York Benjamin Bloom 1967 4 volumes

Ian Campbell, 'A Romanesque Revival and the Early Renaissance in Scotland, c. 1380–1513' in *Journal of the Society of Architectural Historians* Chicago SAH September 1995

A.S. Cameron and J.A. Stones *Aberdeen, An In-depth View of the City's Past*, Edinburgh, Society of Antiquaries of Scotland Monograph 19, 2001

Eamonn Canniffe, *Politics of the Piazza, the History and Meaning of the Italian Square* Farnham Ashgate 2008

Carden Place 1. *Building Warrant* Two Cottages at 25 & 26 Carden Place and Prince Arthur Street, Aberdeen Heritable property Co, by James Valentine Jr 6 Sept 1877

Carden Place 2. *Building Warrant* Additions and Alterations for Mr David Smith Stockbroker, 12 Carden Place, by Wm Smith and Kelly 170 Union Street 12 June 1897

Carmelite Street 1. *Building Warrant* Warehouse for Mr Ogilvie 27 Dec 1883, Ellis and Wilson

Carmelite Street 2. *Building Warrat* Warehouse and Offices for Cruikshank and Sellars May 17 1899, James Barron, civil engineer, 1 Bon Accord Street

Castlegate 1. *Building Warrant* 22–24 Castle Street, New shop fronts and WCs for Mr A Holdsworth Jeweller 15 Castle Street, by Harvey Mennie Architect 33 St Swithin Street April 1905

Luca Cerchai, Lorena Jannelli, Fausto longo, *Greek Cities of Magna Graeca and Sicily* San Giovani Lupatoto, Arsenale 2004

David Clark, 'The Shop Within? An Analysis of Architectural Evidence for Medieval Shops' in *Architectural History 43* Leeds Maney 2000

R.L. Cleary, *The Place Royale and Urban Design in the Ancien Regime* Cambridge CUP 1999

G.R. and C.C. Collins, *Camillo Sitte: The Birth of Modern City Planning, with a translation of the 1889 Austrian edition of his City Planning according to Artistic Principles* New York Rizzoli 1986

Alan Colquhoun, *Modernity and the Classical Tradition; Architectural Essays 1980–1987* Cambridge (USA) and London MIT 1989

H.M. Colvin, *A Biographical Dictionary of British Architects 1600–1840* London Murray 1978

Elias Cornell, 'Going Inside Architecture: A Tentative Synopsis for a history of the Interior' in *Architectural History Journal of the society of Architectural Historians of Great Britain 40* Leeds Maney 1997

Cotton Street 1. *Building Warrant* 4 tenement blocks, by James T. Leilley (approved by William Boulton as engineer) 19 September 1872

Norman Crowe, *Nature and the Idea of a Man-made World* Cambridge (USA) and London MIT 1995

Kitty Cruft and Andrew Fraser (eds) *James Craig 1744–1795,* Edinburgh Mercat 1995

Dan Cruickshank and Neil Burton, *Life in the Georgian City* London Viking 1990

Elizabeth Cumming, *Hand Heart and Soul, The Arts and Crafts Movement in Scotland* Edinburgh Birlinn 2006

D.

David Daiches et al. (eds) *A Hotbed of Genius; The Scottish Enlightenment 1730–90* Edinburgh EUP 1986

Jean-Claude Daufresne, *Louvre & Tuilleries; Architectures de Papier* Leige Pierre Mardaga (nd) c. 1986

E.P. Dennsion et al. (eds) *Aberdeen Before 1800; A New History* Phantassie (East Lothian) Tuckwell 2002

Allan Doig, *Liturgy and Architecture, From the Early Church to the Middle Ages* Farnham Ashgate 2009

John Donald, 'Teaching the Town; Lower Pulteneytown, Wick' in *The Neo-Classical Town; Scottish Contributions to Urban Design since 1750* Edinburgh Rutland Press 1996

J.G. Dunbar, *Scottish Royal Palaces; The Architecture of the Royal Residences during the Late Medieval and Early Renaissance Periods* Phantassie (East Lothian) Tuckwell 1999

E.

Keller Easterling, *American Town Plans; a Comparative Time Line* New York Princeton Architectural Press 1993

William Ellis, 'Type and Context in Urbanism; Colin Rowe's Contextualism' in *Oppositions Reader; Selected Readings from a Journal for Ideas and Criticism in Architecture 1973–1884* New York Princeton Architectural Press 1998

B.M. Evans, 'Respecting the Town; The Office of Urban Architecture' in *The Neo-Classical Town; Scottish Contributions to Urban Design since 1750* Edinburgh Rutland Press 1996

B.M. Evans et al., *Aberdeen Urban Realm Strategy* Glasgow Gillespies 2001

F.

Diane Favro, '*Pater urbis:* Augustus as City Father of Rome' in *Journal of the Society of Architectural Historians* Philadelphia SAH March 1992

Iain Fenlon, *Piazza San Marco* London Profile 2009

John Fleming, *Robert Adam and his Circle in Edinburgh and Rome* London Murray 1962

Thomas Fletcher *Plan showing marches and Freedom Lands of Aberdeen* Town Clerk's Plans A 14 1807

Thomas Fletcher, *Plan of Union Street and Adjacent Town* 1807 (ex Maritime Museum)

M. Flinn (ed) *Scottish population History* Cambridge 1977

Carol Foreman, *Lost Glasgow; Glasgow's Lost Architectural Heritage* Edinburgh Birlinn 2002

Elizabeth Foyster and C.A. Whatley (eds) *A History of Everyday Life in Scotland 1600 to 1800* Edinburgh EUP 2010

A.G. Fraser, *The Building of Old College, Adam Playfair & The University of Edinburgh*, Edinburgh EUP 1989

J.E. Fraser, *The Roman Conquest of Scotland; The Battle of Mons Graupius AD 84* Edinburgh Birlinn 2008

J.E. Fraser, *From Caledonia to Pictland: Scotland to 795* Edinburgh EUP 2009

K.A. Frank and L.H. Shneekloth, *Ordering Space, Types and Architectural Design* New York Von Rostrand Reinhold 1994

W.H. Fraser and C.H. Lee, *Aberdeen 1800–2000; A New History* Phantassie (East Lothian) Tuckwell 2000

Terry Friedman, *James Gibbs* New Haven and London Yale, 1984

G.

Stanley Gale, *Modern Housing Estates* London Batsford 1949

Michel Gallet, *Paris Domestic Architecture of the 18th Century* London Barrie and Jenkins 1972

James Galletly, *The City Could be Made in the Image of Man Who is Made in the Image of…; Report on Andrew Grant Bequest Travelling Scholarship 1933/34* Edinburgh typescript author's copy 1934

Gallowgate 1. Building WarrantHouses in Findlays Court Gallowgate for James Findlay May 1875, William Coutts

Gallowgate 2. Building WarrantHouses at Gallowgate Head for Mr Andrew Craig, James Souttar 16 Mar 77

Gallowgate 3.Building Warrant2875 PB/B Shops Store and Tenement, Gallowgate and Farquhar Place Alexander Mavor 211 Union Street for Northern Cooperative (Gross over building)

Gallowgate 4. Building Warrant (St Margaret's Gallowgate) 7623/PB/E Clergy House, George G Irvine, ARIBA, 231 ½ Union Street Sept 5 1907.

Gallowgate 5. Building Warrant (St Margaret's Gallowgate) New South Aisle, J N Comper 288 Knight's Hill, W Norwood, London SE, per George Irvine.

Gallowgate 6. Building Warrant (Ogston's) F/9626 Ogston and Tennant Offices, J L Simpson, Lever Bros Ltd Port Sunlight, 3 march 1920.

Jane Geddes, *Deeside and the Mearns; An Illustrated Architectural Guide* Edinburgh Rutland 2001

John Gifford, *William Adam 1689–1748 A Life and Times of Scotland's 'Universal Architect'* Edinburgh Mainstream, 1989

Miles Glendinning, 'Modernity, Urbanity and Rationalism: New Towns of the 20th Century' in *The Neo-Classical Town; Scottish Contributions to Urban Design since 1750* Edinburgh Rutland Press 1996

Miles Glendinning and Diane Waters (eds) *Home Builders; Mactaggart & Mickel and the Scottish Housebuilding Industry* Edinburgh RCAHMS 1999

Miles Glendinning, *Modern Architect the Life and Times of Robert Mathew* London RIBA 2008

G. Gordon (ed) *Perspectives of the Scottish City*, Aberdeen AUP, 1985

James Gordon, *Abredoniae utriusque Descriptio; A Description of Both Towns of Aberdeen by James Gordon Parson of Rothemay (sic) with a Selection of the Charters of the Burgh* (1661) Edinburgh Spalding Club 1892

Ian Gow, *The Scottish Interior* Edinburgh EUP 1992

Granton Lodge. Building Warrant 3312 PB/C Ashvale Terrace (or Great Western Road), alterations and additions to Granton Lodge, 17 Sept 1894, Cameron and Matthews Balmoral Terrace

T.A. Greeves, *Bedford Park; the first Garden Suburb* London Anne Bingley 1975

Neil Gregory, 'Monro and Partners: Shopping in Scotland with Marks and Spencer' in *Architectural Heritage XIV* Edinburgh EUP 2003

John Gwynne, *London and Westminster Improved, to which is prefixed a discourse on Public Magnificence* London 1766

H.

Louise Harpman and E.M. Supcoff, *Perspecta 30; Settlement Patterns* Cambridge (USA) MIT 1999

Vaughan Hart and Peter Hicks, *Sebastiano Serlio on Architecture* New Haven and London Yale 1996

Steven Harris and Deborah Berke (eds) *Architecture of the Everyday* New York PAP 1997

J.G. Harrison, 'Wooden-fronted Houses and forestairs in Early Modern Scotland' in *Architectural Heritage IX* Edinburgh EUP 1998

Vaughan Hart, 'Lost Cities and Standing Stones: Stuart London and Georgian Bath' in *Architectural Heritage VI* Edinburgh EUP 1996

Marika Hausen et al., *Eliel Saarinen Projects 1896–1923* Hamburg Ginko 1990

Dolores Hayden, *Building Suburbia; Green Fields and Urban Growth 1820–2000* New York Vintage 2003

Rupert Hebblethwaite, 'The municipal housing programme in Sheffield before 1914' in *Architectural History; The Journal of the Society of Architectural Historians of Great Britain, 30* Leeds Maney 1987

Barbel Hedinger, *C.F. Hansen in Hamburg, Altona und den Elbvororten; ein danischer Architek des Klassizisms* Berlin Deutcher Kunstverlag Munchen 2000

Werner Hegemann and Elbert Peets, *The American Vitruvius: an Architect's Handbook of Civic Art* 1922, A.J. Plattus, ed New York Princeton Architectural Press 1986

George and Isabel Henderson, *The Art of the Picts, Sculpture and Metalwork in Early Medieval Scotland*, London Thames and Hudson, 2004

T.S. Hines, *Burnham of Chicago Architect and Planner* Chicago UCP/Phoenix 1979

Hermann Hipp, *Wohnstadt Hamburg; Meitshauser zwischen Inflation und Weltwirtschaftskrise* Hamburg Christians Verlag 1985

H.-R. Hitchcock and Philip Johnson, *The International Style* New York W.W. Norton, 1966

F.T. Hodgson, *Practical Bungalows and Cottages for Town and Country* Chicago F.J. Drake & Co 1916

Henry Home, Lord Kames, *Elements of Criticism* Edinburgh Kincaid and Bell 1762

John Home, *Aberdeen Harbour* Town Clerk's Plans H 1; displayed at Maritime Museum 1769

Deborah Howard, *Jacopo Sansovino, Architecture and Patronage in Renaissance Venice* New Haven and London Yale 1975

Deborah Howard, *The Architectural History of Venice* New Haven and London 2004

I.

Colin Innes, *Plan of proposed North Entry* (King Street) Town Clerk's Plans K3 1800

Colin Innes, *Plan of the South Entry* (Union Street) Town Clerk's Plans U 1 1800

J.

Mark Jarzombeck, *On Leon Battista Alberti; His Literary and Aesthetic Theories* Cambridge (USA) and London MIT 1989

Jim Johnson and Lou Rosenburg, *Renewing Old Edinburgh;The Enduring Legacy of Patrick Geddes,* Glendaruel (Argyll), 2011

D. Jones and S. McKinstry (eds) *Essays in Scots and English Architetcural History; a Festschrift for John Frew* 2009

D.P. Jordan, *Transforming Paris; the Life and Labours of Baron Hausmann* Chicago UCP 1995

K.

Emil Kaufmann, *Architecture in the Age of Reason; Baroque and Post-Baroque in England Italy and France* Cambridge (USA) Harvard College/Archon 1966

Stuart Kelly, *Scott-land; The Man Who Invented a Nation* Edinburgh Polygon 2010

Kelly Papers, William Kelly manuscripts (incorporating material from John and William Smith) in University of Aberdeen, Special Collections, Kings College

William Kennedy, *Annals of Aberdeen* London Longman 1818, 2 vols

W.H. Kilham *Raymond Hood Architect, Form through Function in the American Skyscraper* New York Architectural Book Publishing 1973

Kingsgate 1. Building Warrant Garden Bungalow, 1922

Kingsgate 2. Building Warrant 8 Bungalows King's Gate (West of Anderson Drive) 1937 J. Bissett and Sons, E.L. Williamson 154 Union Street 15 March 1937

King Street 1. Building Warrant 'Two Cottages at Orchard Street' 14 March 1877

King Street 2. Building Warrant Washington Buildings 2749 PB/B 198–212 King Street for D. Courage Spirit Merchant, Brown and Watt 17 Union Terrace 9 June 1892

King Street 3. Building Warrant Local Authority tenements (20) King Street opp Militia Barracks, J/6559, 26 Dec 1935 A.B. Gardner

King Street 4. Building Warrant (Cottage/House) 466 King Street Road, 2707 PB/B, John Rust City Architect Aberdeen 22 Aug 1892

J.P. Kleihues et al., *Project Report, Internationale Bauausstellung Berlin 1987* Berlin 1991

Christina Kossak, 'Provincial Pretensions: Architecture and Town-Planning in the *Gau*-capital Koblenz 1933-45' in *Architectural History Journal of the Society of Architectural Historians of Great Britain 40* Leeds Maney 1997

Rob Krier, *On Architecture* London Academy/St Martin 1982

L.

Sylvia Lavin, *Quatremere de Quincy and the Invention of a Modern Language of Architecture* Cambridge (USA) and London MIT 1992

LeCorbusier (nom de plume of C.-E. Jenneret) (John Goodman trans) *Towards an Architecture* (Paris 1924) London Francis Lincoln, 2007

LeCorbusier (Frederick Etchells, trans), *The City of To-morrow and its Planning* (New York 1929) Mineola (USA) Dover 1987

W.C. Lehmann, *Henry Home, Lord Kames, and the Scottish Enlightenments; a Study in National Character and the History of Ideas* The Hague Martinus Nijhoff 1971

Gustav Lettstrom (ed) *Nordisk Arkitektur aren 1946–1949* Stockholm TBF 1950

Andrew Logie, *Survey of the cities of Old and New Aberdeen, the harbour and Country adjacent*, Town Clerk's Plans A7 1742

Richard Longstreth, 'The Neighborhood Shopping Center in Washington DC 1930–1941' in *Journal of the Society of Architectural Historians* Philadelphia SAH March 1992

Wolfgang Lotz, *Studies in Italian Renaissance Architecture* Cambridge (USA) and London MIT 1977

J.C. Loudon, *The Encyclopaedia of Cottage Farm and Villa Architecture and Furniture* London Longman et al. 1834

John Lowrey, 'Landscape Design and Edinburgh New Town' in *The Neo-Classical Town; Scottish Contributions to Urban Design since 1750* Edinburgh Rutland Press 1996

M.

M. (Post Office) Building Warrant No 3 (59) Post Office Elevation towards Market Street, Robert Matheson, The Office of Works, Edinburgh 16th Sept 1873

James Macaulay, *The Gothic Revival* Glasgow Blackie 1975

W.L. MacDonald, *The Architecture of the Roman Empire; Volume II An Urban Appraisal* New Haven and London Yale 1986

David Macgibbon and Thomas Ross, *The Castellated and Domestic Architecture of Scotland* Edinburgh 1887–1892 5 volumes James Thin ed nd

Ranald MacInnes, 'Robert Adam's Public Buildings' in *Architectural Heritage IV* Edinburgh EUP 1993

Marshall Mackenzie, *Elevation of Marischal College showing extension of buildings* nd (1890s) TCP U 11 A; Town Clerk's Plans M 5, also *Plans and sections for extension of Marischal College* 1893

H.F. Mallgrave, *Modern Architectural Theory; A Historical Survey, 1673–1968*, Cambridge (UK) CUP 2005

T.A. Marder, 'Alexander VII, Bernini, and the Urban Setting of the Pantheon in the Seventeenth Century' in *Journal of the Society of Architectural Historians* Philadelphia SAH September 1991

T.A. Markus (ed), *Order in Space and Society; Architectural Form and its Context in the Scottish Enlightenment* Edinburgh Mainstream 1982

Robert Maxwell of Arkland, *Transactions of the Honourable the Society for the Improvement of Knowledge in Agriculture in Scotland* Edinburgh 1742

P. May, *Plan of the lands of Ferryhill as surveyed* Town Clerk's Plans F 1 nd (1755)

Debroah Mays (ed) *The Architecture of Scottish Cities*, East Linton, 1997

Niall McCullogh, *A Vision of the City; Dublin and the Wide Streets Commissioners* Dublin Dublin Corporation 1991

I.K. McEwen, *Socrates' Ancestor; an Essay of Architectural Beginnings* Cambridge (USA) and London MIT 1993

I.K. McEwen, *Vitruvius Writing the Body of Architecture*, Cambridge (USA) MIT 2003

Charles McKean, *The Scottish Thirties; an Architetcural Introduction*, Edinburgh Scottish Academic Press, 1987

Charles McKean, 'The Incivility of Edinburgh's New Town' in *The Neo-Classical Town; Scottish Contributions to Urban Design since 1750* Edinburgh Rutland Press 1996

Charles McKean *The Scottish Chateau, The Country House of Renaissance Scotland* Stroud Sutton 2001

Charles McKean, 'Reconsidering the Scottish Town' in *Architectural Heritage XIX* Edinburgh EUP 2008

Christopher Mead, 'Urban Contingency and the Problem of Representation in Second Empire Paris' in *Journal of the Society of Architectural Historians* Philadelphia SAH June 1995

Nicolas Le Camus de Mezieres, *The Genius of Architecture; or, the Analogy that Art with our Sensations* Santa Monica, Getty 1992

David G. Miller, *Archibald Simpson Architect*, Kinloss (Moray) Librario, 2006

David G. Miller, *Tudor Johnny City Architect of Aberdeen*, Kinloss (Moray) Librario, 2007

Henry A. Millon, *The Renaissance from Brunelleschi to Michelangelo: the Representation of Architecture*, London Thames and Hudson 1994

Alexander Milne, *A Plan of the City of Aberdeen, with all the Inclosures Surrounding the Town to the Adjacent Country* engraved by D. Lizars 1789 ex Maritime Museum, copy in Town Clerk's Plans A 12

Diane Morgan, *Lost Aberdeen; Aberdeen's Lost Architectural Heritage* Edinburgh Birlinn 2004

Diane Morgan, *Lost Aberdeen; The Outskirts* Edinburgh Birlinn 2007

Diane Morgan, *Lost Aberdeen; The Freedom Lands* Edinburgh Birlinn 2009

A.E.J. Morris, *History of Urban Form before the Industrial Revolutions* London Longman Scientific and Technical 1994

E.S. Morris, *British Town Planning and Urban Design; Principles and Policies* London Longman 1997

James Mossman, *South Prospect of the City of Aberdeen* 1756 Aberdeen City Art Gallery Macdonald Rooms

A.V. Moudon, *Built for Change; Neighorhood Architecture in San Francisco* Cambridge (USA) MIT post 1985

Eric Mumford, *The CIAM Discourse on Urbanism, 1928–1960* Cambridge (USA) and London MIT 2002

H.K. Murray, J.C. Murray and S.M. Fraser, *A Tale of Unknown Unknowns; a Mesolithic pit alignment and a Neolithic timbers hall at Warren Field, Crathes Aberdeenshire* Oxford and Oakville Oxbow 2009

H.K. Murray et al., *Report on the archaeology of an early (ca 3700 BC) house Garthdee Aberdeen* unpublished draft report provided by authors, 2010

N.

Netherkirkgate 1. Building Warrant Benholm's Lodging (also known as Wallace Tower, or Wallace Neuk) Building Warrants outsize roll 33, tracings and prints of surveys of plans sections and elevations by demolition contractors, Alex Hall & Sons 21 Jan 1964

Netherkirkgate 2. Building WarrantHouse North side (Graham Tiso's), Mackenzie and MacMillan architects 24 March 1881; amendments 4 Feb 1884 Duncan Macmillan Architect 4 Dee Street

Netherkirkgate 3. Building Warrant PB/B 1619 warehouse for Messrs John Fyffe & Sons William Ruxton 84 Union Street 26 Jan 1888

New Streets Trustees Letter Books, Aberdeen City Archives Town House

New Streets Trustees, Minute Books, Aberdeen City Archives Town House

W.F.H. Nicolaisen, *Scottish Place Names* Edinburgh John Donald, 2001

James Nicoll (ed) *Domestic Architecture in Scotland* Aberdeen Daily Journal Offices 1908

Patrick Nuttgens, 'The Planned Villages of North-East Scotland' in *The Neo-Classical Town: Scottish Contributions to Urban Design since 1750* Edinburgh Rutland Press 1996

O.

D.J. Olsen, *The City as a Work of Art; London Paris Vienna* New Haven and London Yale 1986

Richard Oram, *Domination and Lordship; Scotland 1070–1230* Edinburgh EUP 2011

The Poems of Ossian and Related Works H. Gaskill (ed) Edinburgh EUP 2006

P.

Andrea Palladio, *Four Books on Architecture*, trans by Robert Tavernor and Richard Scholfield Cambridge (USA) and London MIT 1997

M.P. Pearson and Colin Richards (eds), *Architecture & Order; Approaches to Social Space* London and New York Routledge 1994

Peddie and Kinnear, *Plans of Town House*, Town Clerk's Plans T 9, also T 10, T 12, T 13 and T 14, plus T 18 (1870) (1–10) 1867–70 and T 19 (1887) : see T 33–40 for works from 1966

Franca Pellegrini (curator) *Giuseppe Jappelli e la nuova Padova* Saonaro Prato 2008

Nikolaus Pevsner, *A History of Building Types* London Thames and Hudson 1976

Antoine Picon, *French Architects and Engineers in the Age of Enlightenment* Cambridge CUP 1992

Stuart Piggott *William Stukely an Eighteenth-Century Antiquary* London Tames and Hudson 1985

Police Commissioners, Minute Books, from 1796 Aberdeen City Archive Town House

Richard Pommer et al., *In the Shadow of Mies; Ludwig Hilberseimer Architect Educator and Urban Planner* Chicago The Art Institute of Chicago 1988

Paolo Portoghesi, Aldo Rossi et al., *Third International Exhibition of Architecture; Venice Project* Milan Electa 1985

Q.

Anthony Quiney, *Town Houses of Medieval Britain* New Haven and London Yale 2003

R.

Raleigh City Council, *Early Raleigh Neighborhoods and Buildings* Raleigh 1983

RCAHMS, see Royal Commission of the Ancient and Historical Monuments of Scotland

Peter Reed (ed) *Glasgow: The Framing of the City*, Edinburgh EUP (1993) 2nd ed 1999

Peter Reed, 'Breaking the Grid; Glasgow's West End' in *The Neo-Classical Town; Scottish Contributions to Urban Design since 1750* Edinburgh Rutland 1996

William Rees Morrissh, *Civilizing Terrains; Mountains Mounds and Mesas* San Francisco William Stout 1996

Terence Riley, *The International Style: Exhibition 15 and the Museum of Modern Art* New York Rizzoli/ Columbia Books of Architecture 1992

Sixten Ringbom, *Stone, Style & Truth, The Vogue for Natural Stone in Nordic Architecture 1880–1910* Helsinki 1987

Alasdair Roberts, 'James Smith and James Gibbs: Seminarians and Architects' in *Architectural Heritage II* Edinburgh EUP 1991

C.M. Robinson, *A City Plan for Raleigh* Raleigh Woman's Club 1913

Rosemount Viaduct. Building Warrant 4931 PB/D 55 Skene Street Corner of Rosemount Viaduct Southside for the Aberdeen Town and County Property Co Ltd Brown and Watt 17 Union Terrace Sept 15 1898

Alistair Rowan, 'Robert Adam's ideas for the North Bridge in Edinburgh' in *Architectural Heritage XV* Edinburgh EUP 2004

Alistair Rowan, Vaulting *Ambition, The Adam Brothers Contractors to the Metropolis in the Reign of George III*, London Sir John Soane's Museum, 2007

General William Roy, The Military Survey of Scotland, 1747–55 is in King's Maps, British Museum as MS. Colour copies available at National Library of Scotland Map Room. It forms the reliable large scale survey of Scotland a century before the Ordnance Survey for which it formed the prototype. It was published at reduced scale as *The Great Map*, Edinburgh 2008 (Birlinn) for British Museum and National Library of Scotland.

Royal Commission on the Ancient and Historical Monuments of Scotland, *Tolbooths and Town-Houses, Civic Architecture in Scotland to 1833* Edinburgh 1996

Royal Commission on the Ancient and Historical Monuments of Scotland, *In the Shadow of Bennachie* Edinburgh 2007

Tatyana Rushinskaya, 'William Hastie and the Reconstruction of Moscow after the 1812 Fire' in *Architectural Heritage V* Edinburgh EUP 1995

S.

Sasines, *Burgh Register Sasines Aberdeen*, 91 Volumes (1484–1809) held at Aberdeen City Archive, Town House

Schoolhill 1. Building Warrant Schoolhill and Harriet Street Warehouse and Shop for Messrs Wm Shirras & Sons 7th Feb 1887, John Rust Architect

Schoolhill 2. Building Warrant Dwelling Houses & Shops Schoolhill, (North Side) for Messrs Wordie 22 March 1886, John Morgan Co and Matthews and Mackenzie Architects

Schoolhill 3. Building Warrant (Rebuilding Jameson's Hs, other half of above) Rebuilding no's 8 and 10, Matthew and Mackenzie Architects 23 May 1887

Schoolhill 4. Building Warrant6667 PB/E et al. Art Gallery & Industrial Museum Schoolhill, 25 Sept 1883, Gray's School of Science and Art 25 Jany 84, and Archway 29 April 1885, Matthews and Mackenzie Architects

Schoolhill 5. Building Warrant Dwelling Houses and Shop Schoolhill,for Messrs Mitchell and Muill Limited 7 Jan '86 and 7 March '87, Matthews and Mackenzie Architects

School Road 1. Building Warrant School Road I/14970, 258 Dwelling Houses 10/8/33, A.B. Gardner

School Road 2 Building Warrant H/12958 392 Dwelling Houses, School Road, Brick (hollow wall) construction noted in pink, and Granite in grey, A.B. Gardner Architect Municipal Offices 11 Broad Street Aberdeen, October 1928 and March 1929

Friederike Schneider (ed) *Floor Plan Manual; Housing* Basel Birkhauser 2004

David Schuyler, *Apostle of Taste; Andrew Jackson Downing 1815–1852* Baltimore Johns Hopkins University Press 1996

Scottish Housing Advisory Committee, *Planning Our New Homes* Edinburgh H.M. Stationery Office 1945

Nancy Seiber, 'The Last Tenement: Confronting Community and Urban Renewal in Boston's West End' review of exhibition in *Journal of the Society of Architectural Historians* Philadelphia SAH March 1994

Cesare de Seta (curator) *L'Architettura a Napoli tra le due Guerre* Naples Electa 1999

Ian Shepherd, *Aberdeenshire Donside and Strathbogie; An Illustrated Architectural Guide*, Edinburgh Rutland 2006

Shiprow 1 Building Warrant (early cinema schemes) P 132, H 13604, and P 125 schemes for Palladium Cinemas Duncan Macmillan Architect 105 Crown Street

1929 and 1930: see also P 249 Regal scheme, William R. Glen ABC Ltd 30 Golden Square London 1938; and K/19673 as built 1939.

Dmitri Shvidcovsky, 'Classical Edinburgh and Russian Town Planning of the late 18th and early 19th centuries: the role of William Hastie' in *Architectural Heritage II* Edinburgh EUP 1991

W. Douglas Simpson, *William Kelly, a Tribute Offered by the University of Aberdeen* Aberdeen AUP 1949

H.G. Slade, 'Craigston and Meldrum Estates, Carriacou, 1769–1841 in *Proceedings of the Society of Antiquaries of Scotland* Edinburgh Vol 114 1984

H.G. Slade, 'James Byres of Tonley: The Architecture of a Scottish Cicerone' in *Architectural Heritage II* Edinburgh EUP 1991

John Slezer, *Theatrum Scotiae* Edinburgh 1693

David Smiley 'Making the Modified Modern' *Perspecta 32; Resurfacing Modernism* Cambridge (USA) MIT 2001

John Smith, *Plan of Aberdeen showing improvements of Wet and Dry Docks and other improvements* Town Clerks Plans H 3, and National library of Scotland Maps, 1810

M.S. Smith and J.C. Moorhouse, 'Architecture and the Housing Market: Nineteenth Century Row Housing in Boston's South End' in *Journal of the Society of Architectural Historians* Philadelphia SAH June 1993

William Smith, *Feuing plan of ground around Skene Street* Town Clerk's Plans S 8 1839

Tony Spawforth, *The Complete Greek Temples* London Thames and Hudson 2006

Basil Spence Architect (Philip Long and Jane Thomas eds) Edinburgh National Galleries of Scotland 2007

Gavin Stamp, 'The Neo-Classical Town in late Victorian and early 20th Century Scotland' in *The Neo-Classical Town; Scottish Contributions to Urban Design since 1750* Edinburgh Rutland Press 1996

K.C. Stevenson and H.W. Jandl, *Houses By Mail; A Guide to Houses from Sears Roebuck and Company* Washington National Trust for Historic Preservation 1986

J.R. Stilgoe, *Borderland; Origins of the American Suburb 1820–1939* New Haven and London Yale 1988

City of Stockholm, *Stockholm City* Stockholm Statens Reproducktionsansatlt 1959

H.E. Stutchbury, *The Architecture of Colen Campbell* Manchester 1967

John Summerson, 'The Beginnings of Regent's Park' in *Architectural History; Journal of the Society of Architectural Historians of Great Britain*, Vol 20, London 1977

Sunnybank Road Building Warrant East side 2764PB/B Cottage for Mr Wm McDonald Oct 17th 1892

Doug Swain (ed) *Carolina Dwelling; Towards Preservation of Place: In Celebration of the North Carolina Vernacular Landscape* Raleigh Vol 26 Student Publication of the School of Design, North Carolina State Univeristy 1978

Stephen Switzer, *Ichnographia Rustica* London D. Browne et al., 1718 3 volumes.

T.

Tacitus, *Life of Agricola* 98 (Oxford, 2009)

Gabrielle Tagliaventi, *Garden City, a Century of Theories, Models, Experiences* Rome Gangemi 1994

George Taylor, City *of Aberdeen The Old Town & The adjacent Country,* Aberdeen Town Clerk's Plans A 11 1773; also reprinted Aberdeen, Taylor and Henderson Adelphi, 1902

George Taylor, *Design Of a New Road, from Aberdeen to Bridge of Dee as a south entry to the Town* 1793 (ex Maritime Museum)

Thistle Street Building Warrant House for Alex. Douglas Feb 1886 (adding wc &c in basement to sewer)

Walter Thom, *The History of Aberdeen* Aberdeen D Chalmers & Co 1811

Duncan Thomson, *The Life and Art of George Jamesone* Oxford Clarendon 1974

Thomson Street 1, Building Warrant 168 Four houses at Thomson St Geo Nicol Dec 10th 1877 no plans; withdrawn 3 houses approved 27 Dec 1877

Thomson Street 2, Building Warrant Cottage (Double) Thomson Street April 1878

Thomson Street 3, Building Warrant Eleven cottages at Thomson Street for Mr George Nicol approved by Street Committee 6 June 1878 (from Mr Lyall feu to Victoria Park)

Thomson Street 4, Building Warrant House in Thomson Street East Side for Mr Alexander Hendry, no architect, 8 oct 1878

Thomson Street 5, Building Warrant House in Thomson Street for George Nicol (north of above) 17 Oct 1878

Thomson Street 6, Building Warrant House at Thomson Street for Mr John S. Sutherland approved 31 Oct 1878 Pirie and Clyne architects

Thomson Street 7, Building Warrant 166 Cottage for Mr Lyall at Thomson St Approved by Street Committee 20 Dec 1877 Ellis and Wilson Architects

Town Clerks Plans, Collection of Drawn and Engraved Maps and Plans, Aberdeen City Archive, Town House: those with known authors are listed alphabetically above and below; anonymous entries follow:

Town Clerk's Plans A7 *Survey of the cities of Old and New Aberdeen, the harbour and Country adjacent,* surveyed by Andrew Logie 1742

Town Clerk's Plans A8 *A Survey of Old and New Aberdeen,* London G. & W. Paterson, 1746 , Also photo-litho facsimile W. & A.K. Johnston, nd

Town Clerk's Plans A 19 *Plan of the crofts of Aberdeen showing Union Street &c* 1846

Town Clerk's Plans A 22 23 *Map of the Cities of Aberdeen* Keith and Gibb 1862

Town Clerk's Plans A 39 *Map of Aberdeen used for Town Planning Scheme* 1933

Town Clerk's Plans B 1 *Plan of land at Bridewell* 1850

Town Clerk's Plans B 2 *Plan of ground at Bannermill* nd (1850)

Town Clerk's Plans B7 *Plan of the Ground around Bridge Street* nd (1850–70)

Town Clerk's Plans B 14 *Fueing plan of the lands of Burnside and Rosehill* 1897

Town Clerk's Plans C 5 *Plan of Castle Street showing tenants in area* 1841

Town Clerk's Plans C 9 *Sketch of Property at top of Castle Street showing Old Record Office &c* nd (1850)

Town Clerk's Plans C 12 *Plan showing ground belonging to Tailor Incorporation of Aberdeen around Chapel Street and vicinity* 1856

Town Clerk's Plans D 2 *Plan of houses and ground in Drum's hospital Close* 1798

Town Clerk's Plans D 10 *Parliamentary plan of Denburn Valley Railway* 1863

Town Clerk's Plans D 11 *Plan of Denburn Junction through City of Aberdeen* 1863

Town Clerk's Plans D 12 *Plans of Denburn area showing Gilcomston Dam* 1867

Town Clerk's Plans D 13 *Sketch plan and Section showing the course of the Denburn from Upper Dock to Skene Street Bridge* 1870

Town Clerk's Plans D 15 *Drawing of sluices to be fitted into Denburn Culverts opposite Messrs Haddens & Sons* 1874

Town Clerk's plans D 18 *Plan of the Proposed Public Park to be presented to Citizens of Aberdeen* (Duthie Park) 1883 *Fueing Plan of south end of Esslemont Avenue* 1883 town Clerk's Plans E 7

Town Clerk's Plans E 8 *Fueing Plan of Northfield Place and south end of Esslemont Avenue* 1884

Town Clerk's Plans E 9 *Plan of ground between Rosemount place and Skene Street for proposed new street, being Esslemont Avenue* 1890 *Plan of ground at Exchequer Row* nd (c1900) Town Clerk's Plans E 10

Town Clerk's Plans F 2 *Plan of Footdee and part of the Harbour* 1787

Town Clerk's Plans F 4 *Fueing plan of Frederick Street, Aberdeen* nd

Town Clerk's Plans F 6 Colin Innes, *Map of Footdee showing names and locations of proprietors* 1803

Town Clerk's Plans F 8 *Sketch of ground at Footdee from York Street to Wellington Street* 1816

Town Clerk's Plans F 10 *Fueing plan of lands of Ferryhill House* nd (1840–60)

Town Clerk's Plans F 17 *Plan of Grand Marine Terrace Footdee* nd (1880)

Town Clerk's Plans G 1 *Survey plan of the Lands of Gilcomston* 1749

Town Clerk's Plans G 2 *Plan of ground at Gilcomston belonging too the Town Of Aberdeen and William Black & Co Brewers* 1779

Town Clerk's Plans G 3 *Plan of river system at Gilcomston Mill* nd (1800)

Town Clerk's Plans G 4 *Plan of Gallowgate from Littlejohn Street to Seamount Place* nd (1890s)

Town Clerks Plans G 7 *Plan of Mill at Gilcomston* 1850

Town Clerk's Plans G 8 *Plan showing proposed widening and improvement of Gallowgate* nd (1890s)

Town Clerk's Plans G 18 *Ground plan of Greyfriars Parish Church as at 1888 with plans of proposed alterations* 1888

Town Clerk's Plans G 19 *Sketch plan, elevation and sections showing proposed improvements to Greyfriars Church* 1888

Town Clerk's Plans G 20 *Plans showing site of Greyfriars Church, Includes plan showing line of university extension* 1893

Town Clerk's Plans G 21 *Site plans of Greyfriars Church showing Marischal College* 1893

Town Clerk's Plans H 2 *Plan of proposed road from Aberdeen to the Bridge of Dee* (Holburn Street) 1807

Town Clerk's Plans H 8 *Plan of the lands of Hazelhead* 1840

Town Clerk's Plans H 9 *Plan of the lands of Hazelhead and Whitemires* nd (1840)

Town Clerk's Plans H 12 *Plan of the proposed road from Castle Street to Hanover Street* 1859

Town Clerk's Plans H 20 *Plan showing proposed alterations on the Carriageway at Heading Hill* 1855

Town Clerk's Plans H 22 *Fueing plan of the lands of Hilton* 1894

Town Clerk's Plans H 23 *Plan of Holburn Street and Hardgate* 1900

Town Clerk's Plans H 27 *Plans of Hilton ad Rosehill Estates showing properties transferred from Common Good, 1926–1938* 1933

Town Clerk's Plans J 10 *Plan of Justice Street* nd (1900)

Town Clerk's Plans K 1 *Plan of Mealmarket Lane leading to King Street* nd (1800)

Town Clerk's Plans K 2 *Plan of King Street from Mealmarket Street to Canal* nd

Town Clerk's Plans K 6 Plan *of East and West sides of King Street between Castle Street and North Street* 1804

Town Clerk's Plans K 20 *Plan of King Street from Castle Street to Merkland Road showing names of those resident in properties from Castle Street to Nelson Street* nd (c. 1830–40)

Town Clerk's Plans L 2 *Plans of school in Little Belmont Street* 1839

Town Clerk's Plans L 3 *Plan and section showing proposed addition to Town's English School* 1853

Town Clerk's Plans L 7 *Plan of proposed new road to Links from Castle Street* 1857

Town Clerk's Plans L 10 *Aberdeen City Improvements- plan of proposed access from Castle Street and East North Street* nd (1880)

Town Clerk's Plans L 12 *Plan of proposed streets at Leadside* 1883

Town Clerk's Plans M 1 *Plan of Marischal Street and ground around it for the Magistrates of Aberdeen* 1788

Town Clerks' Plans M 3 *Plan of proposed bridge over Putachieside and of arches and viaducts leading to an intended Market and connected with improvements in the City* 1838

Town Clerks Plans M 4 *Plan of Market Street showing site of new Post Office* nd (1880)

Town Clerk's Plans P 1 *Sketch plan of the Haugh of Pulmoor* 1763

Town Clerk's Plans P 3 *Plan of the lands of Pulmoor* 1801

Town Clerk's Plans P2 *Plan showing the line of March which divides the property and commonty of the burgh of Aberdeen from the barony of Pitfoddels corresponding to the contract of 1610* 1803

Town Clerk's Plans P 4 *Map of Persley, Grandholm and Woodside* 1817

Town Clerk's Plans P 8 *Plan of Peacock's Close* nd (c. 1875)

Town Clerk's Plans Q 1 *Plan of ground at Queen Street formerly Old Poultry Market* 1869

Town Clerk's Plans R 1 *Sketch plan of part of the lands of Rubislaw* 1748

Town Clerk's Plans R 3 *Feuing plan of part of the lands of Rubislaw* 1849

Town Clerk's Plans R 6 *Plans of lands of Rubislaw* 1868

Town Clerk's Plans R7 *Aberdeen City Improvements fueing plan showing Rosemount access* nd (1880)

Town Clerk's Plans R 8 *Aberdeen Improvements proposed design for elevation of houses on Rosemount Viaduct* nd (1880)

Town Clerk's Plans R 9 *Plan showing proposed continuation of Rosemount Access from Union Terrace to Schoolhill* nd (1880–1900)

Town Clerk's Plans R 12 *Alternative fueing plan to town Council property at Rosemount* 1882

Town Clerk's Plans R 13 *Plan of the lands of Ruthrieston* 1885

Town Clerk's Plans R 16, also R 17 *Fueing Plan of the lands of Rubislaw* 1895

Town Clerk's Plans S 3 *Plan of the Shorelands* 1770

Town Clerk's Plans S 5 *Sketch of properties along St Nicholas Street* 1806

Town Clerk's Plans S 6 *Plan of St Nicholas Churchyard* 1829

Town Clerk's Plans S 8 William Smith, *Feuing plan of ground around Skene Street* 1839

Town Clerk's Plans S 11 *Sketch plan of East elevation of Saint Margaret's Church Hall Gallowgate* 1907

Town Clerk's Plans S 19 *Plan of area around St Nicholas Street* nd (1880)

Town Clerk's Plans S 20 *Plan of Shorelands* 1885

Town Clerk's Plans S 27 *Plan of proposed road from Woodside to Old Aberdeen* (St Machar's Drive) nd (1900)

Town Clerk's Plans T 1 *Plan showing section of Town Hall* 1731

Town Clerk's Plans T 4 *Dr McKay's Plan of Torry* 1797

Town Clerk's Plans T 5 *Sketch of the pier of Torry* 1801

Town Clerk's Plans T 8 *Plan showing ground and property proposed to be acquired for the purpose of erecting a new Court house, Town House and County and Town Hall* 1865

Town Clerk's Plans T 17 *Plan of the feus of Torry* nd (1870)

(Town Clerk's Plans U 1 Colin Innes, *Plan of the South Entry* (Union Street) 1800)

Town Clerk's Plans U 2 *Plan of each side of Union Street between Market Street and Union Place* nd (1840)

Town Clerk's Plans U 4 *Specimen of a new plan of union Street from Union Terrace to Chapel Street* 1842

Town Clerk's Plans U 5 *Plan of ground around Union Street between Belmont Street and Back Wynd* 1850

Town Clerk's Plans U 6 *Plan of ground and property on west corner of Union Bridge* 1864

Town Clerk's Plans U 7 *Plans of west Union Street showing who owned what properties between Union Terrace and Summer Street* nd (1850–70)

Town Clerk's Plans U 8 *Plan of the east side of Union Street between Castle Street and Belmont Street* nd (1880)

Town Clerk's Plans U 10 *Tracing of Union Row* nd (1890)

Town Clerk's Plans U 12 *Plan of Union Street* 1900

Town Clerk's Plans U 13 *Plan of Union Street showing site of Athenaeum* nd (1900)

Town Clerks plans U 14 *Plan of Union Bridge* nd (1905)

Town Clerk's Plans U 15 *Plans sections and elevations &c showing proposed widening of Union Bridge* nd (1906–8)

Town Clerk's Plans V 1 and V 2 *Plan of Glencairn on Glennies Parks Mid Stocket Road* (Victoria Park) 1866

Town Clerk's Plans V 3 *Plan showing ground at east and west sides of new Victoria Public Park as proposed to be feued* 1872

Town Clerk's Plans V 5 *Plan of vaults under St Nicholas Street* nd (1880)

Town Clerk's Plans U 6 *Tracing of Union Street detailing vaults under it between Castle Street and Summer Street* nd (1880)

Town Clerk's Plans U 7 *Plan of vaults under Union Street* nd (1900)

Town Clerk's Plans W 3*Block plan of Weigh House Square* 1869

Town Clerk's Plans W 8 *Westfield fueing plan* 1887

Town Clerk's Plans Y 1 *Plan of York Street and York Place Footdee* nd

P.V. Turner, *Campus an American Planning Tradition* Cambridge (USA) and London MIT 1987

U.

D.K. Underwood, 'Alfred Agache, French Sociology, and Modern Urbanusim in France and Brazil' in *Journal of the Society of Architectural Historians* Philadelphia SAH June 1981

University of Miami Scholl of Architecture, *The New City 1; Foundations* New York PAP 1991

University of Miami School of Architecture, *The New City 2; The American City* New York PAR 1994

University of Miami School of Architecture, *The New City 3; Modern Cities* New York PAR 1996

University College Dublin School of Architecture, *Dublin City Quays; Projects* Dublin UCD 1986

Raymond Unwin, *Town Planning in Practice, An Introduction to the Art of Designing Cities and Suburbs* London TF Unwin 1917

Upperkirkgate 1. Building Warrant 3533 PB/C 6–12 and Rebuilding and in Ross' Court Extension of Premises of the University Press for Messrs A. King & Coy Printers

Upperkirkgate 2. Building Warrant Alteration on House, corner of Upperkirkgate and Gallowgate and new Houses proposed to be built in connection, all being for Mr Henry Gray, James Souttar 4 Nov 73 Architect Aberdeen (not sanctioned 8 March 73 in respect to application of 21 Feb 73)

Urquhart Road, Building Warrant Three half houses for Aberdeen Building Company Ltd, Alexander Ross manager, 15 Dec 1881; also Four Houses on the South Side for the Aberdeen Building Co, 10th June 1884, Alexander Ross and John Sangster; also 35–83, Four Houses on the north side for Aberdeen Building Co, 19th April 1886, James Gordon and John Morgan Co; and Eight Dwelling Houses for the Town Council, 18th May 1897, John Rust City Architect 224 Union Street.

V.

C. van Eesteren, *The idea of the functional city; a lecture with slides 1928* Rotterdam NAi/The Hague EFL 1997

Anthony Vidler, *Histories of the Immediate Past; Inventing Architectural Modernism* Cambridge (USA) and London MIT 2008

Sergio Villari, *J.N.L. Durand (1760–1834); Art and Science of Architecture* New York Rizzoli 1990

W.

F.A. Walker, 'The Emergence of the Grid; Later 18th Century Urban Form in Glasgow' in *The Neo-Classical Town; Scottish Contributions to Urban Design since 1750* Edinburgh Rutland Press 1996

Andrew Wallace-Hadrill, *Houses and Society in Pompeii and Herculaneum* Princeton PUP 1994

David Watkin, *The Roman Forum* London Profile 2009

Watson Street. Building Warrant 4 Houses, 32, 34, 36 & 38 Watson Street, 5th May 1877, Alexander Raeburn 22 Watson Street Tenements between #30 and #48 (John Robb)

Waveley Place. Building Warrant 4578/PB/D 22 Waverley Place (Scott Sutherland's) additions and alterations for W.S. Gill Esq of Fairfield by A.H.L. Mackinnon, Architect, 75 Union Street, 21 Feb 1898.

Weigh House Square 1, Building Warrant 7530 PB, Harbour Offices, 13 April 1883, Matthews and Mackenzie

N.F. Weber, *LeCorbusier; A Life* New York Knopf 2008

Adam Welfare, *Great Crowns of Stone; The Recumbent Stone Circles of Scotland* Edinburgh RCAHMS 2011

V.M. Welter, 'History, Biology and City Deisgn: Patrick Geddes and Edinburgh' in *Architecural Heritage VI* Edinburgh EUP 1996

V.M. Welter, '"Slum, Semi-slum, Super-slum" – Some reflections by Patrick Geddes on Edinburgh's New Town' in *Architectural Heritage X* Edinburgh EUP 1999

V.M. Welter, *Biopolis; Patrick Geddes and the City of Life* Cambridge (USA) and London MIT 2002

Craig Whitaker, *Architecture and the American Dream* New York Three Rivers Press 1996

N.E. Wickberg, *The Senate Square Helsinki* Helsinki Anders Nyborg 1981

Matthew Williams, 'Planning for the Picturesque: Thomas Hamilton's New Roads to the Old Town, 1817–1858' in *Architectural Heritage XX* Edinburgh EUP 2009

H.L. Wilson, *The Wilson Bungalow: The Bungalow Book; A Short Sketch of the Evolution of the Bungalow from its Primitive Crudeness to its Present State of Artistic Beauty and Cozy Convenience* Chicago Henry L. Wilson The Bungalow Man 5th ed nd (c. 1915)

Robert Wilson, *An Historical Account and Delineation of Aberdeen* Aberdeen James Johnstone 1822 with engravings by George Smith

W.H. Wilson, *The City Beautiful Movement* Baltimore Johns Hopkins University Press 1994

William Wood, *Plan of Sow Croft Albion Street* Town Clerk's Plans A 15 1809

William Wood, *Plan of the Cities of Aberdeen* Town Clerk's Plans A 17 1824

Y.

A.L. Youngson, *The Making of Classical Edinburgh* Edinburgh EUP 1966

Illustration Credits

Aberdeen Art Gallery and Museum Collections

1.5	Milne 1789 plan (landscape)
1.6	Milne 1789 plan (town)
2.5	Taylor 1793 Detail of Wharf
2.10	Gibbs 1866 Gallowgatehead to Netherkirkgate
2.22	Guestrow Clearances Plan
2.32	Home south prospect of Aberdeen
3.1	Castlegate, detail of Irvine
3.4	Marischal Street in 1769
3.6	Town House of Old Aberdeen
3.10	R. Seaton Castlegate
4.3	Denburn Bridge (Hamilton)
4.4	James Young of London
4.9	Fletcher 1807
5.1	Henderson King St
5.6	Mercat Cross
5.9	Market St railway
5.15	Gibbs Birds-eye of Western Suburbs 1866
5.17	Gibbs 1866 Short Loanings to Upperkirkgate
5.18	Gibbs 1889 Mount Street to Upperkirkgate
5.20	Extension Plan
5.22	Castlegate, Monumental Gothic Building, c. 1850
6.2	Aberdeen Prototype
7.4	Powis Hs in 1864
8.3	Union Street and Bridge 1830s
8.7	Gibbs 1866 Upper Denburn
8.8	Union Terrace design JF Beattie
8.14	Union Bridge with verdant Denburn slopes

Aberdeen City Archive

2.17 Emporium
2.18 Hutcheson's
2.19 Henry Gray's second premises
2.20 Guestrow Group Ragg's Ln 1
2.21 Guestrow Group Ragg's Ln 2
2.25 New Loan Company
2.26 Esslemont and Macintosh
2.27 'Café Royal'
4.2   Colin Innes's 1798 survey
5.19 Rosemount Design Pattern
7.3   Gallowgate early clearance plan
8.6   Golden Square (1847)

Aberdeen City Library

0.2   Bridge of Dee photo
2.1   St Nicholas print
2.3   Benholm's Lodging
2.4   hiprow
2.7   Bow Brig
2.8   Schoolhill drawing 1865
2.9   Ross Court, (aka Robertson's) Upperkirkgate
2.14 Broadgate, Cistern &c
2.15 Broadgate, drwg
2.16 Broadgate, West side
2.23 Provost Skene's
2.24 Ragg's Lane
2.28 Broadgate, South entry
2.29 Longacre, Broad Street
2.30 Marischal College
3.2   Robert Gordon's Hospital
3.3   Tolbooth Castlegate
3.5   Virginia Street drwg
3.7   Castlegate East view form Rotten Row
3.9   Castlegate North-east corner
3.11 Banking Company in Aberdeen
3.12 Abercrombie canal
5.2   Bridewell
5.3   Assembly Rooms
5.5   Athenaeum/Union Buildings
5.7   St Nicholas and Facade early photo
5.8   Market Street 1840

ILLUSTRATION CREDITS

5.10 New Trades Hall
5.11 Triple Kirks
5.12 Union Street East from Bridge
5.13 Union St Westwards
5.16 City of Aberdeen Land Association Queen's Cross in 1868
5.21 Christ's College City Lib
5.23 New Town House Tower
5.24 Simpson's Marischal College
5.25 Mackenzie's Marischal College
5.26 Schoolhill Marischal College, existing and proposed
5.27 Schoolhill Marischal College, existing and proposed
5.28 Schoolhill Mitchell & Muill
5.29 Jamesone House
5.30 Upperkirkgate and College 1918
6.0 Mrs Yeats of Auquharneys
6.7 Old Rubislaw Hs
6.13 Gilcomston Steps (good crossover)
6.14 Carden Place
7.1 Hardwierd old photo
7.2 Entry to Gallowgate with Grays
7.7 Market Street & Harbour
7.8 Union St-Castlegate
7.9 Old Aberdeen as University Precinct
8.5 Union Bridge Simpson's monumental building
8.9 Denburn Valley gardens photo
8.10 Railway/Denburn/Union St
8.11 Car Park scheme

Nigel Grounds

Cover Nigel Grounds Castlegate after Rain

David MacClean

8.2 David MacClean's Bridge scheme

National Archive of Scotland

3.13 Abercrombie, Aberdeen to the two Bridges over the Rivers Dee and Don NAS (& Duke of Richmond and Gordon)
4.1 Abercrombie, Aberdeen to the two Bridges over the Rivers Dee and Don NAS (& Duke of Richmond and Gordon)

4.8   Abercrombie, Aberdeen to the two Bridges over the Rivers Dee and Don NAS (& Duke of Richmond and Gordon)
4.10   Smith Aberdeen 1810 NAS
4.11   Smith Aberdeen 1810 NAS

National Library of Scotland

1.2   Roy, Great Map aka Military Survey Peterculter and Monymusk
1.4   Roy, Great Map aka Military Survey Peterculter and Monymusk
2.2   Aberdeen, James Gordon 1661
2.6   Aberdeen, James Gordon 1661
2.11   Old Aberdeen (Slezer) detail
2.12   Aberdeen, James Gordon 1661
2.31   Aberdeen, James Gordon 1661
5.4   1st Ed OS Round Table to Justice Port
6.10   1st Ed OS Granton Lodge
8.1   Aberdeen, James Gordon 1661

Robert Gordon University

6.0   Mrs Yeats of Auquharneys

Duke of Richmond and Gordon

3.13   Abercrombie, Aberdeen to the two Bridges over the Rivers Dee and Don NAS (& NLS)
4.1   Abercrombie, Aberdeen to the two Bridges over the Rivers Dee and Don NAS (& NLS)
4.8   Abercrombie, Aberdeen to the two Bridges over the Rivers Dee and Don NAS (& NLS)

Royal Commission on the Ancient and Historic Monuments of Scotland

1.1   Pictish Stone Monymusk
2.13   North Prospect of Aberdeen, Hutton
5.14   Skene's New Town, Elliott Plan
6.11   North Prospect of Aberdeen, Hutton

Soane Museum

3.8 Castlegate Adam Design for Record Office
4.5 Adelphi

W.A. Brogden Consultancy

1.3 Switzer, *Ichnographia Rustica*
4.7 Aisling Shannon View Union Street
6.1 *Early Houses*, Scara Brae, Benholm's Lodging, Skene's House, James Hand
6.3 *Urban Houses*, 20 Castle Street, Gray's site, Marischal Street, Drum's Lane, James Hand
6.4 *Trustee Houses*, a. Young's Union St, b. 21 King St, James Hand
6.5 *Tenements*, Early King St, Rosemount Tenements, Forest Rd, Mitchell and Muill, Wordies, James Hand
6.6 *Local Authority Houses*, Manse types, Modern tenements, King St, and Kincorth and Kaimhill Cottage, James Hand
6.8 *National House Types*, Brighton Place, Fountainhall Rd, 98 Hamilton Pl, 50 Queen's Rd, James Hand
6.9 *Houses*, Granton Lodge, Dalmunzie, Devanha Gardens, James Hand
6.12 *Cottages*, Cross-over cottage, 2 apartment cottage, Cottage, plain, Meston Reid House as cottage, James Hand
6.15 *Bungalows*, Woodcote, Anderson Drive, Garden, 30s bungalow, James Hand
6.16 *High Flats*, Ashgrove Court, Kepplestone Flats, James Hand
7.5 Rosemount Square plan from 1939 booklet
7.6 Kincorth Civic Centre 1939 booklet
8.12 Neo Classical Town scheme
8.13 Neo Classical Town scheme plan, NA Lamb

Every effort has been made to trace and acknowledge all the copyright holders, but if any have been inadvertently overlooked then the publishers will be pleased to make the necessary arrangement at the first opportunity.

Index

Page numbers in *italics* refer to figures.

Abercrombie, Charles
  Aberdeenshire Canal 79, 81
  New Streets designs 85, *86*, 87, 89, 90, 93–4, 148
  New Town plan 81, 105–6, *106*
  roads and bridges *80*, 81
Aberdeen xxvii–xxviii, *12–13*, *56*, *119*, *222*
  landscape 6
  origins of 17
  suburbs *139*, *144*, *145*
  town types 6
  undervalued areas 233
Aberdeen Beyond 2000 246–7
Aberdeen Building Company 207
Aberdeen Hotel 122
Aberdeen Public Realm study 246
Aberdeen School of Architecture
  architecture of the street 224
  Masters course 225–6
  — research project 225–7, 229
Aberdeenshire xxvii–xxviii
Aberdeenshire Canal 10, *79*, 81, 145
Aberdon 6
Adam, James 84–5, *95*
Adam, John 76
Adam, Robert 72, 74, 132
  Adelphi (London) plan *95*
  Edinburgh designs 92, 94, 122
  Glasgow designs 84–5
  Record Office design 72–4, *73*, 75–6, *78*
Adam, William 50, 72
  Dundee Town House design 62
  Robert Gordon's Hospital design 61–2, *62*
  Tolbooth design 61
Aedie's House 29–30
Agricola 4, 5, 14
agriculture xxviii, 7, *7–8*, *8*
Albert, Prince 133
Albert Terrace 140–41
Alberti, L.B. xxiii, 60, 70
Allan, J. Ogg 156
Anderson, Robert Rowand 223, 227
antiquities 11, 14
apartments 23, 164
Architectural Association (AA) 221
architecture
  and economics 229–30
  literature on 60–61, 72, 74, 131, 236
  — pattern books 190, 194
  local information collections 228–9
  project research 227–8
  study of 221–2
  — at Aberdeen School of Architecture *see* Aberdeen School of Architecture
  — and assessment 228–9
  — research of local places 228
  — research of Scottish cities 223–4
  — specialization 225
  — student projects and competitions 222–3, 224, *225*, *248*, *249*, 249
  and theatre xxiv, 236, *237*, 238–9
Art Gallery and Industrial Museum 156
Arts and Crafts movement xxvi, 159, 185, 195, 198
Ashgrove 199, *200*, 201
Assembly Rooms 117–18

association of ideas 11, 132, 133, 149
Athenaeum Rooms 122–3
Auchintoul's House 115, 116
Aulton 38

Back Wynd 29–31, 125, 126, 126–7
Baillie Galen's House 122, 169
Banking Company 78, *78*, 80–81
Barron, James 29
Barron, Patrick 64
Belvidere Place 139–40
Benholm's Lodging 22, *22*, 162, *163*, 164, 238
Bennachie 1, 4
Boece, Hector 3, 37
Bon Accord quarter 135–6
Boulton, Thomas 146
Bow Brig *30*, 146, 239
Bridewell 112, *117*
Bridge of Dee *xxiv*
Broadgate (Broad Street) 34, 39–40, *40*, 46–7, 48–9, *49*, 49–50
  Byron's House 33, *41*, 49–50
  Café Royal *48*, 48
  Cumberland House 46, 178, 180
  Esslemont and Macintosh 47–48, *48*
  Granite City report 208
  Grant's Emporium for Tea 42, *43*
  Gray's warehouses 40, 43, *43*, 45
  Greyfriars' Kirk 50–51, *153*, 158, 158–59
  Guestrow 23, 39, *41*, 43, *44*, *45*, 46–7, 208
  Hutcheson's Bakery 42, 69
  Marischal College *see* Marischal College
  New Loan Company 47, *47*
  proposals for 234
  Provost Skene's House *45*, 46, *163*, 178
Brown and Watt 31, 35, 152–3, 206
bungalows *162*, 185, 193–5, *196*, 197–8
Burn, James
  57 Castlegate 167, 169
  Banking Company 78, 80–81
  Bridewell 112
  King Street 104
Burnet, Thomas 89
Byron's House 33, *41*, 49–50

Café Royal *48*, 48
Cameron's Inn 31
Campbell, Colen 74, 84, 193

Canada 195, 198
Carden Place 141, 181–2, 191–2, *192*
Carmelite Street 29
Carnegie's Brae 22
Castle Hill 6, 18, 226
Castle of Aberdeen 18–19
Castlegate 58, *71*, *77*, *150*, *218*, 234, 238
  18th century changes 77–8
  houses *168*
  John Adam houses 76–7
  King Street junction *116*
  level of 101
  Granite City plan for Union Street junction *218*
  medieval city 51–56, *52*
  Mercat Cross 57–9, 59–60, 61, *63*, *124*, 124–5, 235, 238
  in New Streets plan 85, *88*, 89, 90, 125
  North of Scotland Bank 123–4
  Record Office 72–4, *73*, 75–76, 78, 120, 123
  Salvation Army Citadel 54, 151–2, 203, 217, 235–6
  tenements 167, 169
  Tolbooth *see* Tolbooth
Castlehill 203
Central School 156
Chanonry 38
Chapman and Riley 216, 217, 220
Chapman, R. Dobson 216
Chisolme, John 91
Christ's College *149*, 149–51
churches
  Greyfriars' Kirk 50–51, *153*, 158–9
  North Kirk 120
  St Andrew's Chapel 118, 131
  St Machar 17, 18, 37–8
  St Margaret's mission 35–7
  St Nicholas 17, 18, *18*, 62–3, 125–6, *126*
  Triple Kirks 131, *132*, 133
circular buildings 3–4
city architecture xxi, xxii
  congestion-easing xxiv–xxv
  and power xxii–xxiii
  residential vs. business areas xxv–xxvi
  and stage sets xxiv
City Of Aberdeen Land Association (CALA) 142–3, 144
City of Glasgow Bank 129

city planning xxv–xxvi, 208, 211
  Aberdeen Beyond 2000 246–7
  Aberdeen Public Realm study 246
  assessing projects 250–52
  enterprise agencies 246
  factors to consider
    — climate 231
    — geography 231–2
    — population numbers 232
    — traffic 233
  Granite City report 216, 216–20, 217, 218, 235, 243–5, 244
  grids 89–90
  local authority housing 211–12
  modern design schemes 246–7
  New Streets *see* New Streets
  New Town *see* New Town
  public transport 212
civic clearances 24, 26–7, 217–18, 223, 238
Clydesdale Bank 133
Colclough, Tony 216, 219
Commercial Bank 120
Comper, John Ninian 36–7
Cooper Union School 224
cottages 170–72, *175*, 185–6, *186*, *187*, 188, 192–3
  Blackhouses 189–90
  Carden Place 191–92, *192*
  at Gilcomston *188*
  half cottages 138, 190–91
  Kaimbill cottages 199
  Marine Terrace 191
  prehistoric origins 188–9
  raised 194
  Skene project 140, 143
  St Machar Cottage 193
  urban 190
  Wellington Place 193
  Whitehouses 188
Cotton Street flats 170
Coutts, William 35, 40
The Craftsman 195, 197
Craig, James 85
Crann, Jean 199, 201
Crichton, Richard 91, 91–2
Crimonmogate House 108–9, 116, 117
Cruickshank and Sellars 29
Culter House *5*, 9–10
Cumberland House 46, 178, 180
Cunninghame mansion 84

Cuparston 6

Dalmunzie House 182, *183*, 184–5
De Re Aedificitoria (Alberti) xxiii, 60
Dee Village 6, 138
Denburn Bridge 94–5, *97*, 98, 101, 103, 103–4, 110
  see also Union Bridge
Denburn Valley *132*, 222, 239, 241, *241*
  Granite City report 244, *245*, 245
  health concerns and remedies 145–6
  Robert Gordon University students' proposal 248, *249*
  and Union Bridge 225, *235*, 240, *250*
  and Union Terrace Gardens *242*, 243, *243*
design proposals
  assessing 250–52
  learning from 221
  time lags 230
Devanha Gardens *183*, 185
Don Street 38
Dreghorn, Allan 83
Druidstone 3–4
Drums Lane 32–3
Dundee Town House 62
Dunottar 4
Dyce 6

Earl Marischal's Lodging 55, 65, 180
Ecole des Beaux Arts, Paris 221, 222, 228
economics 229–30
Edinburgh
  Adam's designs in 76, 122, 130
  Charlotte Square 94
  design proposals 223
  High Street 34
  New Town 83, 85
  room sizes 161–2
  Second New Town 106–7
Edwards-McHardy building 169–70
Eisenman, David 224
Elements of Criticism (Kames) 11
Elliott, James 136–7, *137*, 138
Ellis and Wilson 29
encroachment on public domain 26
Essai sur l'architecture (Laugier) 15
Esslemont and Macintosh 47–8, *48*
estates, designed 8–10
Evens Quarter 6, *34*, 83

Ferrara xxiii

Ferryhill Place 138–9, 141
  Belvidere Place 139–40
  Marine Place 139
  Rotunda Place 138
Fingal 14–15
Fingal (Macpherson) 14
Fishcross 58, 60
Fittie Quarter 6, 110–12, *111*, 170
Fleshcross 58–9
Fletcher, Thomas 98, 101, 103, 109–10, *110*
Fontaine, Pierre *96*, 96–7
Forbes Beattie, James 142, 202, 241, *242*

Gaelic Lane 31
Gale, Roger 11, 14
Galletly, James 223
Gallowgate *34*, 34–7, 68, *168*, *208*, 208, *209*, 233
Garden City Movement xxvi–xxvii, 209–10, *215*, 230–31
Garden, James 3
gardening 8–9
gardens 24–5, 54–5, 67
Gardner, A.B. xxvii, 174, 211
Gardner-Medwin, James 215
Gauld, William 45
Geddes, Patrick xxv–xxvi, 223
Georgian style 68
Gibb, John 110, 151
Gibbs, James 61, 62–3, 112
Gilcomston 6, 20, 149, *188*
Gilcomston South 6
Gillespie Graham, James 120
Glasgow 83–5, 94, 95, 162, 223
Golden Square 112, 134–5
Gordon, James 20, 28, 37, 39, 164
Gordon plan of 1661 20, *21*, 164
  Castlegate 52
  Fleshcross 58
  Grammar School 31
  houses 165
  market stalls 165
  Old Aberdeen 37, 38
  St Katherine's Hill 24–5
  Tolbooth 55
Grandhome 10, 177
Granite City report 216, 216–20, *217*, *218*, 235, 243–5, *244*
Grant, Archibald *8*, 8–9
Granton Lodge 182, *183*, *184*
Grant's Emporium for Tea *42*, 43

Gray, John 156
Gray's warehouses 40, *43*, 43, 45
The Green 18, 28–30, *30*, 144, 234
Green Quarter 6, *28*
Greenbogs 4
Greyfriars Kirk 50–51, *153*, 158, 158–59
Guestrow 23, 39, *41*, 43, *44*, *45*, 46–7, 208
Gwynne, John 66

Hadden Street 128, 129
Hamilton, David 91, 92–3, *93*
  Denburn bridge plan *93*, 94–5
  Hutcheson Hospital design 96
  relationship with Trustees 102–3
  street level designs 101–2
Hamilton, William 83
harbour 27–28, 67, 98, 110, 127
Hardgate 6
Hardwierd 6, 144, *206*
Hawksmoor, Nicholas 71
Hazelhead 199, 202
health concerns and remedies xxvi, 145–6, 207–8, 223
Henderson, James *116*, 169–70
high flats 199, 201, 203, 204, 245–6
  Ashgrove 199, *200*, 201
  Castlehill 203
  Hazelhead 199, 202
  Kepplestone *200*
High Street 38
hillforts 4
Hodge, Duncan 48
Hood, Raymond 201
houses
  bungalows *162*, 185, 193–5, *196*, 197–8
  cottages *see* cottages
  country houses
    — Culter House 9–10
    — Grandhome 10, 177
    — Kingswells 178
    — Monymusk *8*, 9
    — Peterculter 177–78
    — Rubislaw House 177, *178*
  early 19, 23, 25–6, 32–3, 35, 38
    — Aedie's House 29–30
    — Benholm's Lodging 22, 22–3, 162, *163*, 164, 238
    — Byron's House 33, *41*, 49–50
    — Cumberland House 46, 178, 180

— Jamesone House 177–8
— Marr Castle 178
— Provost Robertson's House 33
— Provost Ross' House 25, *25*
— Provost Skene's House *45*, *46*, *163*, 178
— Rolland's Lodging 53
Ha'hoose 178
high flats *see* high flats
local authority housing 211–12, 212–13
— Kaimhill 213
— Kincorth Project 213, 215, *215*
— Rosemount Square 213, *214*
— Ruthrieston 212
— The Spital 212
mansions *see* mansions
in North America 194–5
prehistoric 4, *163*
room sizes 161–2
small individual houses 198–9
tenements *see* tenements
Howard, Ebenezer 209–10
Huntly Street 117
hut circles 3–4
Hutcheson's Bakery *42*, 69
Huxtable, Ada Louise 219

Ichnographia Rustica (Switzer) 8
improvements, pre-20th century 11, 57, 87
  Aberdeenshire Canal 81
  Banking Company *78*, 78, 80–81
  Castlegate *77*, 77–8
  Fishcross 60
  houses 65, 67, 76–77
    — Aberdeen Georgian 68–70
    — rounded corners 69
  Marischal Street 65–8, *66*
  Mercat Cross 57–60
  New Streets *see* New Streets
  Record Office 72–3, *73*, *74*, 75–6, 78
  roads and bridges 81
  Robert Gordon's Hospital 61–2
  St Nicholas Kirk nave 62–3
  stance, introduction of 67
  theatrics 71, 73
  Tolbooth 61
  Town House, Old Aberdeen 70–71
India 193–4
industrial suburbs 144–5
Innes, Colin *88*, 90, 99

Irvine, George 36
Irvine, Hugh *58*

Jacobs, Jane 208, 219
Jaffray, John 70–71, 72, 73, 84
Jamesone, George 71, 238
Jamesone House 157, 173
Jeanneret, Charles-Édouard (LeCorbusier) 199, 201, 203, 231
Johnston, James 32

Kaimbill cottages 199
Kaimhill 213
Kames, Henry Home, Lord 11, 15, 132
Keith, George xxvii, 201
Kelly, William 51, 147, 181–2, 198–9, 211, 214
Kepplestone *200*
Kincorth Project 213, *215*, 215
King Street 53, 118, 120–21, 233
  Castlegate junction *116*
  Commercial Bank 120
  Edwards-McHardy building 169–70
  McHardy and Edwards houses 120
  Medico-Chirurgical Society building 118, 120
  naming of 98
  North Kirk 120
  North of Scotland Bank 123–4
  plans and restrictions for 104, 108, 109, 115
  Record Office 120
  St Andrew's Chapel 118
  tenements 174, 205–7
  Washington Buildings 206
King's College 38
Knight, Payne 131

land-sea relationship 1
Laugier, M-A. 15
Law, William 68
LeCorbusier (Charles-Édouard Jeanneret) 199, 201, 203, 231
The Life and Death of Great American Cities (Jacobs) 208
Lindsay, William 60
Littlejohn, James 91, 170
Littlejohn Street 34
Littleways 185
Loch Street 35
London 63, 89–90, *95*, 174
Longacre *50*

MacClean, D.E.D. 225
Mackay, James 152–3
Mackenzie, A. Marshall 147, 153, 156, 182
Mackenzie, A.G.R. 185, 212, 214
Mackenzie and McMillan 23
Mackenzie, Russell 142
Mackenzie, Thomas 141, 149–50, 158
Macmillan, Duncan 198
Macmillan, Ross 185
Macpherson, James 14–15
mansions 84, 140, 178, 180, 181, 182
   12 Carden Place 181–2
   Cumberland House 46, 178, 180
   Cunninghame mansion 84
   Earl Marischal's Lodging 180
   Marischal Street 180
   McMansions 204
   Pitfodel's Lodging 180, 180–81
   Provost Skene's House 178, 180
   Shawfield Mansion 84
   suburban
      — 2 Devanha Gardens 183, 185
      — Dalmunzie House 182, 183, 184–5
      — Granton Lodge 182, 183, 184
      — Littleways 185
      — Powis House 182, 211
Marine Place 139
Marine Terrace 191
Marischal College 49, 50–51, 51, 152, 153, 154–5, 157–9
   sale of ground 108, 135
Marischal Street 65, 65–8, 66, 72, 78, 168, 180
Market building 127–8, 245
market stalls 165
Market Street 127, 127–8
   City of Glasgow Bank 129
   Granite City report 217
   Mechanic's Institute building 128
   Post Office 129
   Railway Terminus 128–9, 129
   Union Club building 129
   Union Street intersection 128
Matthew, Robert 222–3, 223
Matthews and Mackenzie 51, 140, 156, 157, 173
Matthews, James 34, 129, 133, 141, 148, 156
Mavor, Alexander 35

McCann, John 29
Mechanic's Institute building 128
Medico-Chirurgical Society building 118, 120
medieval city 19–20
   castle 18–19
   ecclesiastical buildings 17–18, 18, 35–7, 37–8, 50–51
   feus 19
   houses 19
   layout 20
   streets
      — Back Wynd 30–31, 31
      — Bow Brig 30
      — Broadgate (Broad Street) 34, 39–40, 40, 44, 48–9, 49, 51
         • Byron's House 41
         • Café Royal 48, 48
         • Cumberland House 46
         • Esslemont and Macintosh drapers 47–48, 48
         • Grant's Emporium for Tea 42, 43
         • Gray's warehouses 40, 43, 43, 45–6
         • Guestrow 41, 43, 45
         • Hutcheson's Bakery 42
         • Marischal College 49, 50–51, 51
         • New Loan Company 47, 47
         • Patrick Christie's House 49
         • Provost Skene's House 45, 46
      — Carmelite Street 29
      — Carnegie's Brae 22
      — Castlegate 51–6, 52, 58
      — Chanonry 38
      — Don Street 38
      — Drums Lane 32–3
      — Gaelic Lane 31
      — Gallowgate 34, 34–7
      — Guestrow 23–4
      — High Street 38
      — Littlejohn Street 34
      — Loch Street 35
      — Netherkirkgate (Via Fraxis) 20–23, 25
      — Putachieside 28
      — Ragg's Lane 44, 46–7, 47
      — Schoolhill 31–2, 32
      — Shiprow 24, 25, 25–7
      — Shore Brae 27

— Upperkirkgate 32, 32–4, 33
streets and plots 19
medieval landscape 6–7
Mercat Cross 57–9, 59–60, 61, 63, 124, 124–5, 235, 238
Milne, Alexander 12–13
Milne, Patrick 108–9
Mitchell and Muill's Bakery 156, 156
Modern Movement 177, 185, 199, 204, 212, 228
   Aberdeen version 214–15
modernism 177, 202, 213, 215, 235
Mons Graupius, Battle of 4, 14
Montgomerie, John 58
Monymusk 8, 8–9, 9
Morgan, John 143, 182, 195
Morris, William 195
Morrison, John, of Auchintoul 115–16, 169
The Mounth xxvii, 6
Municipal Arts Foundation 224

Nash, John 192–3
neo-classical style 74–5
Netherkirkgate (Via Fraxis) 20–23, 25
New Inn 63, 64, 67
New Loan Company 47, 47
New Streets 93, 238
   building phase 112–13
   clearances for 89, 98–9
   design problems 93–4
   designs 85, 86, 87, 88
   Fletcher's designs 103–4, 110
   Hamilton's designs
     — Denburn bridge 93, 94–5
     — houses 95–6
     — for various street levels 101–2
   houses 104–5, 107–9, 109
   levels of 100, 101, 103
   masons, appointment of 98
   North Street 49, 89, 90
   — see also King Street
   passage of Bill through Parliament 87, 89
   naming of 98
   search for architects/engineers
     — advertising post 90–91
     — architects/engineers applying 91–3
     — designs accepted 93
   South Street 89, 93, 94, 97–8
   — see also Union Street

stances, sale of 109
superintendent, appointment of 98
survey drawings 88, 90
Trustees
   — difficulties in overseeing project 99–102
   — Hamilton, relationship with 102–3
   — New Town plans 107, 108
   — post-Hamilton confidence 103–4
   Young's designs 97–8
New Town 107
   Abercrombie's plan 105–6, 106
   Bon Accord quarter 135–6
   Crimonmagate House 108–9
   smaller houses 135
   Smith's plan 112, 113
Noble, Ian 229–30
Normandykes 5, 14, 105
Normans, influence of 14, 17–18
North Kirk 120
North of Scotland Bank 123–4
North Street 49, 89, 90, 234
   see also King Street
Northwestern suburbs 144, 145

Odds Quarter 6, 28, 34
Old Aberdeen 6, 20, 36, 37, 37–8
   Town House 69, 70
   University Precinct 219
Ossian 14–15

palace block design 80–81, 94
Palladian style 62, 64, 75, 95
Palladio, Andrea xxiii, 74
Paris 59, 94, 96, 96, 221, 222, 228
Paterson, Ian 202–3
Paul, James 202
Peddie and Kinnear 151–2
Percier, Charles 96, 96–7
Peterculter House 5, 177
The Picturesque (Knight) 131
picturesque style 73–4, 131–3, 148–51, 152, 195, 239
pier 27, 27–8
Pitfodel's Lodging 180, 180–81
Poems of Ossian (Macpherson) 14
Police Commissioners 26, 81, 112, 141
   rounded corners 69, 115, 126
population xxvii, 6, 20, 83, 232, 252
Porthill 6, 34
Powis House 182, 211

prehistory 1–5, *163*
private vs. public life 161
Provost Robertson's House 33
Provost Ross' House 25, *25*
Provost Skene's House 45, 46, *163*, 178
public spaces, use of 233–35
public transport 176, 211–12, 234
Putachieside 108, 127
Putachieside Bridge 102, 103

quay 24, *27*, 27–8
Queen's Gardens 142
Queen's Terrace 141–2

Ragg's Lane 46–7, *47*
railway 128–9, *129*, 143, 145, 210, 227, 241, 249
Record Office 72–74, *73*, 75–6, 78, 120, 123
Regency style 68
Reid, John 90
Reid, Robert 91, *91*–2, 106–7
religious houses 17–18, 50
Riley, Charles 216
Robert Gordon's Hospital 61–2, *62*, 156
Robert Gordon University, students' proposals for Denburn valley 248, 249
see also Aberdeen School of Architecture *et seq.*
Rolland's Lodging 53
Rollo, Leslie 199, 213, 214
Romano-British landscape *5*, 5
Rome xxii–xxiii
Rosemount 143–4
flats and cottages 170–72, *171*
Rosemount Square 176–7, 213, *214*
Rosemount Viaduct project 146–9, *147*, *148*, 153
Art Gallery and Industrial Museum 156
Central School 156
Gordon's Hospital 156
Grammar School site open space 156
Greyfriar's Kirk, demolition of 158–9
Jamesone House, demolition of 157
Mackay's blocks 152–3
Mitchell and Muill's Bakery 156
old buildings, valuing 158–9
School of Art 156
Schoolhill area 156–7, *158*
Souttar's blocks 152

tenements 173
Rossi, Aldo 224
Rotunda Place 138
round houses 3–4
Round Table 23, 24, 26
rounded corners 69, 115, 126
Rubislaw Place 138, 140
Rubislaw Terrace 141
Rue de Rivoli, Paris *96*, 96–7
Ruskin, John xxvi, 195
Russell, Georgiana, Duchess of Bedford 192–3
Rust, John 47, 157, 207
Ruthrieston 6, 212

Sacred Theory of Earth (Burnet) 89
Salvation Army Citadel 54, 151–2, 203, 217, 235–6
Savage, James 91, 92, 93, 95
Scara Brae *163*, 188
School of Art 156
Schoolhill 6, *154*–5, 156–7, *157*, *158*
medieval city 31–2, *32*
Mitchell and Muill's Bakery 156, *156*
Rosemount Viaduct project 146
tenements *171*, 173
Triple Kirks 131, *132*
Scotch Improvers 8
Scott, Walter 132–3
sea-land relationship 1
Serlio, Sebastiano xxiii, xxiv, xxvi, 60–61, 236, *237*, 238
Shawfield Mansion 84
Shiprow 89, 99, 208
Baillie Galen's House 122, 169
medieval city 24, *25*, 25–7, 28–9
Shore Brae 27
Sibbald, William 106–7
Silver Street 134
Simpson, Archibald 112, 114, 115–16, 123
Aberdeen Hotel 122
Assembly Rooms 117–18
Athenaeum Rooms 123
Auchintoul's House 115, *116*
Baillie Galen's House 169
Bon Accord quarter 135–6
Ferryhill designs 137–8
— Belvidere Place 139–40
— Ferryhill Place 138–9
— Marine Place 139
— Rotunda Place 138

Marischal College *152*, 157–8
Market Hall 127–8
Market Street *127*, 127–8
Mechanic's Institute building 128
Medico-Chirurgical Society building 118, 120
North of Scotland Bank 123–4
St Andrew's Chapel 118
Town and County Bank 130
Triple Kirks 131, *132*
Union Buildings *122*, 122–3
Skene, James 136
Smith, John 109, 110, 112, 133
Crimonmogate House 116, 117
Edwards-McHardy building 120
Fittie Quarter improvements *111*
Mercat Cross resiting and restoration *124*, 125
New Town plan 112, *113*
North Kirk 120
Record Office 120
Society of Advocates building 126–7
St Machar Cottage 193
St Nicholas and Façade 125–6, *126*
Trades Hall *130*, 131
Smith, William 127, 129, 151
Society of Advocates building 126–7
Soufllot, Jacques Germain 96
souterrains 4, 6
South Street 89, 93, 94, 97–8
see also Union Street
Souttar, James 34, 40, 151, 152
Spence, Basil 202, 215
Spital 38, *39*, 212
St Andrew's Chapel 118, 131
St Katherine's Hill 6, 24–5, 87
St Machar Cottage 193
St Machar 17, 18, 37–8, 70
St Margaret's mission 35–37
St Nicholas 17, *18*, 18, 62–3, 125–6, *126*
St Nicholas Place 133, 238
St Nicholas Street 32
standing stones 1–3, 2, *2*
Stickley, Gustave 195, 197
Stokes, Leonard 185
stone circles 2–3
Stukely, William 14
sustainability 224, 230
Switzer, Stephen *7*, 8–9, 11, 14

Tacitus 4, 14
Tannery Row 128, 238

Tap o' Noth 4
taxation policies 209
Taylor, George *27*, 85
Ten Books of Architecture (Vitruvius Pollio) 236
tenements xxvi–xxvii, 165–7, *166*, *171*, *175*, 177
architecture of 172–3
bad name of 210–11
Baillie Galen's House 169
Castlegate examples 167, 169
Edwards-McHardy building 169–70
flats 170, 172
King Street 174, 176, 205–7
Manse type 174
Rosemount 170–72
Rosemount Square 176–7
Schoolhill 173
Upperkirkgate 173–4
Urquhart Road 207
Washington Buildings 206–7
Tolbooth 28, 52, 55–6, *63*, *65*, 72, 151
improvements to 61, 62, 63–5
Torry 6, 173, 198
Town and Country Planning Acts xxv–xxvi
Town and County Bank 130
Town House, Old Aberdeen *69*, 70–71
Townhouse 49, 55–6, *63*, 64–5, 123, *151*, 151–2
Trades Hall *130*, 131, 133
Triple Kirks 131, *132*, 133
Trustees Houses 169
Tyrebagger Hill 6

Union Bridge 110, 145, *225*, *235*, 239, *240*, *250*
Union Buildings *122*, 122–3
Union Club building 129
Union Street 112, 121, *134*, *135*, 218
Aberdeen Hotel 122
Assembly Rooms 117–18, *118*
Athenaeum Rooms 122–3
Auchintoul's House 115, 116
and Back Wynd 125, 126
Baillie Galen's House 122, 169
Bridewell 112, *117*
Christ's College *149*, 149–51
Clydesdale Bank 133
Crimonmogate House 108–9, 116, 117
Golden Square 112, 134–5

level of 100, 101, 115, 121–2
Market Street junction 128
naming of 98
North of Scotland Bank 123–4
plans and restrictions for 109, 115
Society of Advocates building 126–7
St Nicholas and Façade 125–6, *126*
Town and County Bank 130
Trades Hall *130*, 131, 133
Union Buildings *122*, 122–3
Union Terrace 112, 146–7, 173, *240*, 241, 243, *243*
Union Terrace Gardens 94, 147, *225*, 239, *240*, 243
  Aberdeen Beyond 2000 scheme 246–7
  Beattie's design *242*, *243*
  parking garage proposal *245*
  proposals for 247–9
United States (USA) 194–5, 198, 220, 232
Unwin, Raymond 210–11
Upperkirkgate *154–55*, *157*, 157, *158*, 168
  medieval city *32*, 32–4, *33*
  tenements 170, 173–4
urban design 52, 59, 66, 74, 80, 141, 252
Urquhart Road 207

Vanbrugh, Sir John 121

Venice xxi–xxii, *xxii*, 80, 238
Venice School of Architecture 224
Victoria Street 140
Victorian style 120, 128, 129–30, 133
Villa d'Este plans xxiii–xxiv
Vitruvius Britannicus (Campbell) 74, 193
Vitruvius Pollio, Marcus 236, 239

Washington Buildings 206
Weighhouse 27, 28
Wellington Place 193
West End 136–42, *137*, *142*
  Albert Terrace 140–41
  CALA additions 142–3
  Carden Place 141
  Queen's Gardens 142
  Queen's Terrace 141–2
  Rubislaw Place 140
  Rubislaw Terrace 141
  Victoria Street 140
Wharf 27, 27–8, *65*, 129
  see also pier, quay
Williamson, E.L. 198
Wilson, R.G. 23, 33, 47–8
Winter, Thomas 63
Wren, Sir Christopher xxv, 89–90

Young, James 91, 92, 93
  South Entry design *94*, 97–8
  Trustees Houses *169*, 169